BURMA CHRONICLES

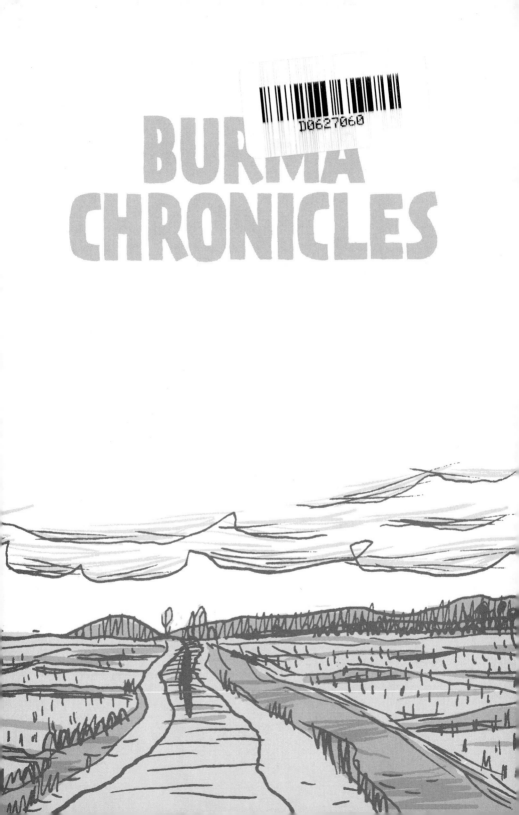

Guy Delisle
BURMA CHRONICLES

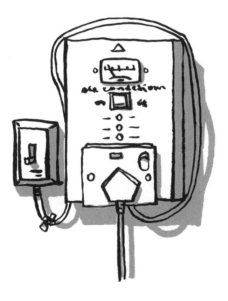

DRAWN AND QUARTERLY

TRANSLATION BY HELGE DASCHER

ALSO BY GUY DELISLE:

PYONGYANG: A JOURNEY IN NORTH KOREA
SHENZHEN: A TRAVELOGUE FROM CHINA
ALBERT & THE OTHERS
ALINE & THE OTHERS

 SPECIAL THANKS TO VIKTOR NÜBEL, CHRISTIAN MAIWALD, AND DIRK REHM.

WWW.GUYDELISLE.COM

DRAWN & QUARTERLY
POST OFFICE BOX 48056
MONTREAL, QUEBEC
CANADA H2V 4S8
WWW.DRAWNANDQUARTERLY.COM

FIRST HARDCOVER EDITION: SEPTEMBER 2008. SECOND PRINTING: OCTOBER 2009.
FIRST PAPERBACK EDITION: NOVEMBER 2010.
ISBN 978-1770460-25-6.
PRINTED IN CANADA.

10 9 8 7 6 5 4 3 2 1

LIBRARY AND ARCHIVES CANADA CATALOGUING IN PUBLICATION
DELISLE, GUY
BURMA CHRONICLES / GUY DELISLE.
TRANSLATION OF: CHRONIQUES BIRMANES.
ISBN 978-1-897299-50-0 (HARDCOVER EDITION); ISBN 978-1770460-25-6 (PAPERBACK EDITION)
1. BURMA--FICTION. I. TITLE.
PN6733.D44C4713 2008 741.5'971 C2008-901257-7

DRAWN & QUARTERLY ACKNOWLEDGES THE FINANCIAL CONTRIBUTION OF THE GOVERNMENT OF CANADA THROUGH THE CANADA BOOK FUND AND THE CANADA COUNCIL FOR THE ARTS FOR OUR PUBLISHING ACTIVITIES AND FOR SUPPORT OF THIS EDITION.

DISTRIBUTED IN THE USA BY:
FARRAR, STRAUS AND GIROUX
18 WEST 18TH STREET
NEW YORK, NY 10011
ORDERS: 888.330.8477

DISTRIBUTED IN CANADA BY:
RAINCOAST BOOKS
9050 SHAUGHNESSY STREET
VANCOUVER, BC V6P 6E5
ORDERS: 800.663.5714

MYANMAR

OFFICIAL NAME SINCE 1989, ADOPTED BY THE UN.

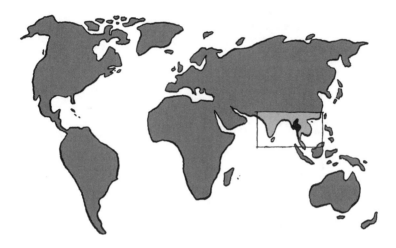

BURMA

FORMER NAME, STILL USED BY COUNTRIES THAT DO NOT ACCEPT THE LEGITIMACY OF THE GOVERNMENT THAT TOOK POWER IN 1989. SUCH AS FRANCE, AUSTRALIA AND THE US.

PAKISTAN
NEPAL
BHUTAN
CHINA
INDIA
MYANMAR
LAOS
BANGLADESH
THAILAND
VIETNAM
CAMBODIA
INDONESIA
MALAYSIA

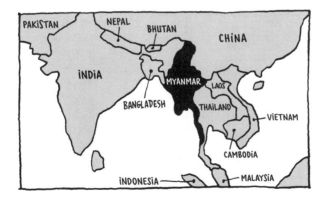

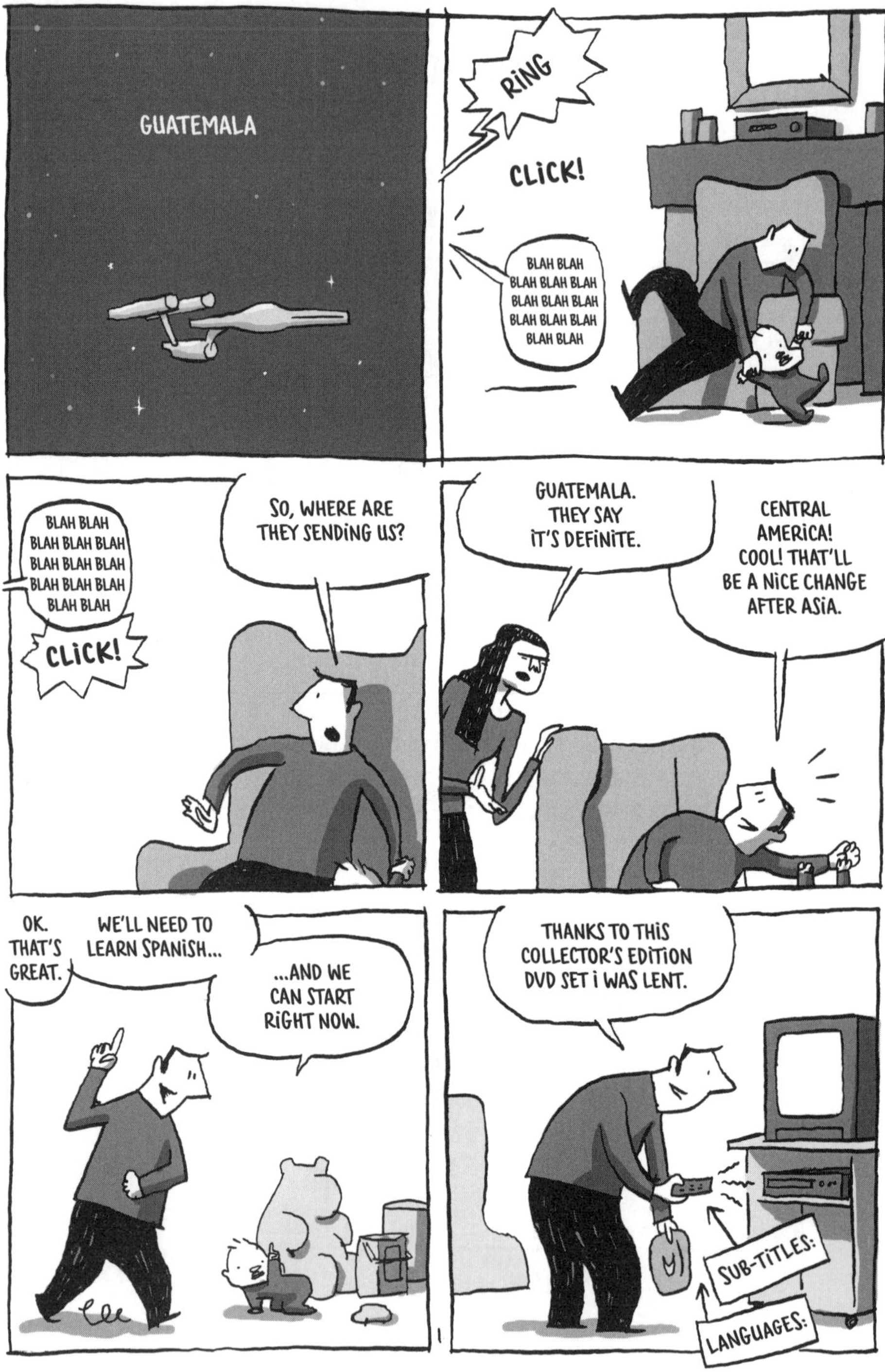
GUATEMALA
RING
CLICK!
BLAH BLAH BLAH BLAH BLAH BLAH BLAH BLAH BLAH BLAH BLAH BLAH BLAH
BLAH BLAH BLAH BLAH BLAH BLAH BLAH BLAH BLAH BLAH BLAH BLAH BLAH
CLICK!
SO, WHERE ARE THEY SENDING US?
GUATEMALA. THEY SAY IT'S DEFINITE.
CENTRAL AMERICA! COOL! THAT'LL BE A NICE CHANGE AFTER ASIA.
OK. THAT'S GREAT.
WE'LL NEED TO LEARN SPANISH...
...AND WE CAN START RIGHT NOW.
THANKS TO THIS COLLECTOR'S EDITION DVD SET I WAS LENT.
SUB-TITLES:
LANGUAGES:

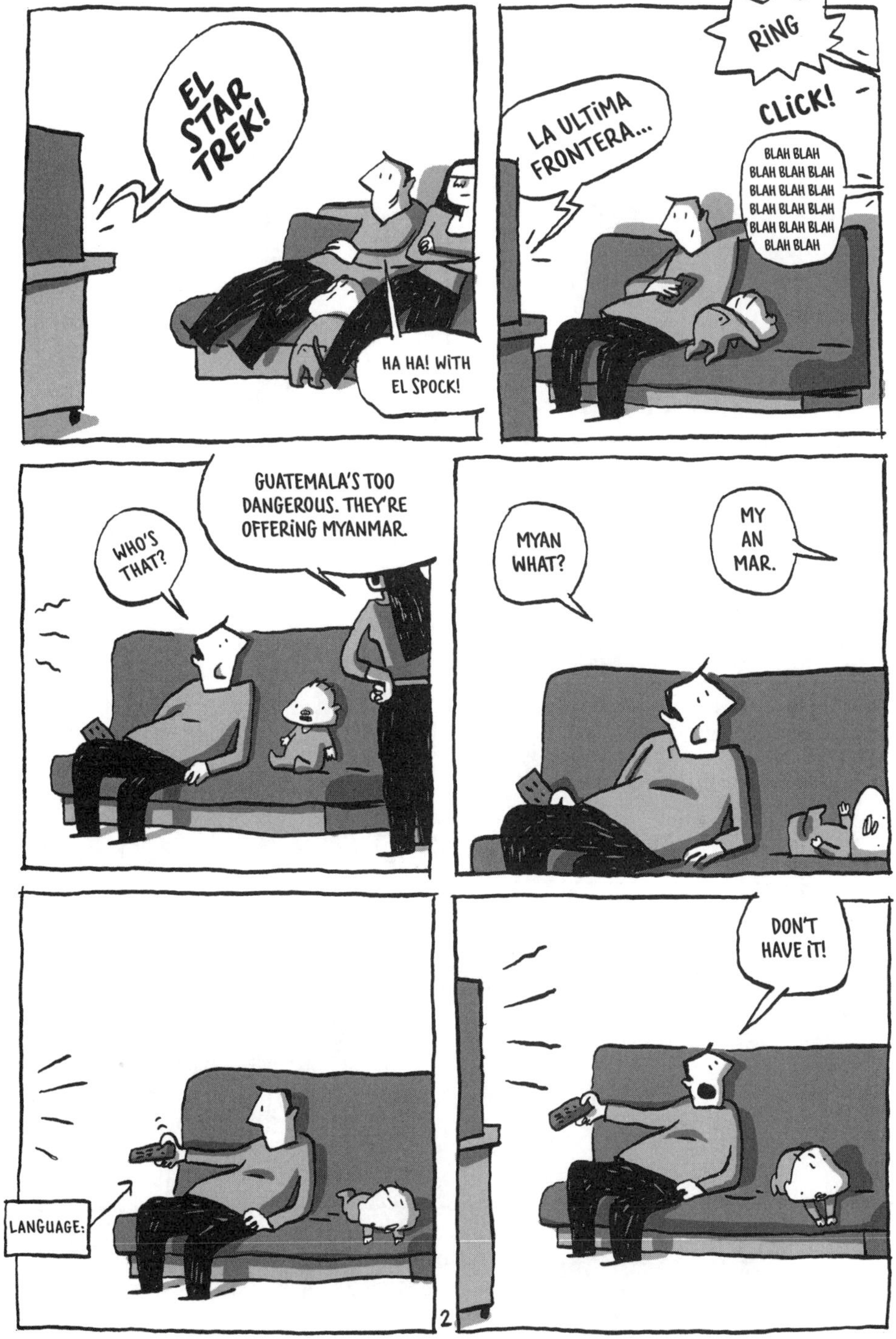

EL STAR TREK!
HA HA! WITH EL SPOCK!
RING
LA ULTIMA FRONTERA...
CLICK!
BLAH BLAH BLAH BLAH BLAH BLAH BLAH BLAH BLAH BLAH BLAH BLAH BLAH BLAH BLAH BLAH
GUATEMALA'S TOO DANGEROUS. THEY'RE OFFERING MYANMAR.
WHO'S THAT?
MYAN WHAT?
MY AN MAR.
LANGUAGE:
DON'T HAVE IT!

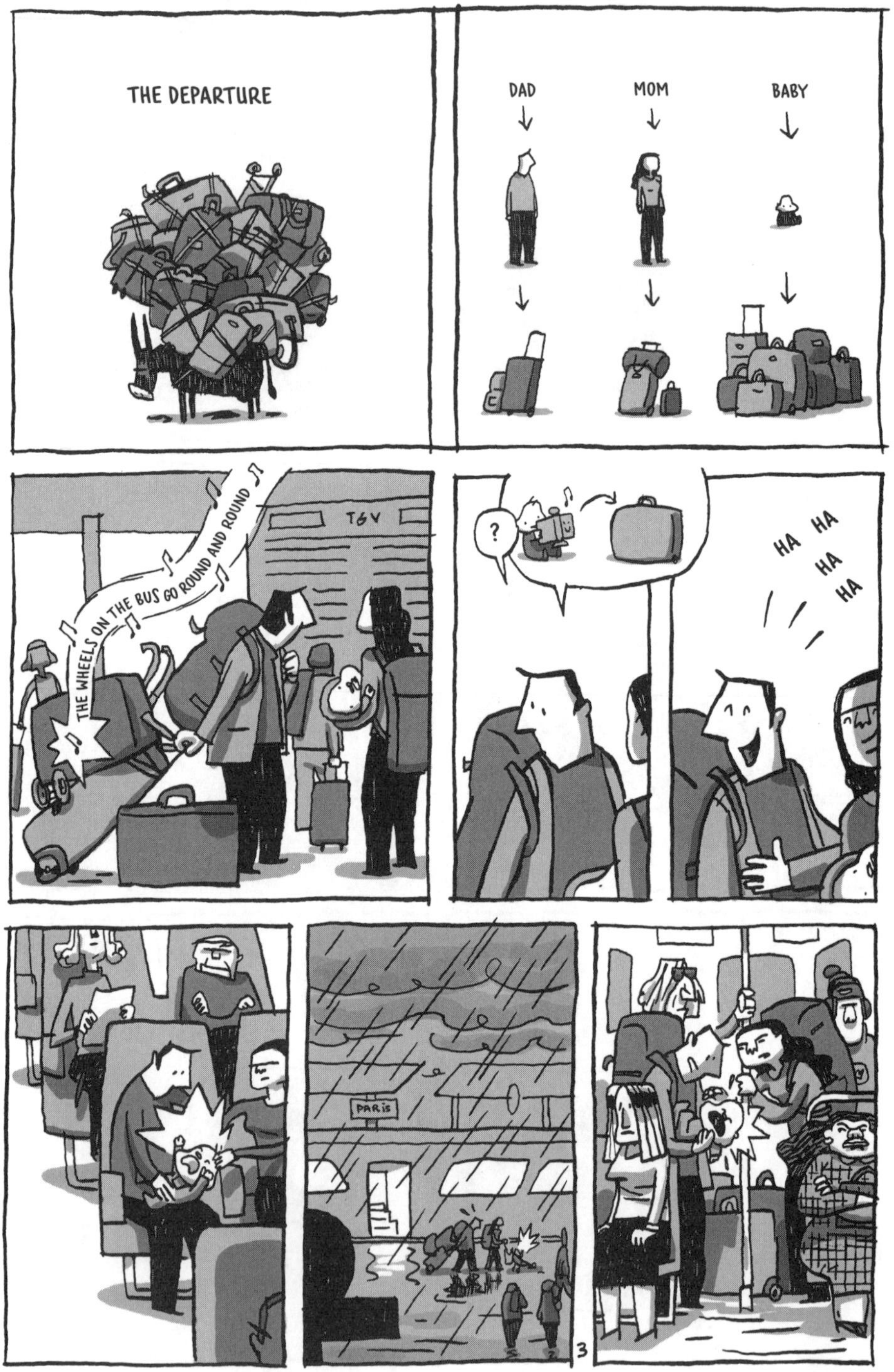
THE DEPARTURE
DAD
MOM
BABY
TGV
THE WHEELS ON THE BUS GO ROUND AND ROUND
?
HA HA
HA
HA
HA
PARIS

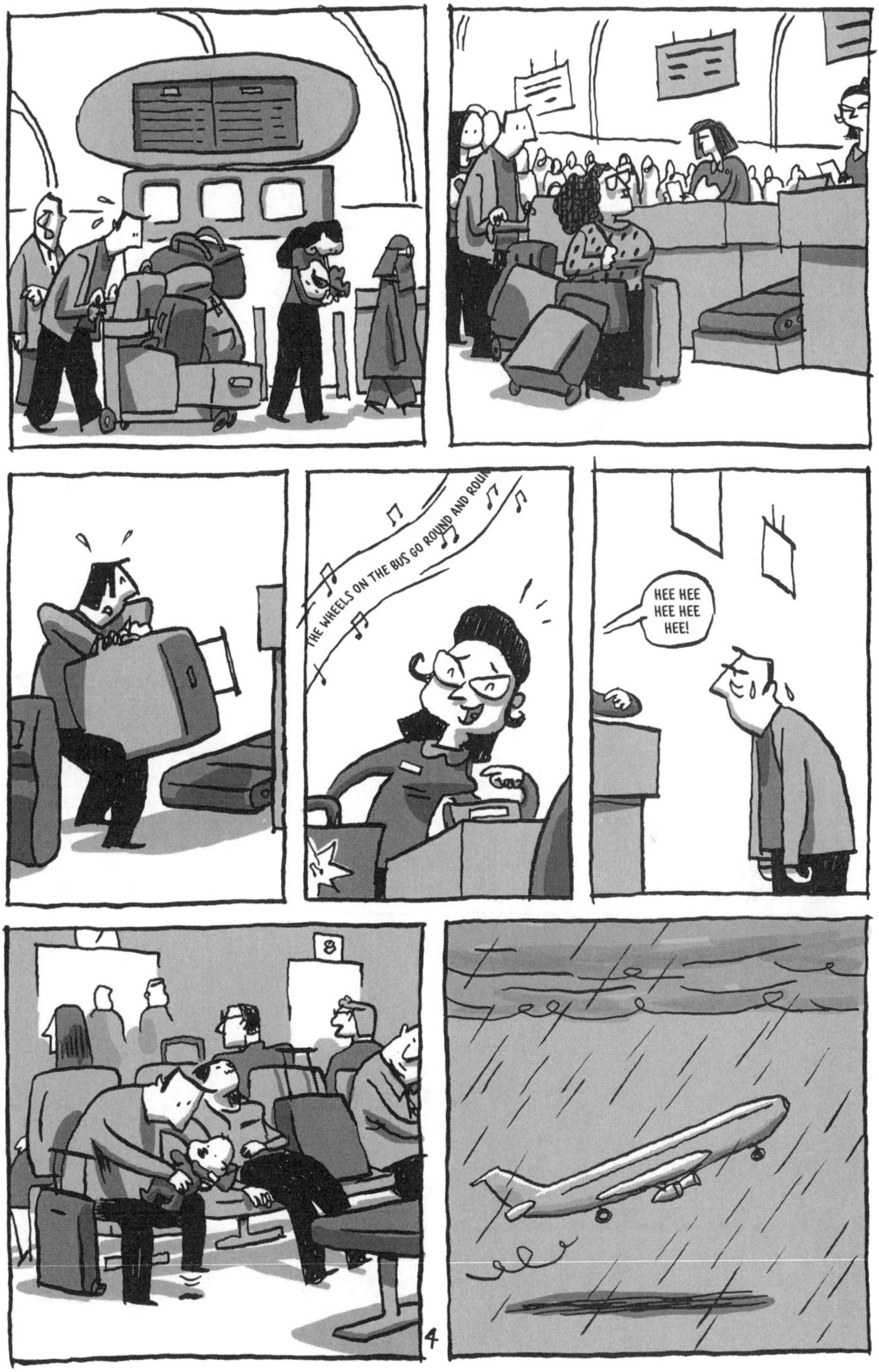
THE WHEELS ON THE BUS GO ROUND AND ROUND
HEE HEE HEE HEE HEE!

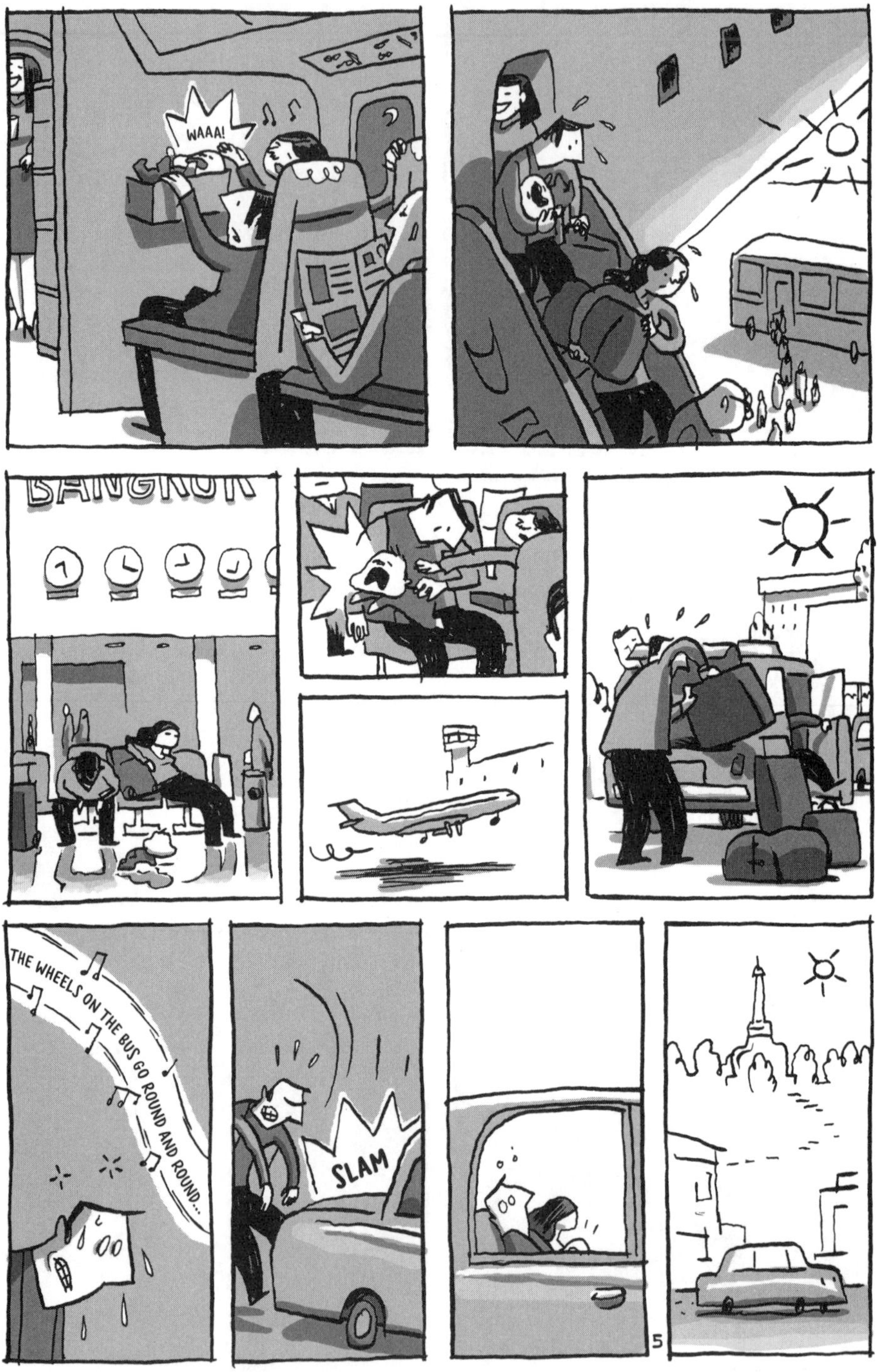
WAAA!
BANGKOK
THE WHEELS ON THE BUS GO ROUND AND ROUND...
SLAM

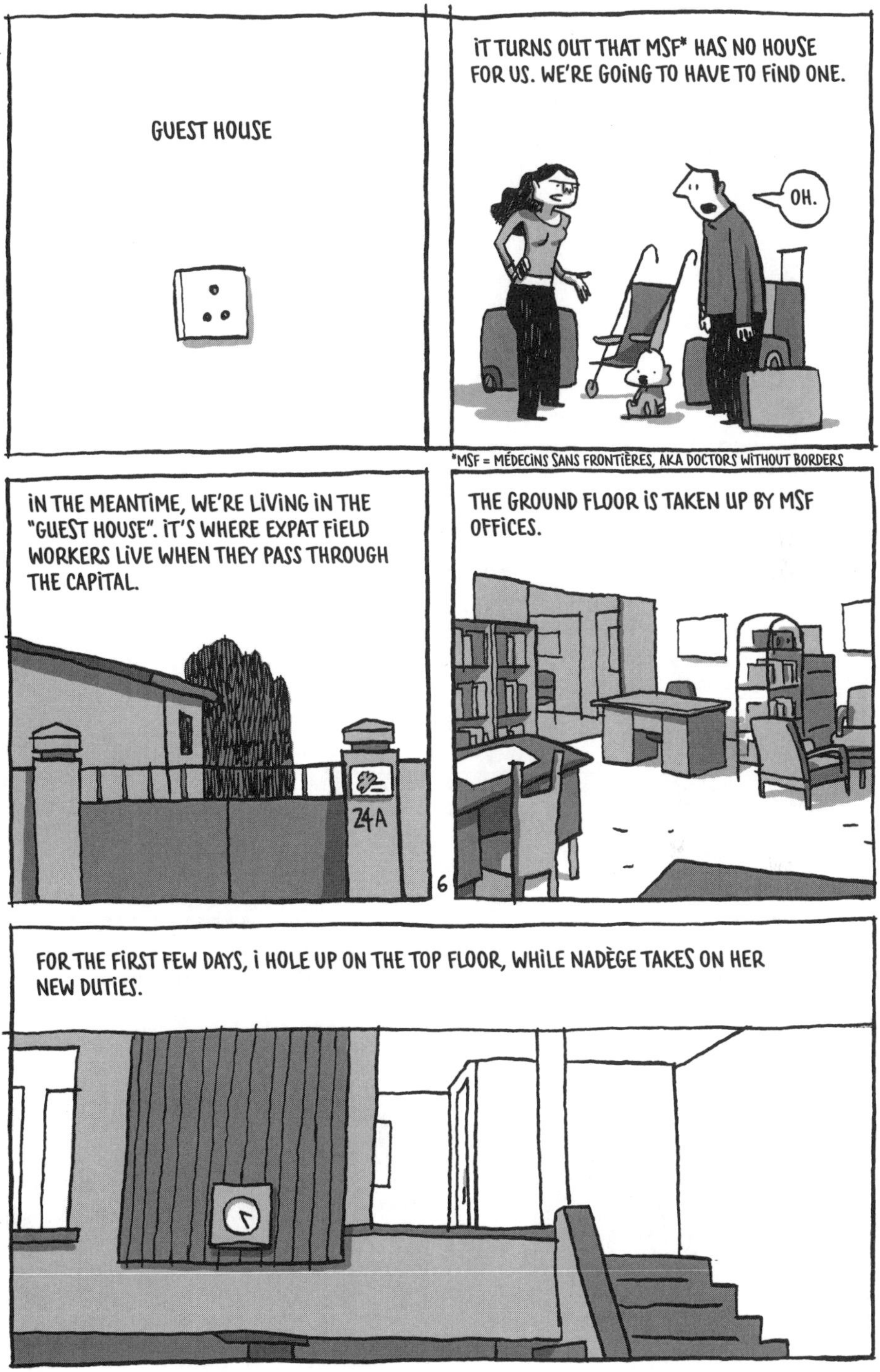
GUEST HOUSE
IT TURNS OUT THAT MSF* HAS NO HOUSE FOR US. WE'RE GOING TO HAVE TO FIND ONE.
OH.
*MSF = MÉDECINS SANS FRONTIÈRES, AKA DOCTORS WITHOUT BORDERS
IN THE MEANTIME, WE'RE LIVING IN THE "GUEST HOUSE". IT'S WHERE EXPAT FIELD WORKERS LIVE WHEN THEY PASS THROUGH THE CAPITAL.
24A
THE GROUND FLOOR IS TAKEN UP BY MSF OFFICES.
FOR THE FIRST FEW DAYS, I HOLE UP ON THE TOP FLOOR, WHILE NADÈGE TAKES ON HER NEW DUTIES.

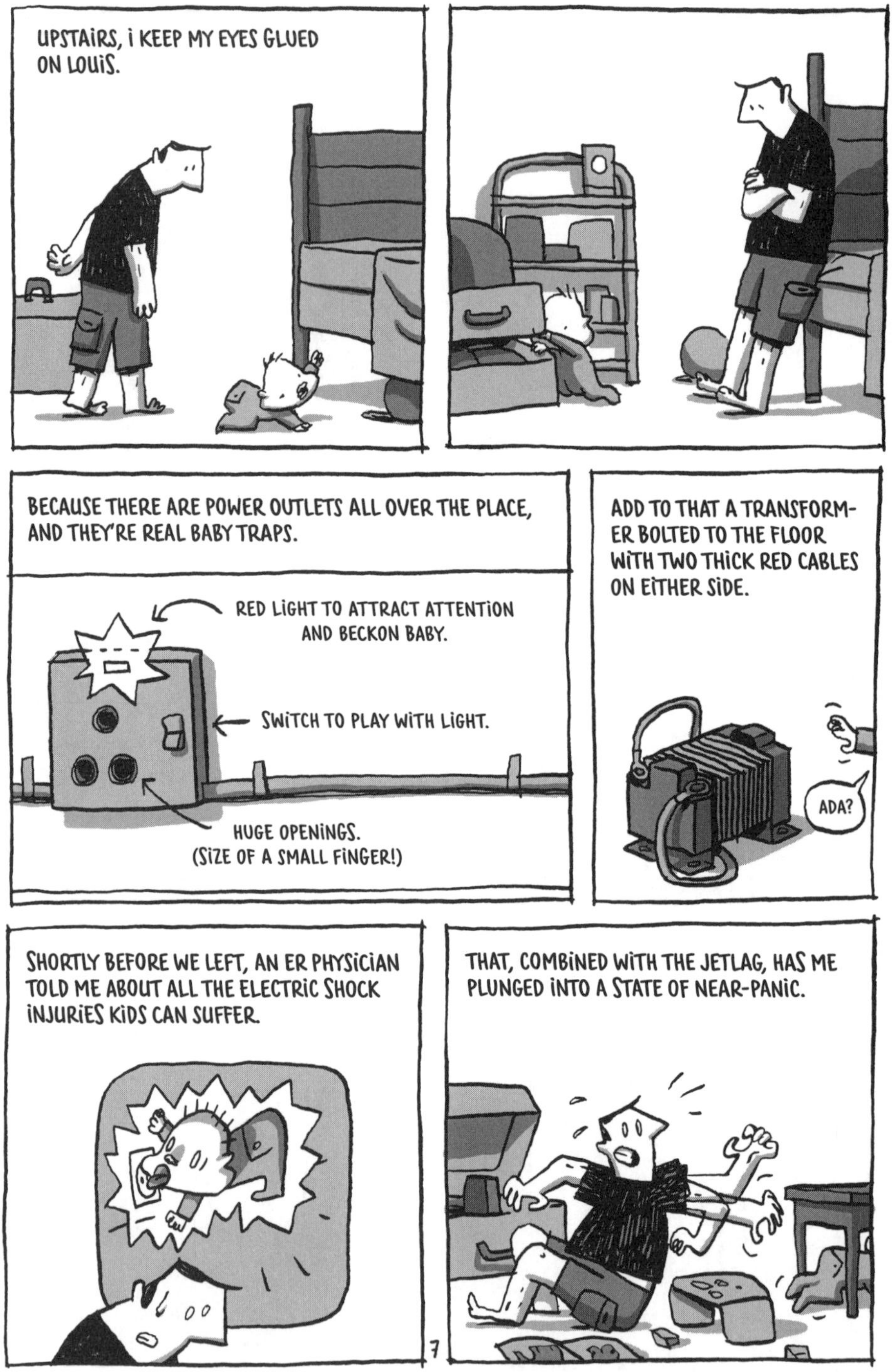
UPSTAIRS, I KEEP MY EYES GLUED ON LOUIS.
BECAUSE THERE ARE POWER OUTLETS ALL OVER THE PLACE, AND THEY'RE REAL BABY TRAPS.
RED LIGHT TO ATTRACT ATTENTION AND BECKON BABY.
SWITCH TO PLAY WITH LIGHT.
HUGE OPENINGS. (SIZE OF A SMALL FINGER!)
ADD TO THAT A TRANSFORMER BOLTED TO THE FLOOR WITH TWO THICK RED CABLES ON EITHER SIDE.
ADA?
SHORTLY BEFORE WE LEFT, AN ER PHYSICIAN TOLD ME ABOUT ALL THE ELECTRIC SHOCK INJURIES KIDS CAN SUFFER.
THAT, COMBINED WITH THE JETLAG, HAS ME PLUNGED INTO A STATE OF NEAR-PANIC.

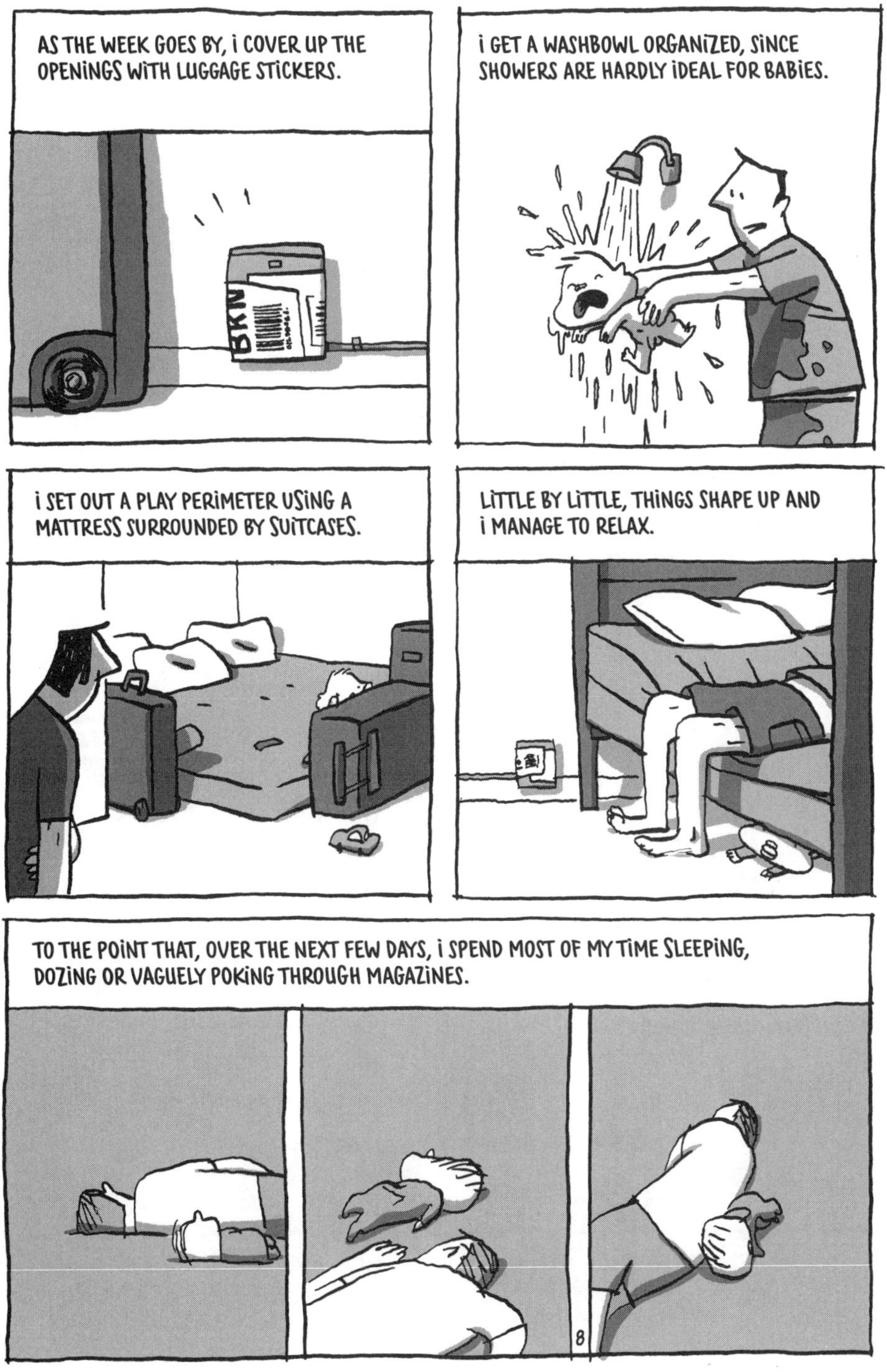
AS THE WEEK GOES BY, I COVER UP THE OPENINGS WITH LUGGAGE STICKERS.
BKN
I GET A WASHBOWL ORGANIZED, SINCE SHOWERS ARE HARDLY IDEAL FOR BABIES.
I SET OUT A PLAY PERIMETER USING A MATTRESS SURROUNDED BY SUITCASES.
LITTLE BY LITTLE, THINGS SHAPE UP AND I MANAGE TO RELAX.
TO THE POINT THAT, OVER THE NEXT FEW DAYS, I SPEND MOST OF MY TIME SLEEPING, DOZING OR VAGUELY POKING THROUGH MAGAZINES.

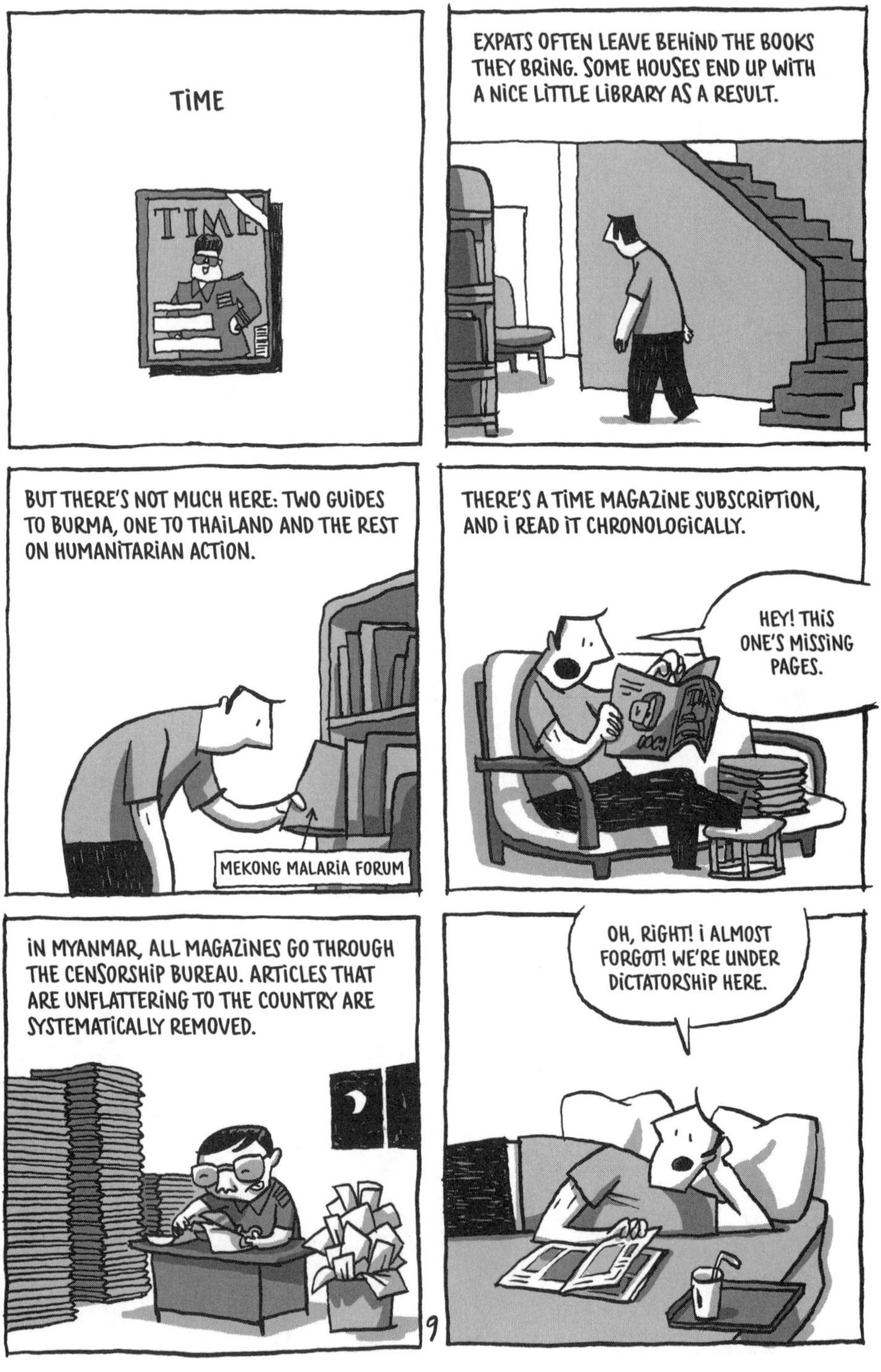
TIME
TIME
EXPATS OFTEN LEAVE BEHIND THE BOOKS THEY BRING. SOME HOUSES END UP WITH A NICE LITTLE LIBRARY AS A RESULT.
BUT THERE'S NOT MUCH HERE: TWO GUIDES TO BURMA, ONE TO THAILAND AND THE REST ON HUMANITARIAN ACTION.
MEKONG MALARIA FORUM
THERE'S A TIME MAGAZINE SUBSCRIPTION, AND I READ IT CHRONOLOGICALLY.
HEY! THIS ONE'S MISSING PAGES.
IN MYANMAR, ALL MAGAZINES GO THROUGH THE CENSORSHIP BUREAU. ARTICLES THAT ARE UNFLATTERING TO THE COUNTRY ARE SYSTEMATICALLY REMOVED.
OH, RIGHT! I ALMOST FORGOT! WE'RE UNDER DICTATORSHIP HERE.

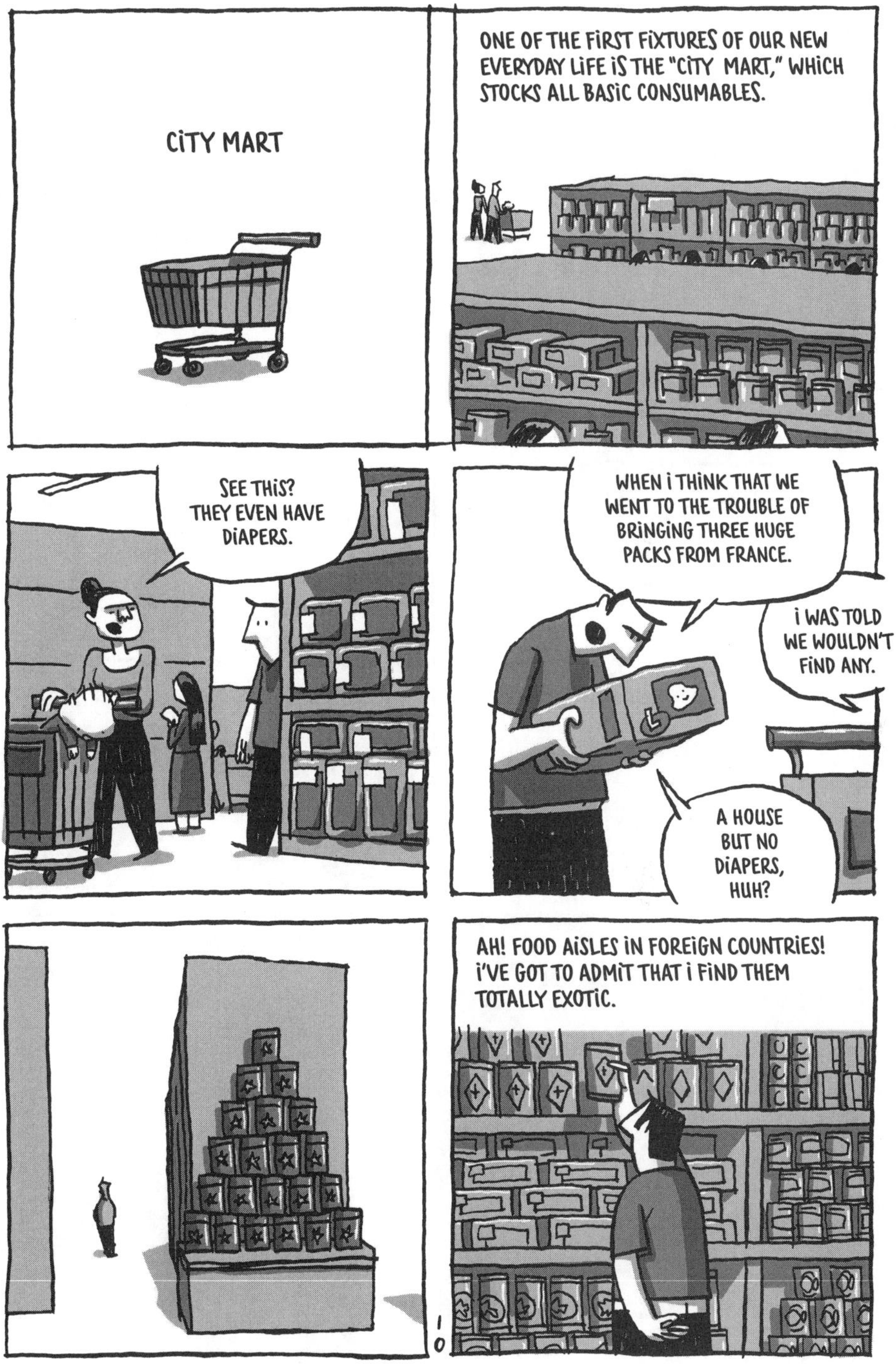
CITY MART
ONE OF THE FIRST FIXTURES OF OUR NEW EVERYDAY LIFE IS THE "CITY MART," WHICH STOCKS ALL BASIC CONSUMABLES.
SEE THIS? THEY EVEN HAVE DIAPERS.
WHEN I THINK THAT WE WENT TO THE TROUBLE OF BRINGING THREE HUGE PACKS FROM FRANCE.
I WAS TOLD WE WOULDN'T FIND ANY.
A HOUSE BUT NO DIAPERS, HUH?
AH! FOOD AISLES IN FOREIGN COUNTRIES! I'VE GOT TO ADMIT THAT I FIND THEM TOTALLY EXOTIC.

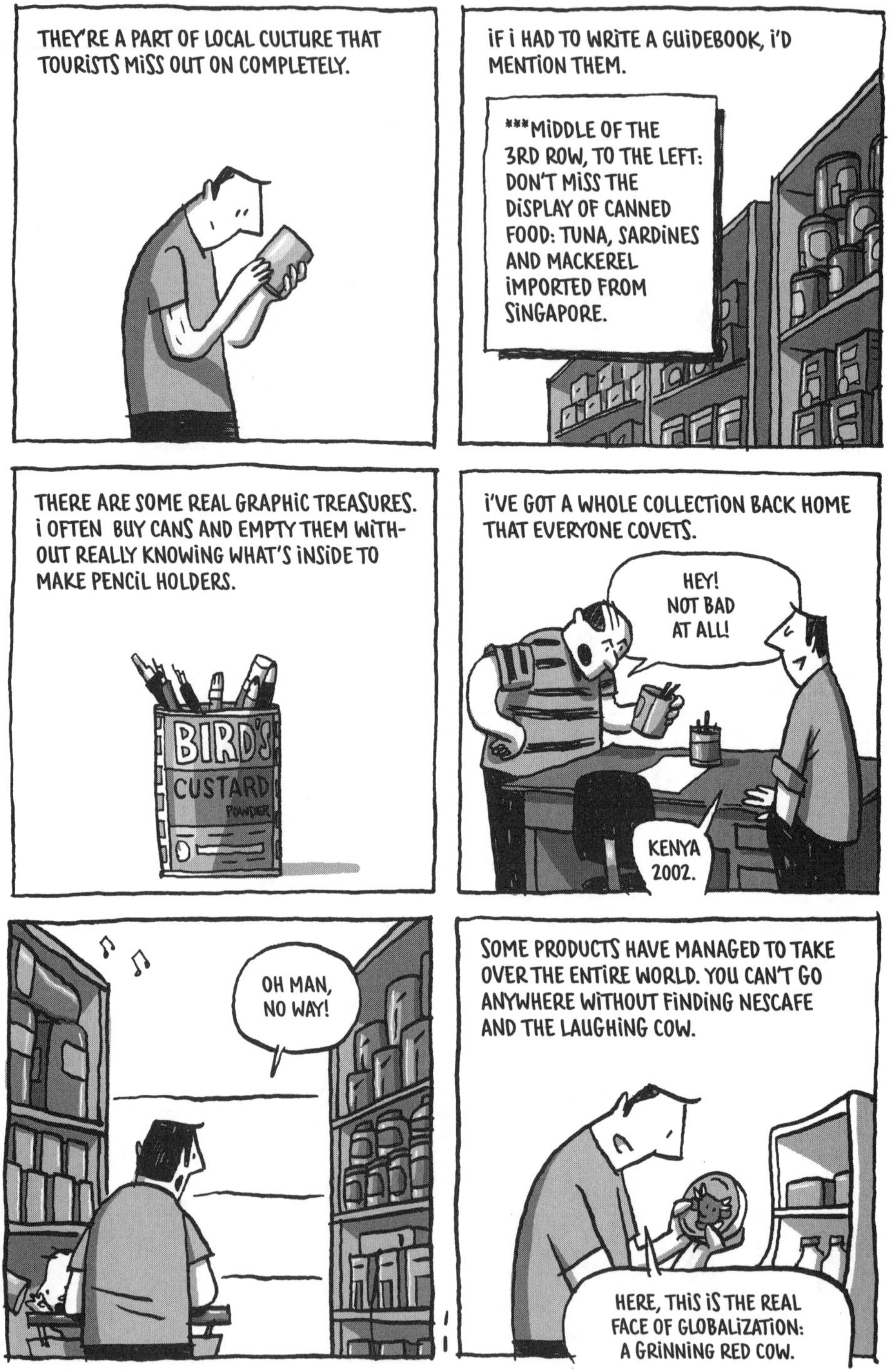
THEY'RE A PART OF LOCAL CULTURE THAT TOURISTS MISS OUT ON COMPLETELY.
IF I HAD TO WRITE A GUIDEBOOK, I'D MENTION THEM.
***MIDDLE OF THE 3RD ROW, TO THE LEFT: DON'T MISS THE DISPLAY OF CANNED FOOD: TUNA, SARDINES AND MACKEREL IMPORTED FROM SINGAPORE.
THERE ARE SOME REAL GRAPHIC TREASURES. I OFTEN BUY CANS AND EMPTY THEM WITHOUT REALLY KNOWING WHAT'S INSIDE TO MAKE PENCIL HOLDERS.
BIRD'S
CUSTARD
POWDER
I'VE GOT A WHOLE COLLECTION BACK HOME THAT EVERYONE COVETS.
HEY! NOT BAD AT ALL!
KENYA 2002.
OH MAN, NO WAY!
SOME PRODUCTS HAVE MANAGED TO TAKE OVER THE ENTIRE WORLD. YOU CAN'T GO ANYWHERE WITHOUT FINDING NESCAFE AND THE LAUGHING COW.
HERE, THIS IS THE REAL FACE OF GLOBALIZATION: A GRINNING RED COW.

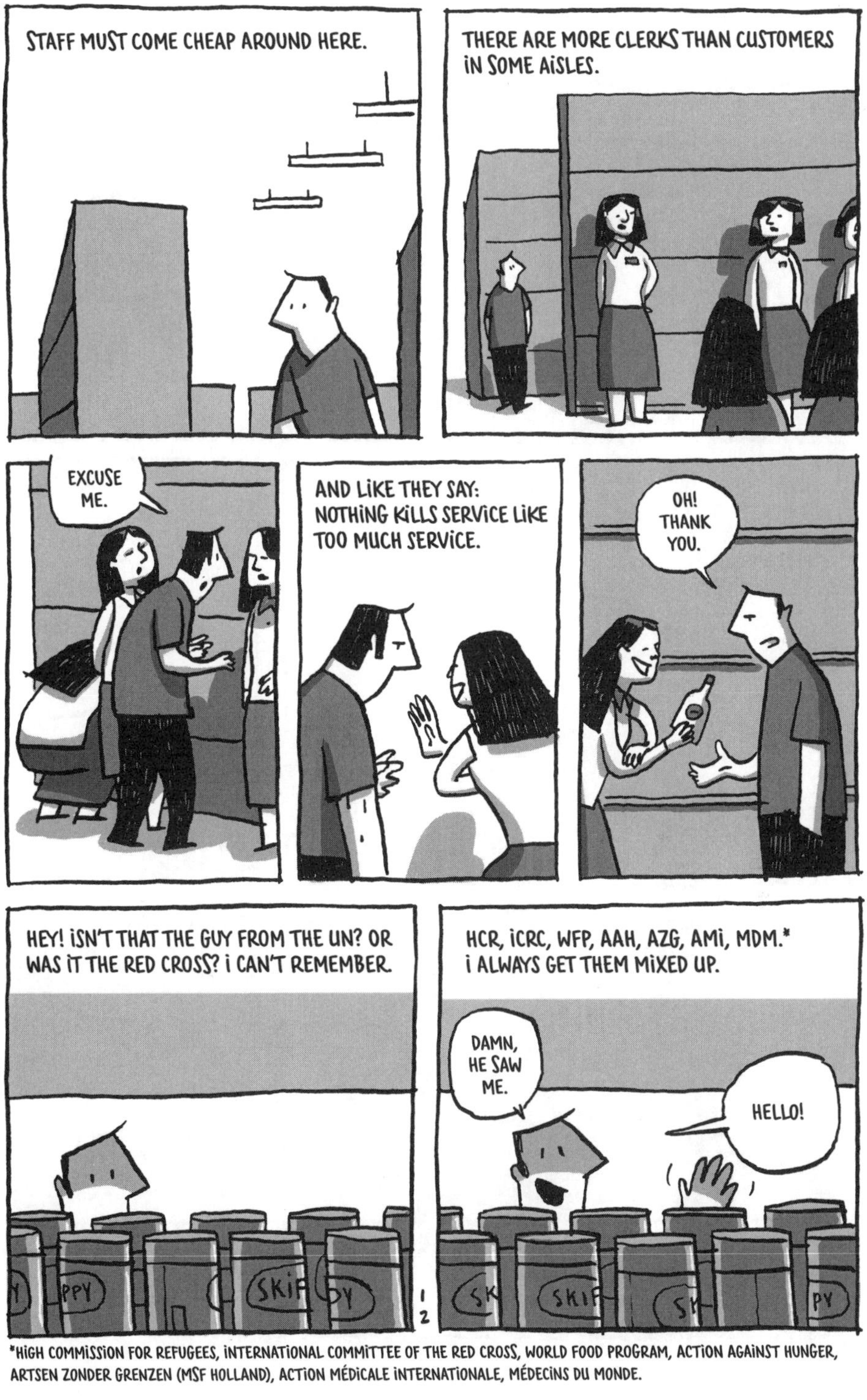
STAFF MUST COME CHEAP AROUND HERE.
THERE ARE MORE CLERKS THAN CUSTOMERS IN SOME AISLES.
EXCUSE ME.
AND LIKE THEY SAY: NOTHING KILLS SERVICE LIKE TOO MUCH SERVICE.
OH! THANK YOU.
HEY! ISN'T THAT THE GUY FROM THE UN? OR WAS IT THE RED CROSS? I CAN'T REMEMBER.
HCR, ICRC, WFP, AAH, AZG, AMI, MDM.* I ALWAYS GET THEM MIXED UP.
DAMN, HE SAW ME.
HELLO!

*HIGH COMMISSION FOR REFUGEES, INTERNATIONAL COMMITTEE OF THE RED CROSS, WORLD FOOD PROGRAM, ACTION AGAINST HUNGER, ARTSEN ZONDER GRENZEN (MSF HOLLAND), ACTION MÉDICALE INTERNATIONALE, MÉDECINS DU MONDE.

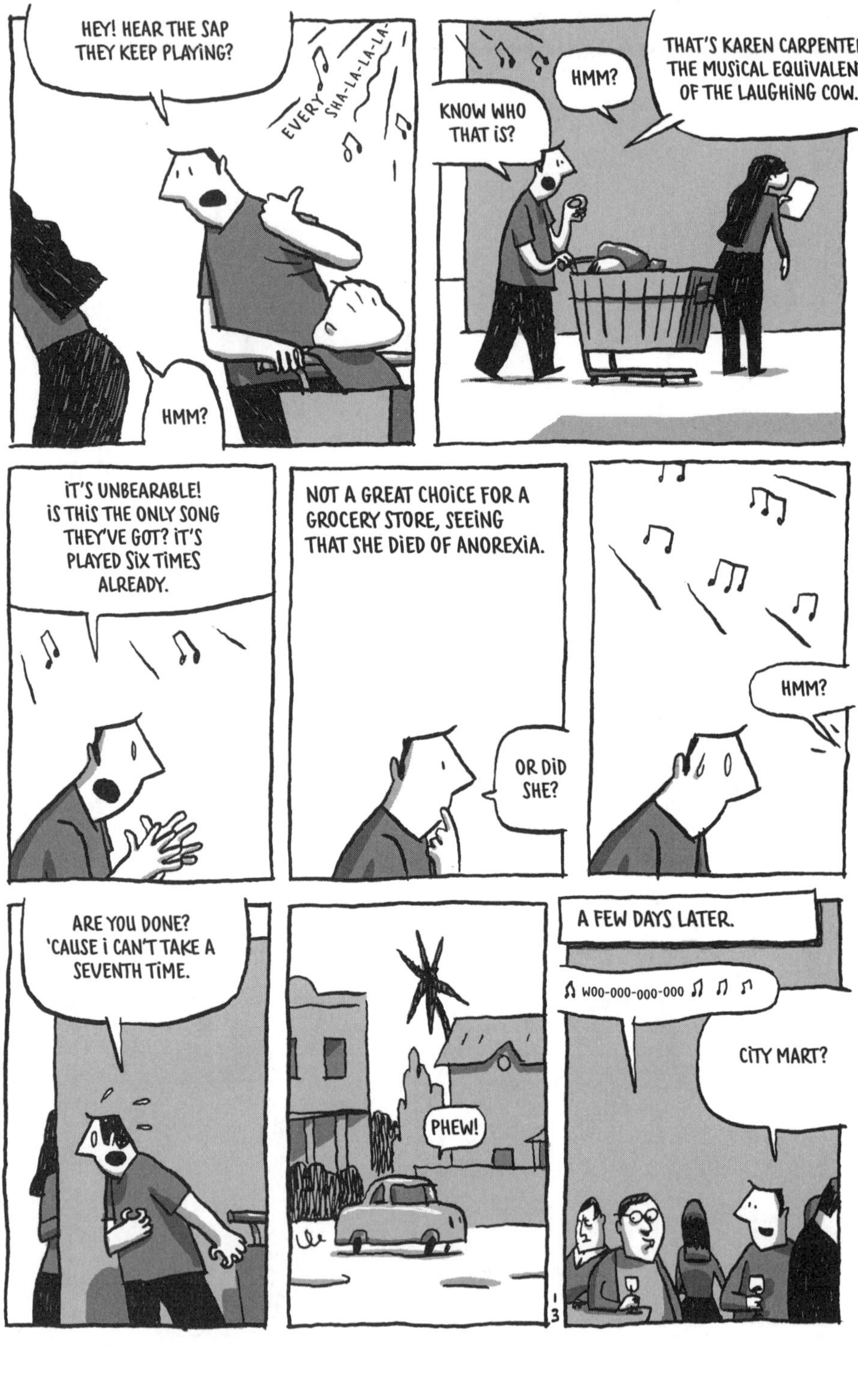
HEY! HEAR THE SAP THEY KEEP PLAYING?
EVERY SHA-LA-LA-LA-
HMM?
KNOW WHO THAT IS?
HMM?
THAT'S KAREN CARPENTER. THE MUSICAL EQUIVALENT OF THE LAUGHING COW.
IT'S UNBEARABLE! IS THIS THE ONLY SONG THEY'VE GOT? IT'S PLAYED SIX TIMES ALREADY.
NOT A GREAT CHOICE FOR A GROCERY STORE, SEEING THAT SHE DIED OF ANOREXIA.
OR DID SHE?
HMM?
ARE YOU DONE? 'CAUSE I CAN'T TAKE A SEVENTH TIME.
PHEW!
A FEW DAYS LATER.
WOO-000-000-000
CITY MART?

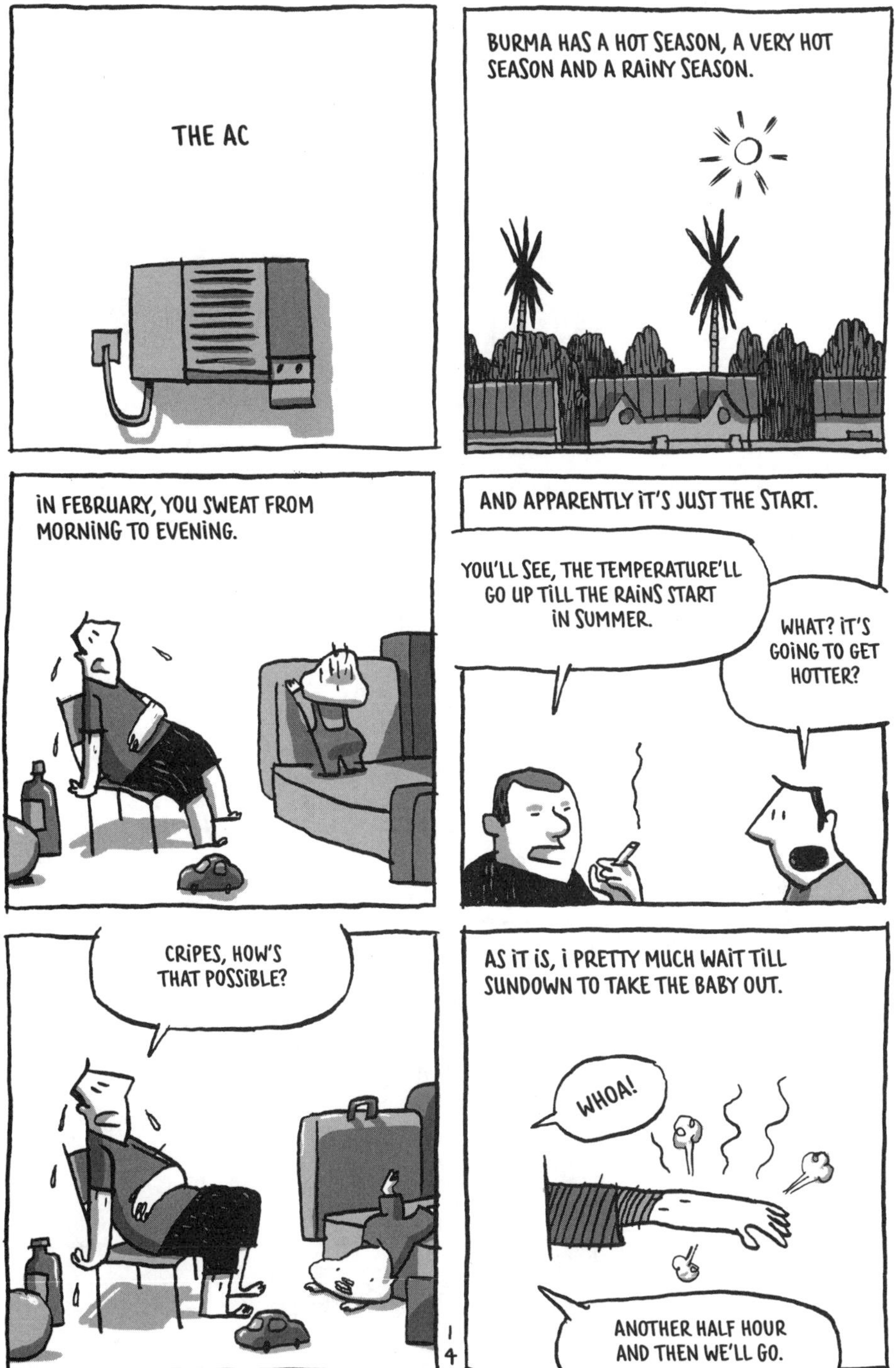
THE AC
BURMA HAS A HOT SEASON, A VERY HOT SEASON AND A RAINY SEASON.
IN FEBRUARY, YOU SWEAT FROM MORNING TO EVENING.
AND APPARENTLY IT'S JUST THE START.
YOU'LL SEE, THE TEMPERATURE'LL GO UP TILL THE RAINS START IN SUMMER.
WHAT? IT'S GOING TO GET HOTTER?
CRIPES, HOW'S THAT POSSIBLE?
AS IT IS, I PRETTY MUCH WAIT TILL SUNDOWN TO TAKE THE BABY OUT.
WHOA!
ANOTHER HALF HOUR AND THEN WE'LL GO.

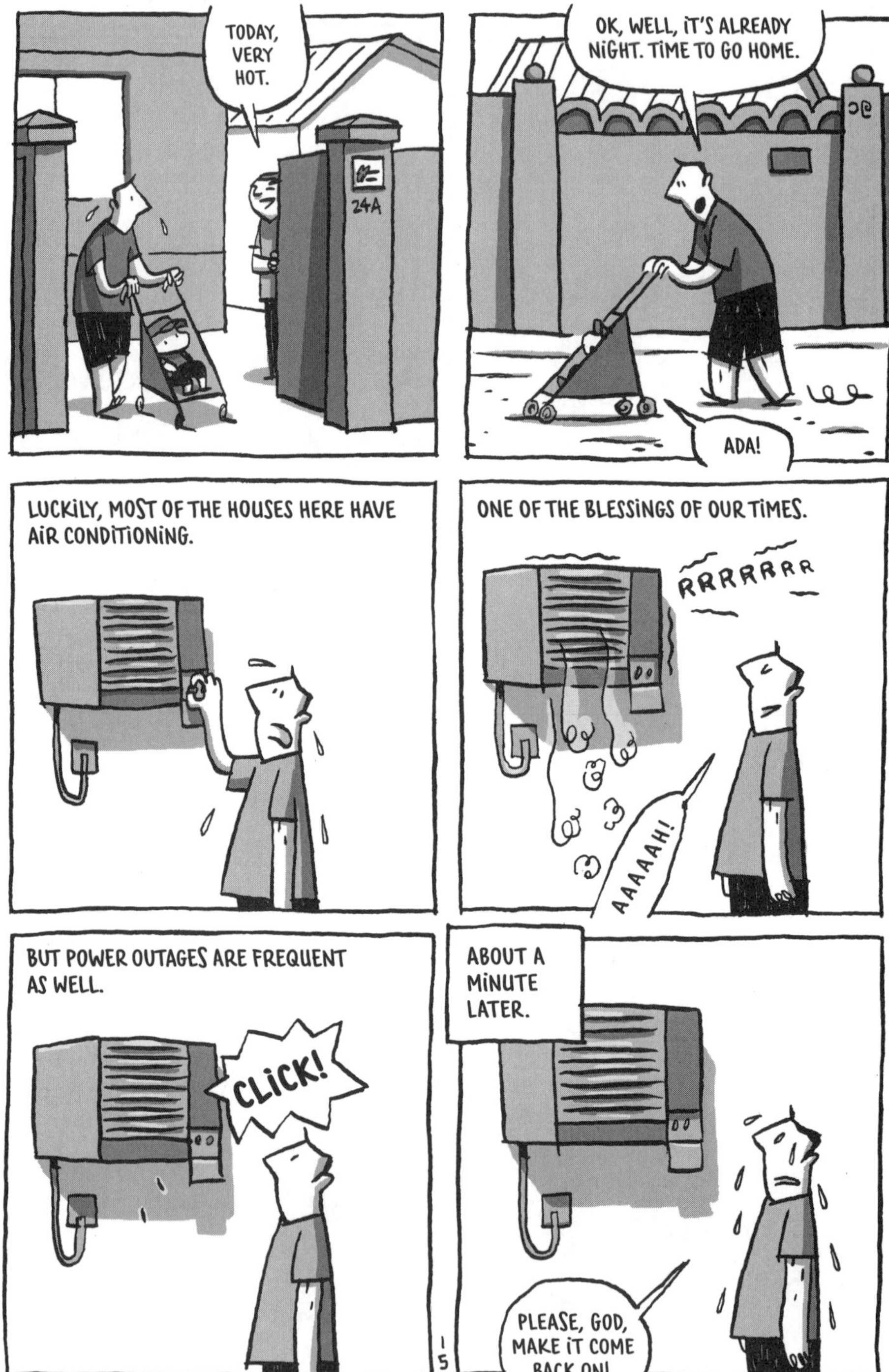

TODAY, VERY HOT.
24A
OK, WELL, IT'S ALREADY NIGHT. TIME TO GO HOME.
ADA!
LUCKILY, MOST OF THE HOUSES HERE HAVE AIR CONDITIONING.
ONE OF THE BLESSINGS OF OUR TIMES.
RRRRRRRR
AAAAAAH!
BUT POWER OUTAGES ARE FREQUENT AS WELL.
CLICK!
ABOUT A MINUTE LATER.
PLEASE, GOD, MAKE IT COME BACK ON!

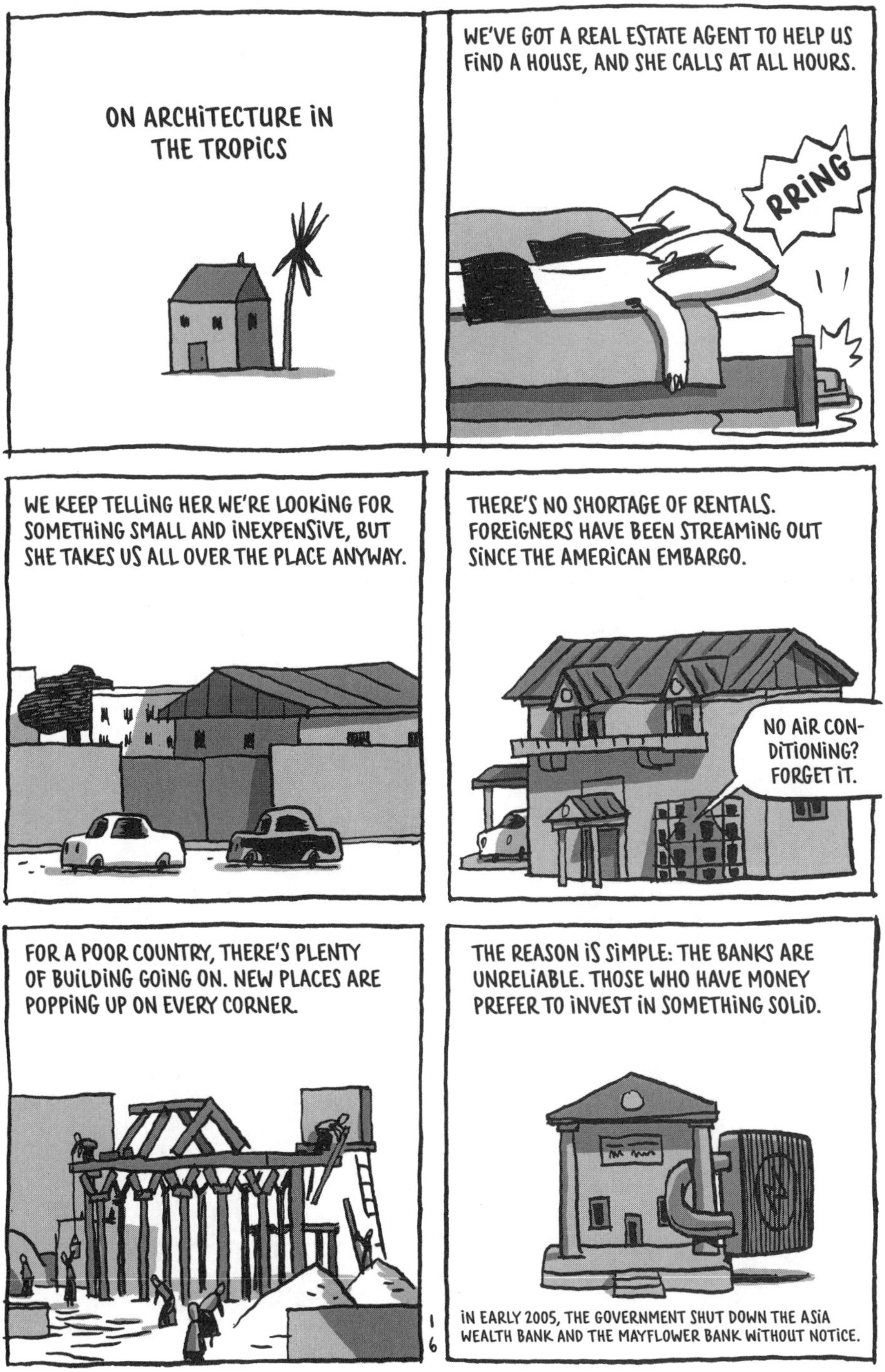
ON ARCHITECTURE IN THE TROPICS
WE'VE GOT A REAL ESTATE AGENT TO HELP US FIND A HOUSE, AND SHE CALLS AT ALL HOURS.
RRING
WE KEEP TELLING HER WE'RE LOOKING FOR SOMETHING SMALL AND INEXPENSIVE, BUT SHE TAKES US ALL OVER THE PLACE ANYWAY.
THERE'S NO SHORTAGE OF RENTALS. FOREIGNERS HAVE BEEN STREAMING OUT SINCE THE AMERICAN EMBARGO.
NO AIR CONDITIONING? FORGET IT.
FOR A POOR COUNTRY, THERE'S PLENTY OF BUILDING GOING ON. NEW PLACES ARE POPPING UP ON EVERY CORNER.
THE REASON IS SIMPLE: THE BANKS ARE UNRELIABLE. THOSE WHO HAVE MONEY PREFER TO INVEST IN SOMETHING SOLID.
IN EARLY 2005, THE GOVERNMENT SHUT DOWN THE ASIA WEALTH BANK AND THE MAYFLOWER BANK WITHOUT NOTICE.

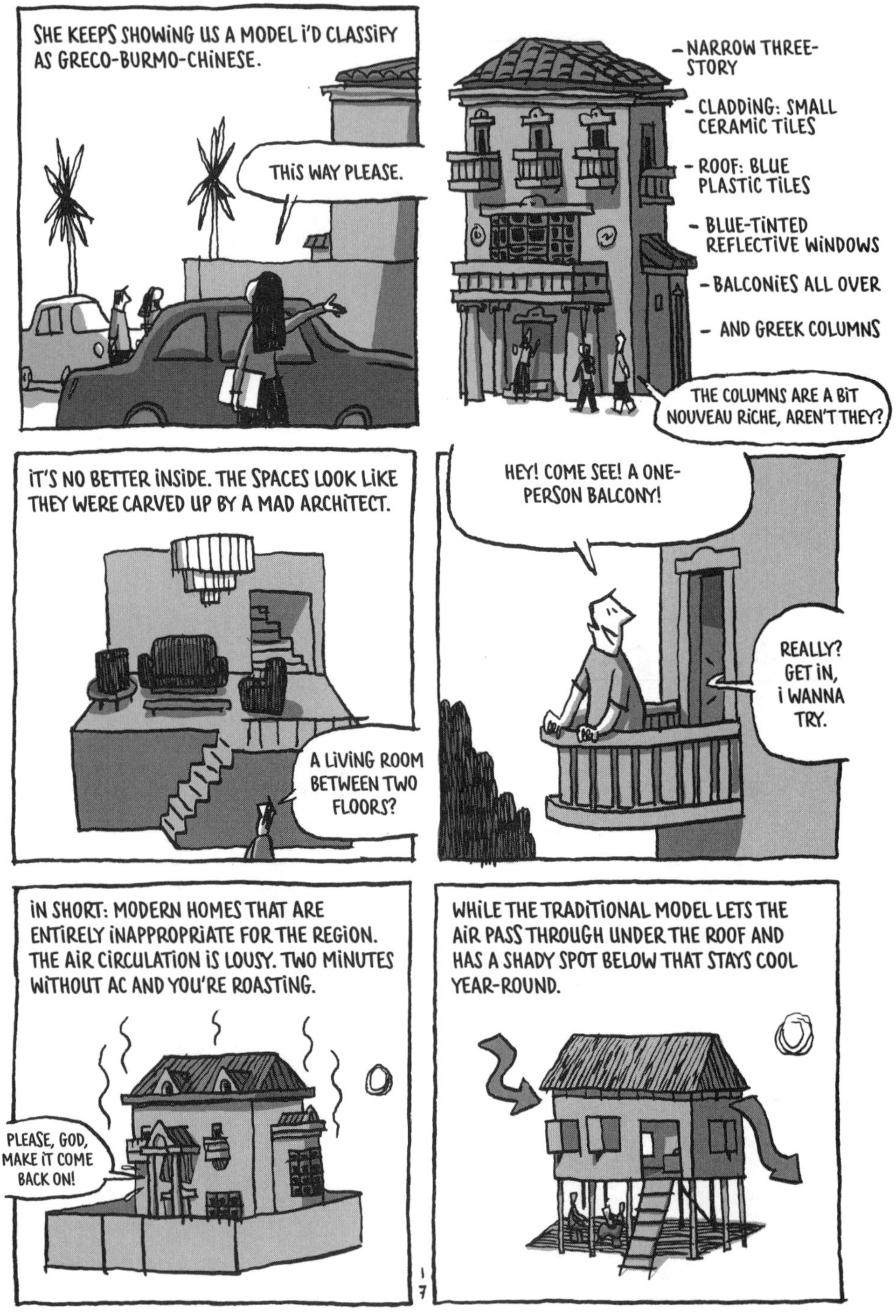
SHE KEEPS SHOWING US A MODEL I'D CLASSIFY AS GRECO-BURMO-CHINESE.
THIS WAY PLEASE.
- NARROW THREE-STORY
- CLADDING: SMALL CERAMIC TILES
- ROOF: BLUE PLASTIC TILES
- BLUE-TINTED REFLECTIVE WINDOWS
- BALCONIES ALL OVER
- AND GREEK COLUMNS
THE COLUMNS ARE A BIT NOUVEAU RICHE, AREN'T THEY?
IT'S NO BETTER INSIDE. THE SPACES LOOK LIKE THEY WERE CARVED UP BY A MAD ARCHITECT.
A LIVING ROOM BETWEEN TWO FLOORS?
HEY! COME SEE! A ONE-PERSON BALCONY!
REALLY? GET IN, I WANNA TRY.
IN SHORT: MODERN HOMES THAT ARE ENTIRELY INAPPROPRIATE FOR THE REGION. THE AIR CIRCULATION IS LOUSY. TWO MINUTES WITHOUT AC AND YOU'RE ROASTING.
PLEASE, GOD, MAKE IT COME BACK ON!
WHILE THE TRADITIONAL MODEL LETS THE AIR PASS THROUGH UNDER THE ROOF AND HAS A SHADY SPOT BELOW THAT STAYS COOL YEAR-ROUND.

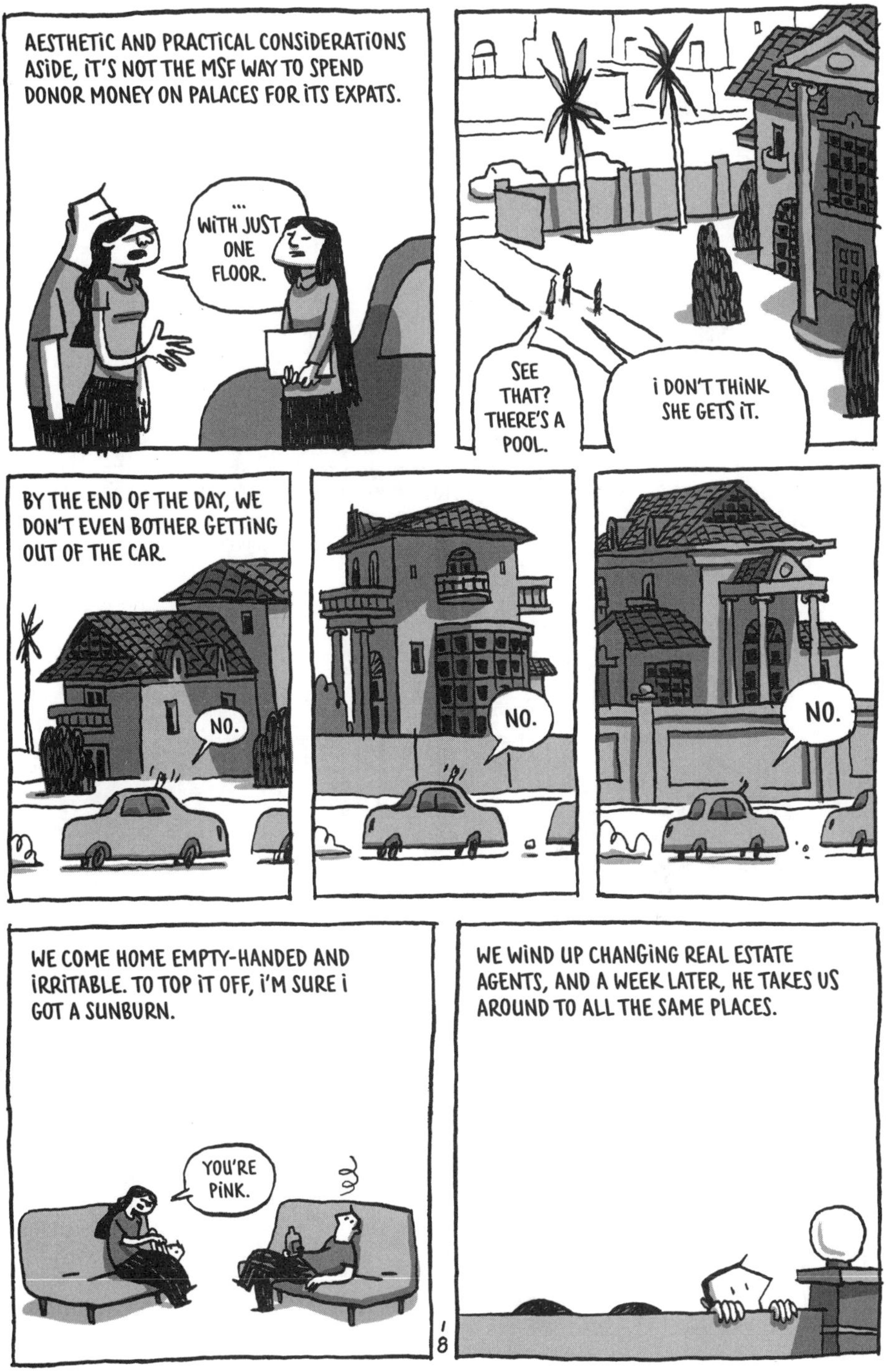
AESTHETIC AND PRACTICAL CONSIDERATIONS ASIDE, IT'S NOT THE MSF WAY TO SPEND DONOR MONEY ON PALACES FOR ITS EXPATS.
... WITH JUST ONE FLOOR.
SEE THAT? THERE'S A POOL.
I DON'T THINK SHE GETS IT.
BY THE END OF THE DAY, WE DON'T EVEN BOTHER GETTING OUT OF THE CAR.
NO.
NO.
NO.
WE COME HOME EMPTY-HANDED AND IRRITABLE. TO TOP IT OFF, I'M SURE I GOT A SUNBURN.
YOU'RE PINK.
WE WIND UP CHANGING REAL ESTATE AGENTS, AND A WEEK LATER, HE TAKES US AROUND TO ALL THE SAME PLACES.

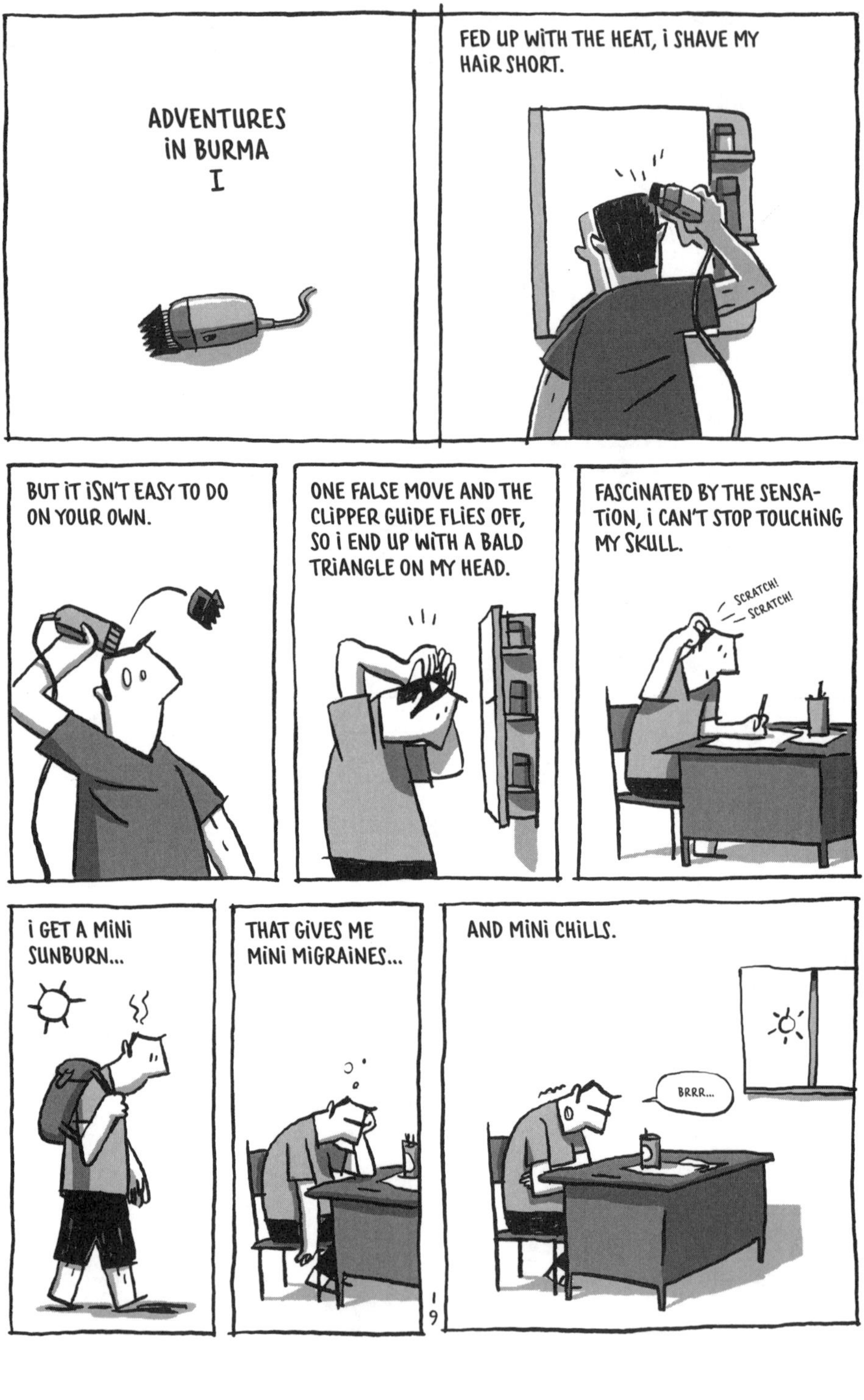
ADVENTURES IN BURMA
I
FED UP WITH THE HEAT, I SHAVE MY HAIR SHORT.
BUT IT ISN'T EASY TO DO ON YOUR OWN.
ONE FALSE MOVE AND THE CLIPPER GUIDE FLIES OFF, SO I END UP WITH A BALD TRIANGLE ON MY HEAD.
FASCINATED BY THE SENSATION, I CAN'T STOP TOUCHING MY SKULL.
SCRATCH!
SCRATCH!
I GET A MINI SUNBURN...
THAT GIVES ME MINI MIGRAINES...
AND MINI CHILLS.
BRRR...

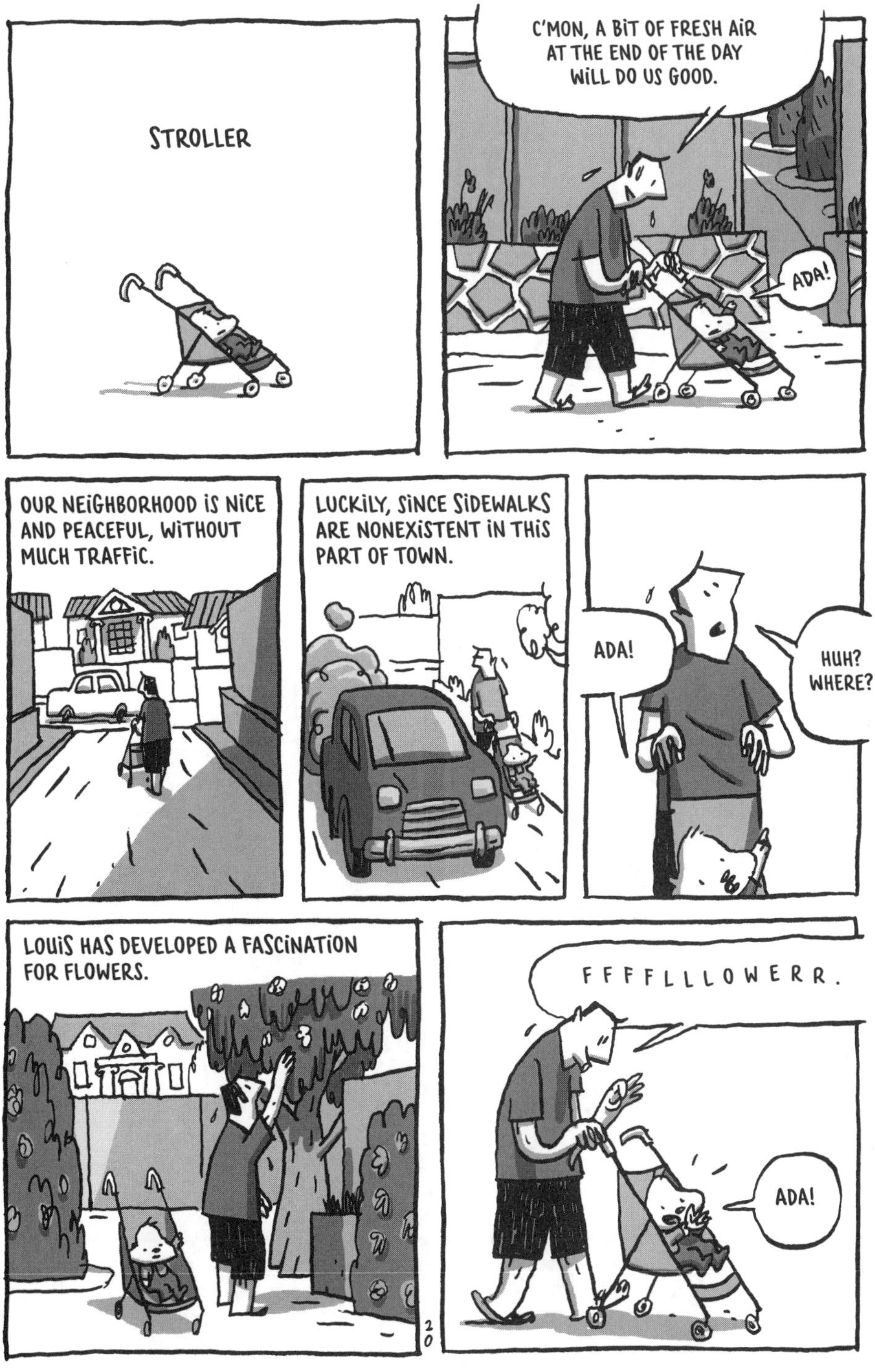
STROLLER
C'MON, A BIT OF FRESH AIR AT THE END OF THE DAY WILL DO US GOOD.
ADA!
OUR NEIGHBORHOOD IS NICE AND PEACEFUL, WITHOUT MUCH TRAFFIC.
LUCKILY, SINCE SIDEWALKS ARE NONEXISTENT IN THIS PART OF TOWN.
ADA!
HUH? WHERE?
LOUIS HAS DEVELOPED A FASCINATION FOR FLOWERS.
FFFFLLLOWERR.
ADA!

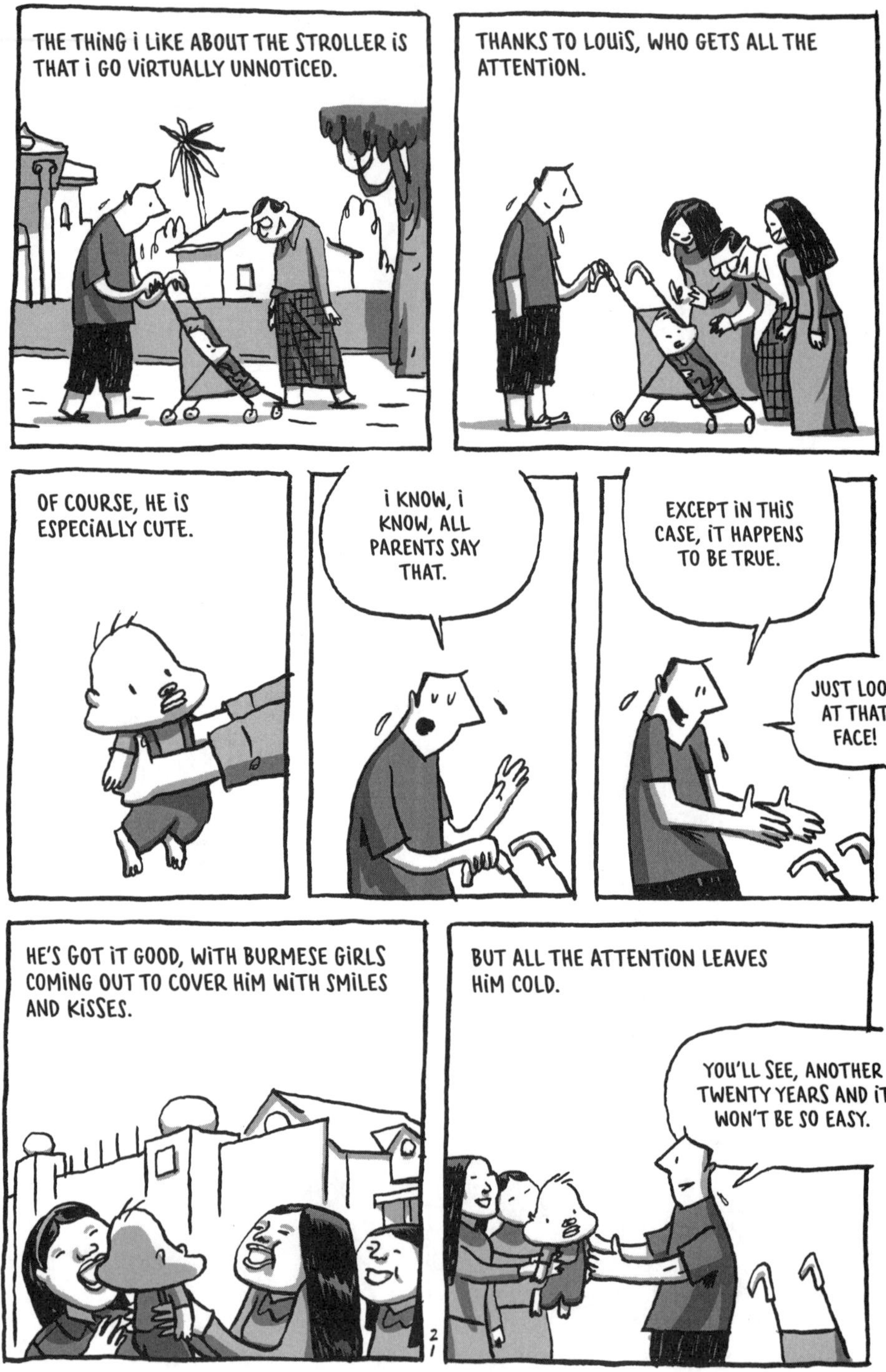
THE THING I LIKE ABOUT THE STROLLER IS THAT I GO VIRTUALLY UNNOTICED.
THANKS TO LOUIS, WHO GETS ALL THE ATTENTION.
OF COURSE, HE IS ESPECIALLY CUTE.
I KNOW, I KNOW, ALL PARENTS SAY THAT.
EXCEPT IN THIS CASE, IT HAPPENS TO BE TRUE.
JUST LOOK AT THAT FACE!
HE'S GOT IT GOOD, WITH BURMESE GIRLS COMING OUT TO COVER HIM WITH SMILES AND KISSES.
BUT ALL THE ATTENTION LEAVES HIM COLD.
YOU'LL SEE, ANOTHER TWENTY YEARS AND IT WON'T BE SO EASY.

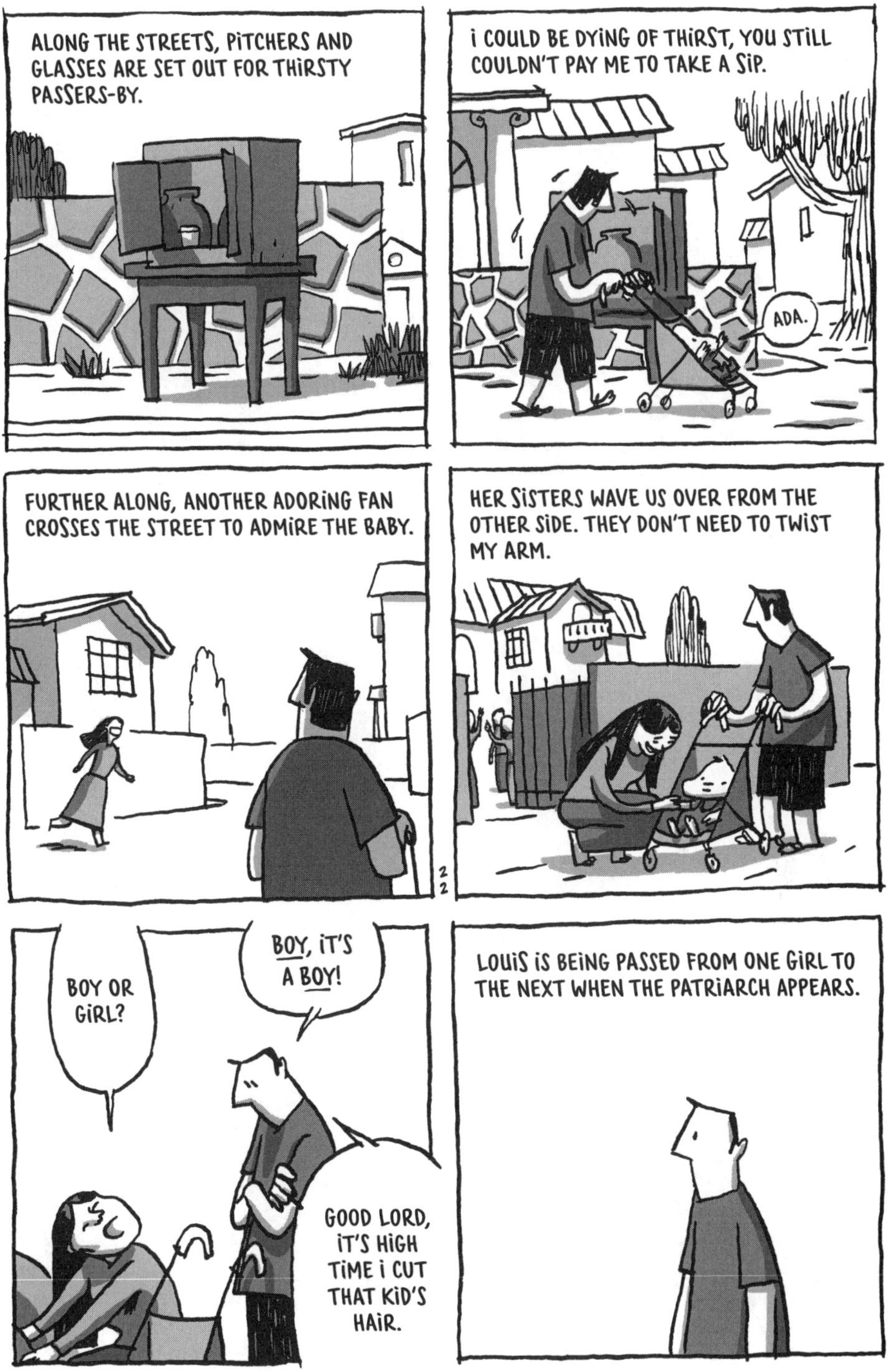

ALONG THE STREETS, PITCHERS AND GLASSES ARE SET OUT FOR THIRSTY PASSERS-BY.
I COULD BE DYING OF THIRST, YOU STILL COULDN'T PAY ME TO TAKE A SIP.
ADA.
FURTHER ALONG, ANOTHER ADORING FAN CROSSES THE STREET TO ADMIRE THE BABY.
HER SISTERS WAVE US OVER FROM THE OTHER SIDE. THEY DON'T NEED TO TWIST MY ARM.
BOY OR GIRL?
BOY, IT'S A BOY!
GOOD LORD, IT'S HIGH TIME I CUT THAT KID'S HAIR.
LOUIS IS BEING PASSED FROM ONE GIRL TO THE NEXT WHEN THE PATRIARCH APPEARS.

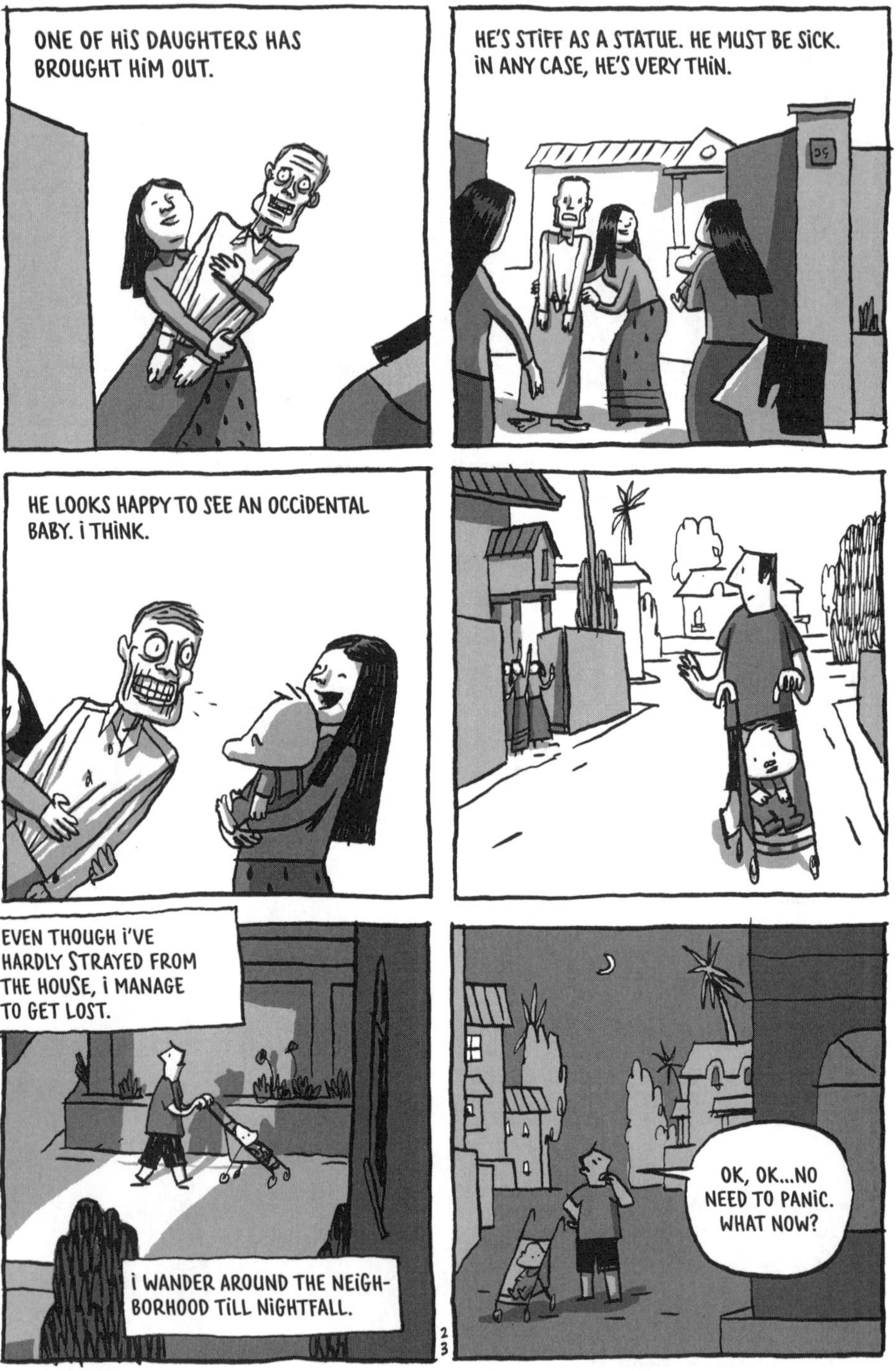
ONE OF HIS DAUGHTERS HAS BROUGHT HIM OUT.
HE'S STIFF AS A STATUE. HE MUST BE SICK. IN ANY CASE, HE'S VERY THIN.
HE LOOKS HAPPY TO SEE AN OCCIDENTAL BABY. I THINK.
EVEN THOUGH I'VE HARDLY STRAYED FROM THE HOUSE, I MANAGE TO GET LOST.
I WANDER AROUND THE NEIGHBORHOOD TILL NIGHTFALL.
OK, OK...NO NEED TO PANIC. WHAT NOW?

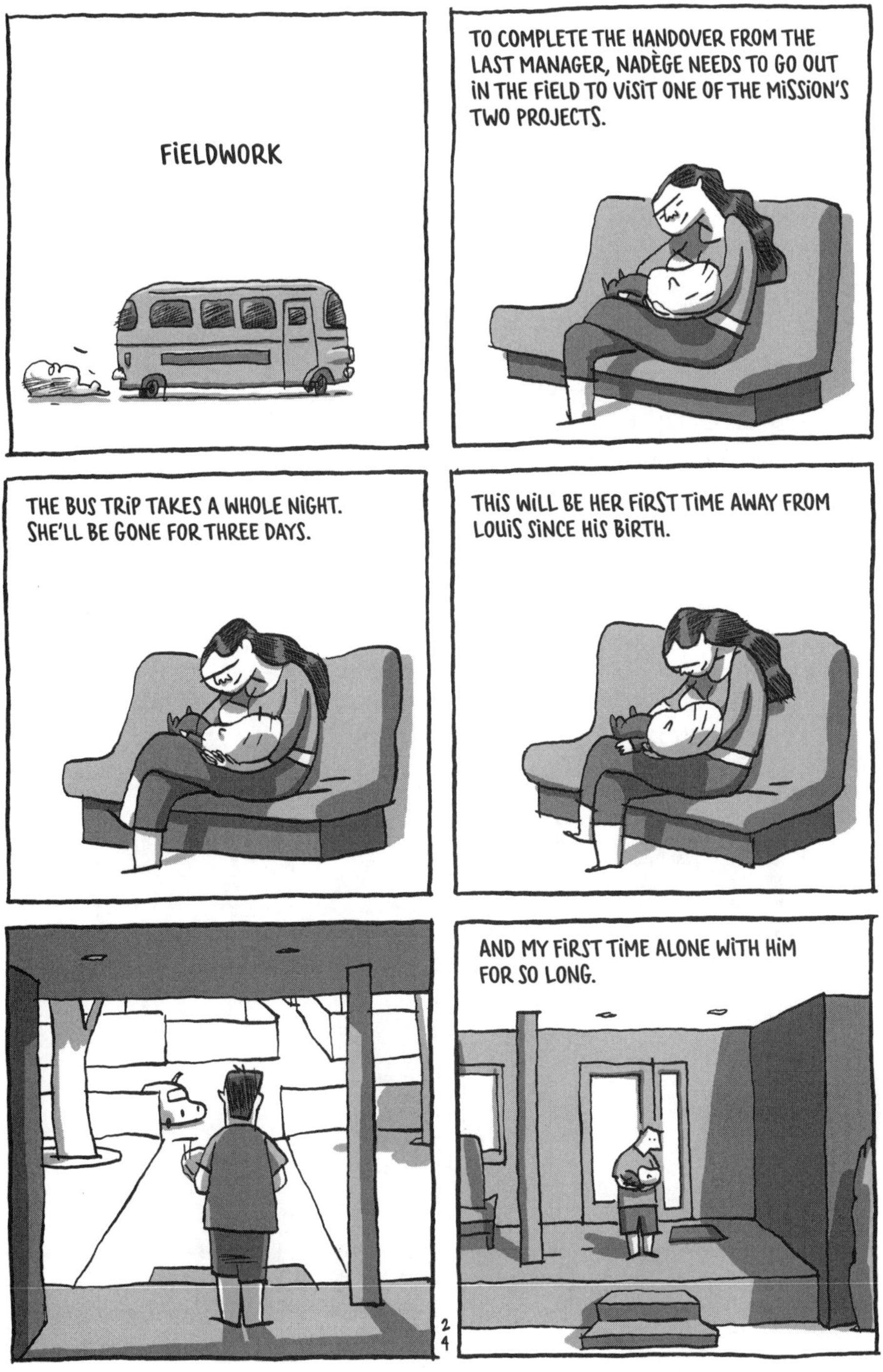
FIELDWORK
TO COMPLETE THE HANDOVER FROM THE LAST MANAGER, NADÈGE NEEDS TO GO OUT IN THE FIELD TO VISIT ONE OF THE MISSION'S TWO PROJECTS.
THE BUS TRIP TAKES A WHOLE NIGHT. SHE'LL BE GONE FOR THREE DAYS.
THIS WILL BE HER FIRST TIME AWAY FROM LOUIS SINCE HIS BIRTH.
AND MY FIRST TIME ALONE WITH HIM FOR SO LONG.

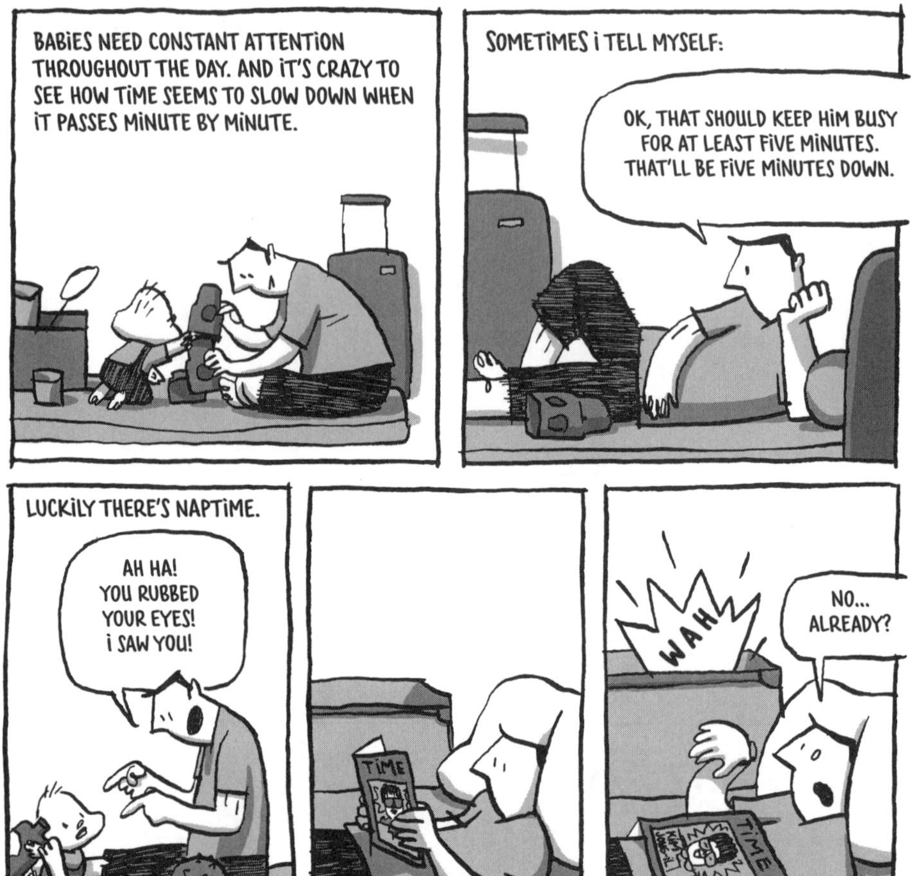
BABIES NEED CONSTANT ATTENTION THROUGHOUT THE DAY. AND IT'S CRAZY TO SEE HOW TIME SEEMS TO SLOW DOWN WHEN IT PASSES MINUTE BY MINUTE.
SOMETIMES I TELL MYSELF:
OK, THAT SHOULD KEEP HIM BUSY FOR AT LEAST FIVE MINUTES. THAT'LL BE FIVE MINUTES DOWN.
LUCKILY THERE'S NAPTIME.
AH HA! YOU RUBBED YOUR EYES! I SAW YOU!
TIME
WAH
NO... ALREADY?
TIME
LOUIS' LATEST GAME INVOLVES LETTING SMALL OBJECTS FALL INTO HARD-TO-REACH PLACES.
AND THEN CRYING FOR THEM.
ADA
ADA
ADA
ADA
HANG ON, I'M COMING.

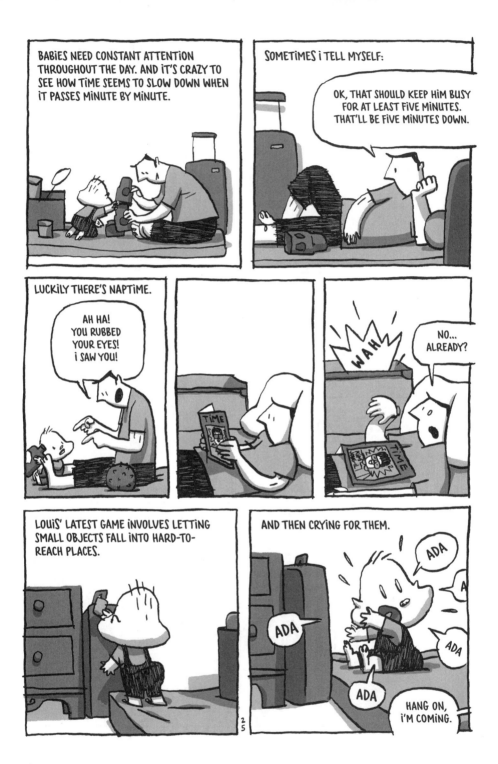

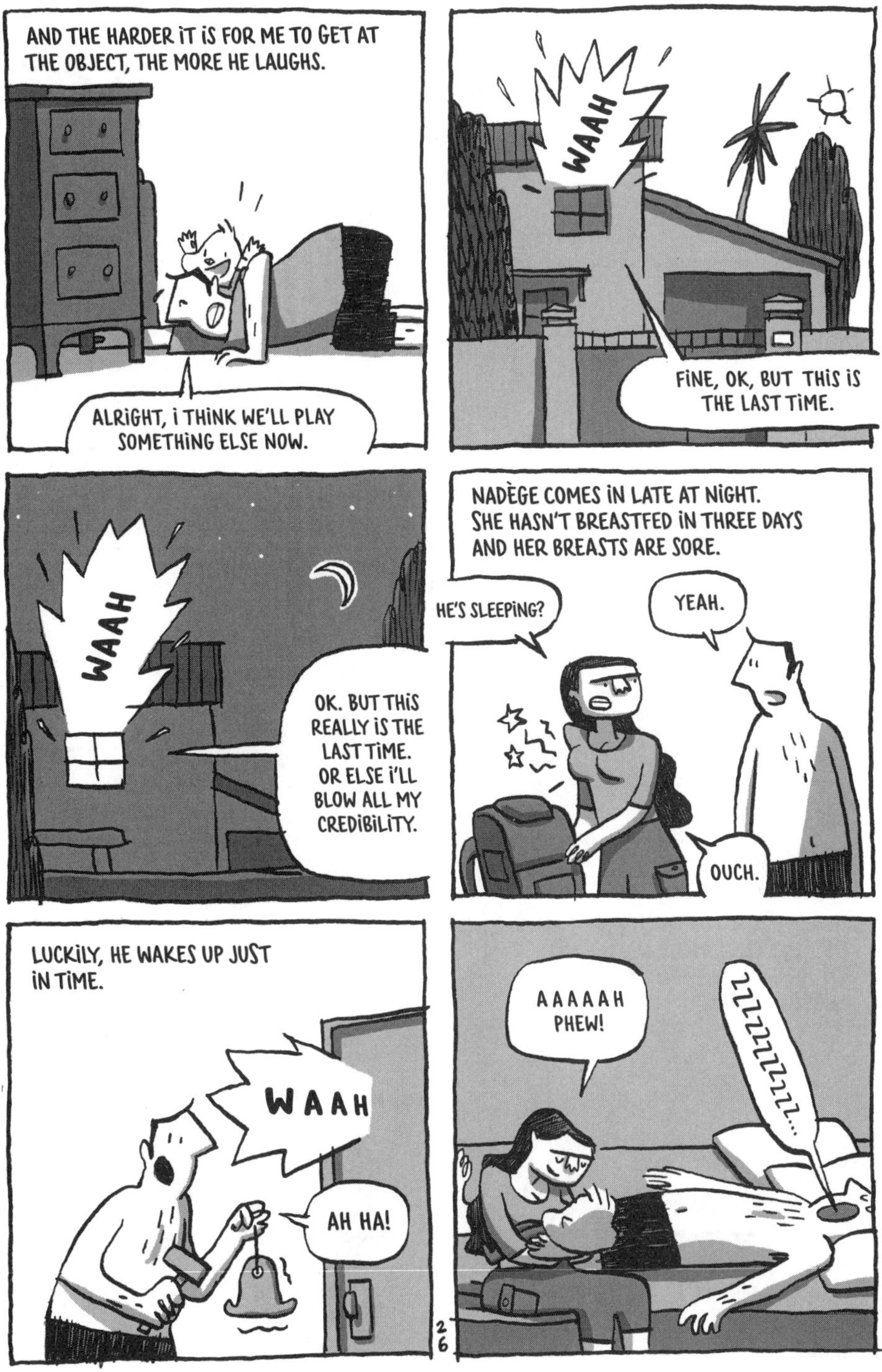
AND THE HARDER IT IS FOR ME TO GET AT THE OBJECT, THE MORE HE LAUGHS.
ALRIGHT, I THINK WE'LL PLAY SOMETHING ELSE NOW.
WAAH
FINE, OK, BUT THIS IS THE LAST TIME.
WAAH
OK. BUT THIS REALLY IS THE LAST TIME. OR ELSE I'LL BLOW ALL MY CREDIBILITY.
NADÈGE COMES IN LATE AT NIGHT. SHE HASN'T BREASTFED IN THREE DAYS AND HER BREASTS ARE SORE.
HE'S SLEEPING?
YEAH.
OUCH.
LUCKILY, HE WAKES UP JUST IN TIME.
WAAH
AH HA!
AAAAAH PHEW!
ZZZZZZZZZ...

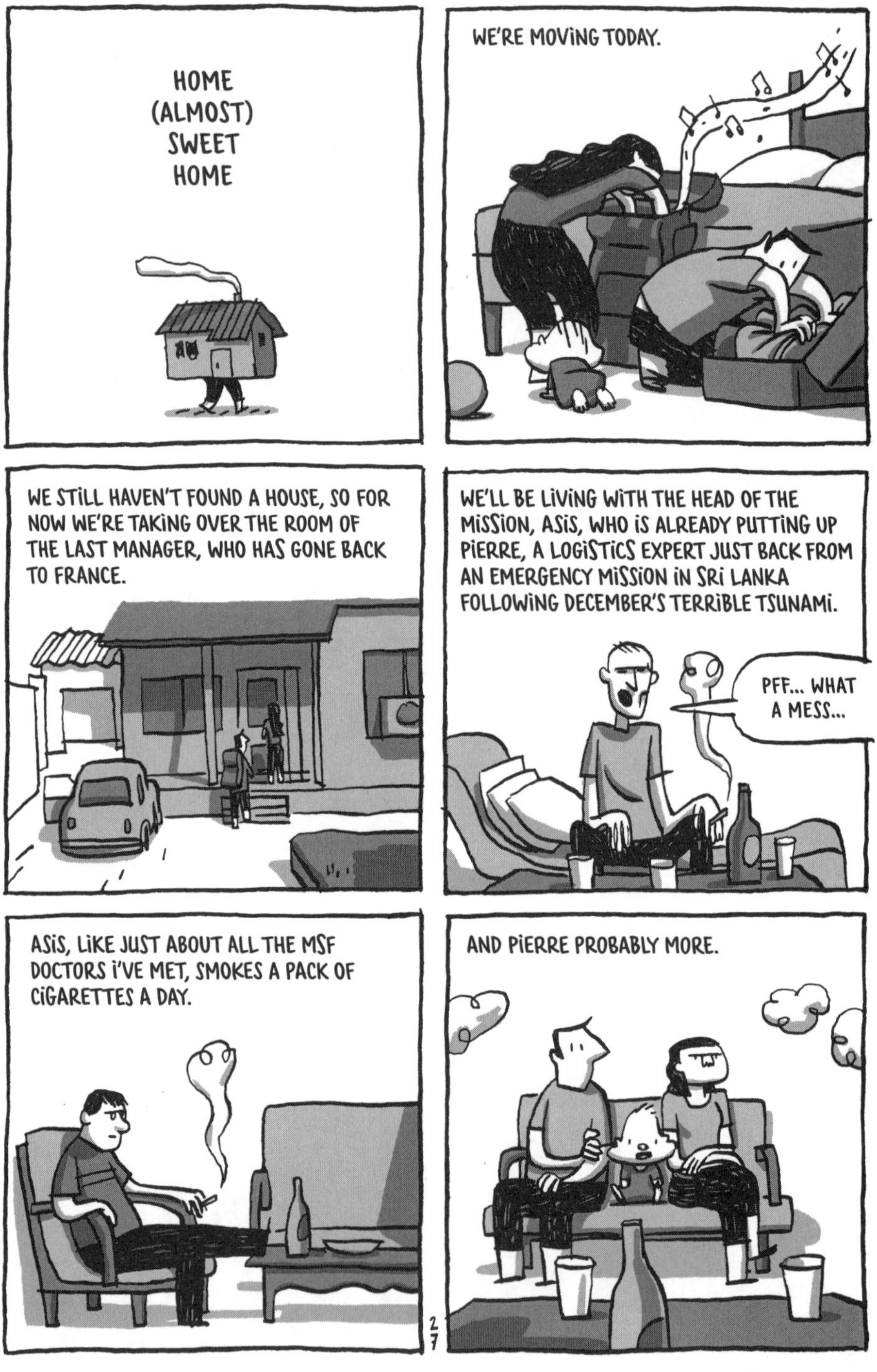
HOME (ALMOST) SWEET HOME
WE'RE MOVING TODAY.
WE STILL HAVEN'T FOUND A HOUSE, SO FOR NOW WE'RE TAKING OVER THE ROOM OF THE LAST MANAGER, WHO HAS GONE BACK TO FRANCE.
WE'LL BE LIVING WITH THE HEAD OF THE MISSION, ASIS, WHO IS ALREADY PUTTING UP PIERRE, A LOGISTICS EXPERT JUST BACK FROM AN EMERGENCY MISSION IN SRI LANKA FOLLOWING DECEMBER'S TERRIBLE TSUNAMI.
PFF... WHAT A MESS...
ASIS, LIKE JUST ABOUT ALL THE MSF DOCTORS I'VE MET, SMOKES A PACK OF CIGARETTES A DAY.
AND PIERRE PROBABLY MORE.

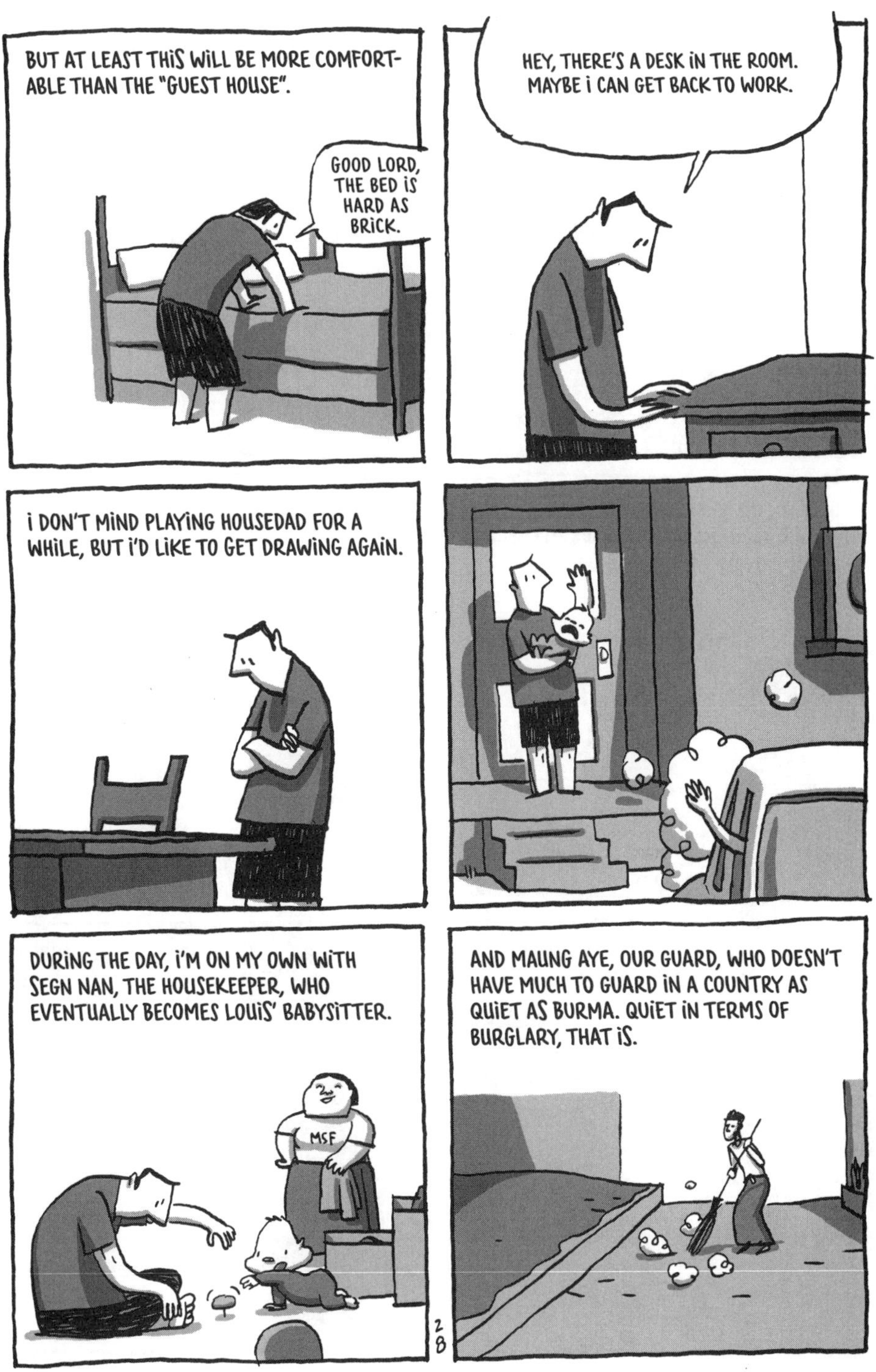
BUT AT LEAST THIS WILL BE MORE COMFORTABLE THAN THE "GUEST HOUSE".
GOOD LORD, THE BED IS HARD AS BRICK.
HEY, THERE'S A DESK IN THE ROOM. MAYBE I CAN GET BACK TO WORK.
I DON'T MIND PLAYING HOUSEDAD FOR A WHILE, BUT I'D LIKE TO GET DRAWING AGAIN.
DURING THE DAY, I'M ON MY OWN WITH SEGN NAN, THE HOUSEKEEPER, WHO EVENTUALLY BECOMES LOUIS' BABYSITTER.
MSF
AND MAUNG AYE, OUR GUARD, WHO DOESN'T HAVE MUCH TO GUARD IN A COUNTRY AS QUIET AS BURMA. QUIET IN TERMS OF BURGLARY, THAT IS.

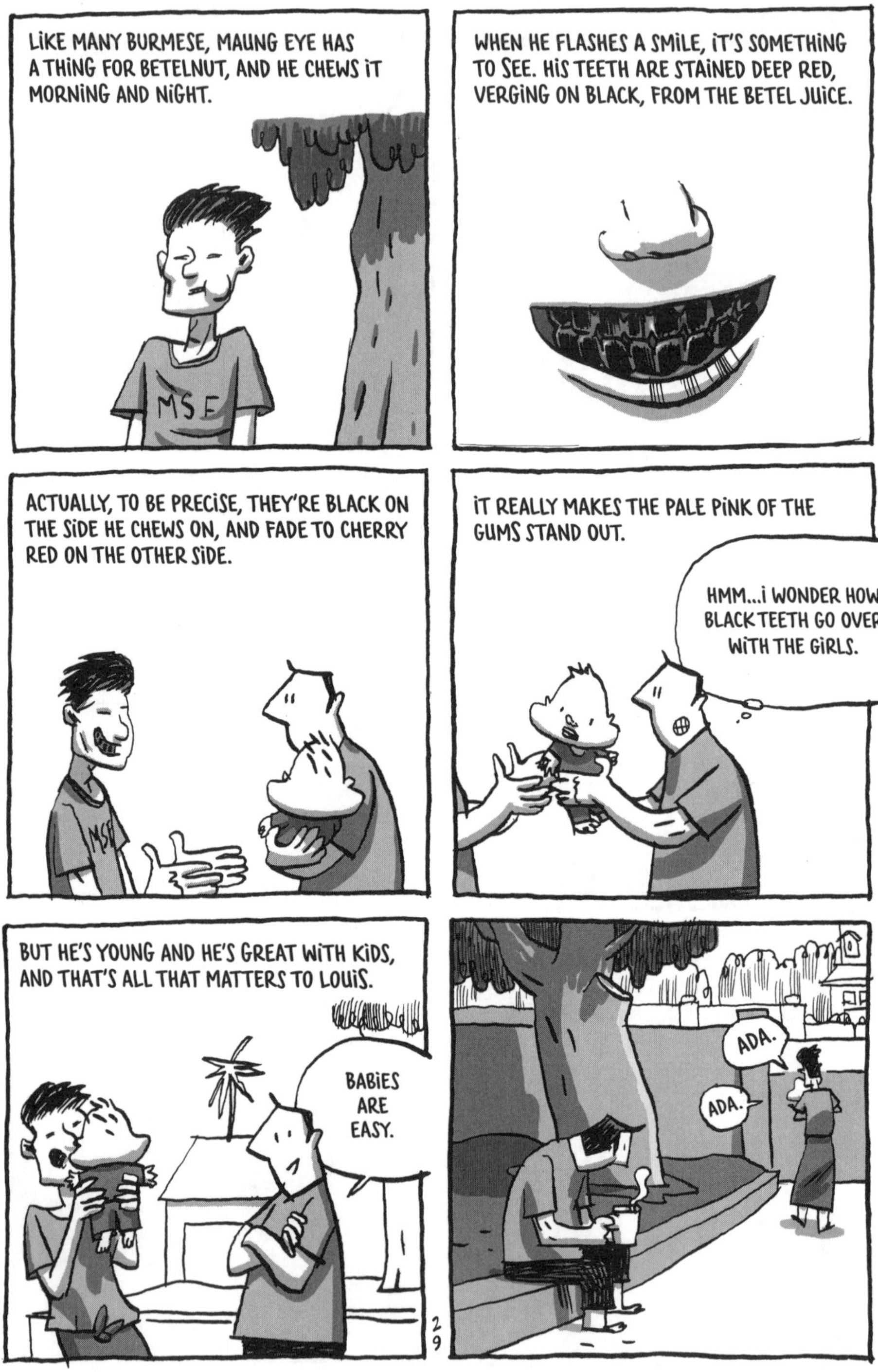
LIKE MANY BURMESE, MAUNG EYE HAS A THING FOR BETELNUT, AND HE CHEWS IT MORNING AND NIGHT.
MSF
WHEN HE FLASHES A SMILE, IT'S SOMETHING TO SEE. HIS TEETH ARE STAINED DEEP RED, VERGING ON BLACK, FROM THE BETEL JUICE.
ACTUALLY, TO BE PRECISE, THEY'RE BLACK ON THE SIDE HE CHEWS ON, AND FADE TO CHERRY RED ON THE OTHER SIDE.
IT REALLY MAKES THE PALE PINK OF THE GUMS STAND OUT.
HMM...I WONDER HOW BLACK TEETH GO OVER WITH THE GIRLS.
BUT HE'S YOUNG AND HE'S GREAT WITH KIDS, AND THAT'S ALL THAT MATTERS TO LOUIS.
BABIES ARE EASY.
ADA.
ADA.

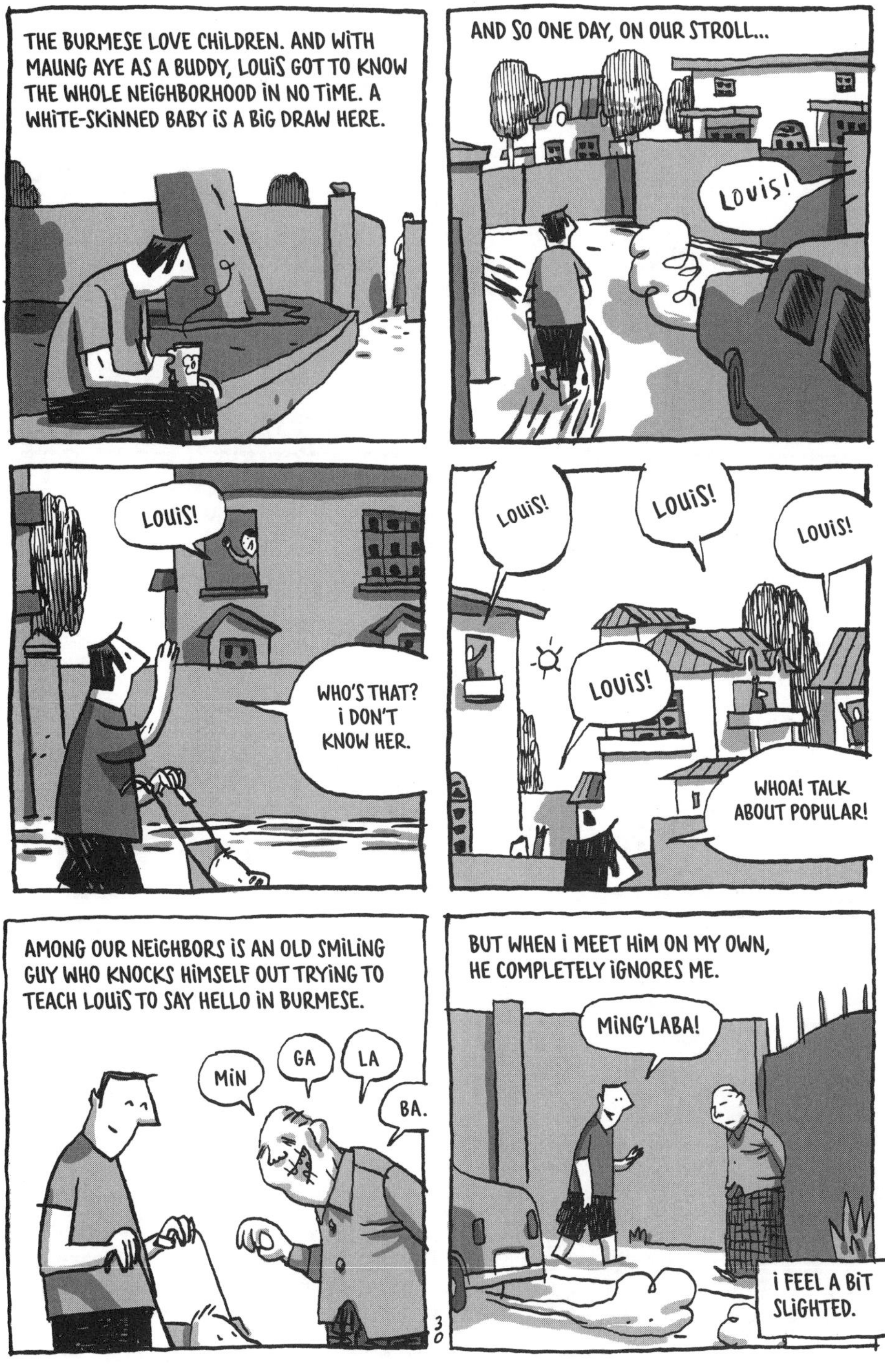
THE BURMESE LOVE CHILDREN. AND WITH MAUNG AYE AS A BUDDY, LOUIS GOT TO KNOW THE WHOLE NEIGHBORHOOD IN NO TIME. A WHITE-SKINNED BABY IS A BIG DRAW HERE.
AND SO ONE DAY, ON OUR STROLL...
LOUIS!
LOUIS!
WHO'S THAT? I DON'T KNOW HER.
LOUIS!
LOUIS!
LOUIS!
LOUIS!
WHOA! TALK ABOUT POPULAR!
AMONG OUR NEIGHBORS IS AN OLD SMILING GUY WHO KNOCKS HIMSELF OUT TRYING TO TEACH LOUIS TO SAY HELLO IN BURMESE.
MIN
GA
LA
BA.
BUT WHEN I MEET HIM ON MY OWN, HE COMPLETELY IGNORES ME.
MING'LABA!
I FEEL A BIT SLIGHTED.

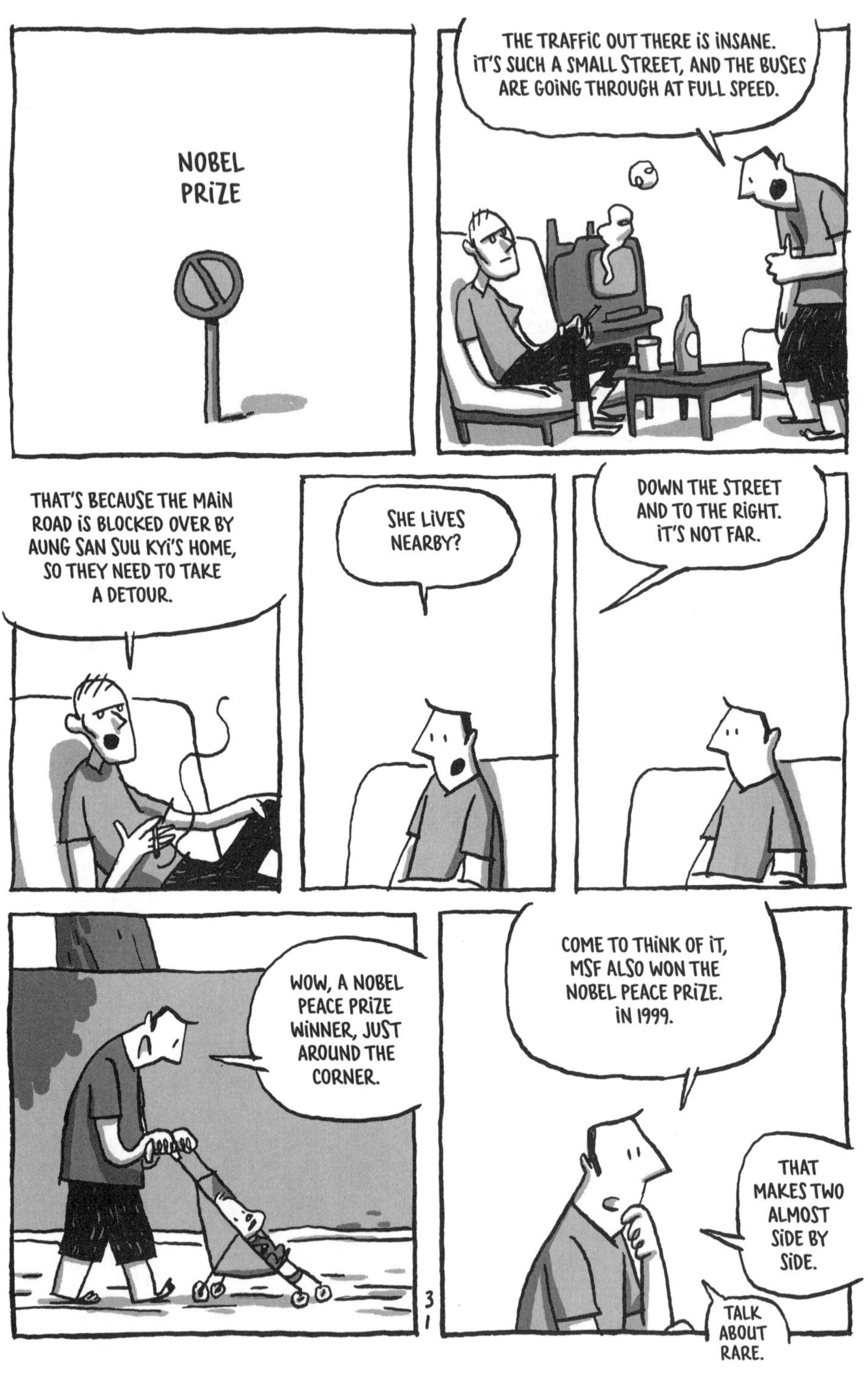
NOBEL PRIZE
THE TRAFFIC OUT THERE IS INSANE. IT'S SUCH A SMALL STREET, AND THE BUSES ARE GOING THROUGH AT FULL SPEED.
THAT'S BECAUSE THE MAIN ROAD IS BLOCKED OVER BY AUNG SAN SUU KYI'S HOME, SO THEY NEED TO TAKE A DETOUR.
SHE LIVES NEARBY?
DOWN THE STREET AND TO THE RIGHT. IT'S NOT FAR.
WOW, A NOBEL PEACE PRIZE WINNER, JUST AROUND THE CORNER.
COME TO THINK OF IT, MSF ALSO WON THE NOBEL PEACE PRIZE. IN 1999.
THAT MAKES TWO ALMOST SIDE BY SIDE.
TALK ABOUT RARE.

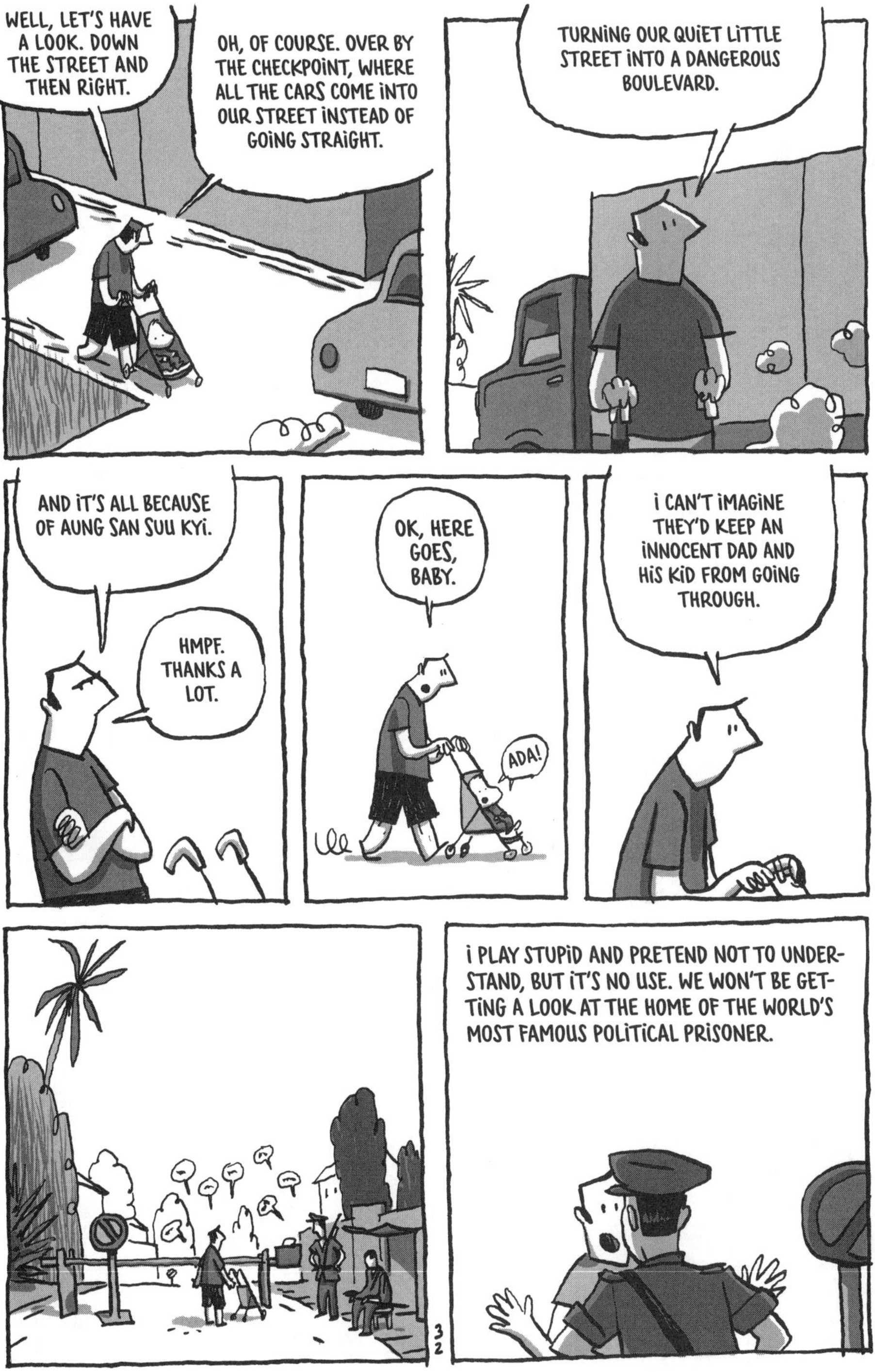

WELL, LET'S HAVE A LOOK. DOWN THE STREET AND THEN RIGHT.
OH, OF COURSE. OVER BY THE CHECKPOINT, WHERE ALL THE CARS COME INTO OUR STREET INSTEAD OF GOING STRAIGHT.
TURNING OUR QUIET LITTLE STREET INTO A DANGEROUS BOULEVARD.
AND IT'S ALL BECAUSE OF AUNG SAN SUU KYI.
HMPF. THANKS A LOT.
OK, HERE GOES, BABY.
ADA!
I CAN'T IMAGINE THEY'D KEEP AN INNOCENT DAD AND HIS KID FROM GOING THROUGH.
I PLAY STUPID AND PRETEND NOT TO UNDERSTAND, BUT IT'S NO USE. WE WON'T BE GETTING A LOOK AT THE HOME OF THE WORLD'S MOST FAMOUS POLITICAL PRISONER.

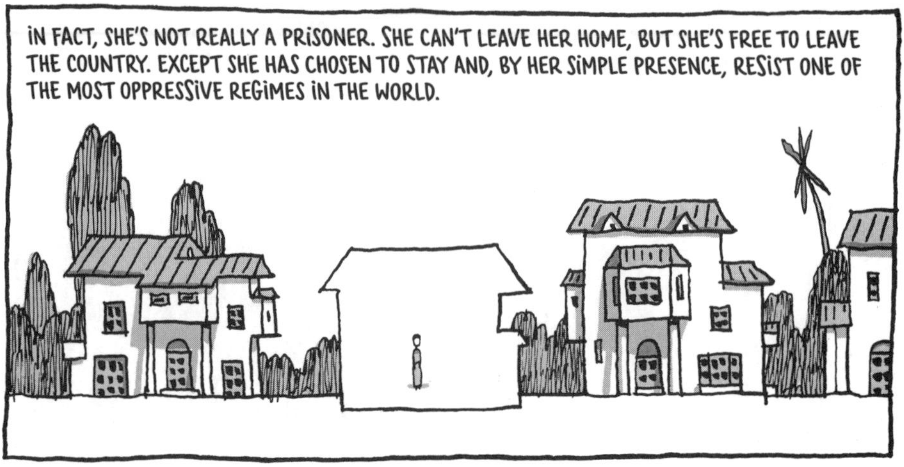
IN FACT, SHE'S NOT REALLY A PRISONER. SHE CAN'T LEAVE HER HOME, BUT SHE'S FREE TO LEAVE THE COUNTRY. EXCEPT SHE HAS CHOSEN TO STAY AND, BY HER SIMPLE PRESENCE, RESIST ONE OF THE MOST OPPRESSIVE REGIMES IN THE WORLD.

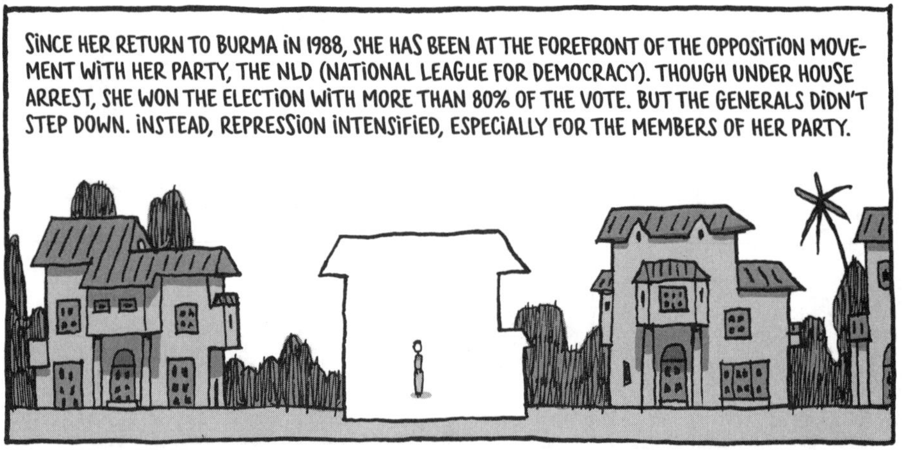
SINCE HER RETURN TO BURMA IN 1988, SHE HAS BEEN AT THE FOREFRONT OF THE OPPOSITION MOVEMENT WITH HER PARTY, THE NLD (NATIONAL LEAGUE FOR DEMOCRACY). THOUGH UNDER HOUSE ARREST, SHE WON THE ELECTION WITH MORE THAN 80% OF THE VOTE. BUT THE GENERALS DIDN'T STEP DOWN. INSTEAD, REPRESSION INTENSIFIED, ESPECIALLY FOR THE MEMBERS OF HER PARTY.

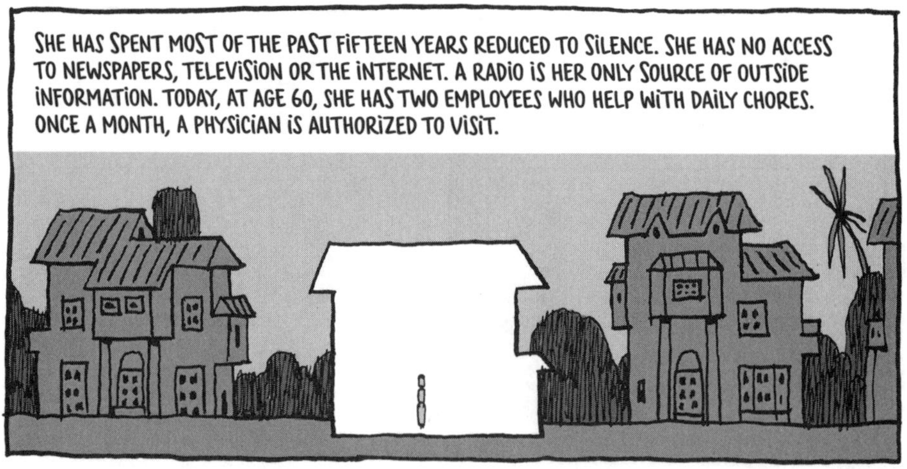
SHE HAS SPENT MOST OF THE PAST FIFTEEN YEARS REDUCED TO SILENCE. SHE HAS NO ACCESS TO NEWSPAPERS, TELEVISION OR THE INTERNET. A RADIO IS HER ONLY SOURCE OF OUTSIDE INFORMATION. TODAY, AT AGE 60, SHE HAS TWO EMPLOYEES WHO HELP WITH DAILY CHORES. ONCE A MONTH, A PHYSICIAN IS AUTHORIZED TO VISIT.

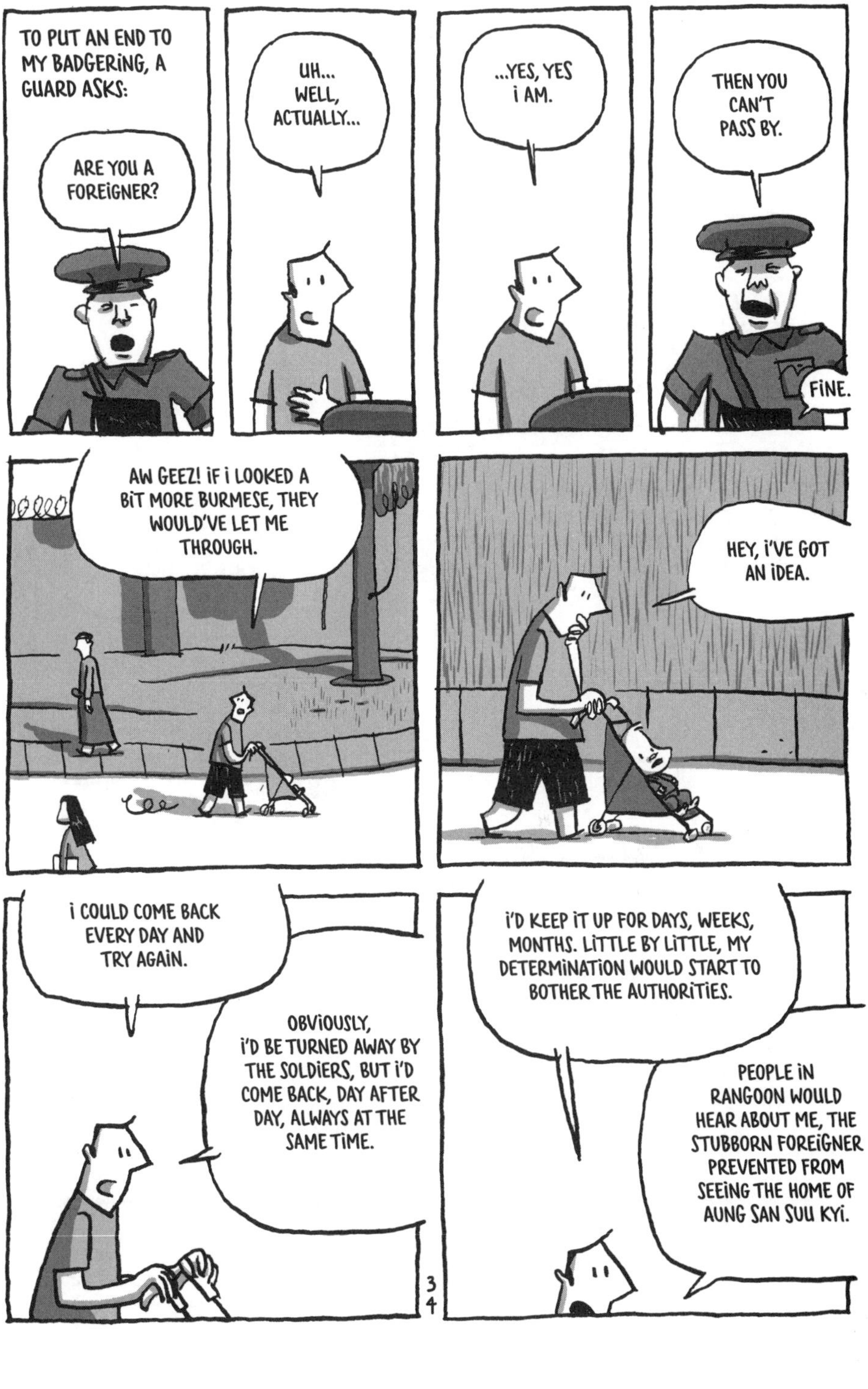
TO PUT AN END TO MY BADGERING, A GUARD ASKS:
ARE YOU A FOREIGNER?
UH... WELL, ACTUALLY...
...YES, YES I AM.
THEN YOU CAN'T PASS BY.
FINE.
AW GEEZ! IF I LOOKED A BIT MORE BURMESE, THEY WOULD'VE LET ME THROUGH.
HEY, I'VE GOT AN IDEA.
I COULD COME BACK EVERY DAY AND TRY AGAIN.
OBVIOUSLY, I'D BE TURNED AWAY BY THE SOLDIERS, BUT I'D COME BACK, DAY AFTER DAY, ALWAYS AT THE SAME TIME.
I'D KEEP IT UP FOR DAYS, WEEKS, MONTHS. LITTLE BY LITTLE, MY DETERMINATION WOULD START TO BOTHER THE AUTHORITIES.
PEOPLE IN RANGOON WOULD HEAR ABOUT ME, THE STUBBORN FOREIGNER PREVENTED FROM SEEING THE HOME OF AUNG SAN SUU KYI.

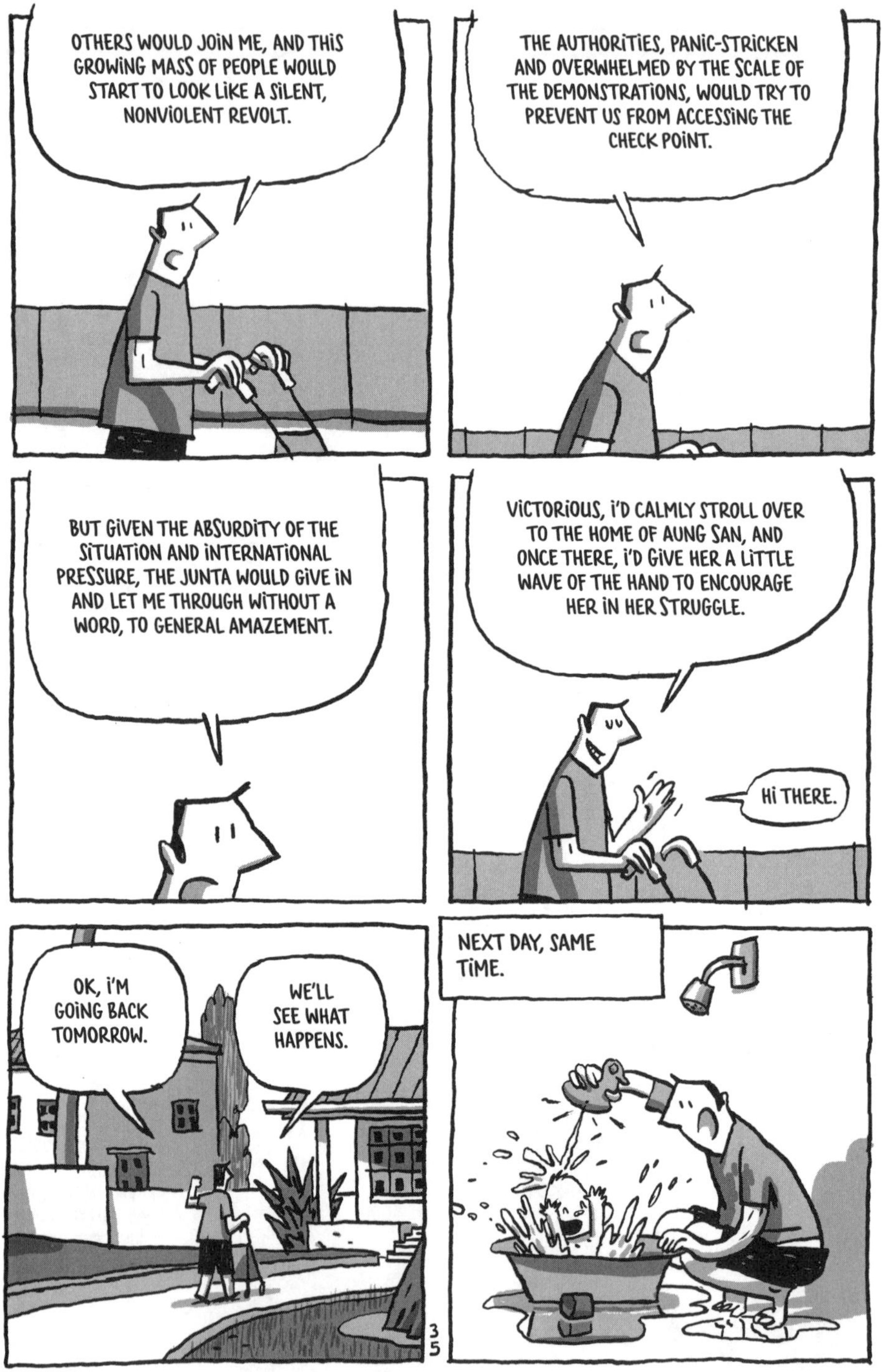
OTHERS WOULD JOIN ME, AND THIS GROWING MASS OF PEOPLE WOULD START TO LOOK LIKE A SILENT, NONVIOLENT REVOLT.
THE AUTHORITIES, PANIC-STRICKEN AND OVERWHELMED BY THE SCALE OF THE DEMONSTRATIONS, WOULD TRY TO PREVENT US FROM ACCESSING THE CHECK POINT.
BUT GIVEN THE ABSURDITY OF THE SITUATION AND INTERNATIONAL PRESSURE, THE JUNTA WOULD GIVE IN AND LET ME THROUGH WITHOUT A WORD, TO GENERAL AMAZEMENT.
VICTORIOUS, I'D CALMLY STROLL OVER TO THE HOME OF AUNG SAN, AND ONCE THERE, I'D GIVE HER A LITTLE WAVE OF THE HAND TO ENCOURAGE HER IN HER STRUGGLE.
HI THERE.
OK, I'M GOING BACK TOMORROW.
WE'LL SEE WHAT HAPPENS.
NEXT DAY, SAME TIME.

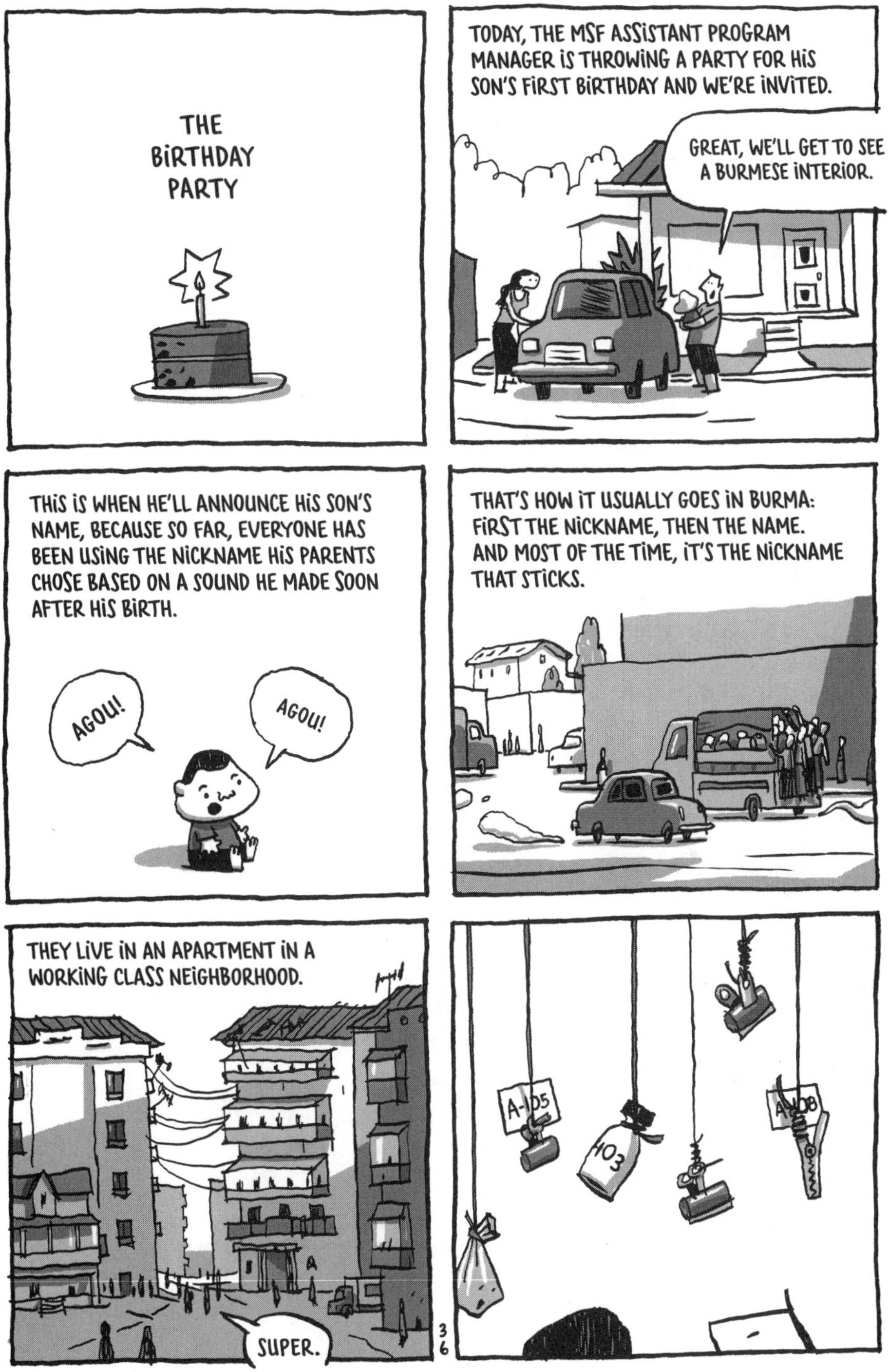
THE BIRTHDAY PARTY
TODAY, THE MSF ASSISTANT PROGRAM MANAGER IS THROWING A PARTY FOR HIS SON'S FIRST BIRTHDAY AND WE'RE INVITED.
GREAT, WE'LL GET TO SEE A BURMESE INTERIOR.
THIS IS WHEN HE'LL ANNOUNCE HIS SON'S NAME, BECAUSE SO FAR, EVERYONE HAS BEEN USING THE NICKNAME HIS PARENTS CHOSE BASED ON A SOUND HE MADE SOON AFTER HIS BIRTH.
AGOU!
AGOU!
THAT'S HOW IT USUALLY GOES IN BURMA: FIRST THE NICKNAME, THEN THE NAME. AND MOST OF THE TIME, IT'S THE NICKNAME THAT STICKS.
THEY LIVE IN AN APARTMENT IN A WORKING CLASS NEIGHBORHOOD.
SUPER.
A-105
403
A-108

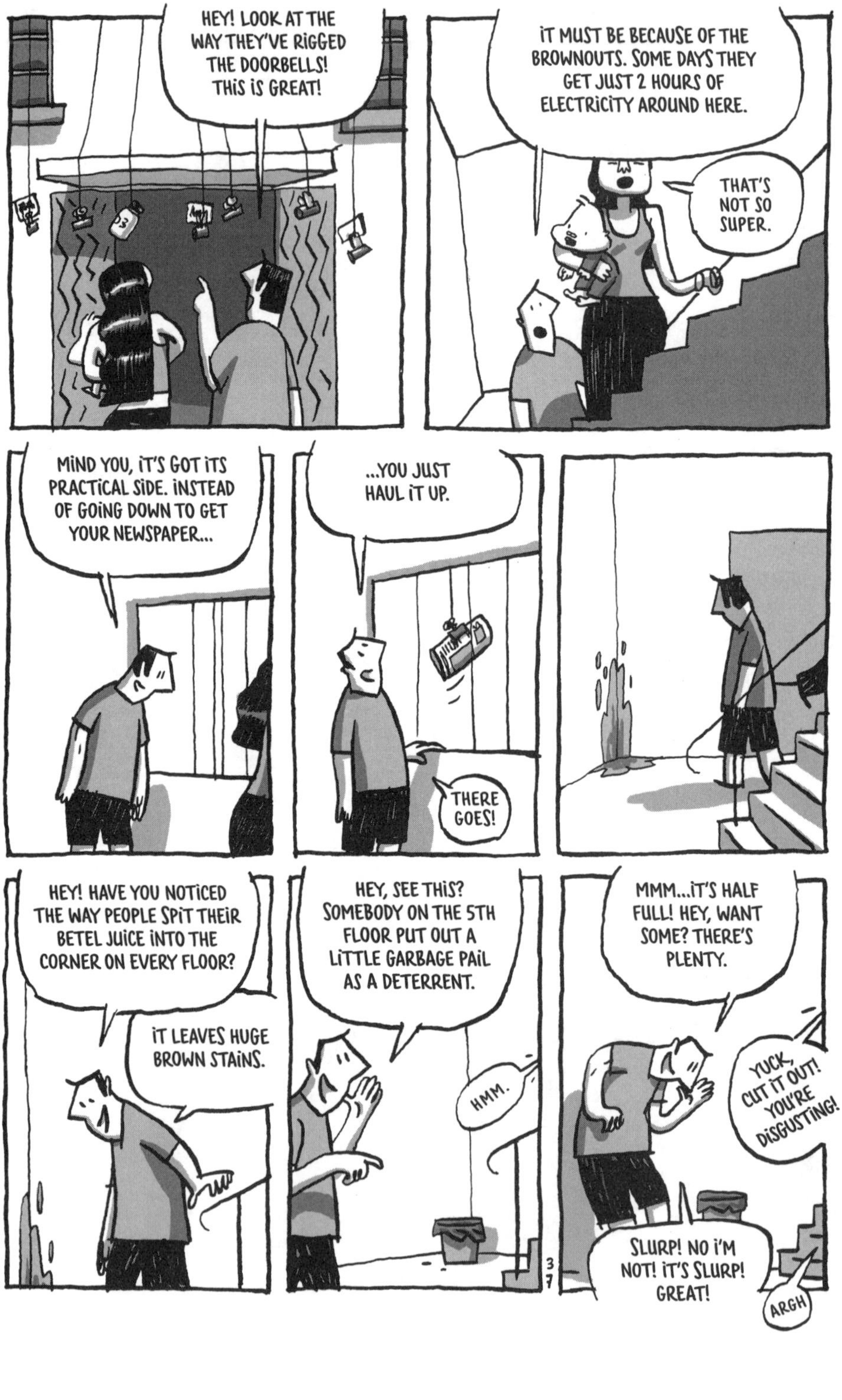
HEY! LOOK AT THE WAY THEY'VE RIGGED THE DOORBELLS! THIS IS GREAT!
IT MUST BE BECAUSE OF THE BROWNOUTS. SOME DAYS THEY GET JUST 2 HOURS OF ELECTRICITY AROUND HERE.
THAT'S NOT SO SUPER.
MIND YOU, IT'S GOT ITS PRACTICAL SIDE. INSTEAD OF GOING DOWN TO GET YOUR NEWSPAPER...
...YOU JUST HAUL IT UP.
THERE GOES!
HEY! HAVE YOU NOTICED THE WAY PEOPLE SPIT THEIR BETEL JUICE INTO THE CORNER ON EVERY FLOOR?
IT LEAVES HUGE BROWN STAINS.
HEY, SEE THIS? SOMEBODY ON THE 5TH FLOOR PUT OUT A LITTLE GARBAGE PAIL AS A DETERRENT.
HMM.
MMM...IT'S HALF FULL! HEY, WANT SOME? THERE'S PLENTY.
YUCK, CUT IT OUT! YOU'RE DISGUSTING!
SLURP! NO I'M NOT! IT'S SLURP! GREAT!
ARGH

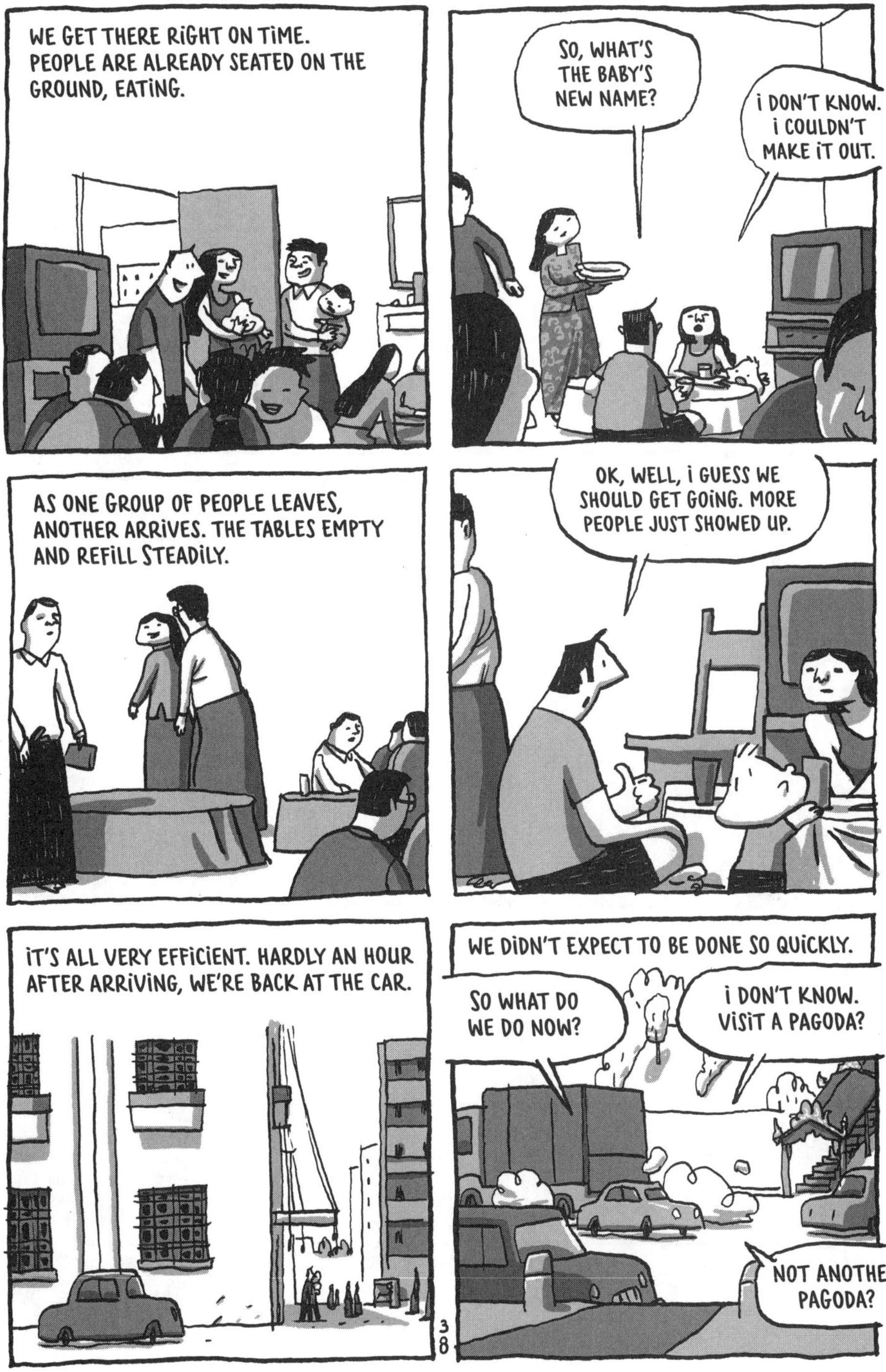
WE GET THERE RIGHT ON TIME. PEOPLE ARE ALREADY SEATED ON THE GROUND, EATING.
SO, WHAT'S THE BABY'S NEW NAME?
I DON'T KNOW. I COULDN'T MAKE IT OUT.
AS ONE GROUP OF PEOPLE LEAVES, ANOTHER ARRIVES. THE TABLES EMPTY AND REFILL STEADILY.
OK, WELL, I GUESS WE SHOULD GET GOING. MORE PEOPLE JUST SHOWED UP.
IT'S ALL VERY EFFICIENT. HARDLY AN HOUR AFTER ARRIVING, WE'RE BACK AT THE CAR.
WE DIDN'T EXPECT TO BE DONE SO QUICKLY.
SO WHAT DO WE DO NOW?
I DON'T KNOW. VISIT A PAGODA?
NOT ANOTHER PAGODA?

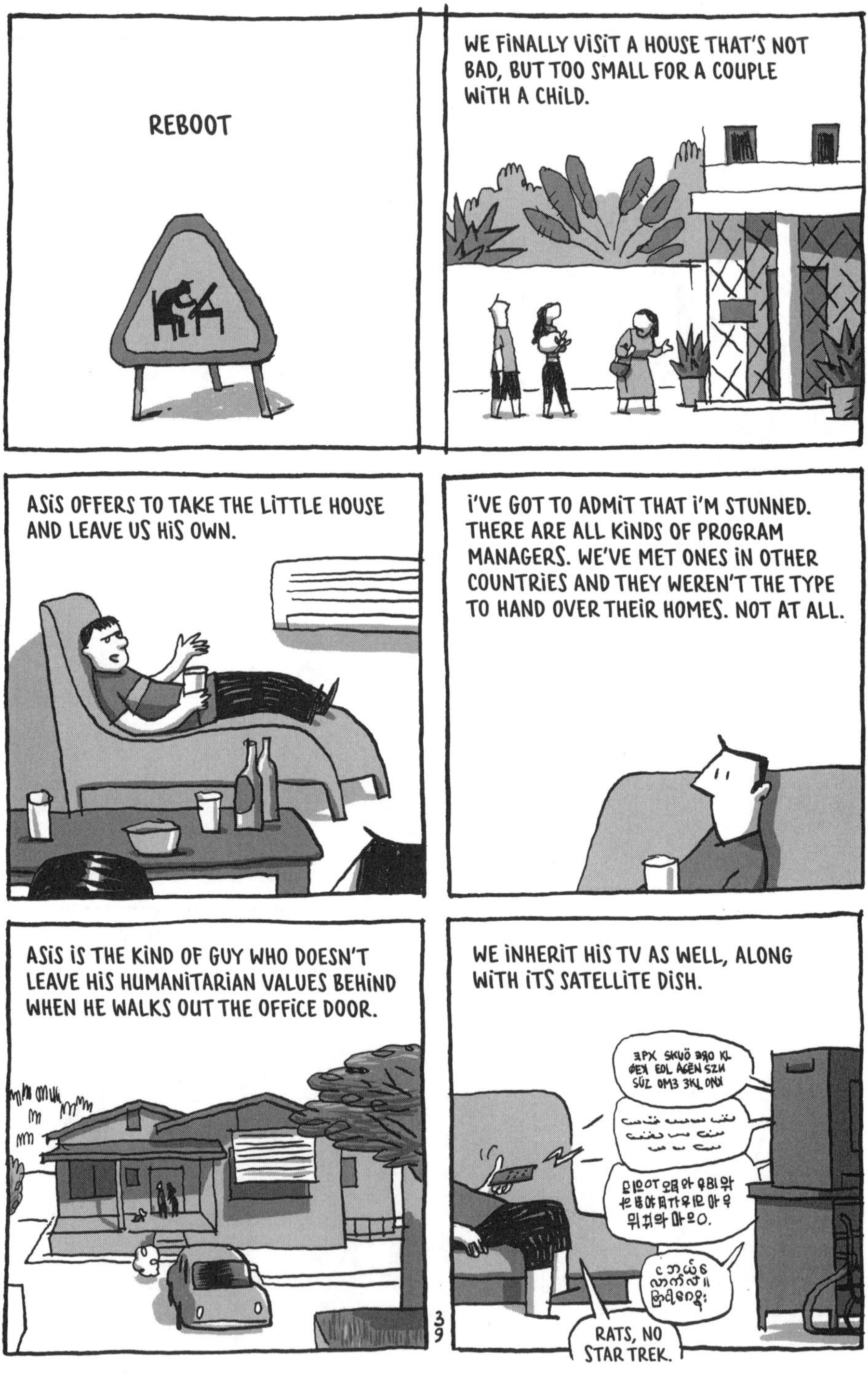
REBOOT
WE FINALLY VISIT A HOUSE THAT'S NOT BAD, BUT TOO SMALL FOR A COUPLE WITH A CHILD.
ASIS OFFERS TO TAKE THE LITTLE HOUSE AND LEAVE US HIS OWN.
I'VE GOT TO ADMIT THAT I'M STUNNED. THERE ARE ALL KINDS OF PROGRAM MANAGERS. WE'VE MET ONES IN OTHER COUNTRIES AND THEY WEREN'T THE TYPE TO HAND OVER THEIR HOMES. NOT AT ALL.
ASIS IS THE KIND OF GUY WHO DOESN'T LEAVE HIS HUMANITARIAN VALUES BEHIND WHEN HE WALKS OUT THE OFFICE DOOR.
WE INHERIT HIS TV AS WELL, ALONG WITH ITS SATELLITE DISH.
RATS, NO STAR TREK.

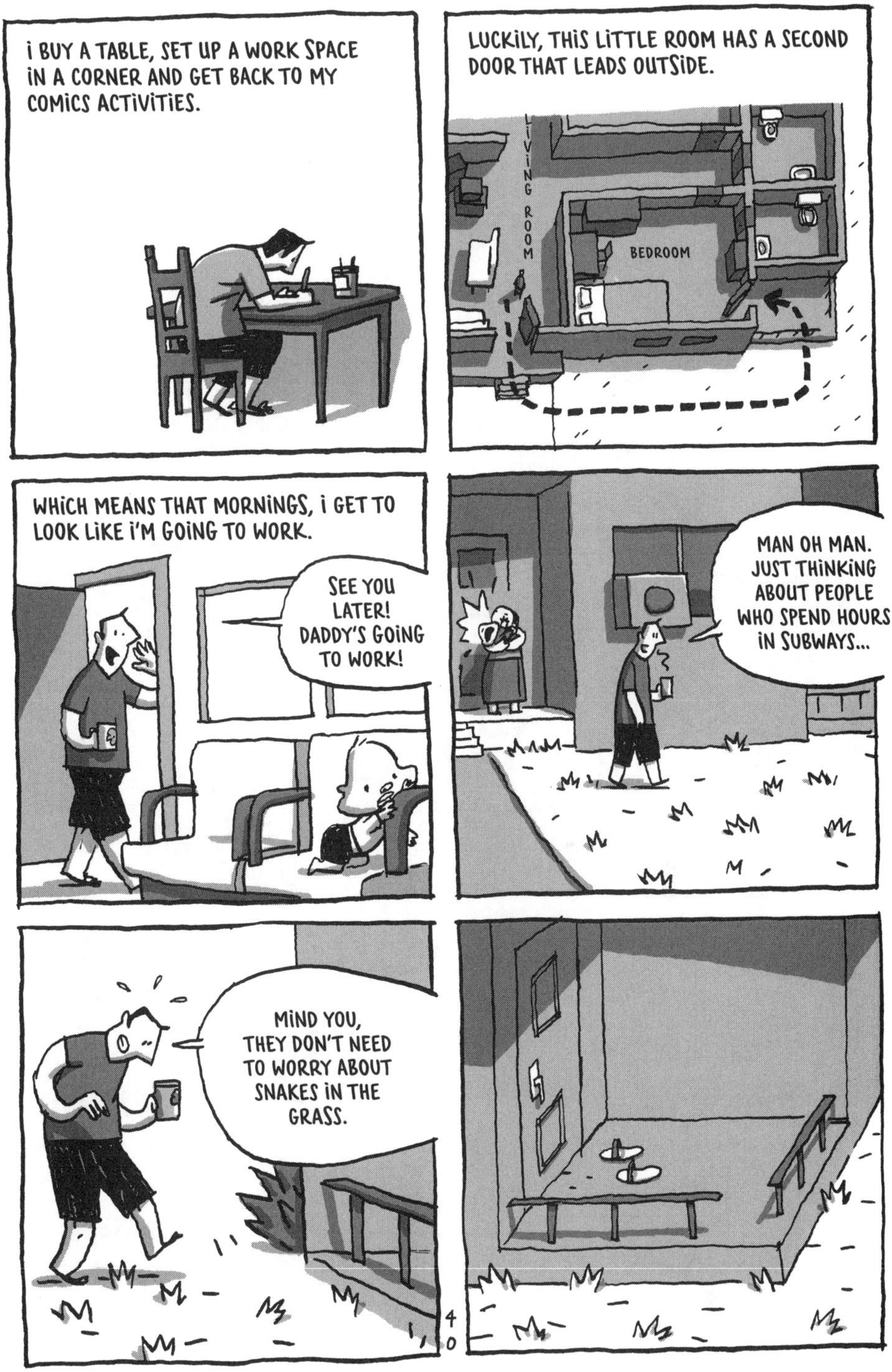
I BUY A TABLE, SET UP A WORK SPACE IN A CORNER AND GET BACK TO MY COMICS ACTIVITIES.
LUCKILY, THIS LITTLE ROOM HAS A SECOND DOOR THAT LEADS OUTSIDE.
LIVING ROOM
BEDROOM
WHICH MEANS THAT MORNINGS, I GET TO LOOK LIKE I'M GOING TO WORK.
SEE YOU LATER! DADDY'S GOING TO WORK!
MAN OH MAN. JUST THINKING ABOUT PEOPLE WHO SPEND HOURS IN SUBWAYS...
MIND YOU, THEY DON'T NEED TO WORRY ABOUT SNAKES IN THE GRASS.

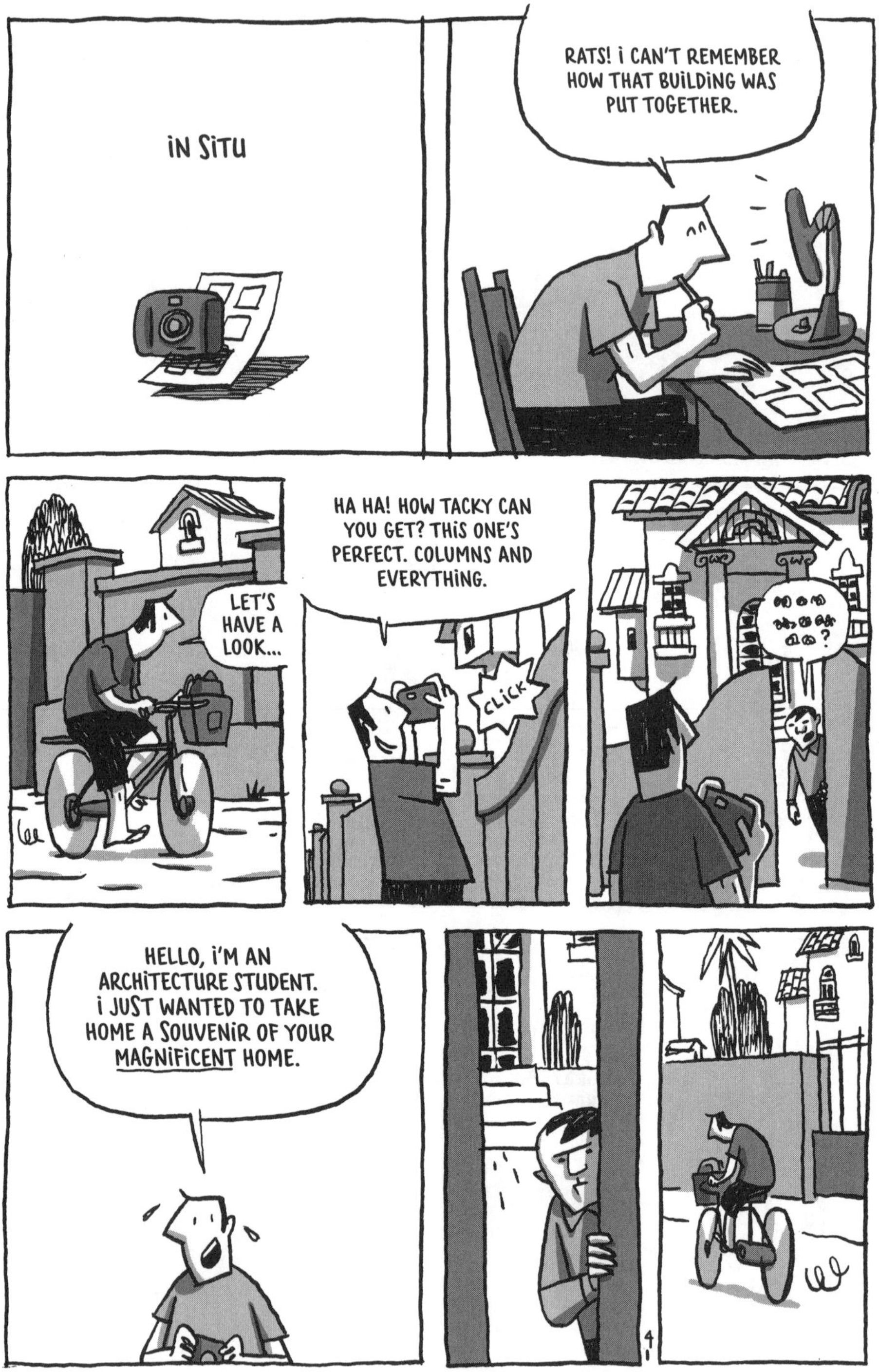

IN SITU
RATS! I CAN'T REMEMBER HOW THAT BUILDING WAS PUT TOGETHER.
LET'S HAVE A LOOK...
HA HA! HOW TACKY CAN YOU GET? THIS ONE'S PERFECT. COLUMNS AND EVERYTHING.
CLICK
HELLO, I'M AN ARCHITECTURE STUDENT. I JUST WANTED TO TAKE HOME A SOUVENIR OF YOUR MAGNIFICENT HOME.

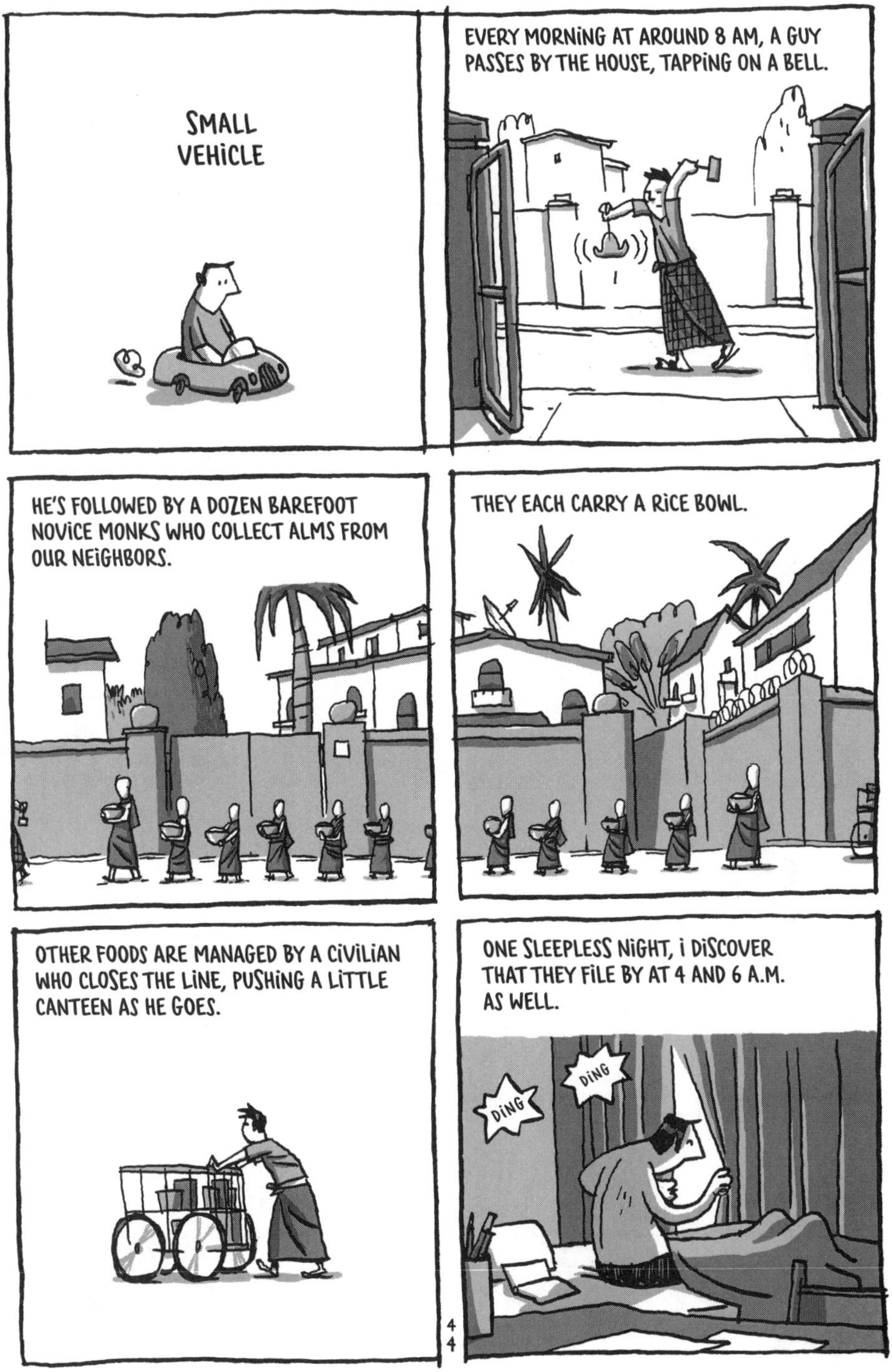
SMALL VEHICLE
EVERY MORNING AT AROUND 8 AM, A GUY PASSES BY THE HOUSE, TAPPING ON A BELL.
HE'S FOLLOWED BY A DOZEN BAREFOOT NOVICE MONKS WHO COLLECT ALMS FROM OUR NEIGHBORS.
THEY EACH CARRY A RICE BOWL.
OTHER FOODS ARE MANAGED BY A CIVILIAN WHO CLOSES THE LINE, PUSHING A LITTLE CANTEEN AS HE GOES.
ONE SLEEPLESS NIGHT, I DISCOVER THAT THEY FILE BY AT 4 AND 6 A.M. AS WELL.
DING
DING

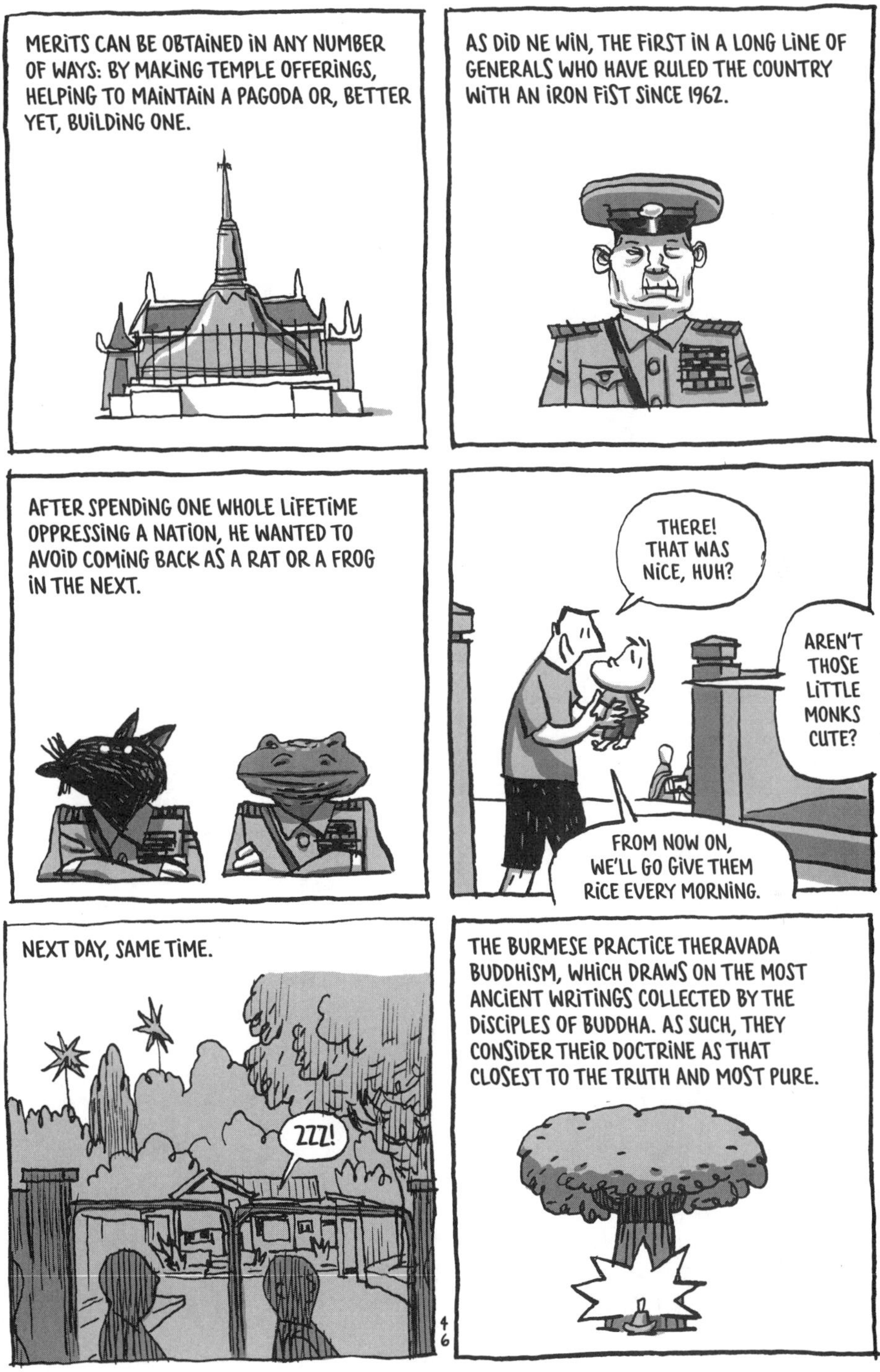
MERITS CAN BE OBTAINED IN ANY NUMBER OF WAYS: BY MAKING TEMPLE OFFERINGS, HELPING TO MAINTAIN A PAGODA OR, BETTER YET, BUILDING ONE.
AS DID NE WIN, THE FIRST IN A LONG LINE OF GENERALS WHO HAVE RULED THE COUNTRY WITH AN IRON FIST SINCE 1962.
AFTER SPENDING ONE WHOLE LIFETIME OPPRESSING A NATION, HE WANTED TO AVOID COMING BACK AS A RAT OR A FROG IN THE NEXT.
THERE! THAT WAS NICE, HUH?
AREN'T THOSE LITTLE MONKS CUTE?
FROM NOW ON, WE'LL GO GIVE THEM RICE EVERY MORNING.
NEXT DAY, SAME TIME.
ZZZ!
THE BURMESE PRACTICE THERAVADA BUDDHISM, WHICH DRAWS ON THE MOST ANCIENT WRITINGS COLLECTED BY THE DISCIPLES OF BUDDHA. AS SUCH, THEY CONSIDER THEIR DOCTRINE AS THAT CLOSEST TO THE TRUTH AND MOST PURE.

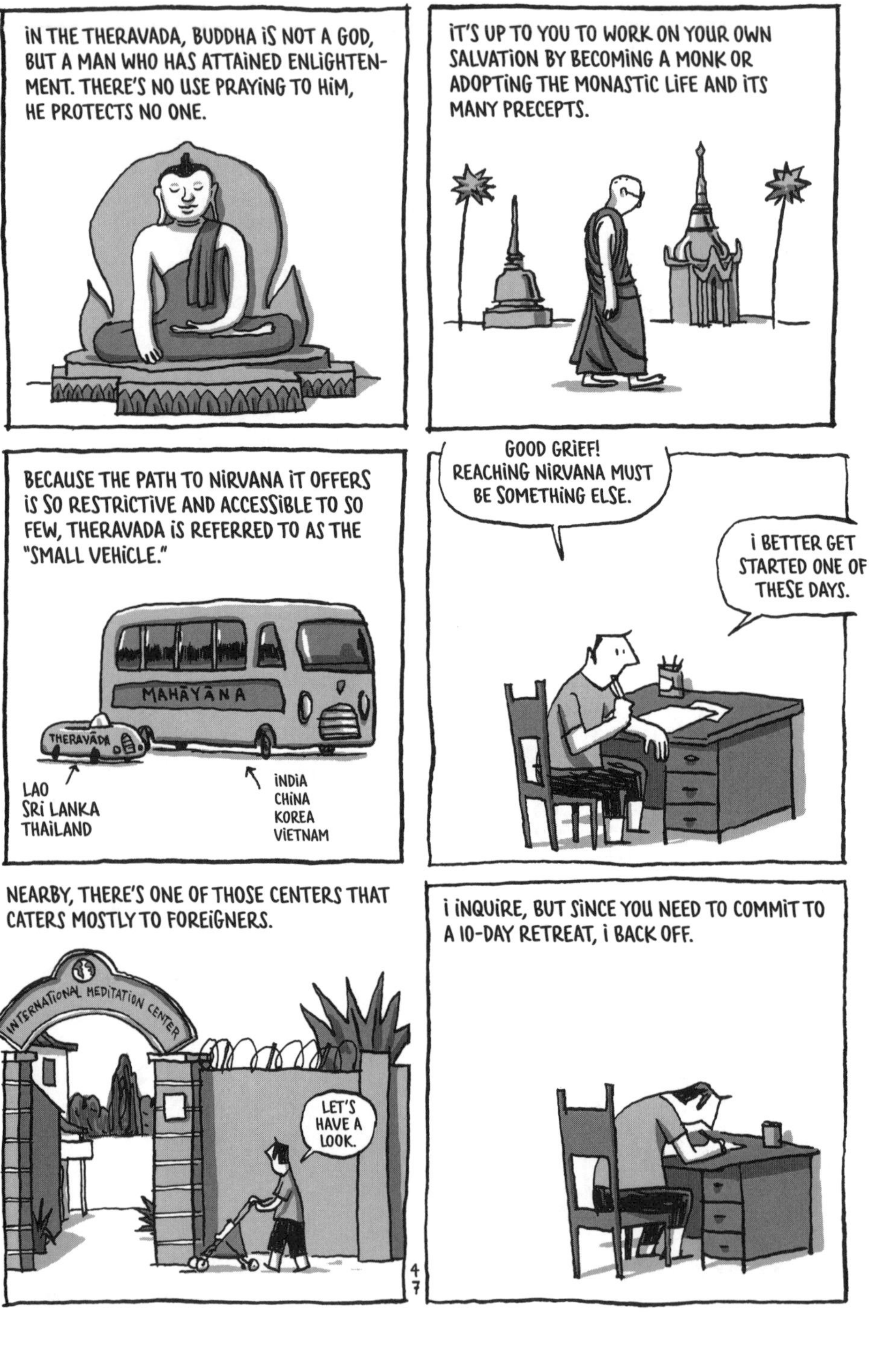
IN THE THERAVADA, BUDDHA IS NOT A GOD, BUT A MAN WHO HAS ATTAINED ENLIGHTENMENT. THERE'S NO USE PRAYING TO HIM, HE PROTECTS NO ONE.
IT'S UP TO YOU TO WORK ON YOUR OWN SALVATION BY BECOMING A MONK OR ADOPTING THE MONASTIC LIFE AND ITS MANY PRECEPTS.
BECAUSE THE PATH TO NIRVANA IT OFFERS IS SO RESTRICTIVE AND ACCESSIBLE TO SO FEW, THERAVADA IS REFERRED TO AS THE "SMALL VEHICLE."
MAHĀYĀNA
THERAVĀDA
LAO
SRI LANKA
THAILAND
INDIA
CHINA
KOREA
VIETNAM
GOOD GRIEF! REACHING NIRVANA MUST BE SOMETHING ELSE.
I BETTER GET STARTED ONE OF THESE DAYS.
NEARBY, THERE'S ONE OF THOSE CENTERS THAT CATERS MOSTLY TO FOREIGNERS.
INTERNATIONAL MEDITATION CENTER
LET'S HAVE A LOOK.
I INQUIRE, BUT SINCE YOU NEED TO COMMIT TO A 10-DAY RETREAT, I BACK OFF.

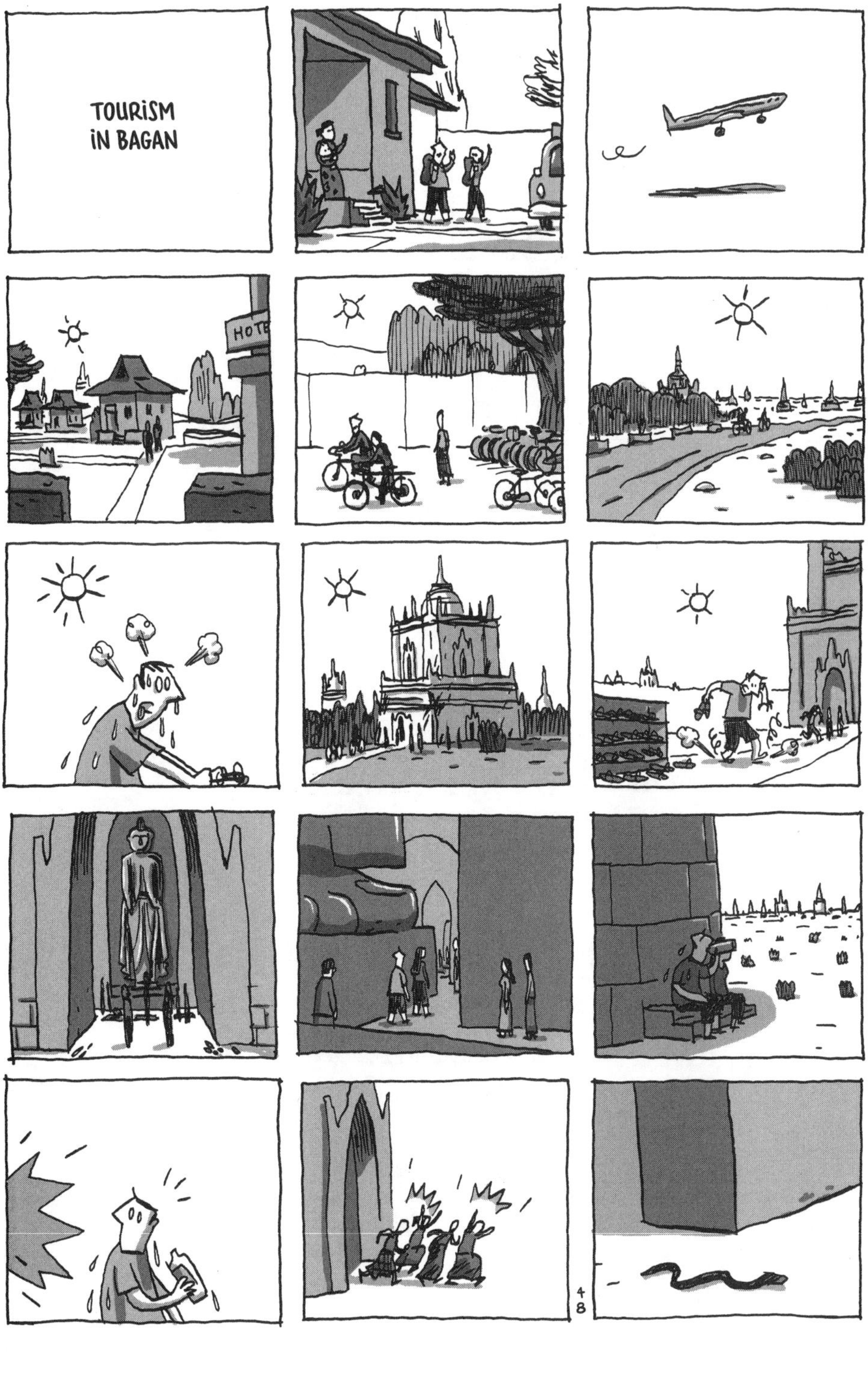
TOURISM
IN BAGAN
HOTE

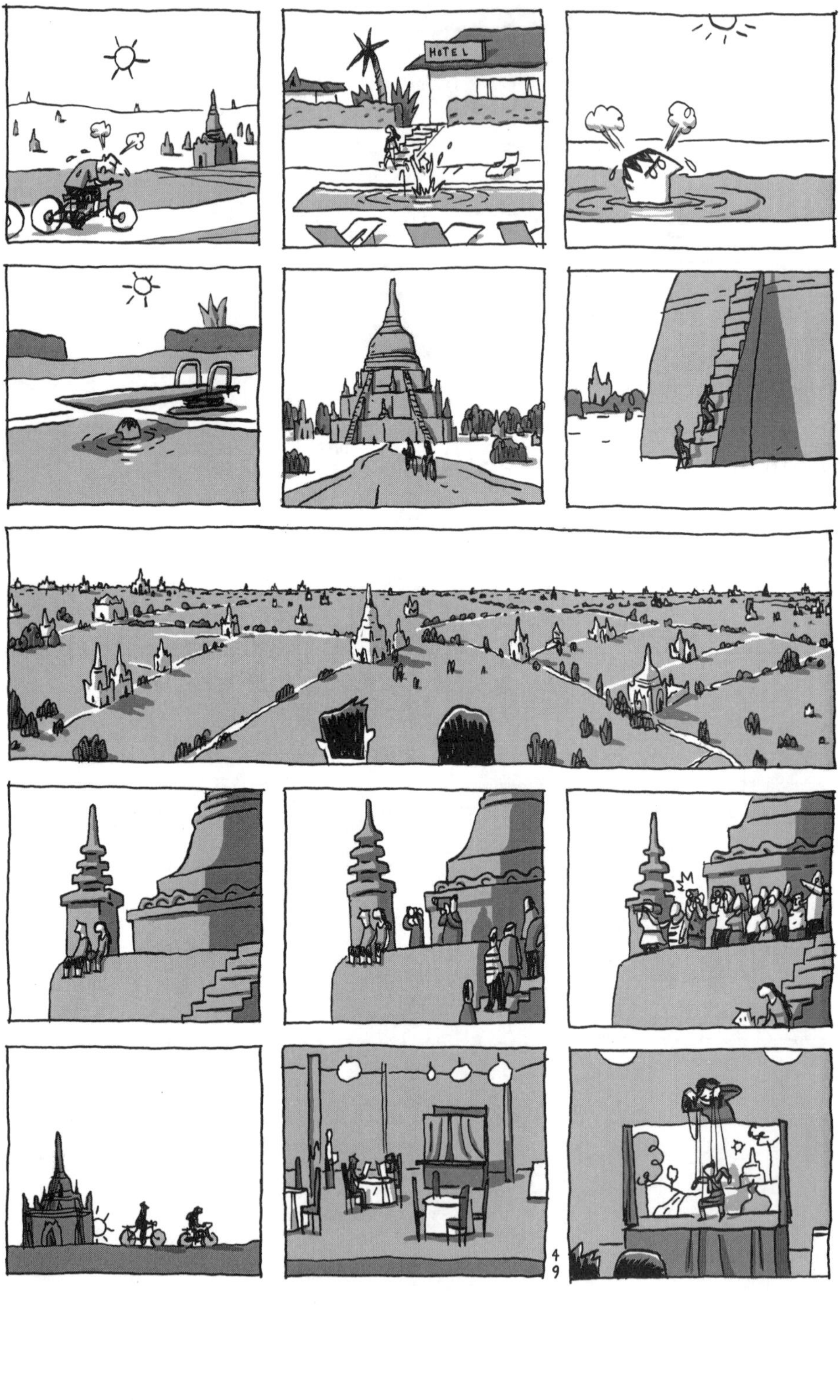
HOTEL
M

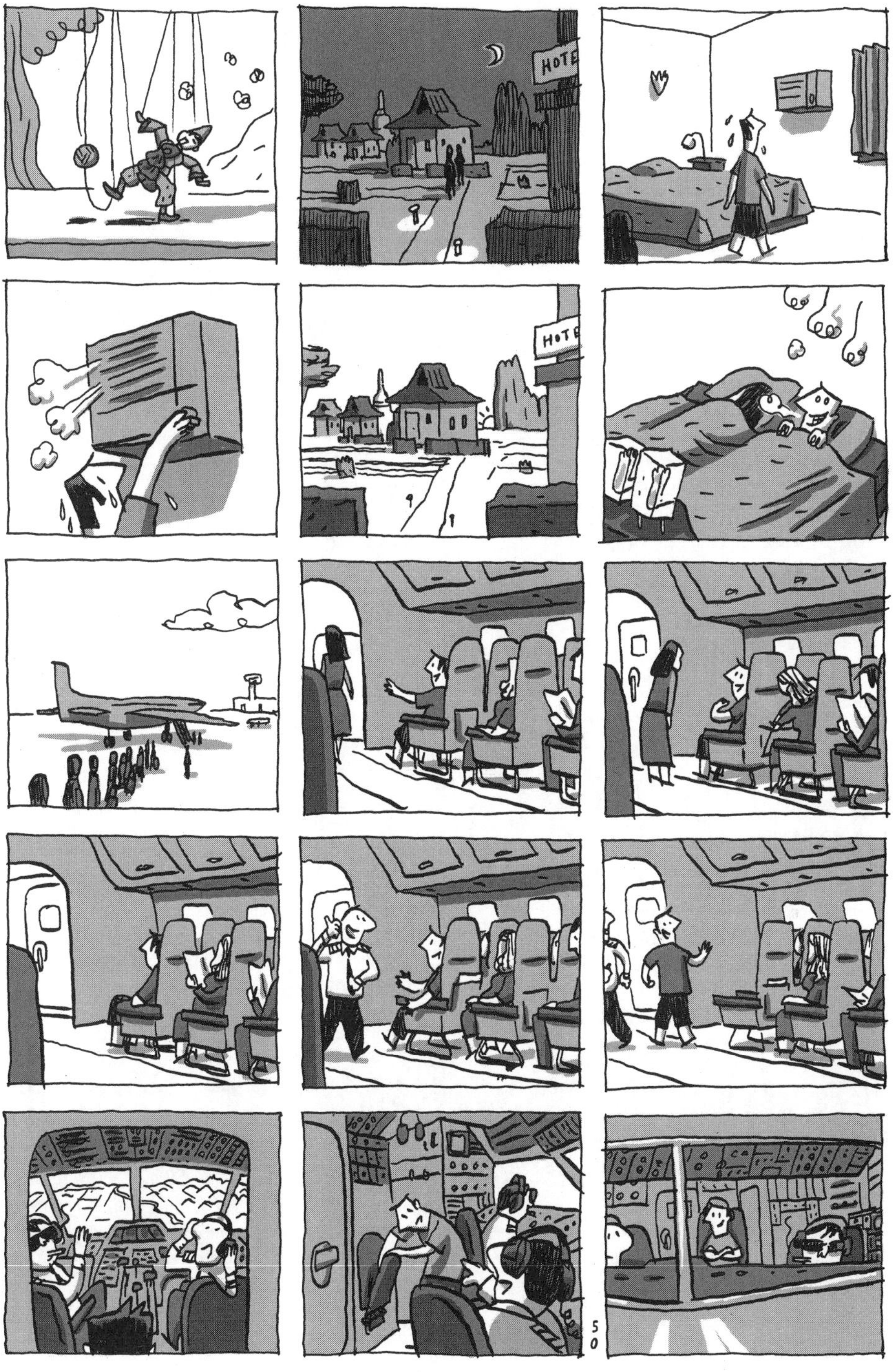
HOTE
HOTE

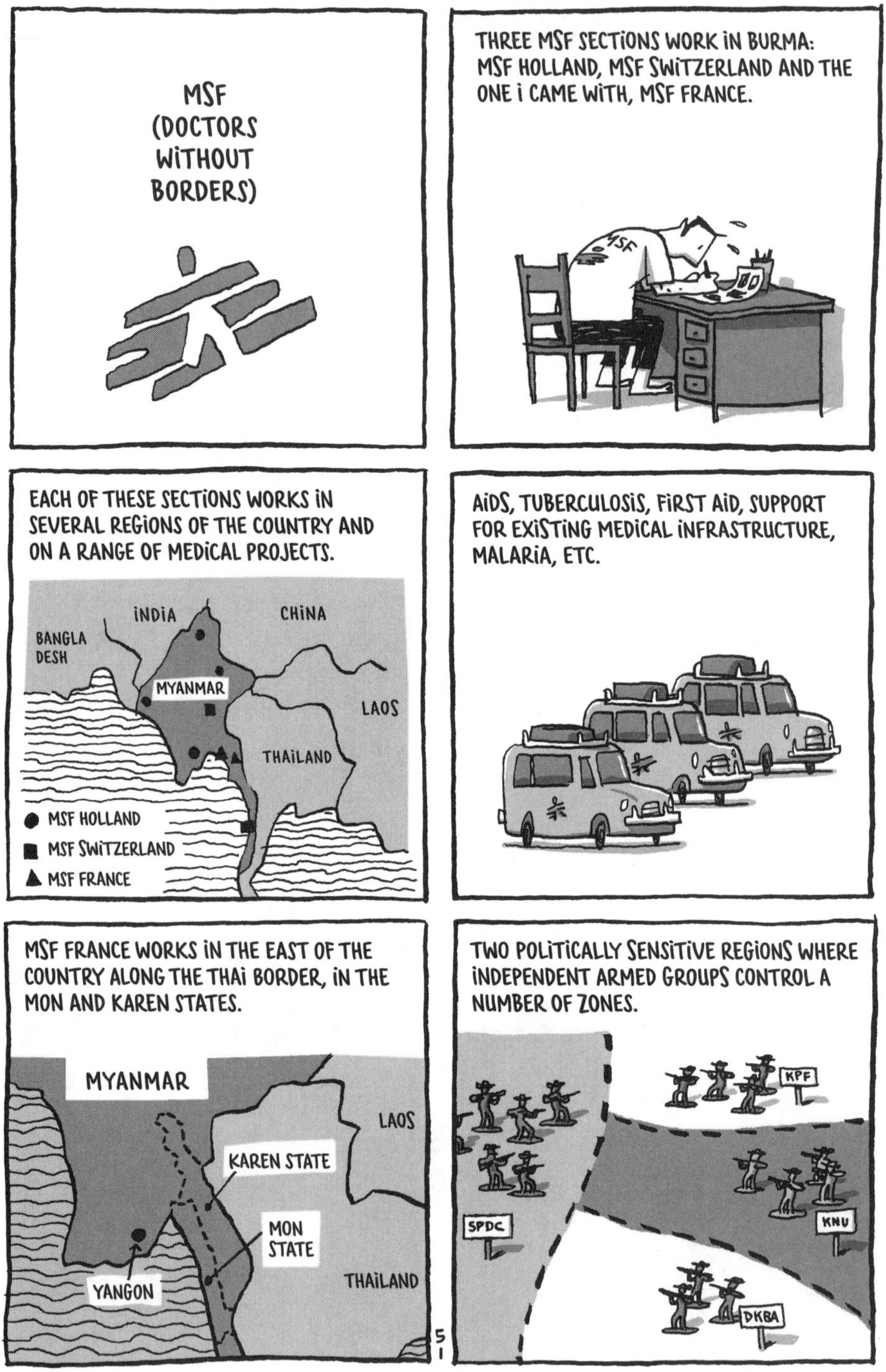
MSF
(DOCTORS WITHOUT BORDERS)
THREE MSF SECTIONS WORK IN BURMA: MSF HOLLAND, MSF SWITZERLAND AND THE ONE I CAME WITH, MSF FRANCE.
MSF
EACH OF THESE SECTIONS WORKS IN SEVERAL REGIONS OF THE COUNTRY AND ON A RANGE OF MEDICAL PROJECTS.
INDIA
CHINA
BANGLA DESH
MYANMAR
LAOS
THAILAND
MSF HOLLAND
MSF SWITZERLAND
MSF FRANCE
AIDS, TUBERCULOSIS, FIRST AID, SUPPORT FOR EXISTING MEDICAL INFRASTRUCTURE, MALARIA, ETC.
MSF FRANCE WORKS IN THE EAST OF THE COUNTRY ALONG THE THAI BORDER, IN THE MON AND KAREN STATES.
MYANMAR
LAOS
KAREN STATE
MON STATE
YANGON
THAILAND
TWO POLITICALLY SENSITIVE REGIONS WHERE INDEPENDENT ARMED GROUPS CONTROL A NUMBER OF ZONES.
KPF
KNU
SPDC
DKBA

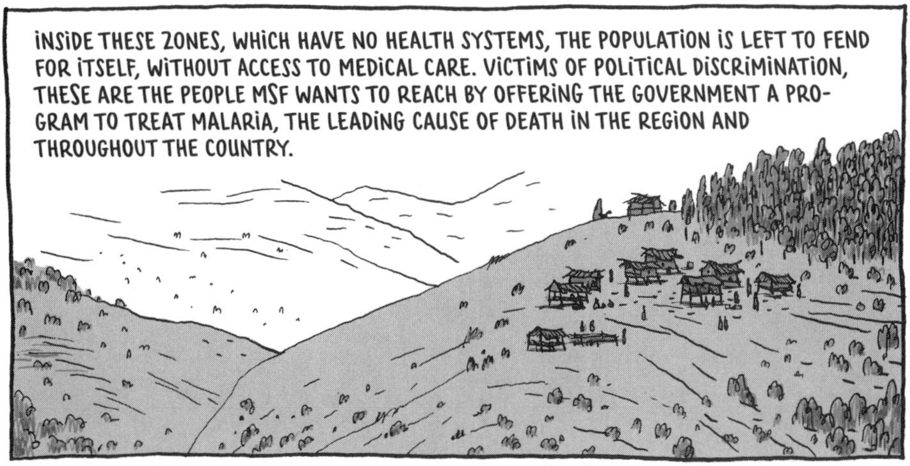
INSIDE THESE ZONES, WHICH HAVE NO HEALTH SYSTEMS, THE POPULATION IS LEFT TO FEND FOR ITSELF, WITHOUT ACCESS TO MEDICAL CARE. VICTIMS OF POLITICAL DISCRIMINATION, THESE ARE THE PEOPLE MSF WANTS TO REACH BY OFFERING THE GOVERNMENT A PROGRAM TO TREAT MALARIA, THE LEADING CAUSE OF DEATH IN THE REGION AND THROUGHOUT THE COUNTRY.

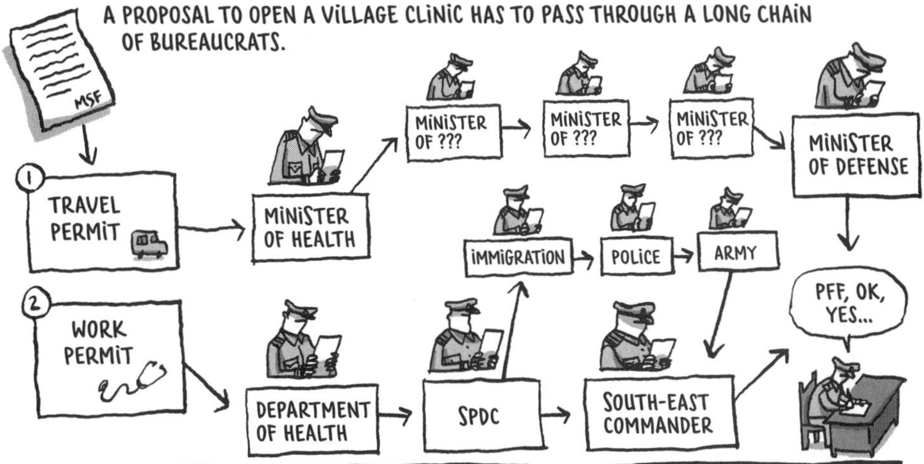
A PROPOSAL TO OPEN A VILLAGE CLINIC HAS TO PASS THROUGH A LONG CHAIN OF BUREAUCRATS.
MSF
1
TRAVEL PERMIT
MINISTER OF HEALTH
MINISTER OF ???
MINISTER OF ???
MINISTER OF ???
MINISTER OF DEFENSE
2
WORK PERMIT
DEPARTMENT OF HEALTH
SPDC
IMMIGRATION
POLICE
ARMY
SOUTH-EAST COMMANDER
PFF, OK, YES...

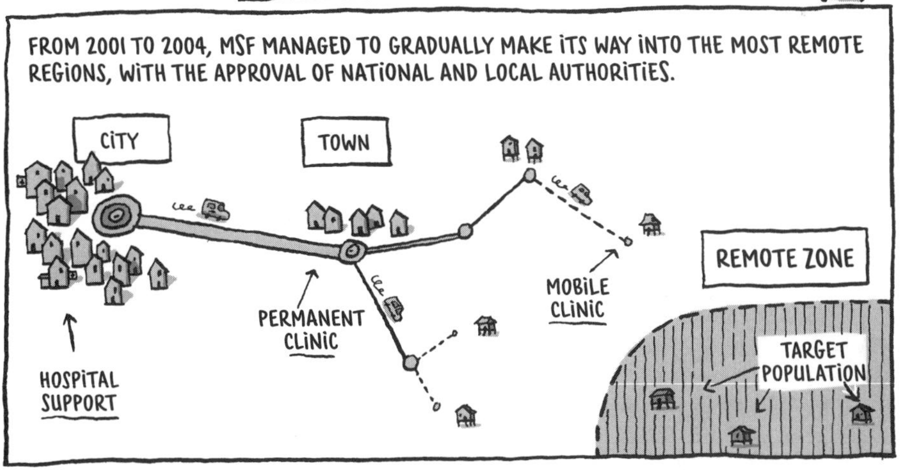
FROM 2001 TO 2004, MSF MANAGED TO GRADUALLY MAKE ITS WAY INTO THE MOST REMOTE REGIONS, WITH THE APPROVAL OF NATIONAL AND LOCAL AUTHORITIES.
CITY
TOWN
REMOTE ZONE
HOSPITAL SUPPORT
PERMANENT CLINIC
MOBILE CLINIC
TARGET POPULATION

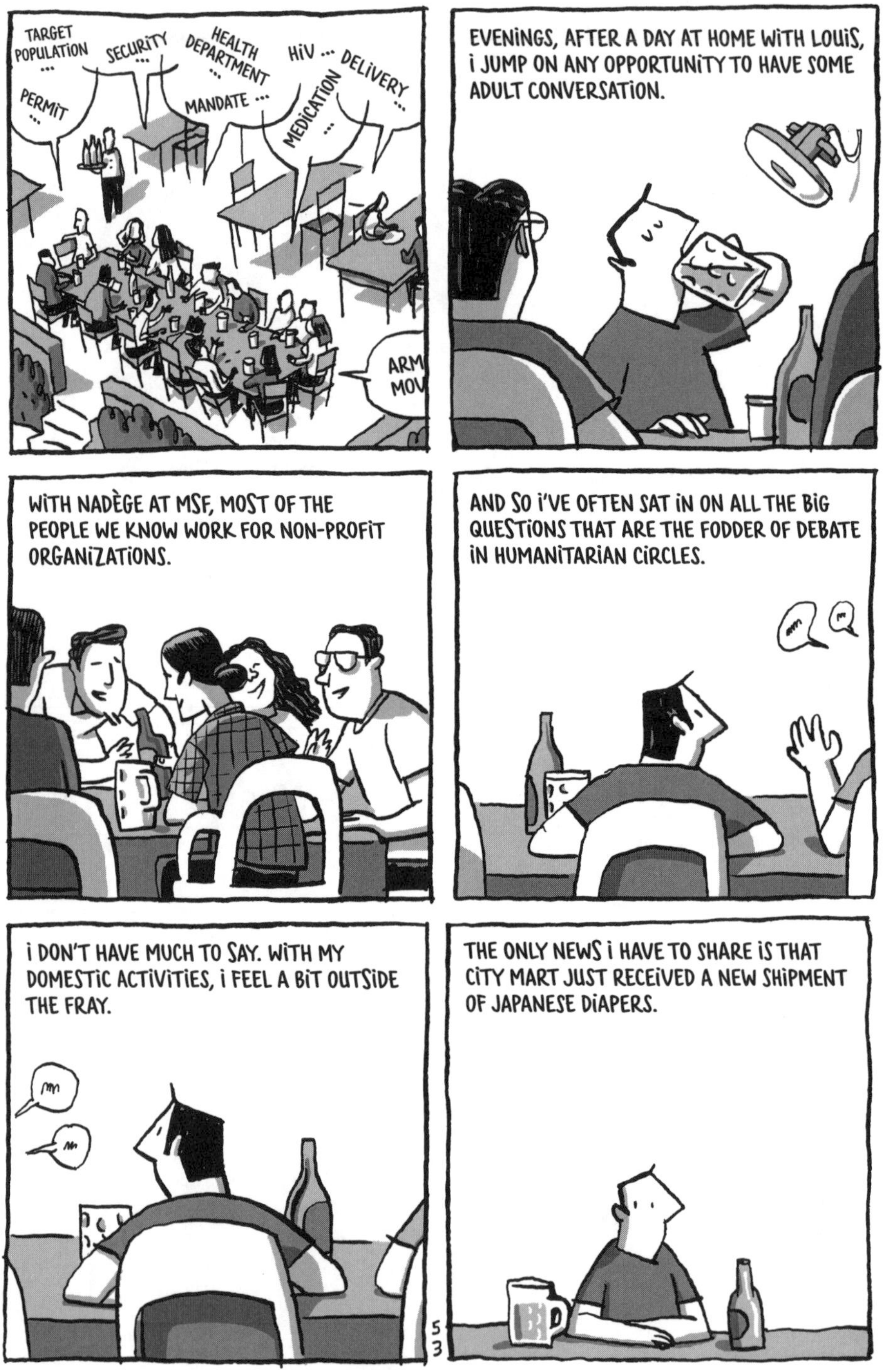
TARGET POPULATION ...
PERMIT ...
SECURITY ...
HEALTH DEPARTMENT ...
MANDATE ...
HIV ...
MEDICATION ...
DELIVERY ...
ARM
MOV
EVENINGS, AFTER A DAY AT HOME WITH LOUIS, I JUMP ON ANY OPPORTUNITY TO HAVE SOME ADULT CONVERSATION.
WITH NADÈGE AT MSF, MOST OF THE PEOPLE WE KNOW WORK FOR NON-PROFIT ORGANIZATIONS.
AND SO I'VE OFTEN SAT IN ON ALL THE BIG QUESTIONS THAT ARE THE FODDER OF DEBATE IN HUMANITARIAN CIRCLES.
I DON'T HAVE MUCH TO SAY. WITH MY DOMESTIC ACTIVITIES, I FEEL A BIT OUTSIDE THE FRAY.
THE ONLY NEWS I HAVE TO SHARE IS THAT CITY MART JUST RECEIVED A NEW SHIPMENT OF JAPANESE DIAPERS.

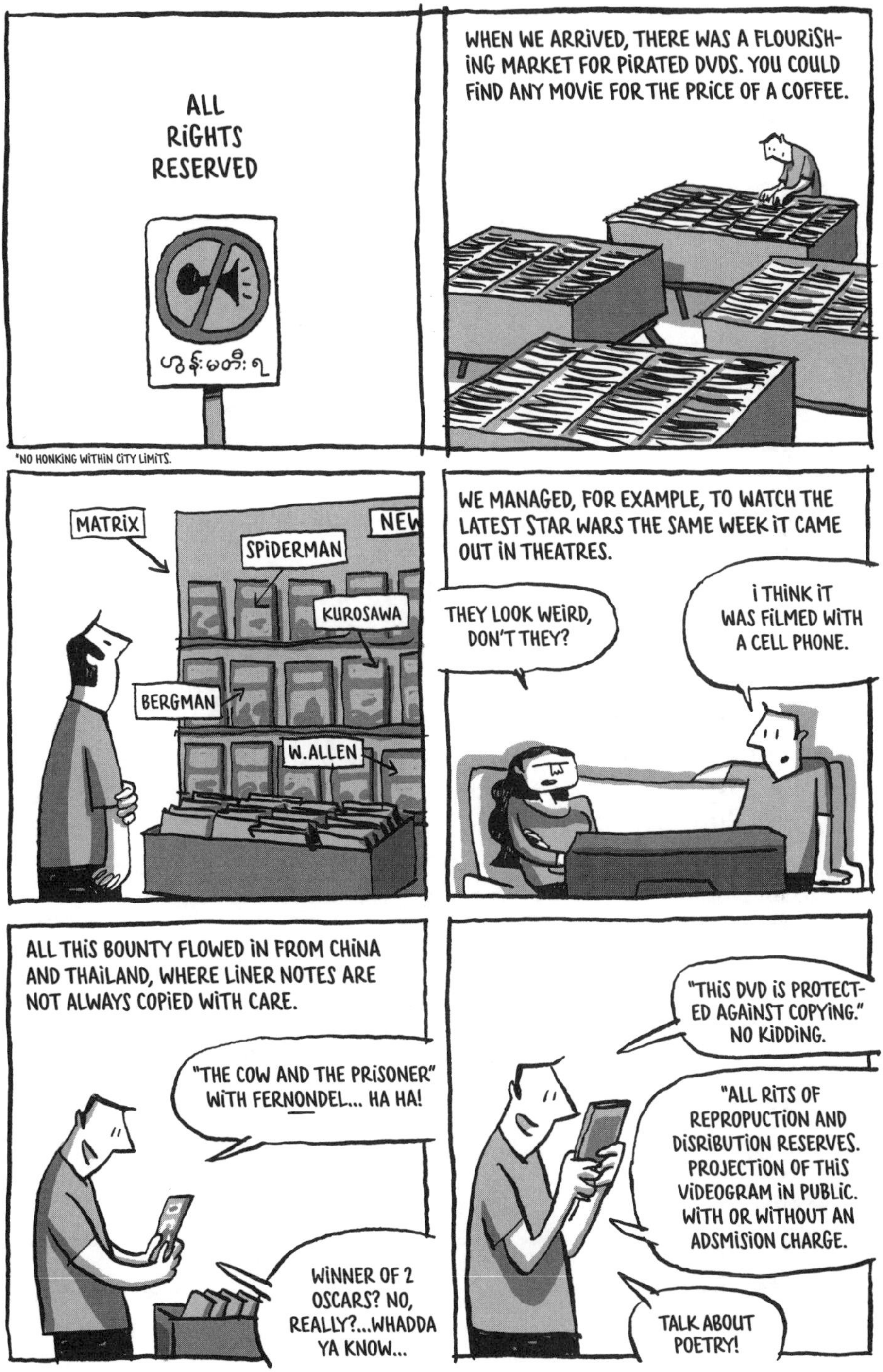
ALL RIGHTS RESERVED
ဟွန်းမတီးရ
*NO HONKING WITHIN CITY LIMITS.
WHEN WE ARRIVED, THERE WAS A FLOURISHING MARKET FOR PIRATED DVDS. YOU COULD FIND ANY MOVIE FOR THE PRICE OF A COFFEE.
MATRIX
SPIDERMAN
NEW
KUROSAWA
BERGMAN
W.ALLEN
WE MANAGED, FOR EXAMPLE, TO WATCH THE LATEST STAR WARS THE SAME WEEK IT CAME OUT IN THEATRES.
THEY LOOK WEIRD, DON'T THEY?
I THINK IT WAS FILMED WITH A CELL PHONE.
ALL THIS BOUNTY FLOWED IN FROM CHINA AND THAILAND, WHERE LINER NOTES ARE NOT ALWAYS COPIED WITH CARE.
"THE COW AND THE PRISONER" WITH FERNONDEL... HA HA!
WINNER OF 2 OSCARS? NO, REALLY?...WHADDA YA KNOW...
"THIS DVD IS PROTECTED AGAINST COPYING." NO KIDDING.
"ALL RITS OF REPROPUCTION AND DISRIBUTION RESERVES. PROJECTION OF THIS VIDEOGRAM IN PUBLIC. WITH OR WITHOUT AN ADSMISION CHARGE.
TALK ABOUT POETRY!

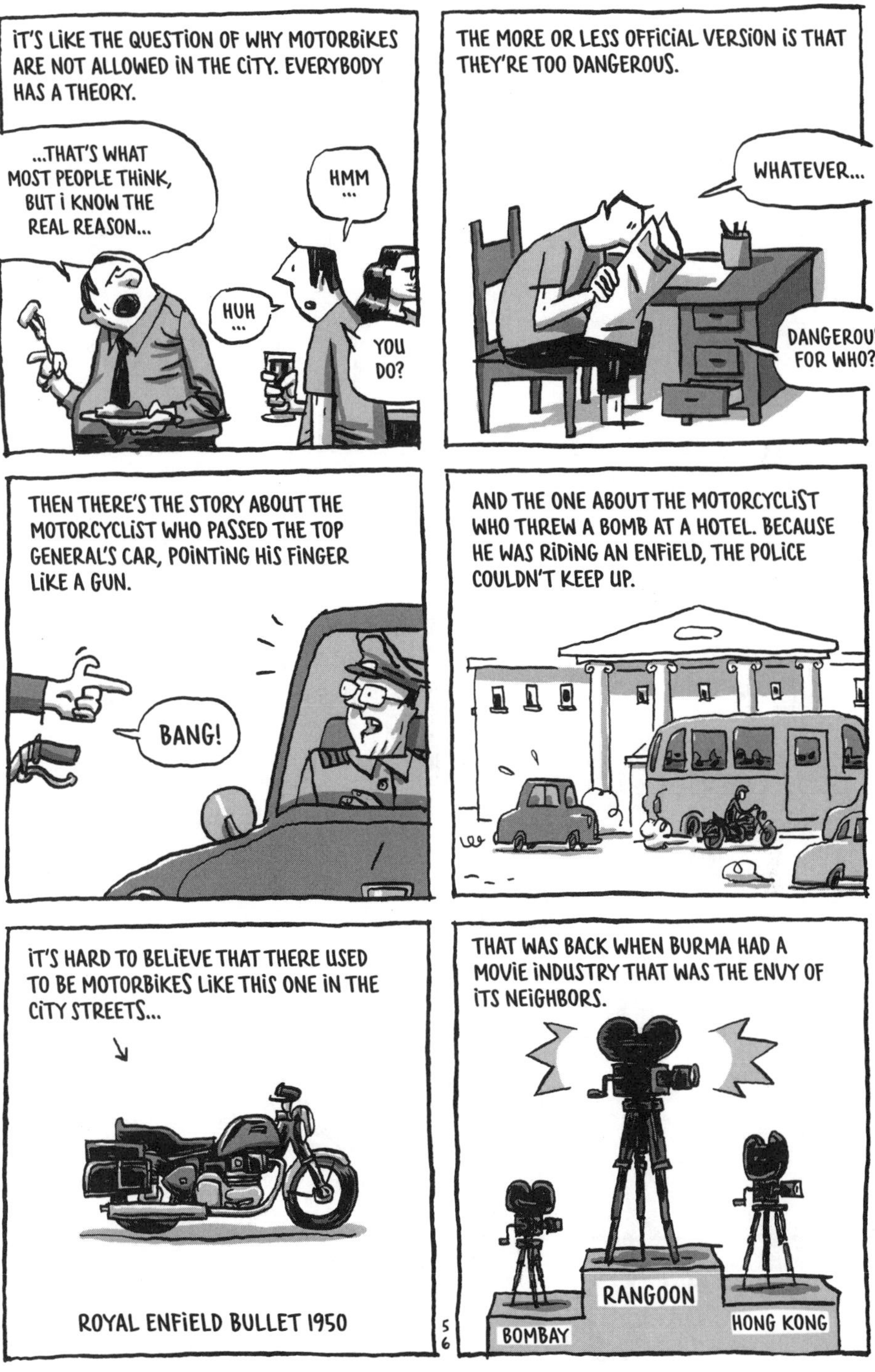
IT'S LIKE THE QUESTION OF WHY MOTORBIKES ARE NOT ALLOWED IN THE CITY. EVERYBODY HAS A THEORY.
...THAT'S WHAT MOST PEOPLE THINK, BUT I KNOW THE REAL REASON...
HMM ...
HUH ...
YOU DO?
THE MORE OR LESS OFFICIAL VERSION IS THAT THEY'RE TOO DANGEROUS.
WHATEVER...
DANGEROUS FOR WHO?
THEN THERE'S THE STORY ABOUT THE MOTORCYCLIST WHO PASSED THE TOP GENERAL'S CAR, POINTING HIS FINGER LIKE A GUN.
BANG!
AND THE ONE ABOUT THE MOTORCYCLIST WHO THREW A BOMB AT A HOTEL. BECAUSE HE WAS RIDING AN ENFIELD, THE POLICE COULDN'T KEEP UP.
IT'S HARD TO BELIEVE THAT THERE USED TO BE MOTORBIKES LIKE THIS ONE IN THE CITY STREETS...
ROYAL ENFIELD BULLET 1950
THAT WAS BACK WHEN BURMA HAD A MOVIE INDUSTRY THAT WAS THE ENVY OF ITS NEIGHBORS.
RANGOON
BOMBAY
HONG KONG

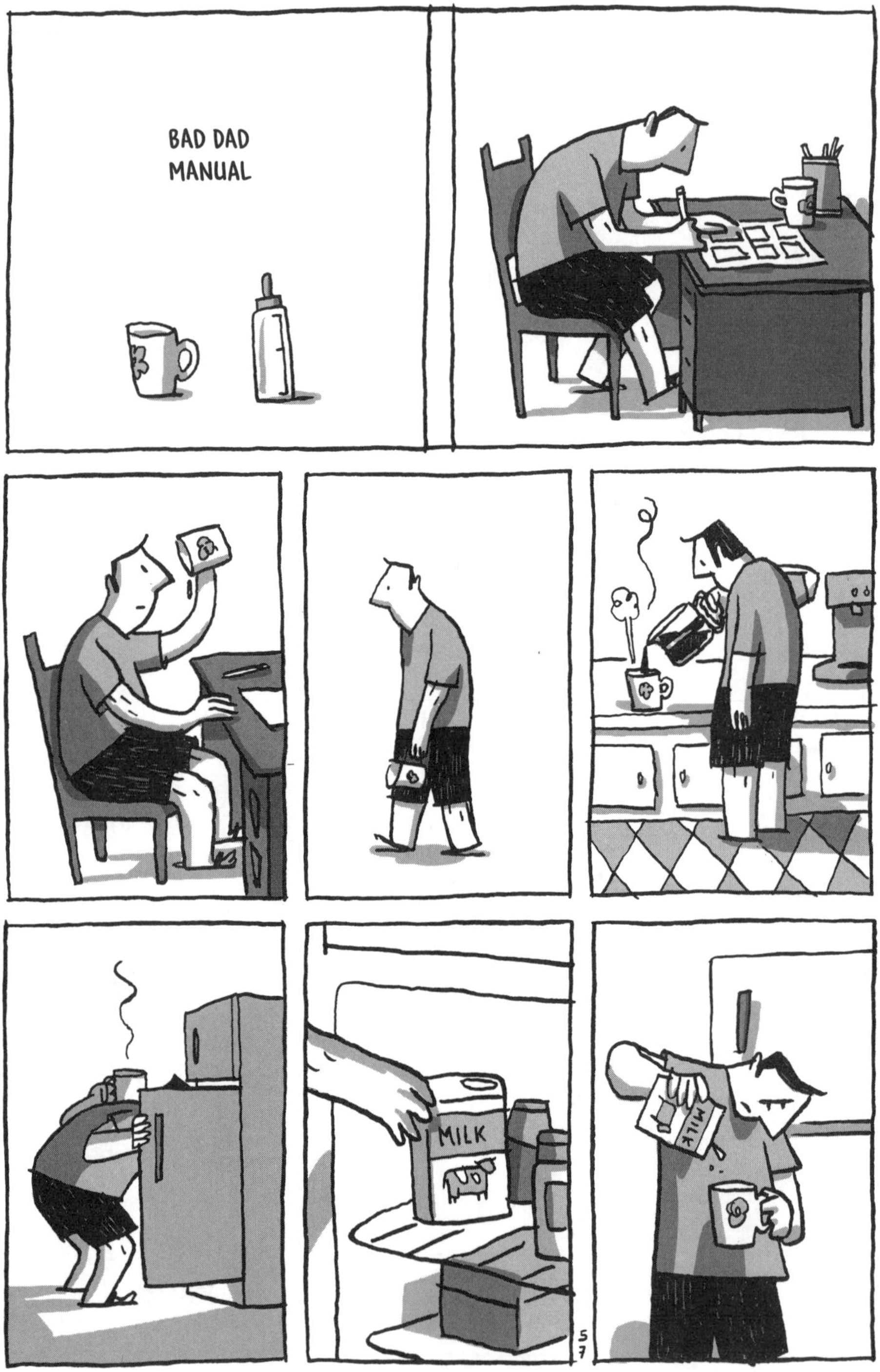
BAD DAD
MANUAL
MILK
MILK

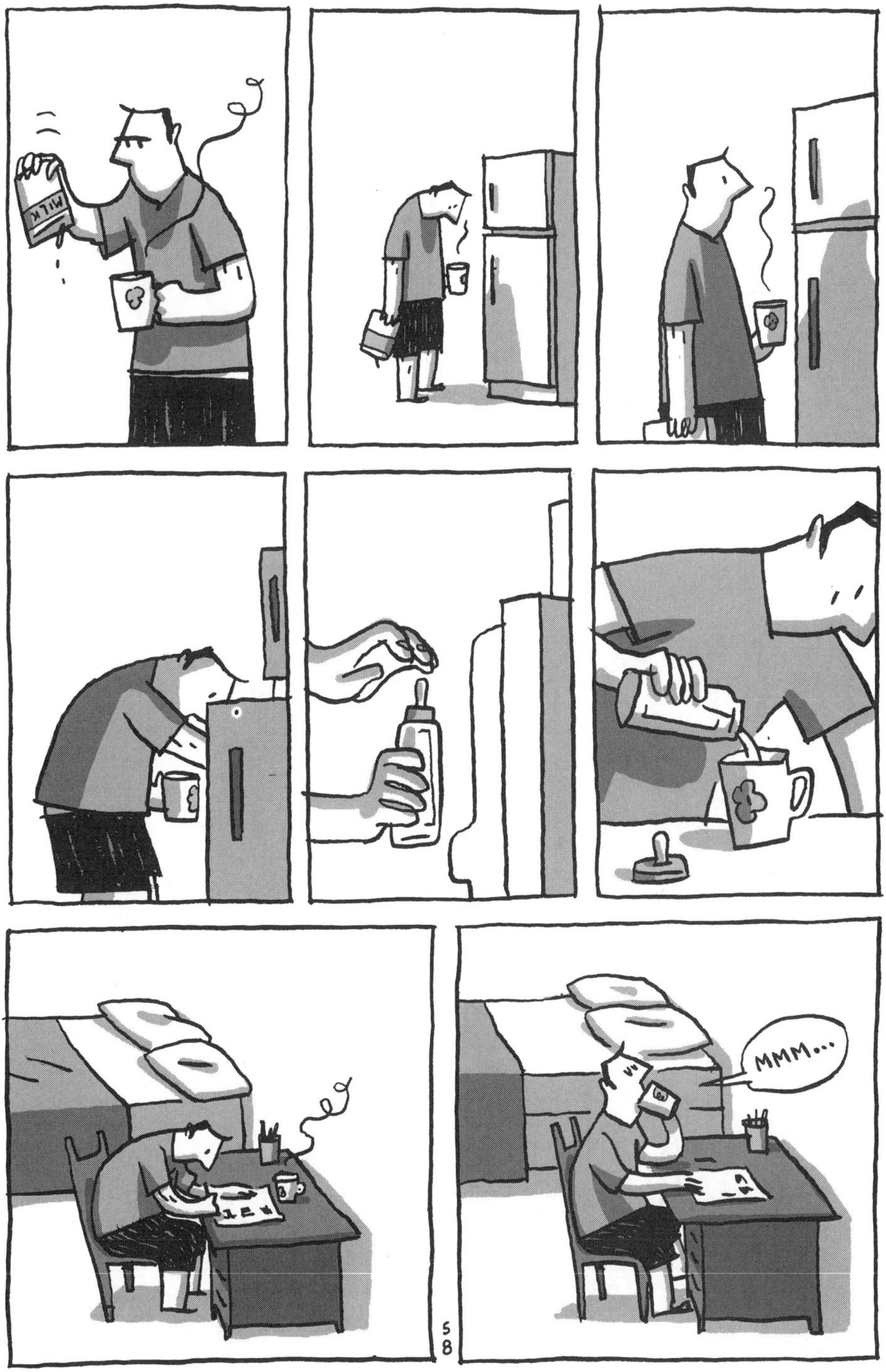
MILK
MMM...

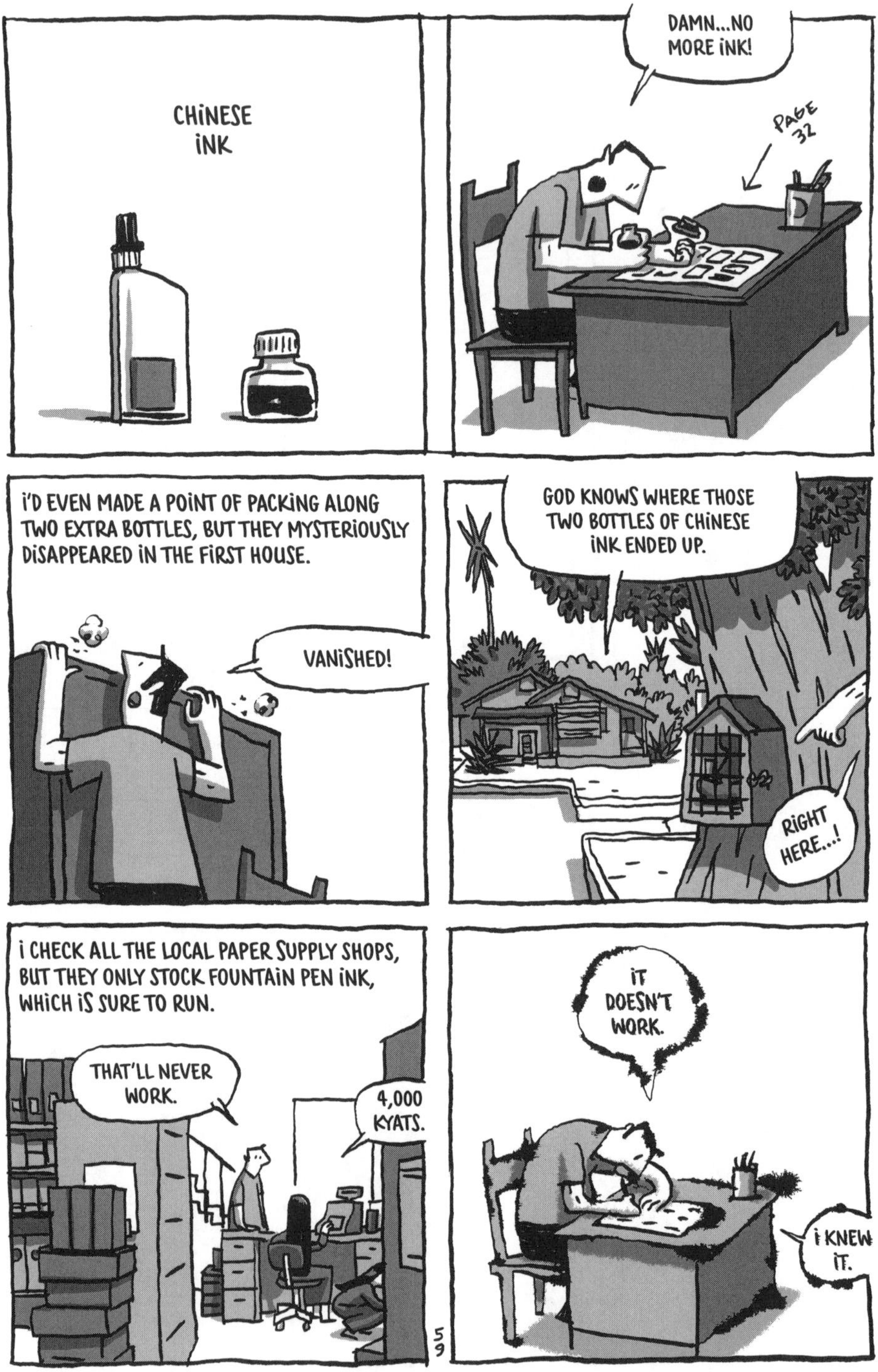

CHINESE INK
DAMN...NO MORE INK!
PAGE 32
I'D EVEN MADE A POINT OF PACKING ALONG TWO EXTRA BOTTLES, BUT THEY MYSTERIOUSLY DISAPPEARED IN THE FIRST HOUSE.
VANISHED!
GOD KNOWS WHERE THOSE TWO BOTTLES OF CHINESE INK ENDED UP.
RIGHT HERE...!
I CHECK ALL THE LOCAL PAPER SUPPLY SHOPS, BUT THEY ONLY STOCK FOUNTAIN PEN INK, WHICH IS SURE TO RUN.
THAT'LL NEVER WORK.
4,000 KYATS.
IT DOESN'T WORK.
I KNEW IT.

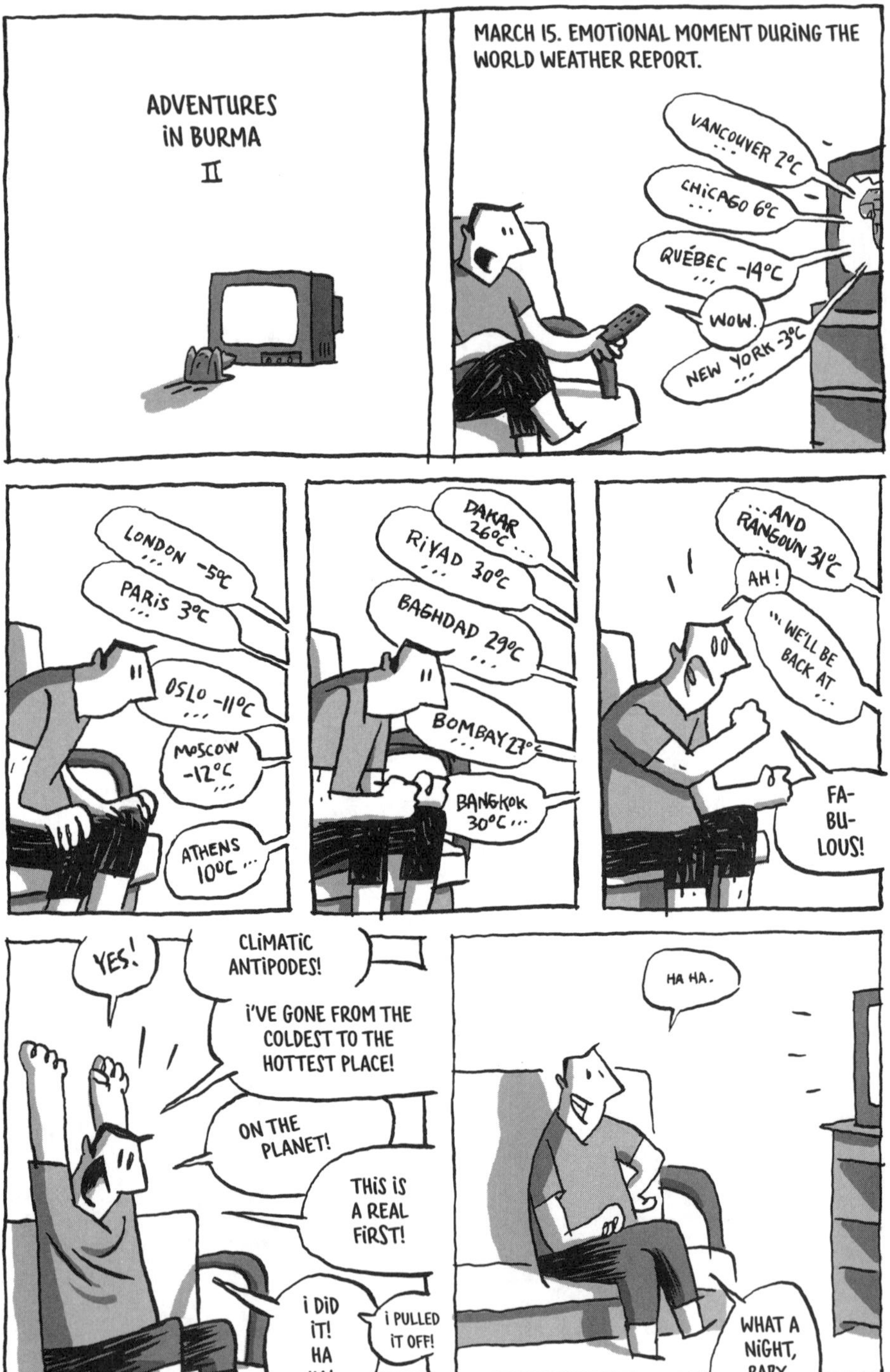
ADVENTURES IN BURMA II
MARCH 15. EMOTIONAL MOMENT DURING THE WORLD WEATHER REPORT.
VANCOUVER 2°C ...
CHICAGO 6°C ...
QUÉBEC -14°C ...
WOW.
NEW YORK -3°C ...
LONDON -5°C ...
PARIS 3°C ...
OSLO -11°C ...
MOSCOW -12°C ...
ATHENS 10°C ...
DAKAR 26°C ...
RIYAD 30°C ...
BAGHDAD 29°C ...
BOMBAY 27°C ...
BANGKOK 30°C ...
...AND RANGOUN 31°C ...
AH!
... WE'LL BE BACK AT ...
FA-BU-LOUS!
YES!
CLIMATIC ANTIPODES!
I'VE GONE FROM THE COLDEST TO THE HOTTEST PLACE!
ON THE PLANET!
THIS IS A REAL FIRST!
I DID IT! HA HA!
I PULLED IT OFF!
HA HA.
WHAT A NIGHT, BABY.

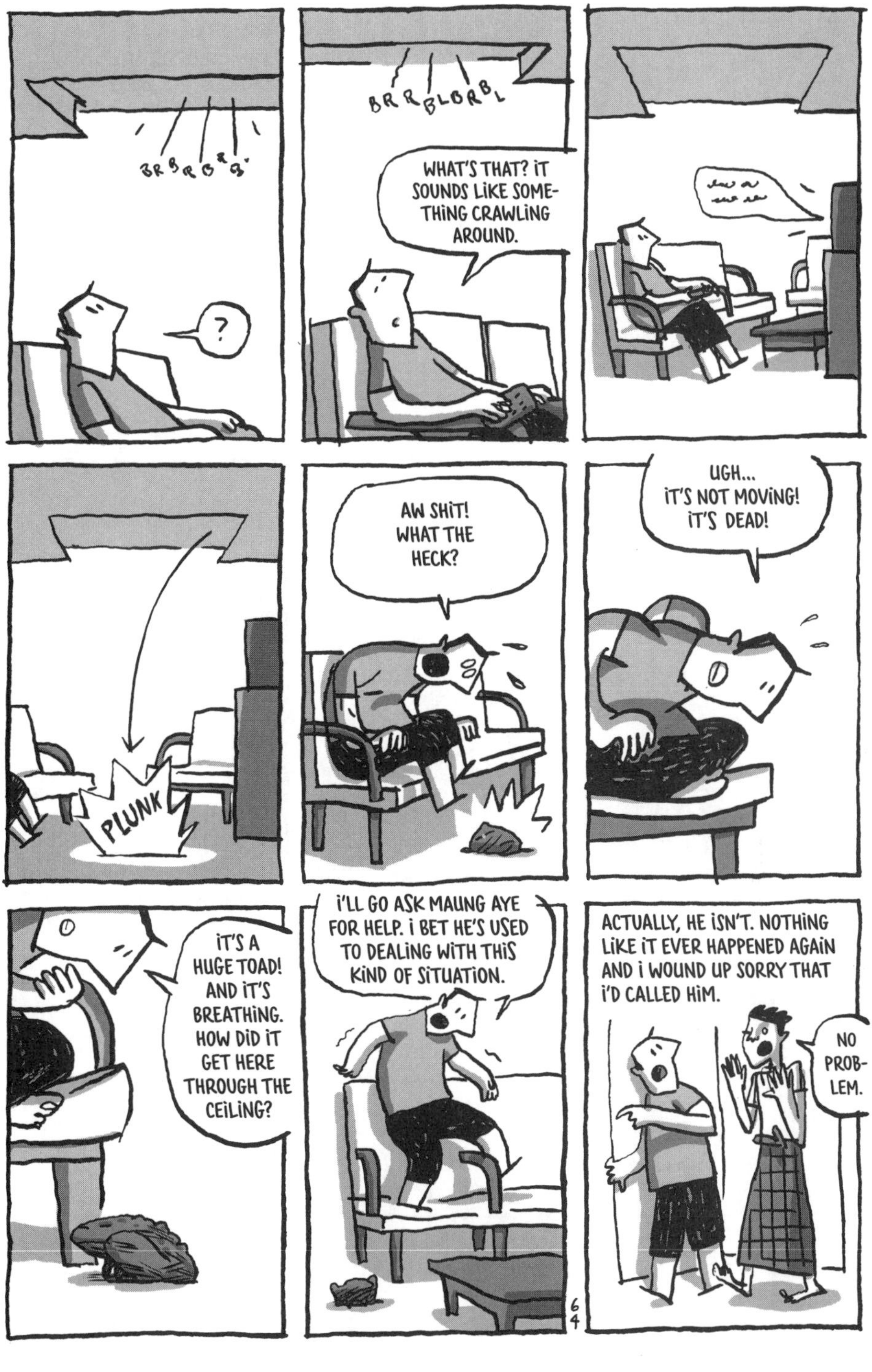
BRBRBRB
?
BRRBLORBL
WHAT'S THAT? IT SOUNDS LIKE SOME-THING CRAWLING AROUND.
PLUNK
AW SHIT! WHAT THE HECK?
UGH... IT'S NOT MOVING! IT'S DEAD!
IT'S A HUGE TOAD! AND IT'S BREATHING. HOW DID IT GET HERE THROUGH THE CEILING?
I'LL GO ASK MAUNG AYE FOR HELP. I BET HE'S USED TO DEALING WITH THIS KIND OF SITUATION.
ACTUALLY, HE ISN'T. NOTHING LIKE IT EVER HAPPENED AGAIN AND I WOUND UP SORRY THAT I'D CALLED HIM.
NO PROB-LEM.

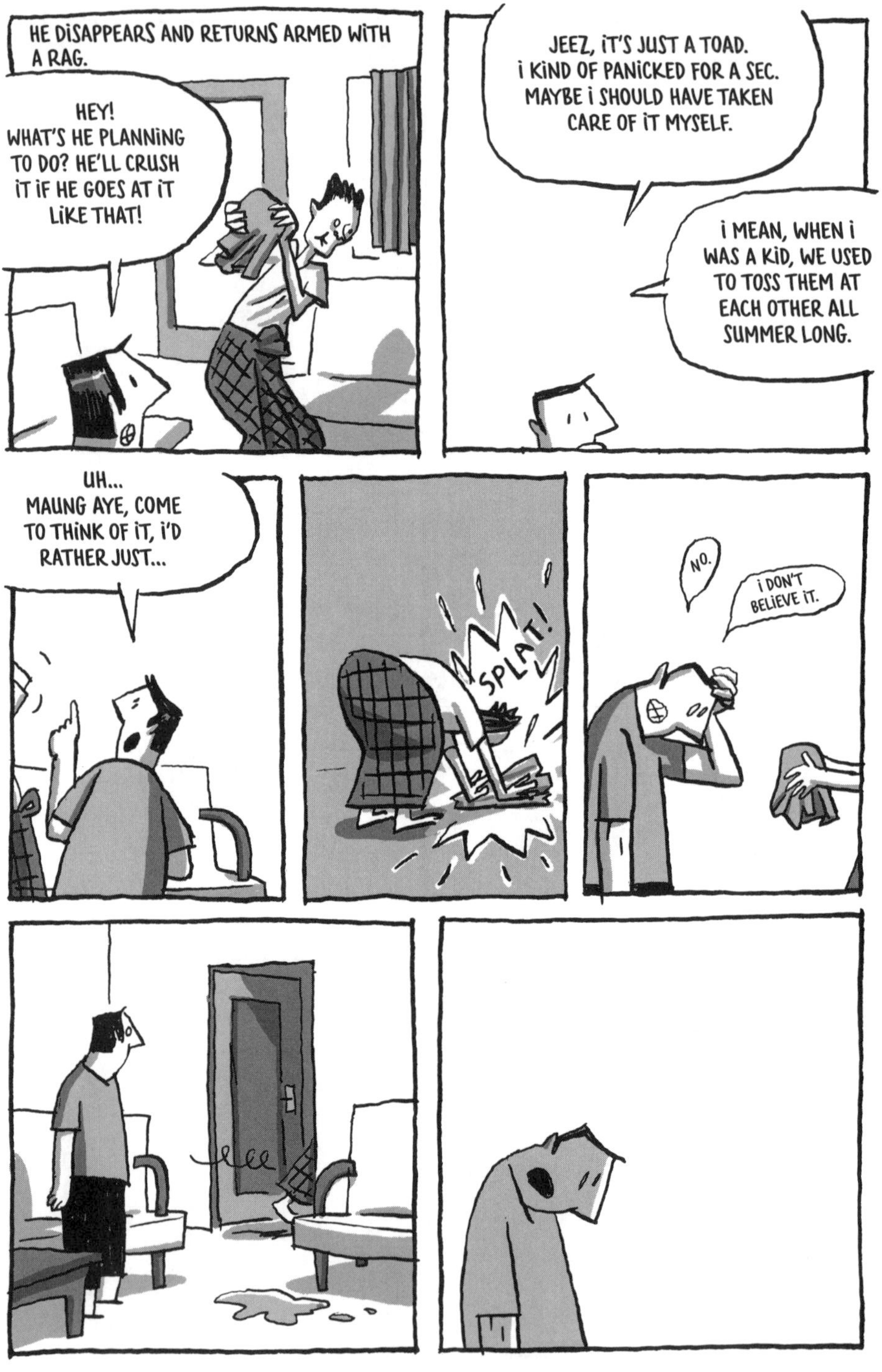
HE DISAPPEARS AND RETURNS ARMED WITH A RAG.
HEY! WHAT'S HE PLANNING TO DO? HE'LL CRUSH IT IF HE GOES AT IT LIKE THAT!
JEEZ, IT'S JUST A TOAD. I KIND OF PANICKED FOR A SEC. MAYBE I SHOULD HAVE TAKEN CARE OF IT MYSELF.
I MEAN, WHEN I WAS A KID, WE USED TO TOSS THEM AT EACH OTHER ALL SUMMER LONG.
UH... MAUNG AYE, COME TO THINK OF IT, I'D RATHER JUST...
SPLAT!
NO.
I DON'T BELIEVE IT.

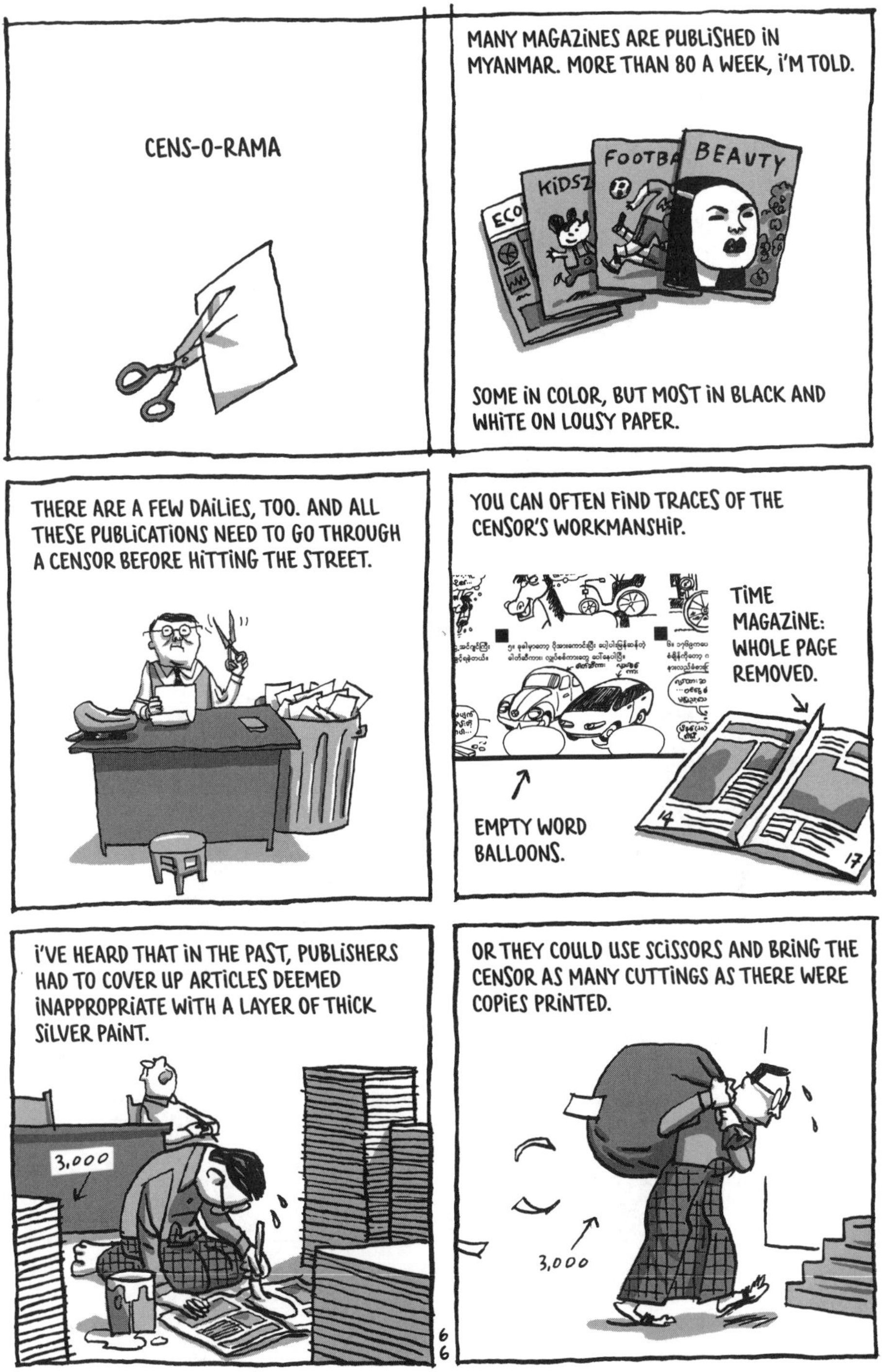
CENS-O-RAMA
MANY MAGAZINES ARE PUBLISHED IN MYANMAR. MORE THAN 80 A WEEK, I'M TOLD.
ECO
KIDSZ
FOOTBA
BEAUTY
SOME IN COLOR, BUT MOST IN BLACK AND WHITE ON LOUSY PAPER.
THERE ARE A FEW DAILIES, TOO. AND ALL THESE PUBLICATIONS NEED TO GO THROUGH A CENSOR BEFORE HITTING THE STREET.
YOU CAN OFTEN FIND TRACES OF THE CENSOR'S WORKMANSHIP.
TIME MAGAZINE: WHOLE PAGE REMOVED.
14
17
EMPTY WORD BALLOONS.
I'VE HEARD THAT IN THE PAST, PUBLISHERS HAD TO COVER UP ARTICLES DEEMED INAPPROPRIATE WITH A LAYER OF THICK SILVER PAINT.
3,000
OR THEY COULD USE SCISSORS AND BRING THE CENSOR AS MANY CUTTINGS AS THERE WERE COPIES PRINTED.
3,000

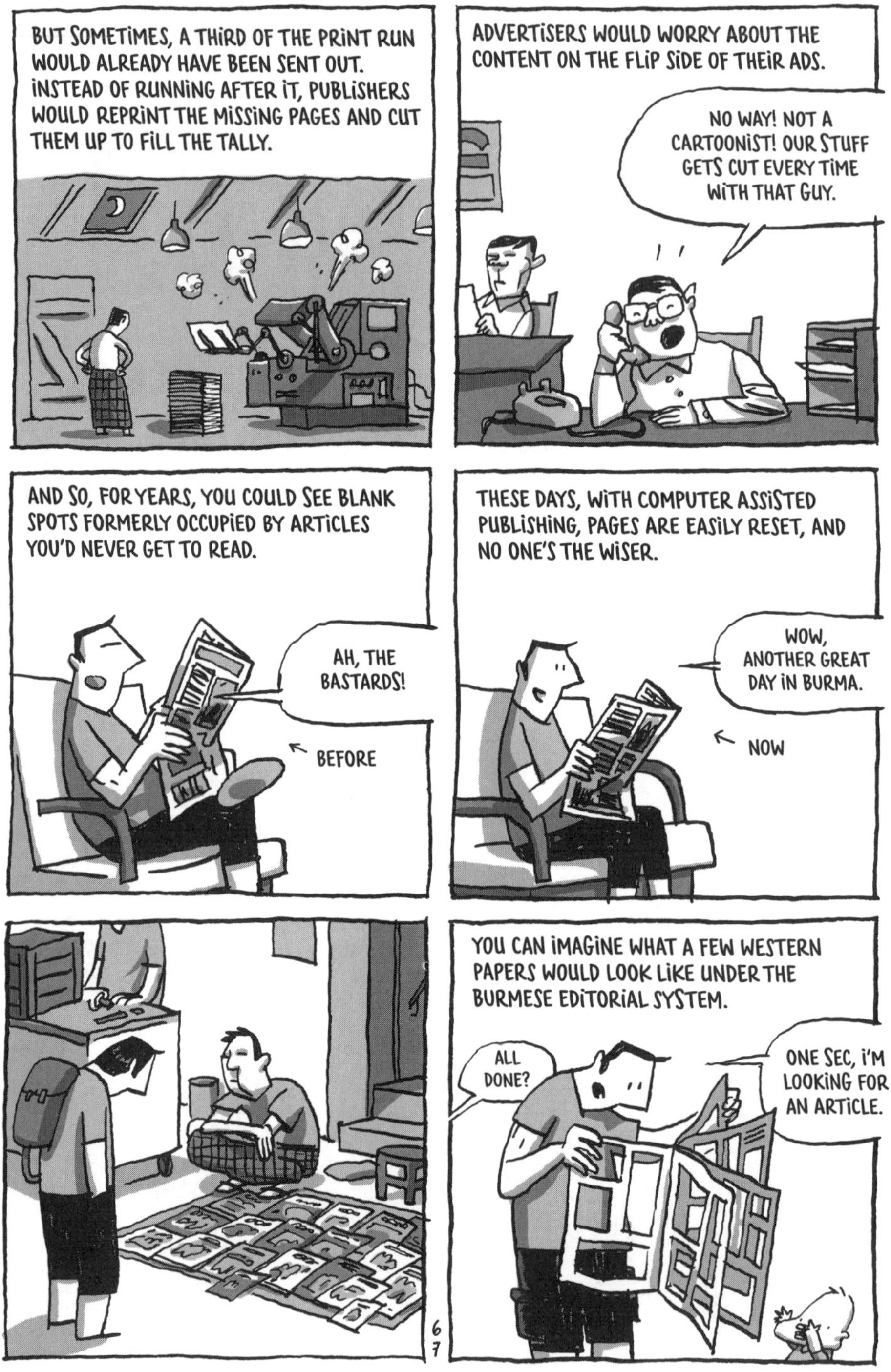
BUT SOMETIMES, A THIRD OF THE PRINT RUN WOULD ALREADY HAVE BEEN SENT OUT. INSTEAD OF RUNNING AFTER IT, PUBLISHERS WOULD REPRINT THE MISSING PAGES AND CUT THEM UP TO FILL THE TALLY.
ADVERTISERS WOULD WORRY ABOUT THE CONTENT ON THE FLIP SIDE OF THEIR ADS.
NO WAY! NOT A CARTOONIST! OUR STUFF GETS CUT EVERY TIME WITH THAT GUY.
AND SO, FOR YEARS, YOU COULD SEE BLANK SPOTS FORMERLY OCCUPIED BY ARTICLES YOU'D NEVER GET TO READ.
AH, THE BASTARDS!
BEFORE
THESE DAYS, WITH COMPUTER ASSISTED PUBLISHING, PAGES ARE EASILY RESET, AND NO ONE'S THE WISER.
WOW, ANOTHER GREAT DAY IN BURMA.
NOW
YOU CAN IMAGINE WHAT A FEW WESTERN PAPERS WOULD LOOK LIKE UNDER THE BURMESE EDITORIAL SYSTEM.
ALL DONE?
ONE SEC, I'M LOOKING FOR AN ARTICLE.

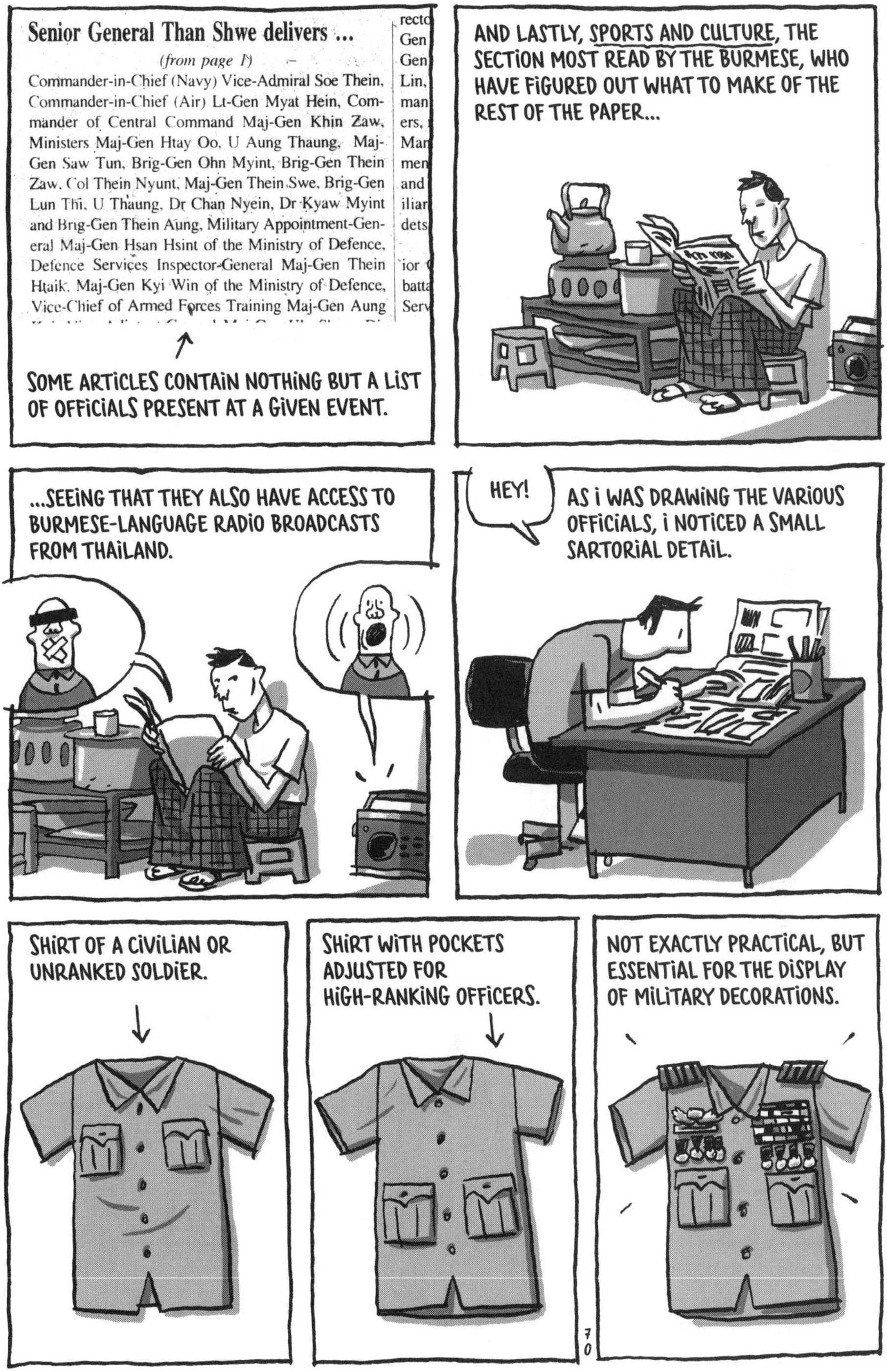
Senior General Than Shwe delivers ...
(from page 1)
Commander-in-Chief (Navy) Vice-Admiral Soe Thein, Commander-in-Chief (Air) Lt-Gen Myat Hein, Commander of Central Command Maj-Gen Khin Zaw, Ministers Maj-Gen Htay Oo, U Aung Thaung, Maj-Gen Saw Tun, Brig-Gen Ohn Myint, Brig-Gen Thein Zaw, Col Thein Nyunt, Maj-Gen Thein Swe, Brig-Gen Lun Thi, U Thaung, Dr Chan Nyein, Dr Kyaw Myint and Brig-Gen Thein Aung, Military Appointment-General Maj-Gen Hsan Hsint of the Ministry of Defence, Defence Services Inspector-General Maj-Gen Thein Htaik, Maj-Gen Kyi Win of the Ministry of Defence, Vice-Chief of Armed Forces Training Maj-Gen Aung
SOME ARTICLES CONTAIN NOTHING BUT A LIST OF OFFICIALS PRESENT AT A GIVEN EVENT.
AND LASTLY, SPORTS AND CULTURE, THE SECTION MOST READ BY THE BURMESE, WHO HAVE FIGURED OUT WHAT TO MAKE OF THE REST OF THE PAPER...
...SEEING THAT THEY ALSO HAVE ACCESS TO BURMESE-LANGUAGE RADIO BROADCASTS FROM THAILAND.
HEY!
AS I WAS DRAWING THE VARIOUS OFFICIALS, I NOTICED A SMALL SARTORIAL DETAIL.
SHIRT OF A CIVILIAN OR UNRANKED SOLDIER.
SHIRT WITH POCKETS ADJUSTED FOR HIGH-RANKING OFFICERS.
NOT EXACTLY PRACTICAL, BUT ESSENTIAL FOR THE DISPLAY OF MILITARY DECORATIONS.

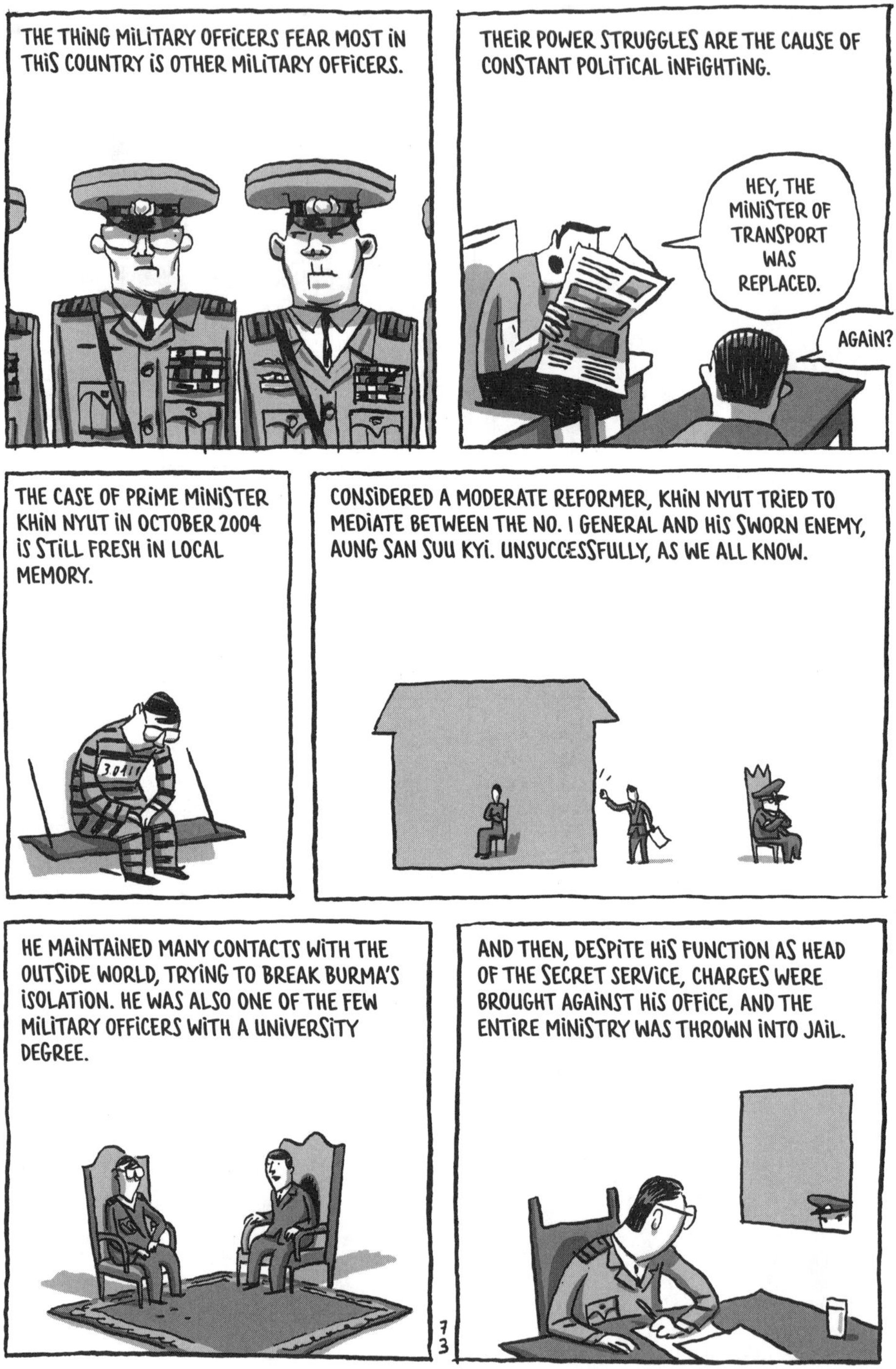
THE THING MILITARY OFFICERS FEAR MOST IN THIS COUNTRY IS OTHER MILITARY OFFICERS.
THEIR POWER STRUGGLES ARE THE CAUSE OF CONSTANT POLITICAL INFIGHTING.
HEY, THE MINISTER OF TRANSPORT WAS REPLACED.
AGAIN?
THE CASE OF PRIME MINISTER KHIN NYUT IN OCTOBER 2004 IS STILL FRESH IN LOCAL MEMORY.
3.04.11
CONSIDERED A MODERATE REFORMER, KHIN NYUT TRIED TO MEDIATE BETWEEN THE NO. 1 GENERAL AND HIS SWORN ENEMY, AUNG SAN SUU KYI. UNSUCCESSFULLY, AS WE ALL KNOW.
HE MAINTAINED MANY CONTACTS WITH THE OUTSIDE WORLD, TRYING TO BREAK BURMA'S ISOLATION. HE WAS ALSO ONE OF THE FEW MILITARY OFFICERS WITH A UNIVERSITY DEGREE.
AND THEN, DESPITE HIS FUNCTION AS HEAD OF THE SECRET SERVICE, CHARGES WERE BROUGHT AGAINST HIS OFFICE, AND THE ENTIRE MINISTRY WAS THROWN INTO JAIL.

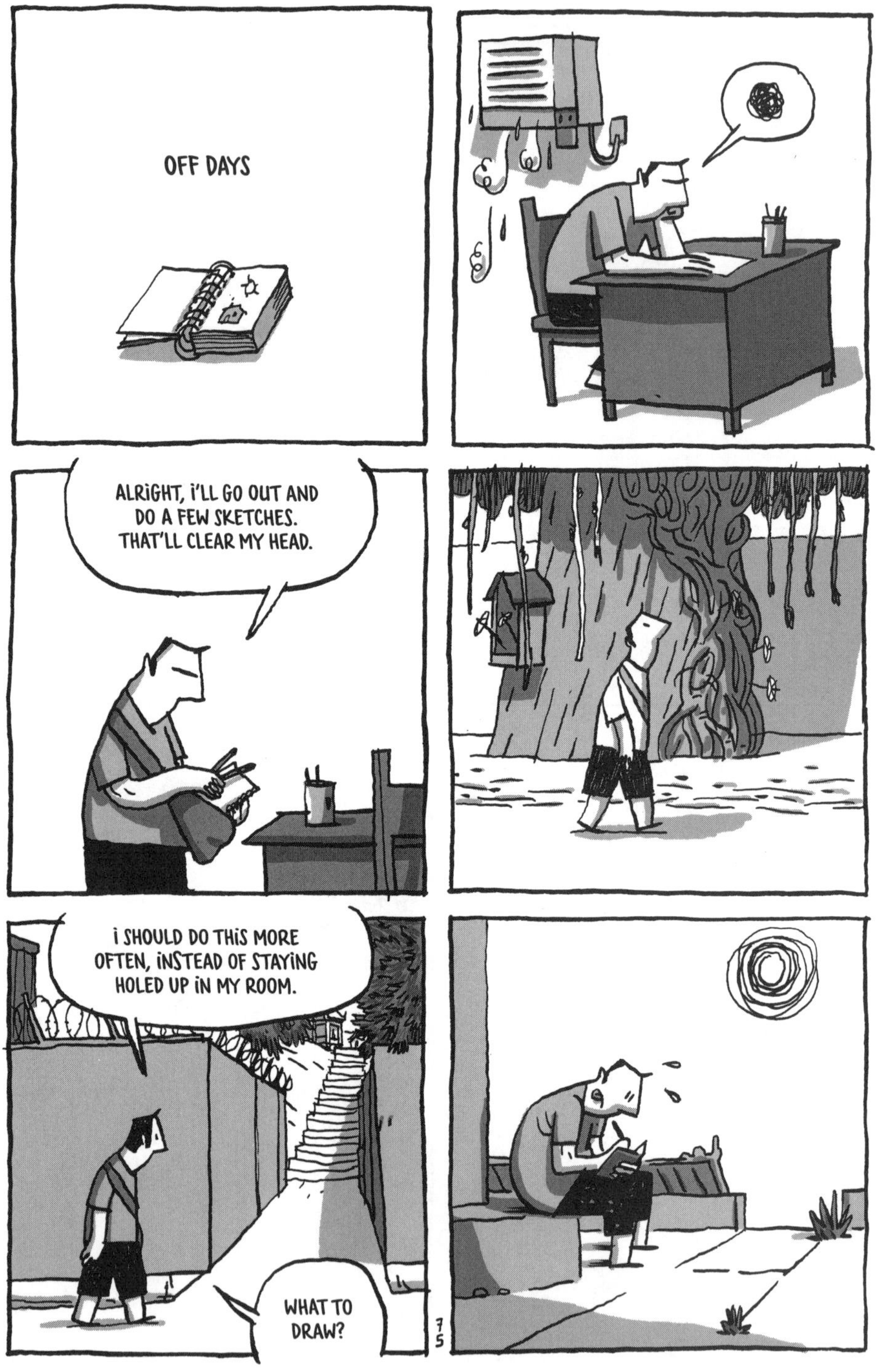
OFF DAYS
ALRIGHT, I'LL GO OUT AND DO A FEW SKETCHES. THAT'LL CLEAR MY HEAD.
I SHOULD DO THIS MORE OFTEN, INSTEAD OF STAYING HOLED UP IN MY ROOM.
WHAT TO DRAW?

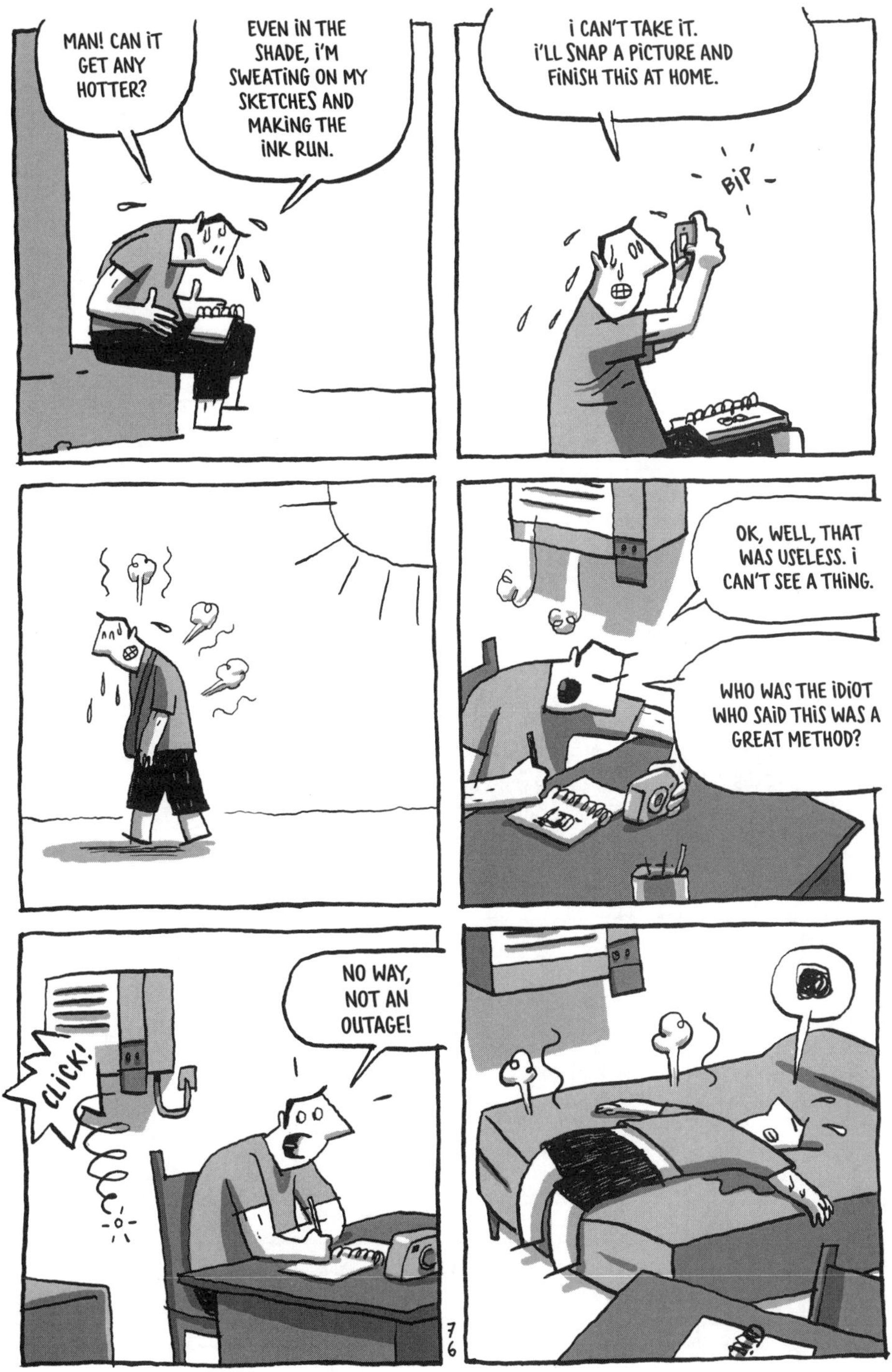
MAN! CAN IT GET ANY HOTTER?
EVEN IN THE SHADE, I'M SWEATING ON MY SKETCHES AND MAKING THE INK RUN.
I CAN'T TAKE IT. I'LL SNAP A PICTURE AND FINISH THIS AT HOME.
BIP
OK, WELL, THAT WAS USELESS. I CAN'T SEE A THING.
WHO WAS THE IDIOT WHO SAID THIS WAS A GREAT METHOD?
CLICK!
NO WAY, NOT AN OUTAGE!

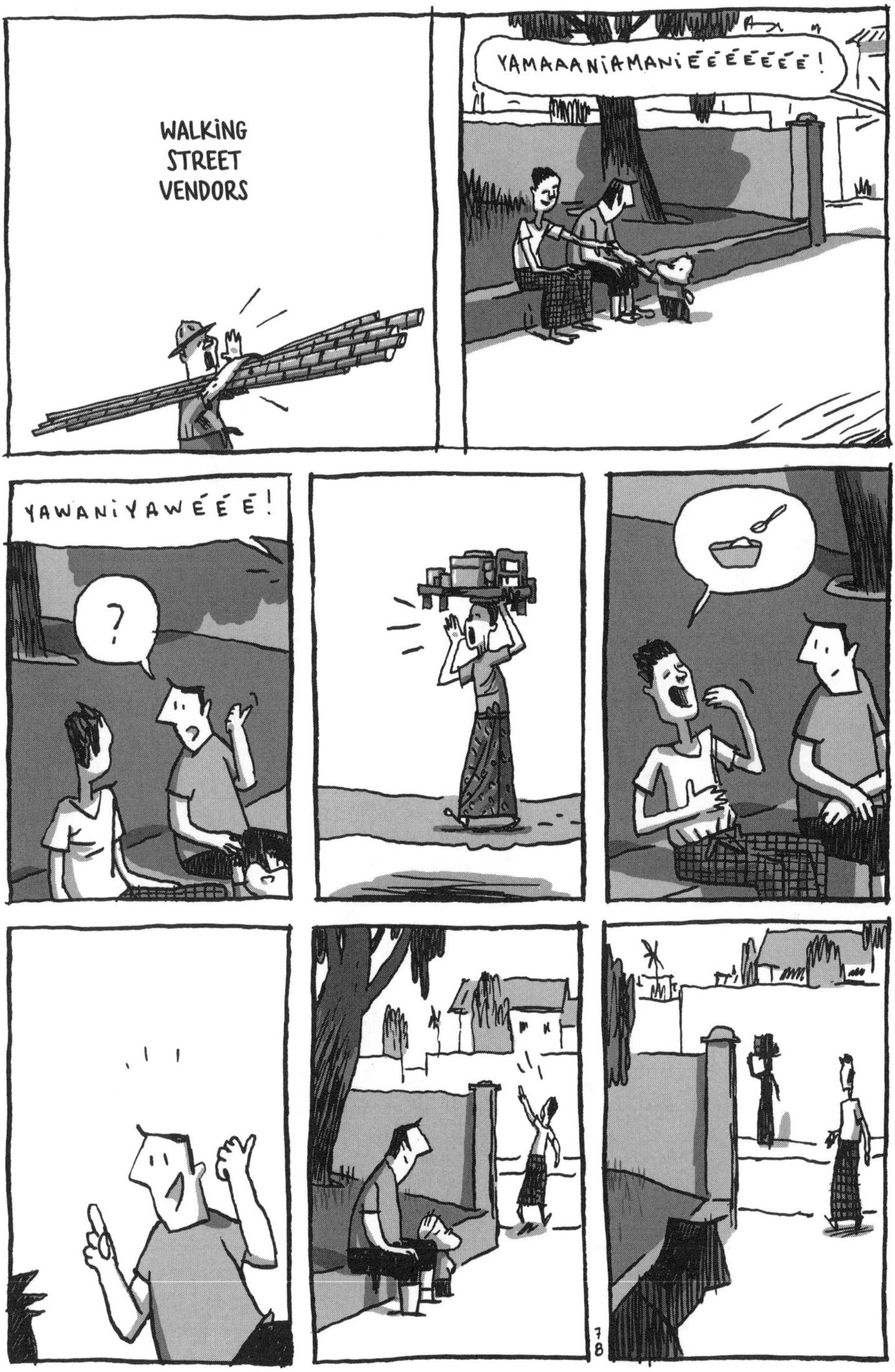
WALKING STREET VENDORS
YAMAAANIAMANIÉÉÉÉÉÉÉ!
YAWANIYAWÉÉÉ!
?

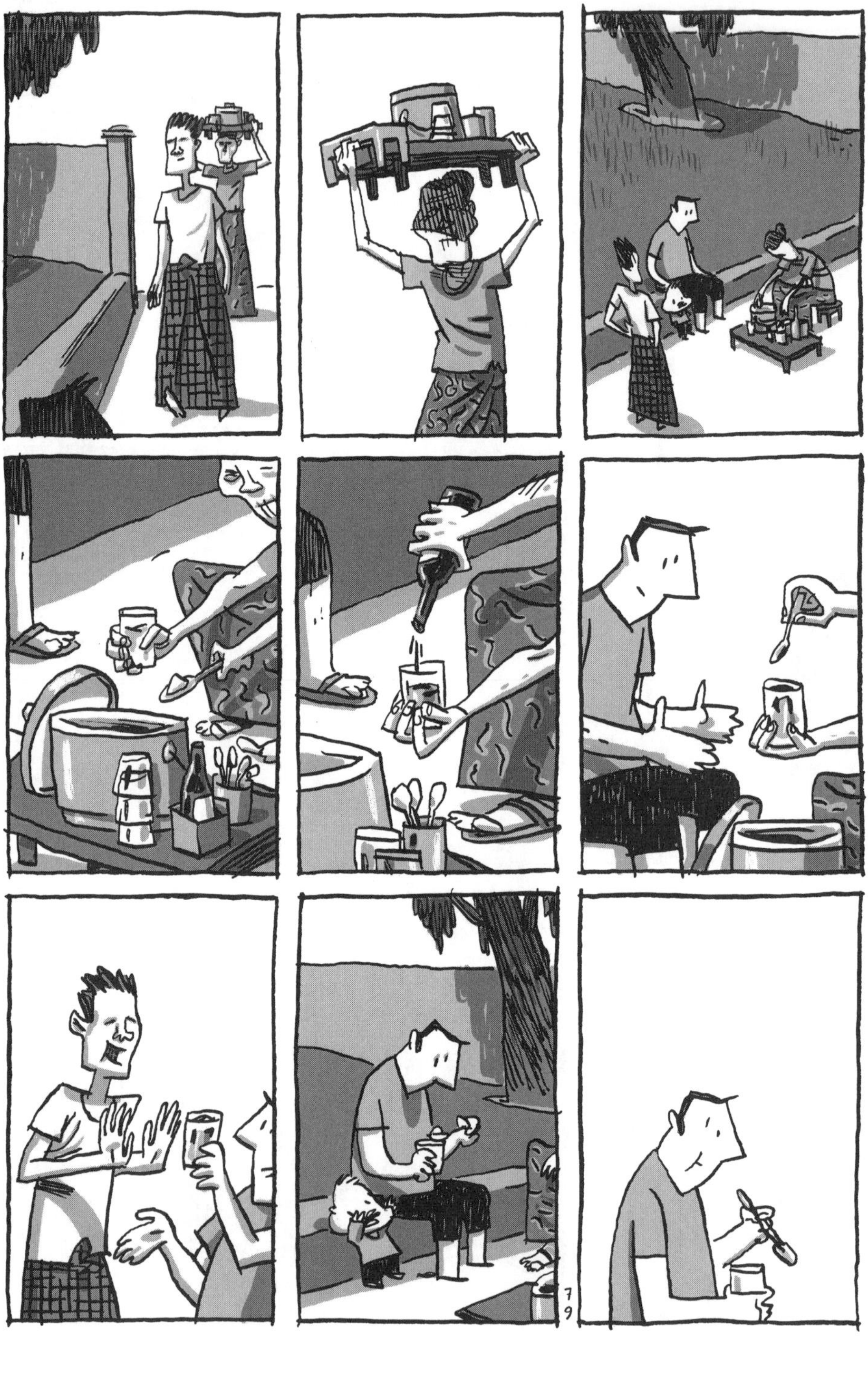

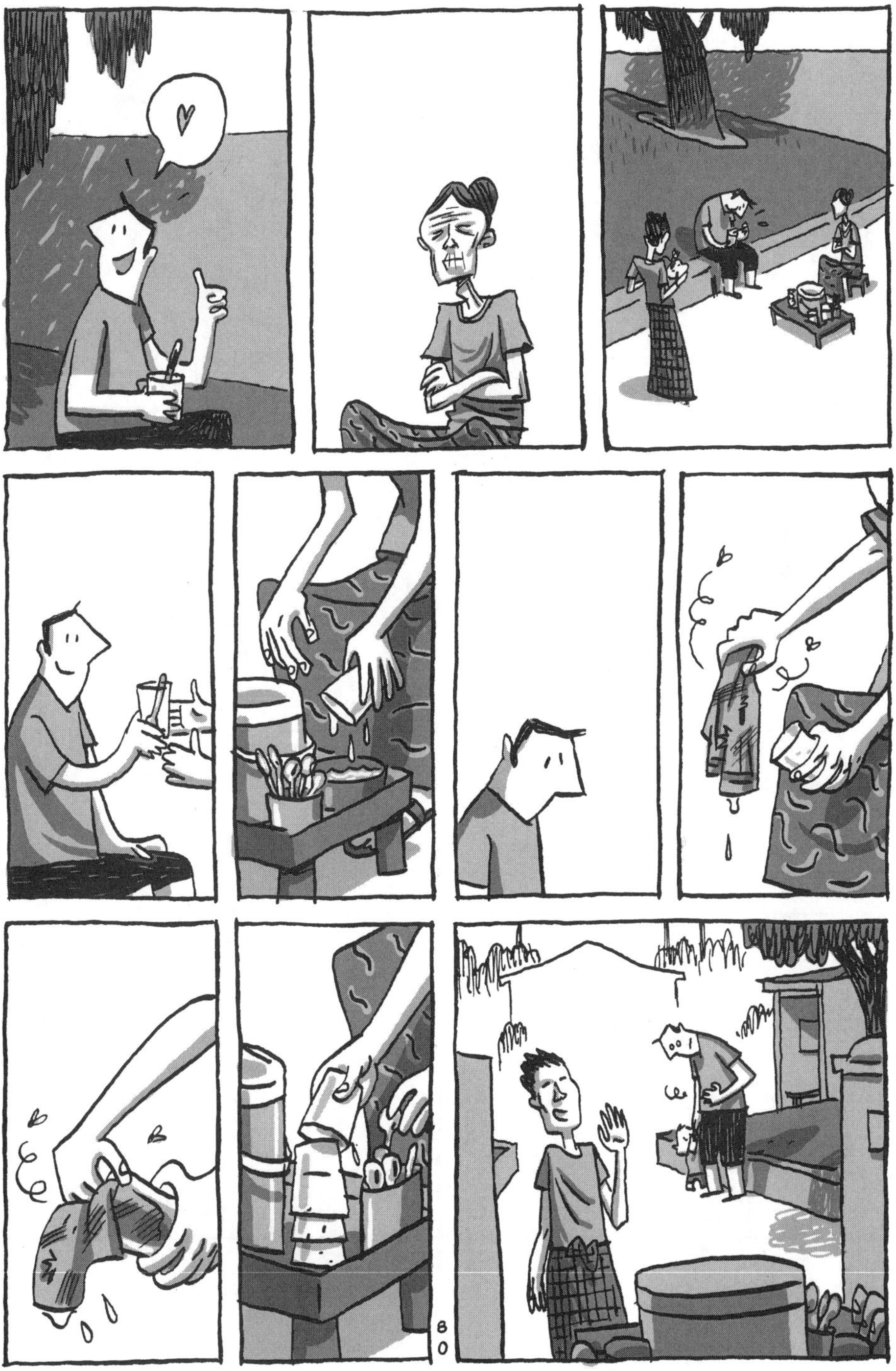

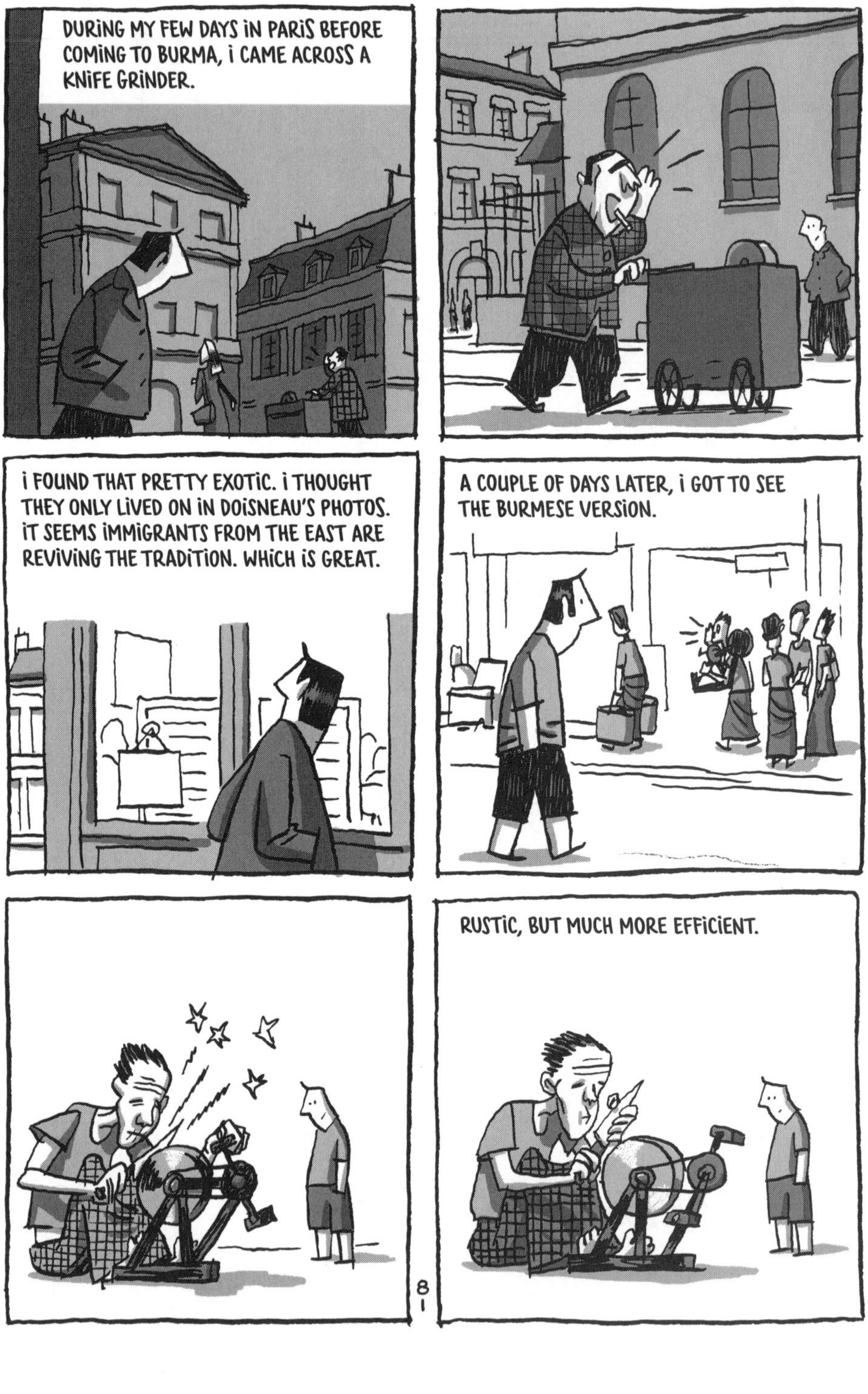
DURING MY FEW DAYS IN PARIS BEFORE COMING TO BURMA, I CAME ACROSS A KNIFE GRINDER.
I FOUND THAT PRETTY EXOTIC. I THOUGHT THEY ONLY LIVED ON IN DOISNEAU'S PHOTOS. IT SEEMS IMMIGRANTS FROM THE EAST ARE REVIVING THE TRADITION. WHICH IS GREAT.
A COUPLE OF DAYS LATER, I GOT TO SEE THE BURMESE VERSION.
RUSTIC, BUT MUCH MORE EFFICIENT.

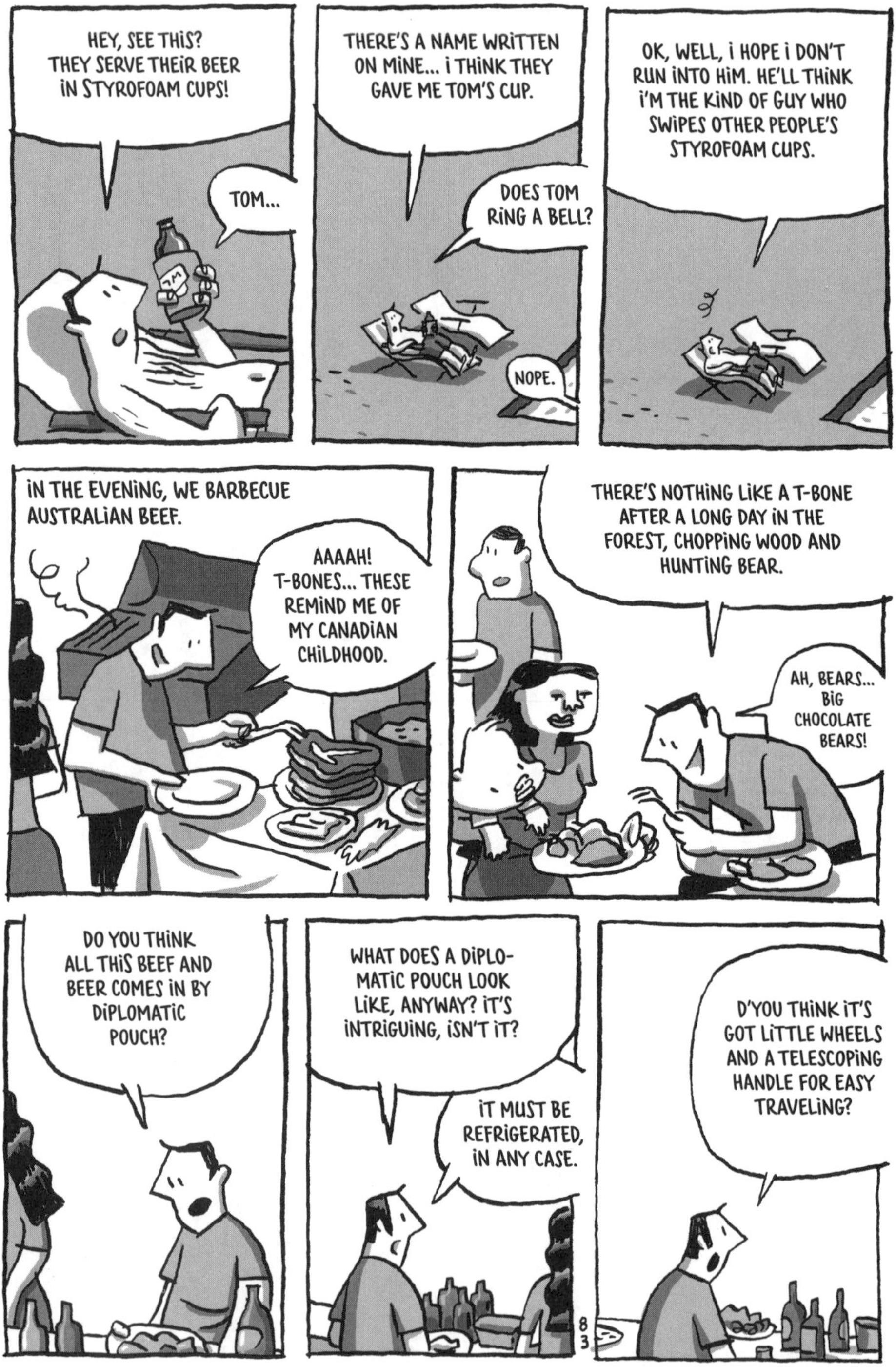
HEY, SEE THIS? THEY SERVE THEIR BEER IN STYROFOAM CUPS!
TOM...
THERE'S A NAME WRITTEN ON MINE... I THINK THEY GAVE ME TOM'S CUP.
DOES TOM RING A BELL?
NOPE.
OK, WELL, I HOPE I DON'T RUN INTO HIM. HE'LL THINK I'M THE KIND OF GUY WHO SWIPES OTHER PEOPLE'S STYROFOAM CUPS.
IN THE EVENING, WE BARBECUE AUSTRALIAN BEEF.
AAAAH! T-BONES... THESE REMIND ME OF MY CANADIAN CHILDHOOD.
THERE'S NOTHING LIKE A T-BONE AFTER A LONG DAY IN THE FOREST, CHOPPING WOOD AND HUNTING BEAR.
AH, BEARS... BIG CHOCOLATE BEARS!
DO YOU THINK ALL THIS BEEF AND BEER COMES IN BY DIPLOMATIC POUCH?
WHAT DOES A DIPLOMATIC POUCH LOOK LIKE, ANYWAY? IT'S INTRIGUING, ISN'T IT?
IT MUST BE REFRIGERATED, IN ANY CASE.
D'YOU THINK IT'S GOT LITTLE WHEELS AND A TELESCOPING HANDLE FOR EASY TRAVELING?

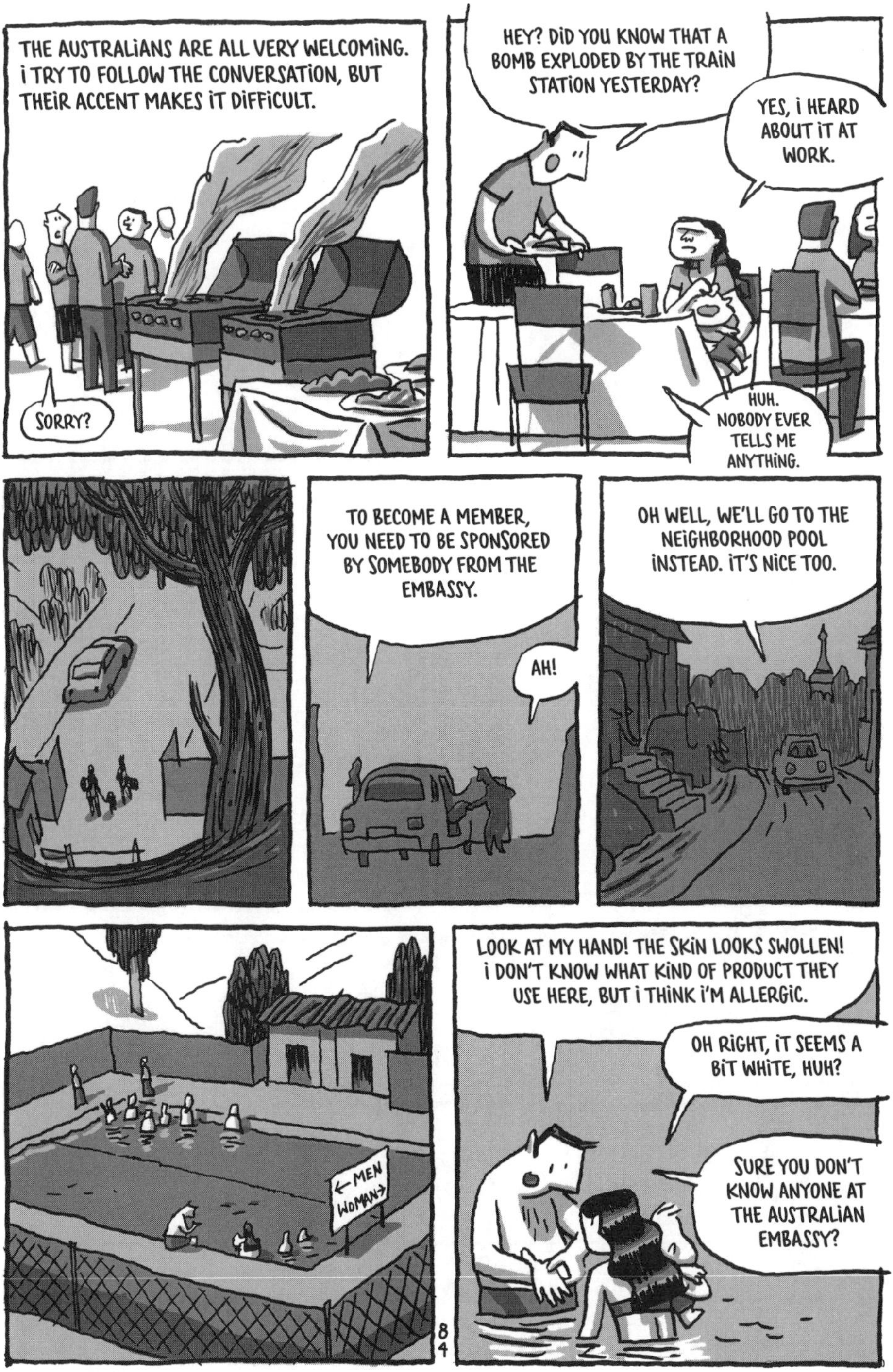
THE AUSTRALIANS ARE ALL VERY WELCOMING. I TRY TO FOLLOW THE CONVERSATION, BUT THEIR ACCENT MAKES IT DIFFICULT.
SORRY?
HEY? DID YOU KNOW THAT A BOMB EXPLODED BY THE TRAIN STATION YESTERDAY?
YES, I HEARD ABOUT IT AT WORK.
HUH. NOBODY EVER TELLS ME ANYTHING.
TO BECOME A MEMBER, YOU NEED TO BE SPONSORED BY SOMEBODY FROM THE EMBASSY.
AH!
OH WELL, WE'LL GO TO THE NEIGHBORHOOD POOL INSTEAD. IT'S NICE TOO.
← MEN
WOMAN →
LOOK AT MY HAND! THE SKIN LOOKS SWOLLEN! I DON'T KNOW WHAT KIND OF PRODUCT THEY USE HERE, BUT I THINK I'M ALLERGIC.
OH RIGHT, IT SEEMS A BIT WHITE, HUH?
SURE YOU DON'T KNOW ANYONE AT THE AUSTRALIAN EMBASSY?

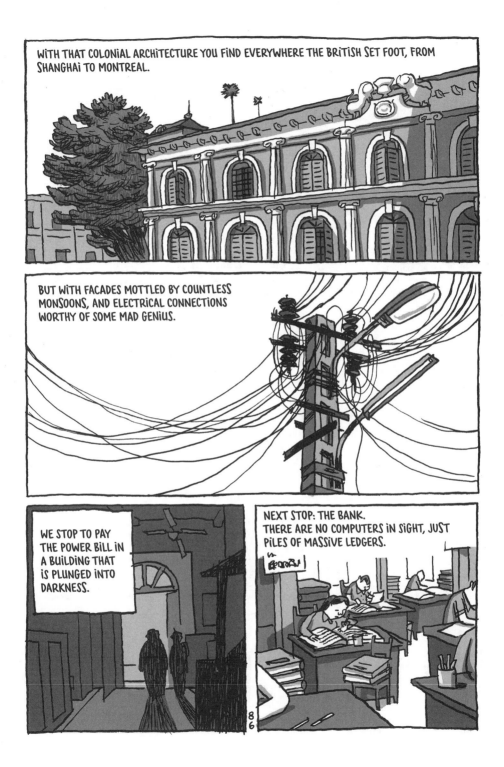

WITH THAT COLONIAL ARCHITECTURE YOU FIND EVERYWHERE THE BRITISH SET FOOT, FROM SHANGHAI TO MONTREAL.

BUT WITH FACADES MOTTLED BY COUNTLESS MONSOONS, AND ELECTRICAL CONNECTIONS WORTHY OF SOME MAD GENIUS.

WE STOP TO PAY THE POWER BILL IN A BUILDING THAT IS PLUNGED INTO DARKNESS.

NEXT STOP: THE BANK. THERE ARE NO COMPUTERS IN SIGHT, JUST PILES OF MASSIVE LEDGERS.

8
6

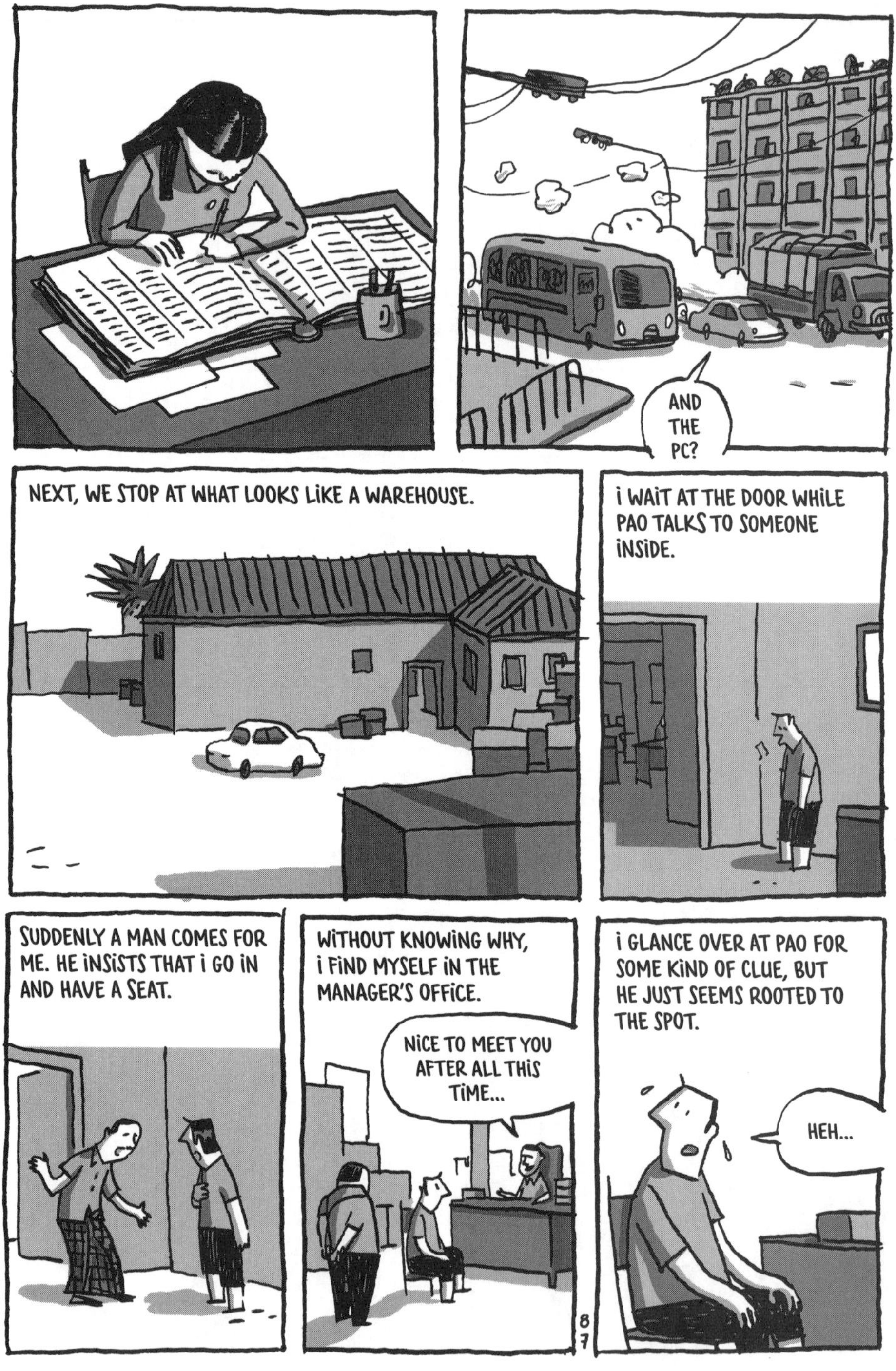
AND THE PC?
NEXT, WE STOP AT WHAT LOOKS LIKE A WAREHOUSE.
I WAIT AT THE DOOR WHILE PAO TALKS TO SOMEONE INSIDE.
SUDDENLY A MAN COMES FOR ME. HE INSISTS THAT I GO IN AND HAVE A SEAT.
WITHOUT KNOWING WHY, I FIND MYSELF IN THE MANAGER'S OFFICE.
NICE TO MEET YOU AFTER ALL THIS TIME...
I GLANCE OVER AT PAO FOR SOME KIND OF CLUE, BUT HE JUST SEEMS ROOTED TO THE SPOT.
HEH...

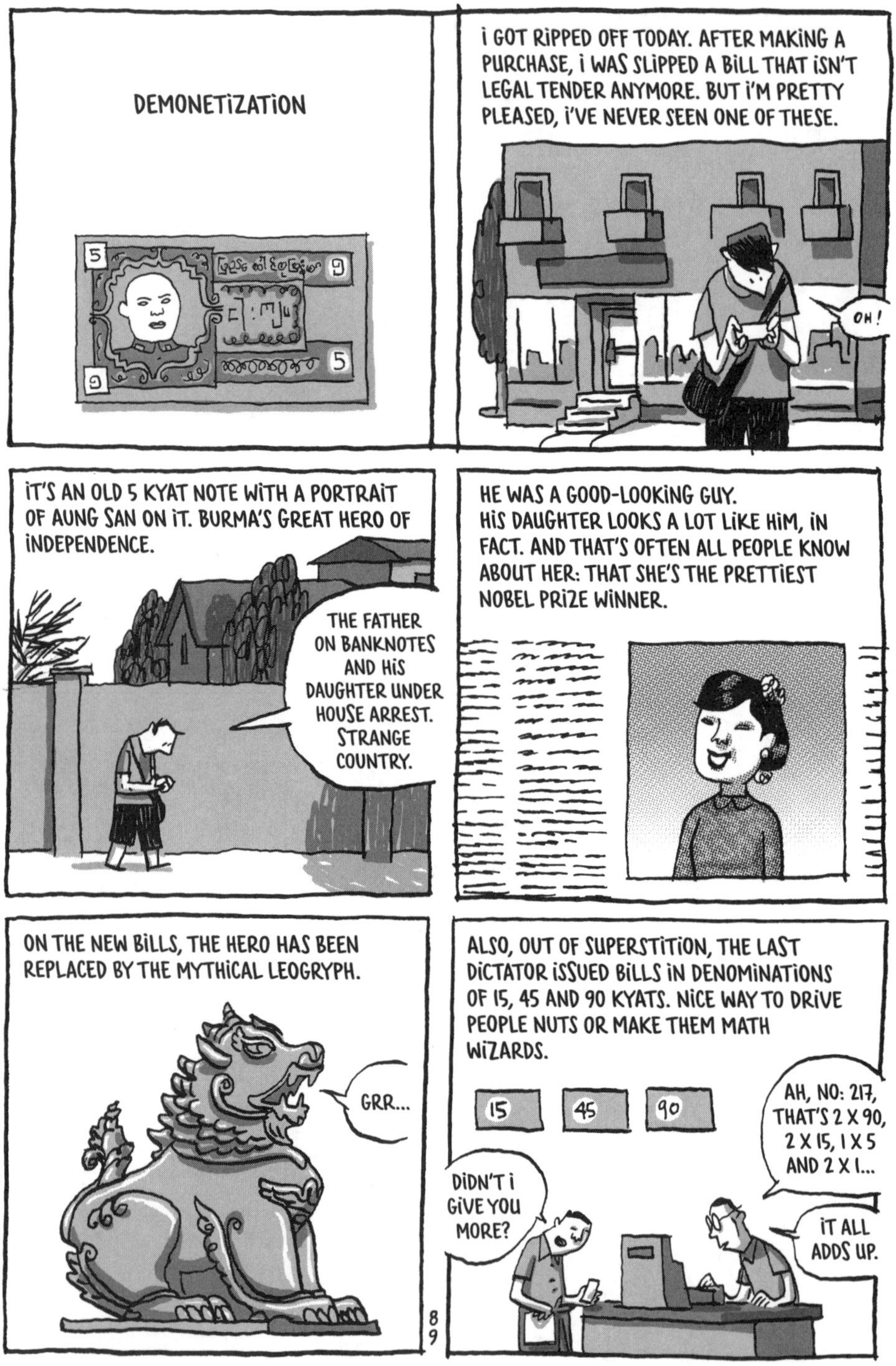
DEMONETIZATION
I GOT RIPPED OFF TODAY. AFTER MAKING A PURCHASE, I WAS SLIPPED A BILL THAT ISN'T LEGAL TENDER ANYMORE. BUT I'M PRETTY PLEASED, I'VE NEVER SEEN ONE OF THESE.
OH!
IT'S AN OLD 5 KYAT NOTE WITH A PORTRAIT OF AUNG SAN ON IT. BURMA'S GREAT HERO OF INDEPENDENCE.
THE FATHER ON BANKNOTES AND HIS DAUGHTER UNDER HOUSE ARREST. STRANGE COUNTRY.
HE WAS A GOOD-LOOKING GUY. HIS DAUGHTER LOOKS A LOT LIKE HIM, IN FACT. AND THAT'S OFTEN ALL PEOPLE KNOW ABOUT HER: THAT SHE'S THE PRETTIEST NOBEL PRIZE WINNER.
ON THE NEW BILLS, THE HERO HAS BEEN REPLACED BY THE MYTHICAL LEOGRYPH.
GRR...
ALSO, OUT OF SUPERSTITION, THE LAST DICTATOR ISSUED BILLS IN DENOMINATIONS OF 15, 45 AND 90 KYATS. NICE WAY TO DRIVE PEOPLE NUTS OR MAKE THEM MATH WIZARDS.
15
45
90
AH, NO: 217, THAT'S 2 X 90, 2 X 15, 1 X 5 AND 2 X 1...
DIDN'T I GIVE YOU MORE?
IT ALL ADDS UP.

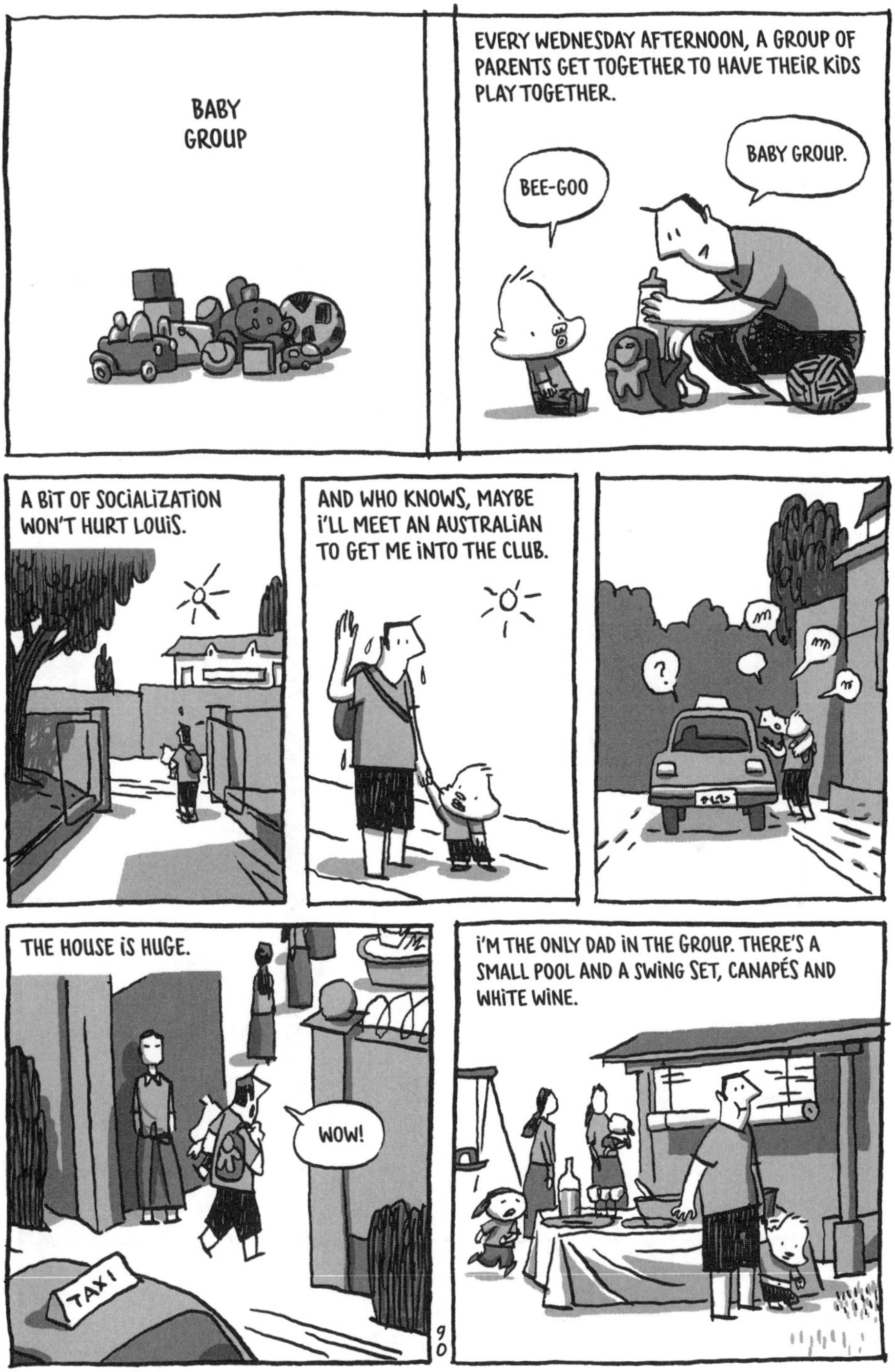
BABY GROUP
EVERY WEDNESDAY AFTERNOON, A GROUP OF PARENTS GET TOGETHER TO HAVE THEIR KIDS PLAY TOGETHER.
BEE-GOO
BABY GROUP.
A BIT OF SOCIALIZATION WON'T HURT LOUIS.
AND WHO KNOWS, MAYBE I'LL MEET AN AUSTRALIAN TO GET ME INTO THE CLUB.
?
THE HOUSE IS HUGE.
WOW!
TAXI
I'M THE ONLY DAD IN THE GROUP. THERE'S A SMALL POOL AND A SWING SET, CANAPÉS AND WHITE WINE.

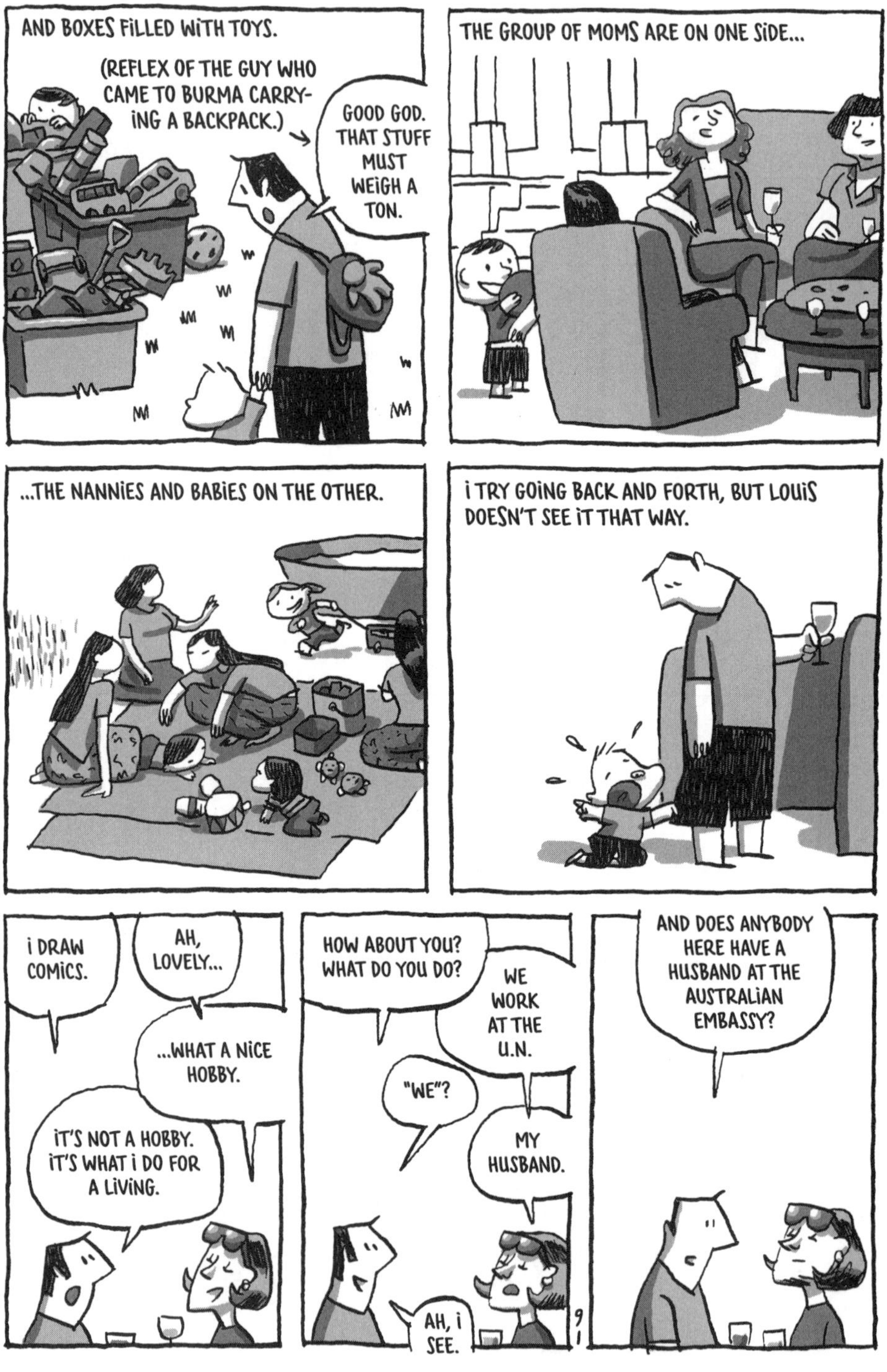
AND BOXES FILLED WITH TOYS.
(REFLEX OF THE GUY WHO CAME TO BURMA CARRYING A BACKPACK.)
GOOD GOD. THAT STUFF MUST WEIGH A TON.
THE GROUP OF MOMS ARE ON ONE SIDE...
...THE NANNIES AND BABIES ON THE OTHER.
I TRY GOING BACK AND FORTH, BUT LOUIS DOESN'T SEE IT THAT WAY.
I DRAW COMICS.
AH, LOVELY...
...WHAT A NICE HOBBY.
IT'S NOT A HOBBY. IT'S WHAT I DO FOR A LIVING.
HOW ABOUT YOU? WHAT DO YOU DO?
WE WORK AT THE U.N.
"WE"?
MY HUSBAND.
AH, I SEE.
AND DOES ANYBODY HERE HAVE A HUSBAND AT THE AUSTRALIAN EMBASSY?

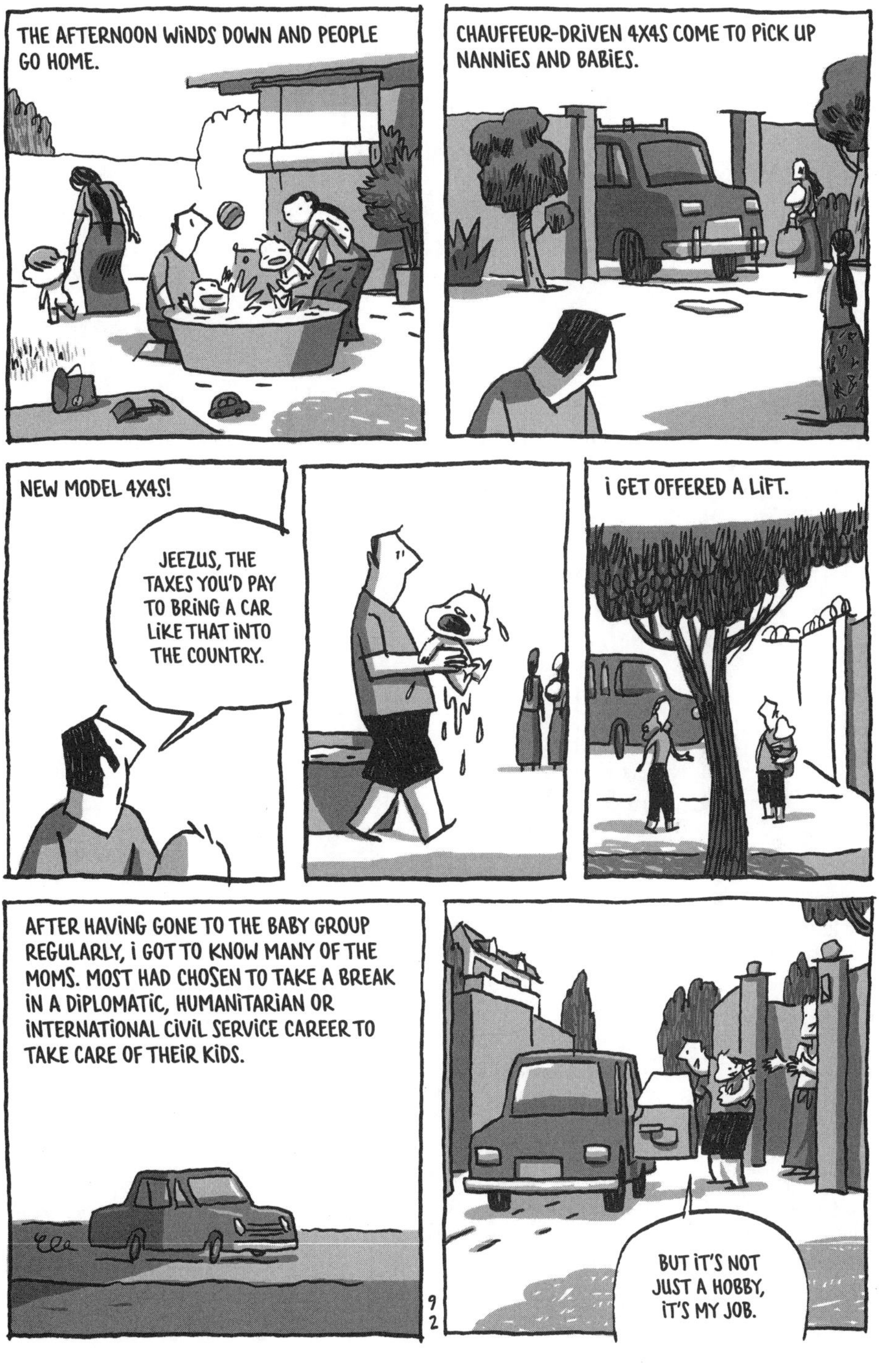

THE AFTERNOON WINDS DOWN AND PEOPLE GO HOME.
CHAUFFEUR-DRIVEN 4X4S COME TO PICK UP NANNIES AND BABIES.
NEW MODEL 4X4S!
JEEZUS, THE TAXES YOU'D PAY TO BRING A CAR LIKE THAT INTO THE COUNTRY.
I GET OFFERED A LIFT.
AFTER HAVING GONE TO THE BABY GROUP REGULARLY, I GOT TO KNOW MANY OF THE MOMS. MOST HAD CHOSEN TO TAKE A BREAK IN A DIPLOMATIC, HUMANITARIAN OR INTERNATIONAL CIVIL SERVICE CAREER TO TAKE CARE OF THEIR KIDS.
BUT IT'S NOT JUST A HOBBY, IT'S MY JOB.

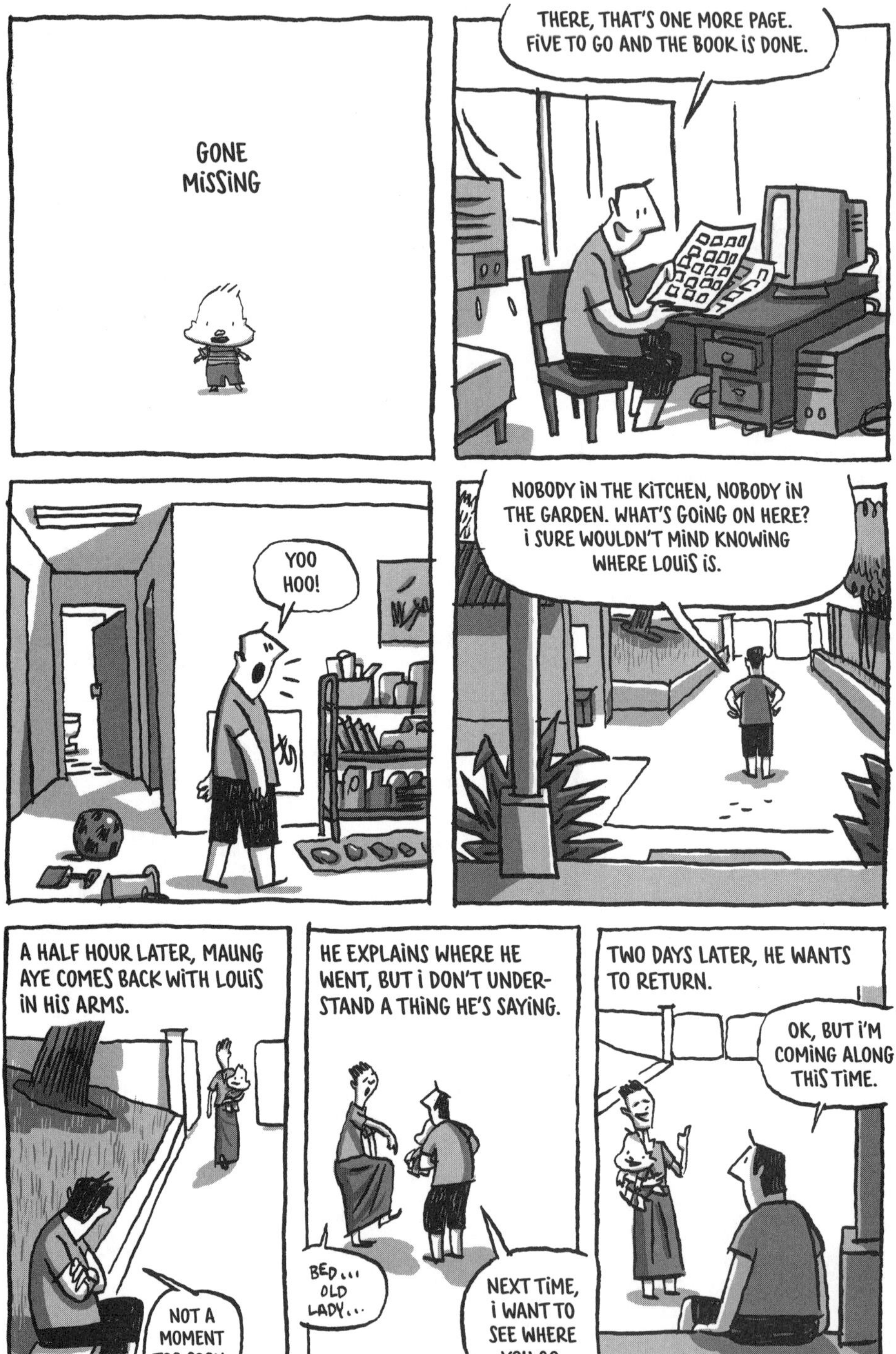
GONE
MISSING
THERE, THAT'S ONE MORE PAGE. FIVE TO GO AND THE BOOK IS DONE.
YOO HOO!
NOBODY IN THE KITCHEN, NOBODY IN THE GARDEN. WHAT'S GOING ON HERE? I SURE WOULDN'T MIND KNOWING WHERE LOUIS IS.
A HALF HOUR LATER, MAUNG AYE COMES BACK WITH LOUIS IN HIS ARMS.
NOT A MOMENT TOO SOON.
HE EXPLAINS WHERE HE WENT, BUT I DON'T UNDERSTAND A THING HE'S SAYING.
BED... OLD LADY...
NEXT TIME, I WANT TO SEE WHERE YOU GO.
TWO DAYS LATER, HE WANTS TO RETURN.
OK, BUT I'M COMING ALONG THIS TIME.

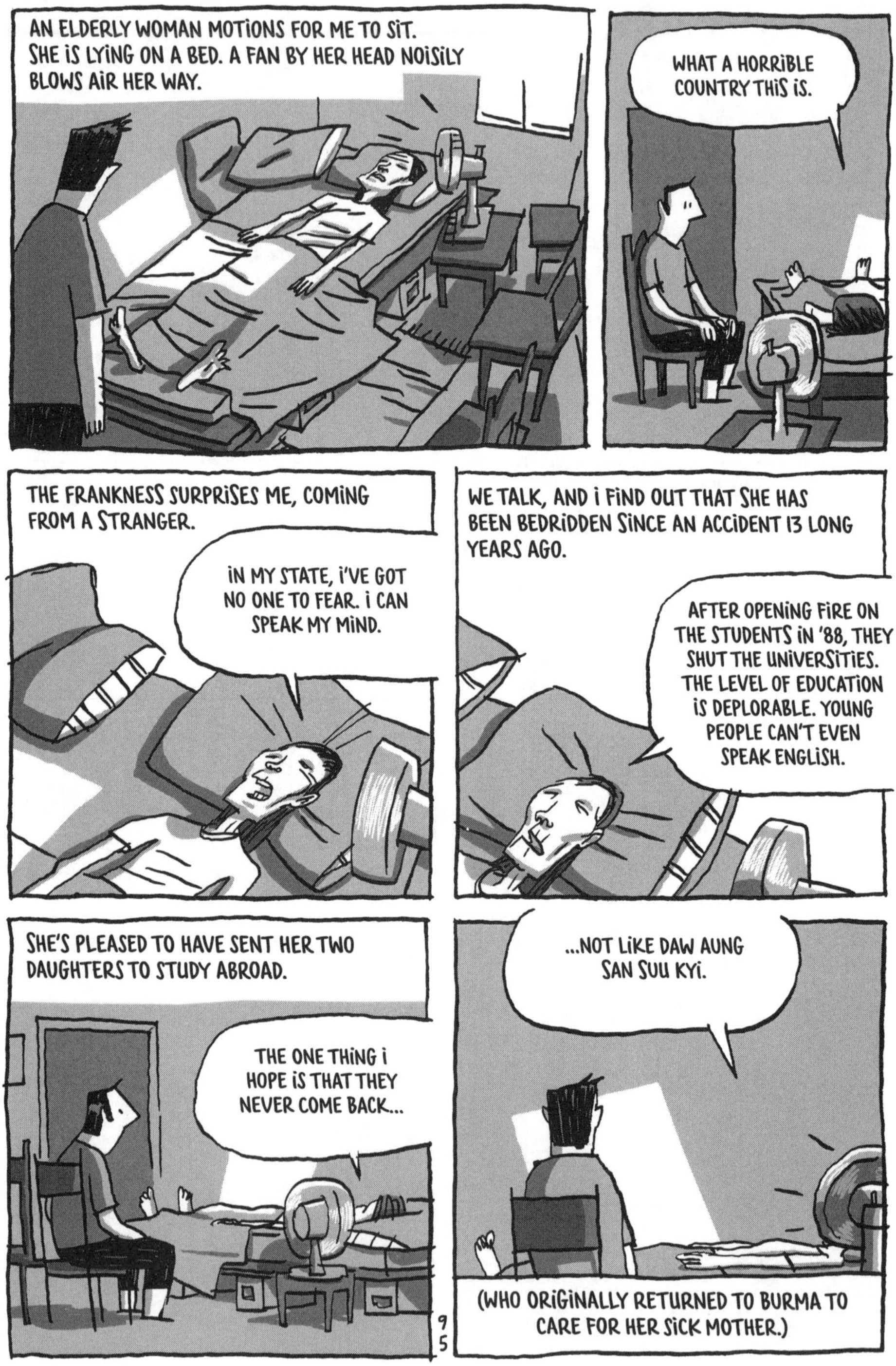
AN ELDERLY WOMAN MOTIONS FOR ME TO SIT. SHE IS LYING ON A BED. A FAN BY HER HEAD NOISILY BLOWS AIR HER WAY.
WHAT A HORRIBLE COUNTRY THIS IS.
THE FRANKNESS SURPRISES ME, COMING FROM A STRANGER.
IN MY STATE, I'VE GOT NO ONE TO FEAR. I CAN SPEAK MY MIND.
WE TALK, AND I FIND OUT THAT SHE HAS BEEN BEDRIDDEN SINCE AN ACCIDENT 13 LONG YEARS AGO.
AFTER OPENING FIRE ON THE STUDENTS IN '88, THEY SHUT THE UNIVERSITIES. THE LEVEL OF EDUCATION IS DEPLORABLE. YOUNG PEOPLE CAN'T EVEN SPEAK ENGLISH.
SHE'S PLEASED TO HAVE SENT HER TWO DAUGHTERS TO STUDY ABROAD.
THE ONE THING I HOPE IS THAT THEY NEVER COME BACK...
...NOT LIKE DAW AUNG SAN SUU KYI.
(WHO ORIGINALLY RETURNED TO BURMA TO CARE FOR HER SICK MOTHER.)

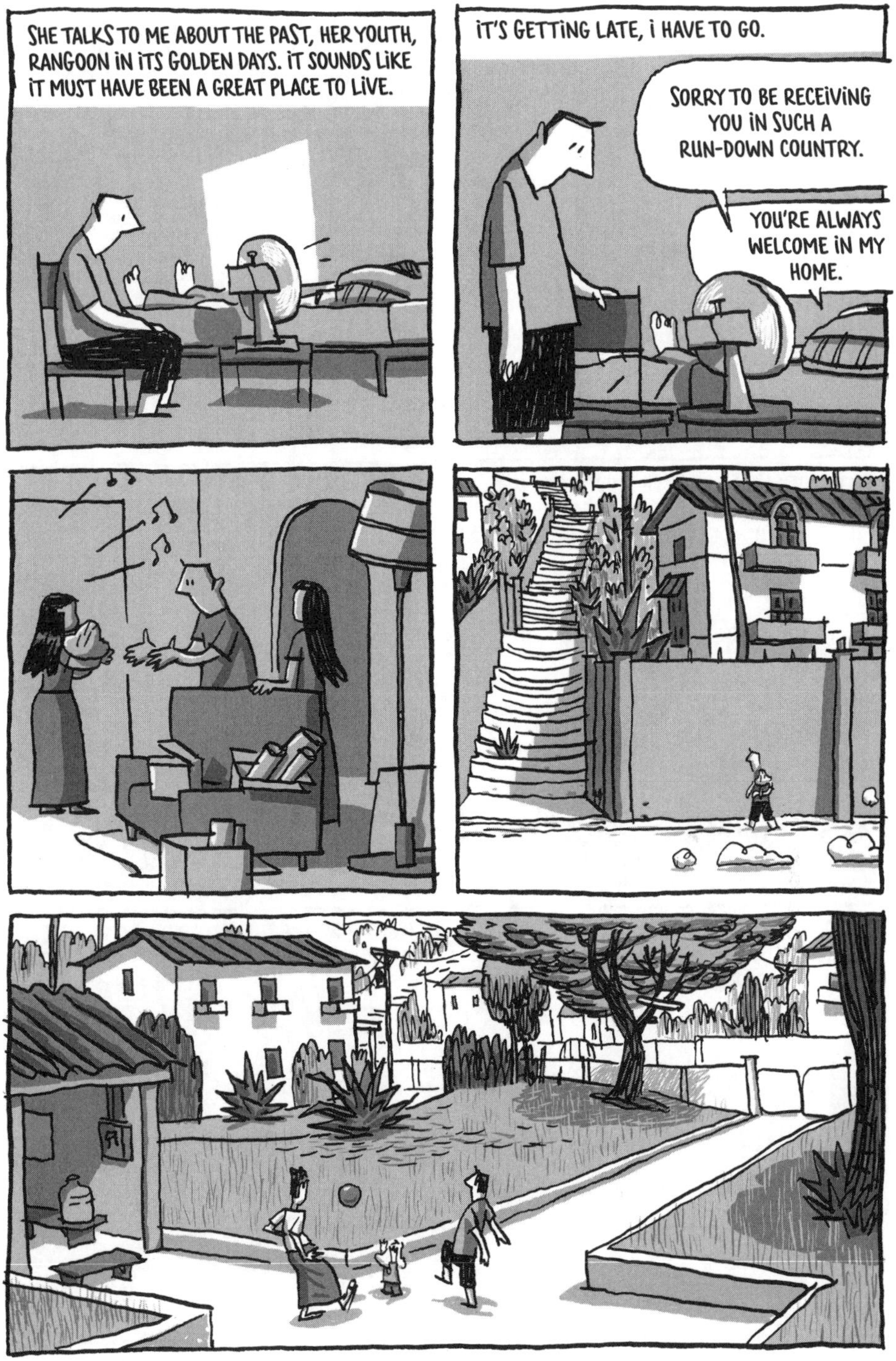
SHE TALKS TO ME ABOUT THE PAST, HER YOUTH, RANGOON IN ITS GOLDEN DAYS. IT SOUNDS LIKE IT MUST HAVE BEEN A GREAT PLACE TO LIVE.
IT'S GETTING LATE, I HAVE TO GO.
SORRY TO BE RECEIVING YOU IN SUCH A RUN-DOWN COUNTRY.
YOU'RE ALWAYS WELCOME IN MY HOME.

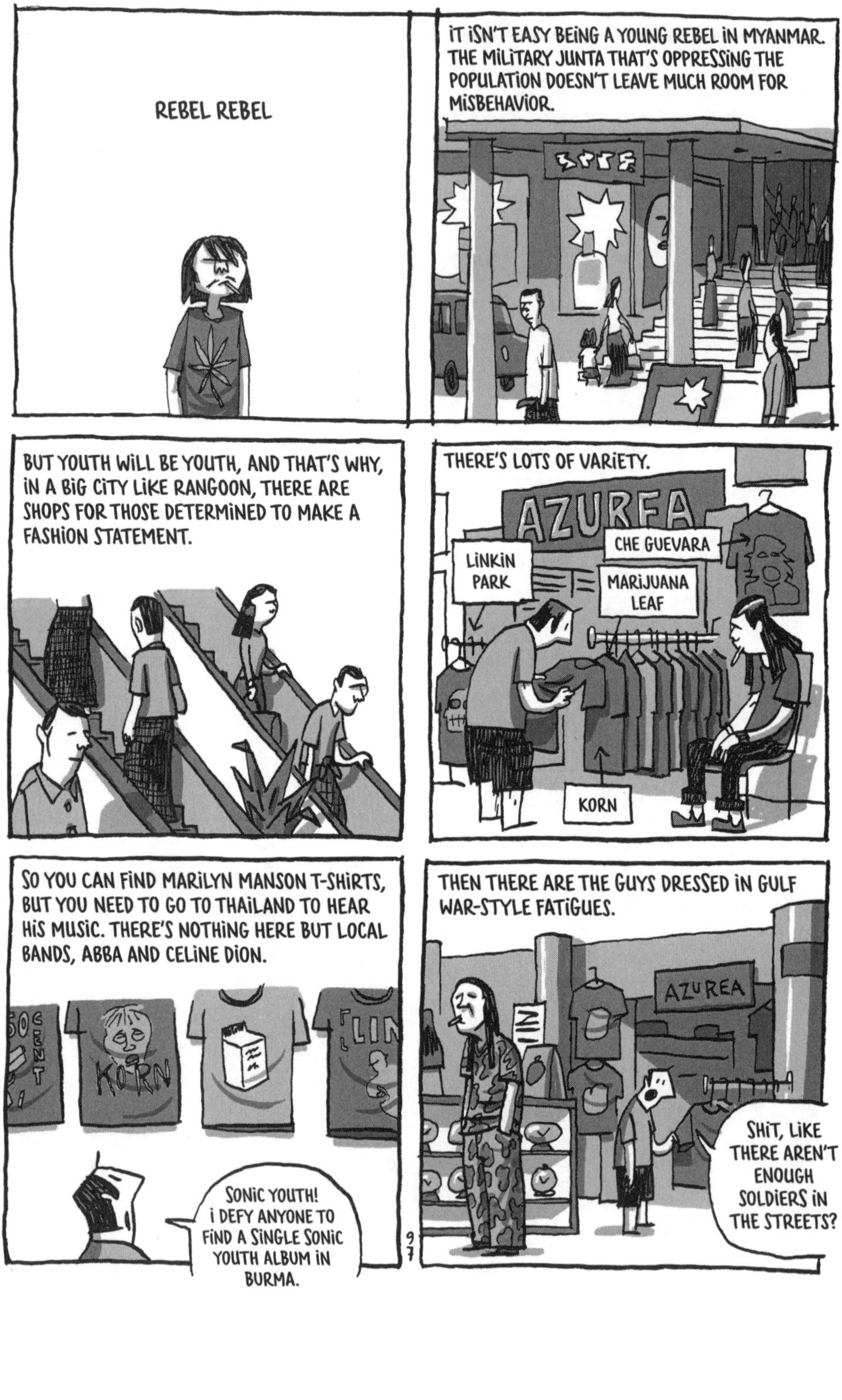
REBEL REBEL
IT ISN'T EASY BEING A YOUNG REBEL IN MYANMAR. THE MILITARY JUNTA THAT'S OPPRESSING THE POPULATION DOESN'T LEAVE MUCH ROOM FOR MISBEHAVIOR.
BUT YOUTH WILL BE YOUTH, AND THAT'S WHY, IN A BIG CITY LIKE RANGOON, THERE ARE SHOPS FOR THOSE DETERMINED TO MAKE A FASHION STATEMENT.
THERE'S LOTS OF VARIETY.
CHE GUEVARA
LINKIN PARK
MARIJUANA LEAF
KORN
SO YOU CAN FIND MARILYN MANSON T-SHIRTS, BUT YOU NEED TO GO TO THAILAND TO HEAR HIS MUSIC. THERE'S NOTHING HERE BUT LOCAL BANDS, ABBA AND CELINE DION.
KORN
SONIC YOUTH! I DEFY ANYONE TO FIND A SINGLE SONIC YOUTH ALBUM IN BURMA.
THEN THERE ARE THE GUYS DRESSED IN GULF WAR-STYLE FATIGUES.
AZUREA
SHIT, LIKE THERE AREN'T ENOUGH SOLDIERS IN THE STREETS?

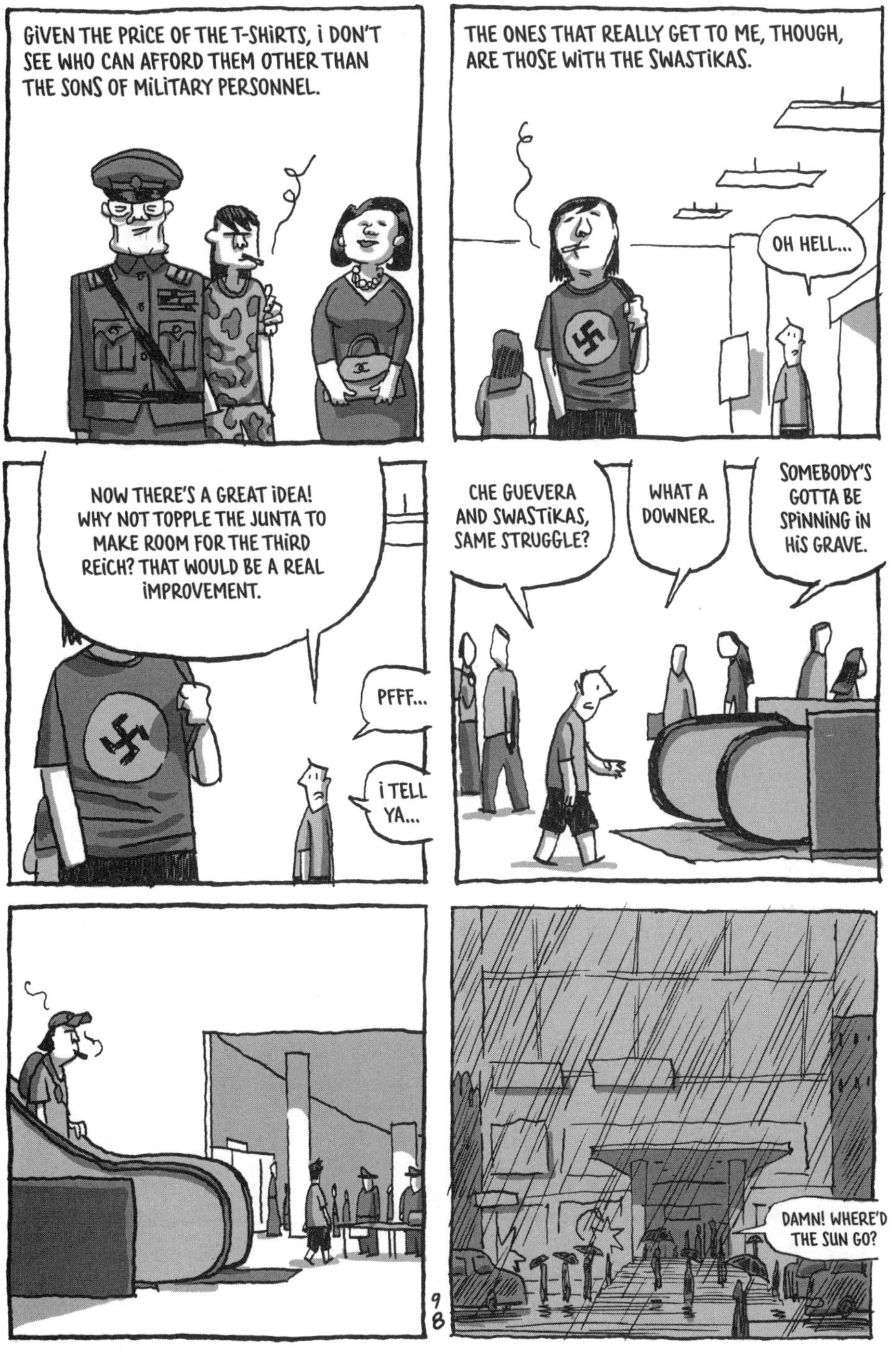
GIVEN THE PRICE OF THE T-SHIRTS, I DON'T SEE WHO CAN AFFORD THEM OTHER THAN THE SONS OF MILITARY PERSONNEL.
THE ONES THAT REALLY GET TO ME, THOUGH, ARE THOSE WITH THE SWASTIKAS.
OH HELL...
NOW THERE'S A GREAT IDEA! WHY NOT TOPPLE THE JUNTA TO MAKE ROOM FOR THE THIRD REICH? THAT WOULD BE A REAL IMPROVEMENT.
PFFF...
I TELL YA...
CHE GUEVERA AND SWASTIKAS, SAME STRUGGLE?
WHAT A DOWNER.
SOMEBODY'S GOTTA BE SPINNING IN HIS GRAVE.
DAMN! WHERE'D THE SUN GO?

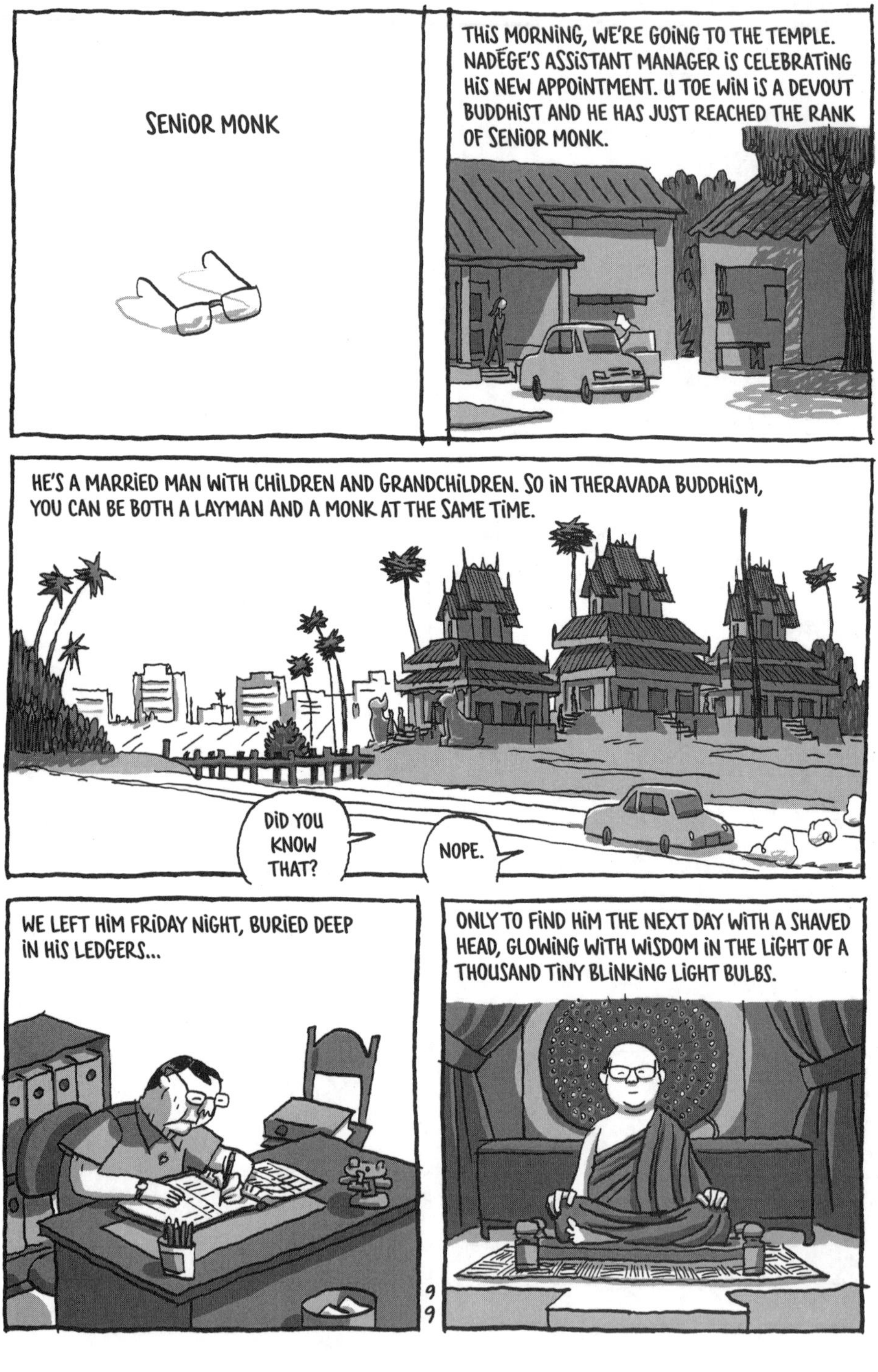
SENIOR MONK
THIS MORNING, WE'RE GOING TO THE TEMPLE. NADÉGE'S ASSISTANT MANAGER IS CELEBRATING HIS NEW APPOINTMENT. U TOE WIN IS A DEVOUT BUDDHIST AND HE HAS JUST REACHED THE RANK OF SENIOR MONK.
HE'S A MARRIED MAN WITH CHILDREN AND GRANDCHILDREN. SO IN THERAVADA BUDDHISM, YOU CAN BE BOTH A LAYMAN AND A MONK AT THE SAME TIME.
DID YOU KNOW THAT?
NOPE.
WE LEFT HIM FRIDAY NIGHT, BURIED DEEP IN HIS LEDGERS...
ONLY TO FIND HIM THE NEXT DAY WITH A SHAVED HEAD, GLOWING WITH WISDOM IN THE LIGHT OF A THOUSAND TINY BLINKING LIGHT BULBS.

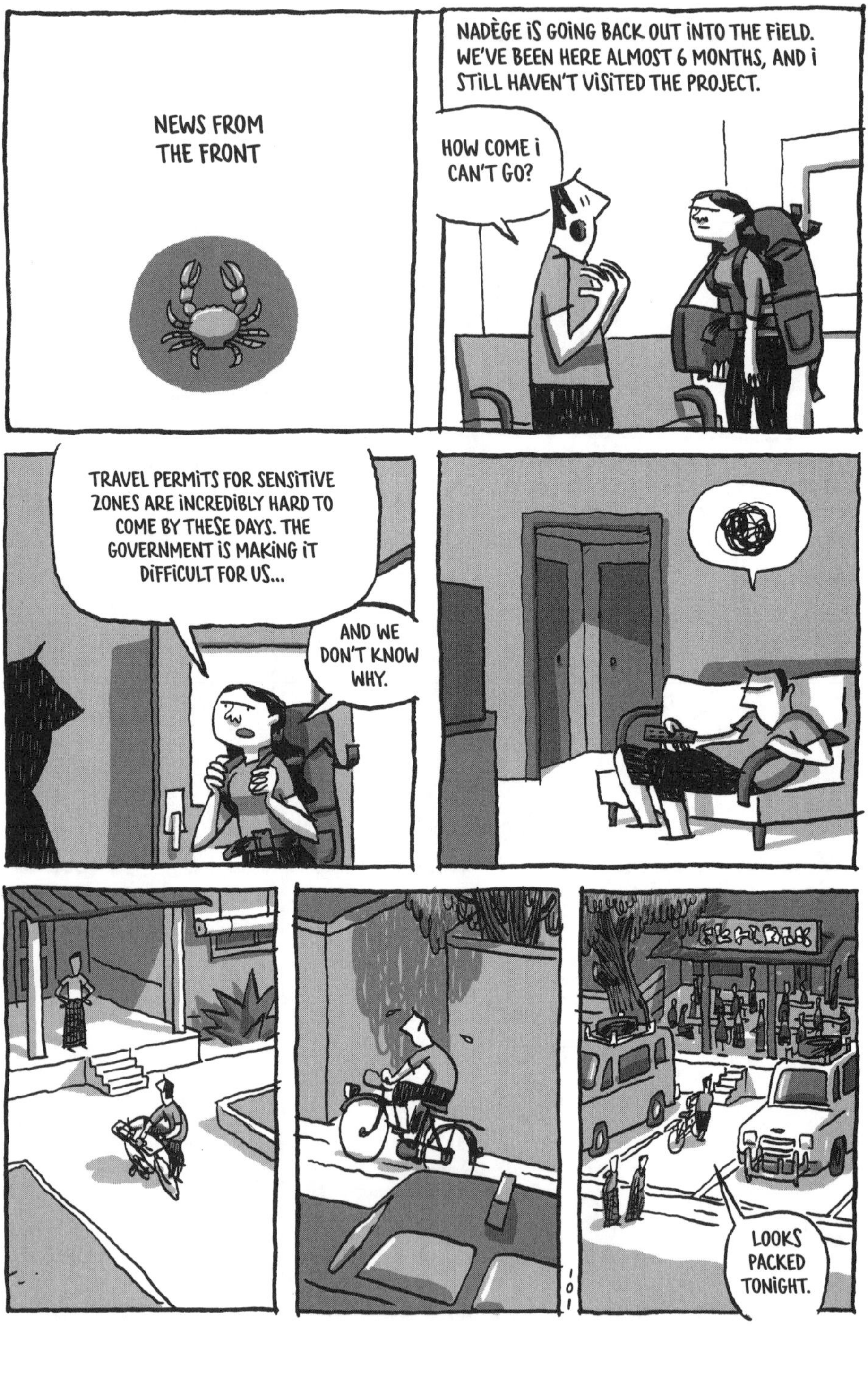
NEWS FROM THE FRONT
NADÈGE IS GOING BACK OUT INTO THE FIELD. WE'VE BEEN HERE ALMOST 6 MONTHS, AND I STILL HAVEN'T VISITED THE PROJECT.
HOW COME I CAN'T GO?
TRAVEL PERMITS FOR SENSITIVE ZONES ARE INCREDIBLY HARD TO COME BY THESE DAYS. THE GOVERNMENT IS MAKING IT DIFFICULT FOR US...
AND WE DON'T KNOW WHY.
LOOKS PACKED TONIGHT.

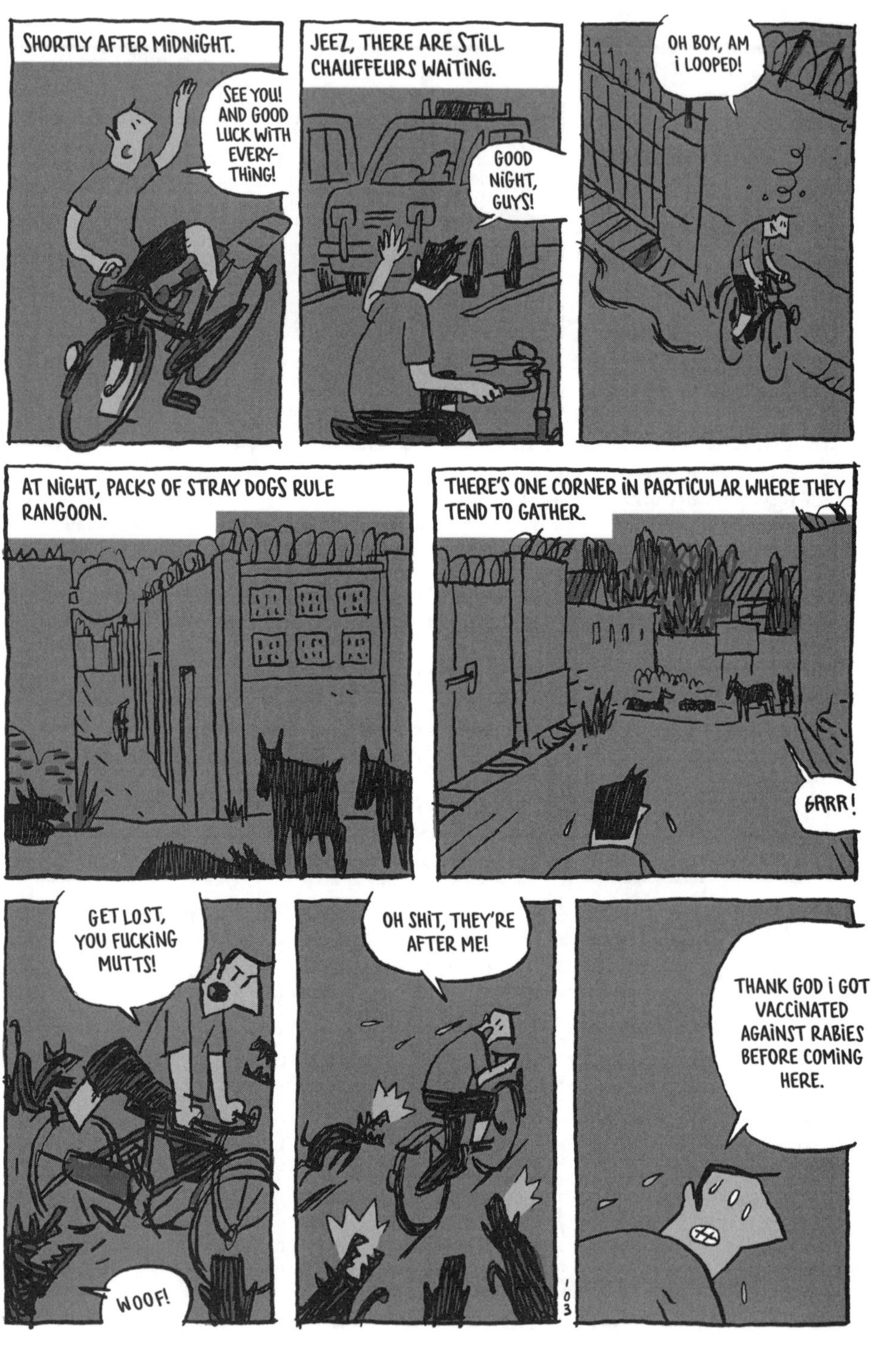

SHORTLY AFTER MIDNIGHT.
SEE YOU! AND GOOD LUCK WITH EVERY-THING!
JEEZ, THERE ARE STILL CHAUFFEURS WAITING.
GOOD NIGHT, GUYS!
OH BOY, AM I LOOPED!
AT NIGHT, PACKS OF STRAY DOGS RULE RANGOON.
THERE'S ONE CORNER IN PARTICULAR WHERE THEY TEND TO GATHER.
GRRR!
GET LOST, YOU FUCKING MUTTS!
WOOF!
OH SHIT, THEY'RE AFTER ME!
THANK GOD I GOT VACCINATED AGAINST RABIES BEFORE COMING HERE.

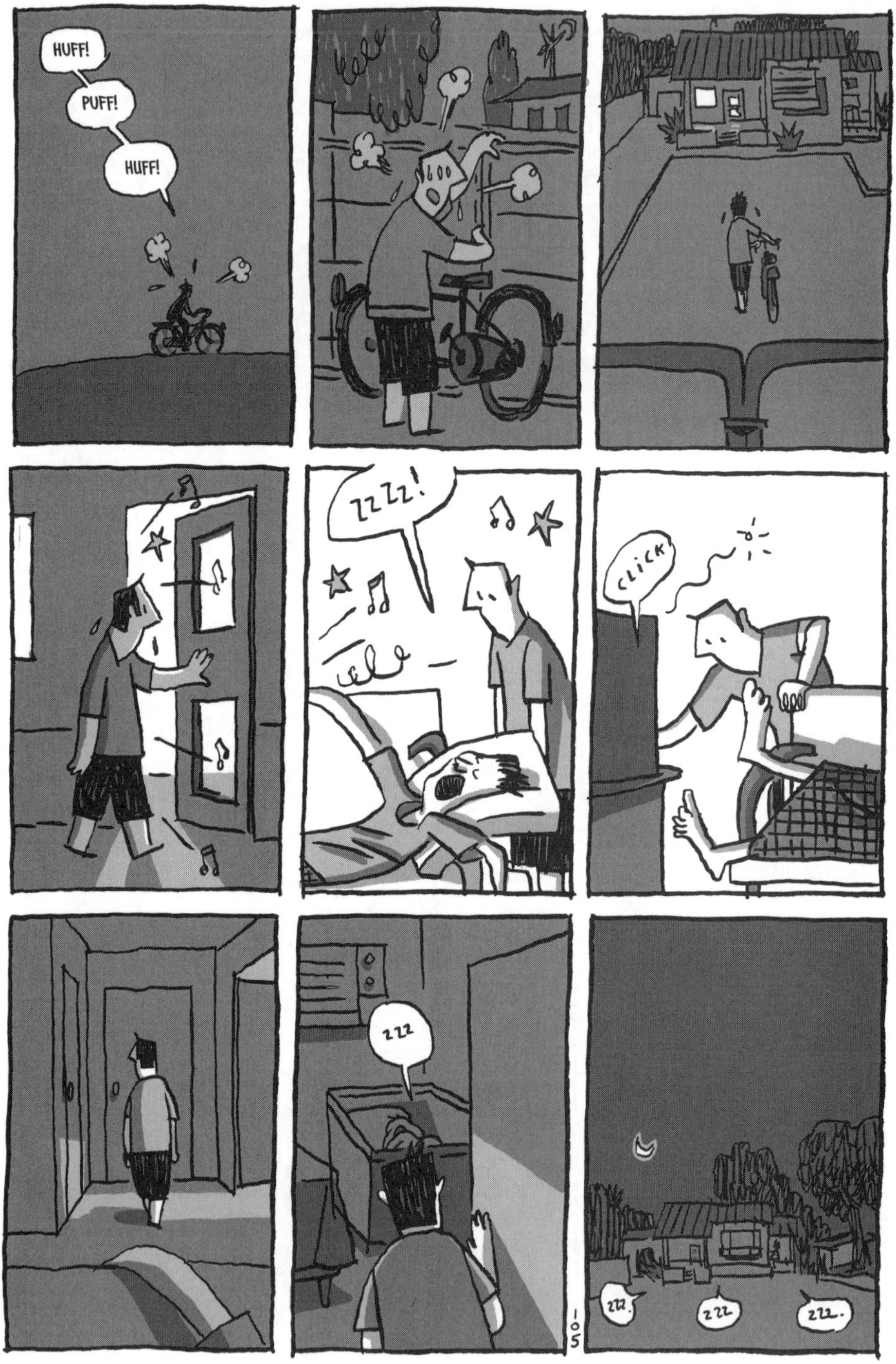
HUFF!
PUFF!
HUFF!
ZZZZ!
CLICK
ZZZ
ZZZ.
ZZZ
ZZZ.

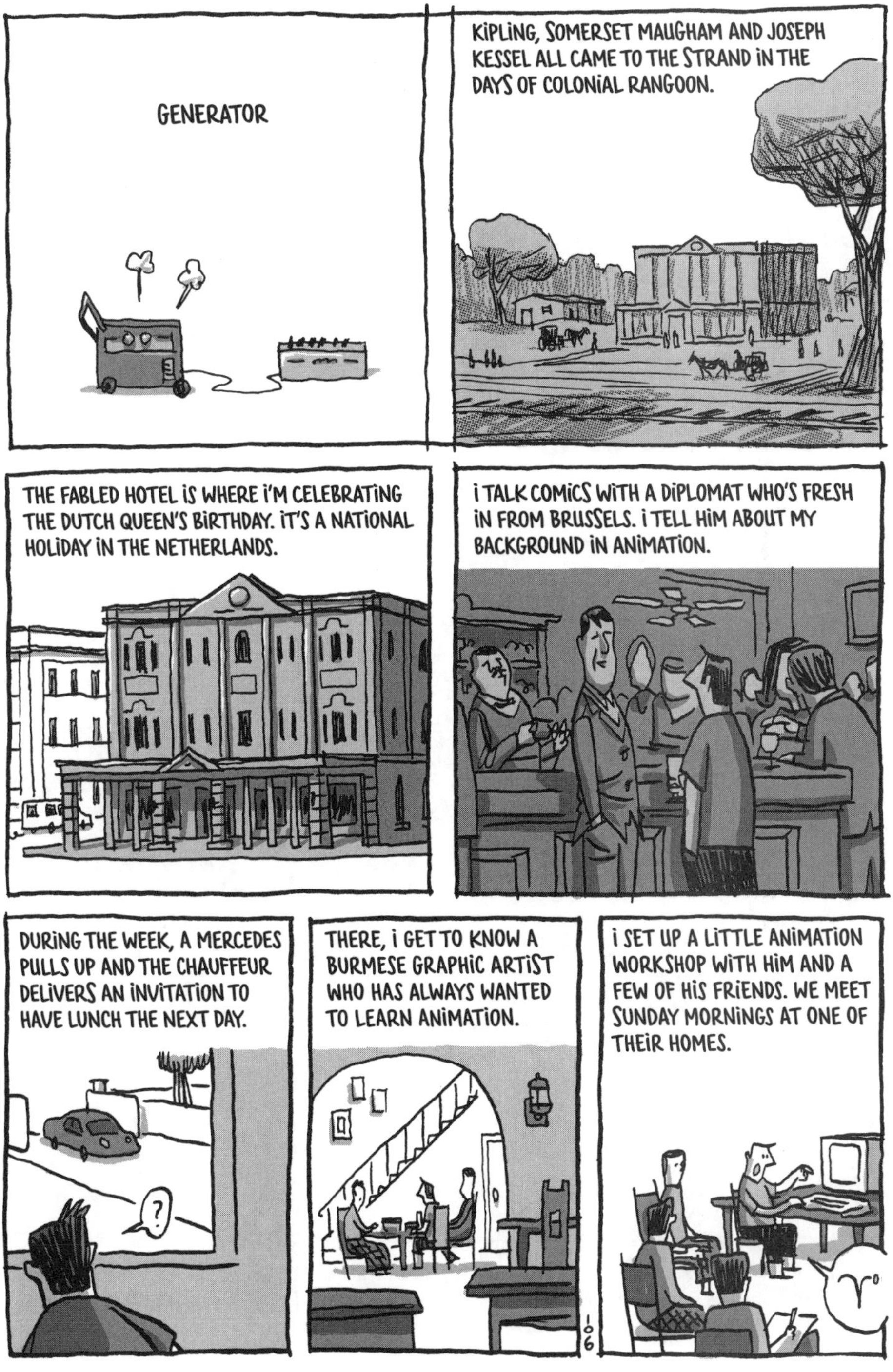
GENERATOR
KIPLING, SOMERSET MAUGHAM AND JOSEPH KESSEL ALL CAME TO THE STRAND IN THE DAYS OF COLONIAL RANGOON.
THE FABLED HOTEL IS WHERE I'M CELEBRATING THE DUTCH QUEEN'S BIRTHDAY. IT'S A NATIONAL HOLIDAY IN THE NETHERLANDS.
I TALK COMICS WITH A DIPLOMAT WHO'S FRESH IN FROM BRUSSELS. I TELL HIM ABOUT MY BACKGROUND IN ANIMATION.
DURING THE WEEK, A MERCEDES PULLS UP AND THE CHAUFFEUR DELIVERS AN INVITATION TO HAVE LUNCH THE NEXT DAY.
?
THERE, I GET TO KNOW A BURMESE GRAPHIC ARTIST WHO HAS ALWAYS WANTED TO LEARN ANIMATION.
I SET UP A LITTLE ANIMATION WORKSHOP WITH HIM AND A FEW OF HIS FRIENDS. WE MEET SUNDAY MORNINGS AT ONE OF THEIR HOMES.

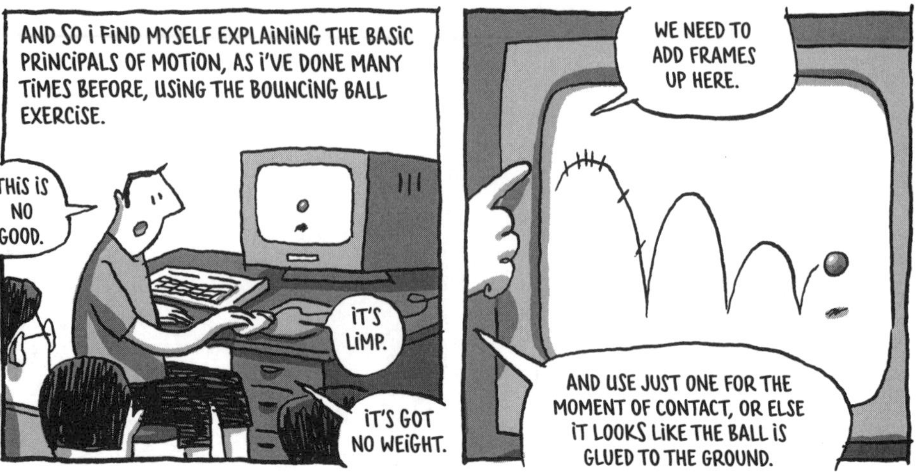
AND SO I FIND MYSELF EXPLAINING THE BASIC PRINCIPALS OF MOTION, AS I'VE DONE MANY TIMES BEFORE, USING THE BOUNCING BALL EXERCISE.
THIS IS NO GOOD.
IT'S LIMP.
IT'S GOT NO WEIGHT.
WE NEED TO ADD FRAMES UP HERE.
AND USE JUST ONE FOR THE MOMENT OF CONTACT, OR ELSE IT LOOKS LIKE THE BALL IS GLUED TO THE GROUND.

FOR TECHNICAL REASONS, WE DON'T GET VERY FAR. WE'RE IN A WORKING CLASS NEIGHBORHOOD AND THESE DAYS, THEY GET ONLY 4 HOURS OF POWER A DAY. JUST ENOUGH TO RECHARGE THE BATTERY, BUT SINCE IT'S NOT EXACTLY NEW ANYMORE, IT DOESN'T HOLD ITS CHARGE FOR LONG.

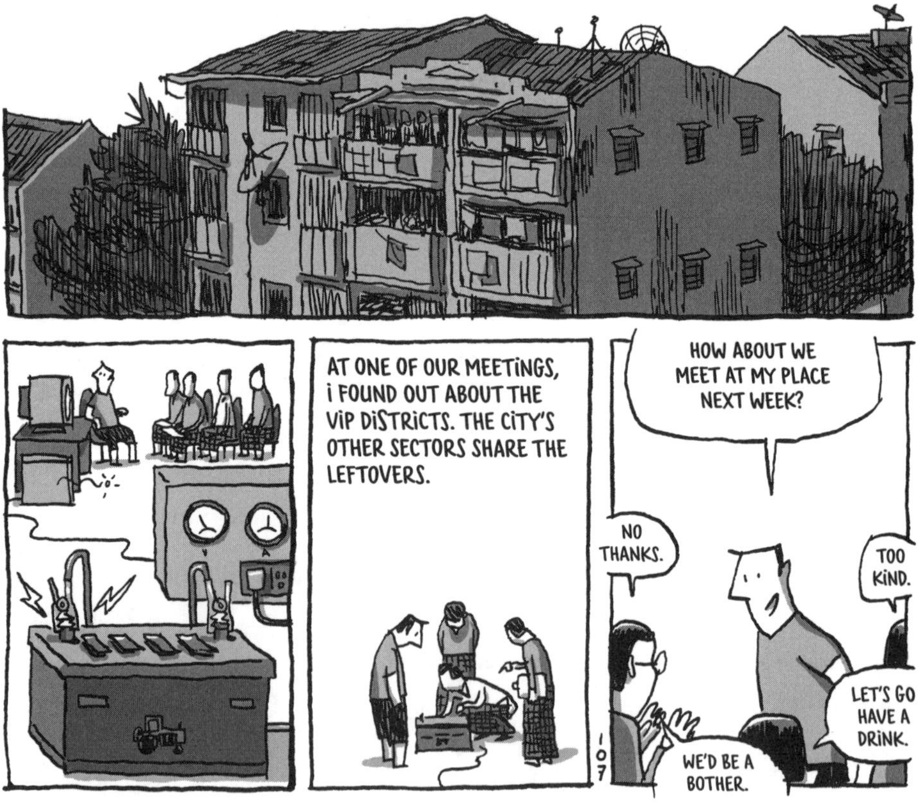
AT ONE OF OUR MEETINGS, I FOUND OUT ABOUT THE VIP DISTRICTS. THE CITY'S OTHER SECTORS SHARE THE LEFTOVERS.
HOW ABOUT WE MEET AT MY PLACE NEXT WEEK?
NO THANKS.
TOO KIND.
LET'S GO HAVE A DRINK.
WE'D BE A BOTHER.

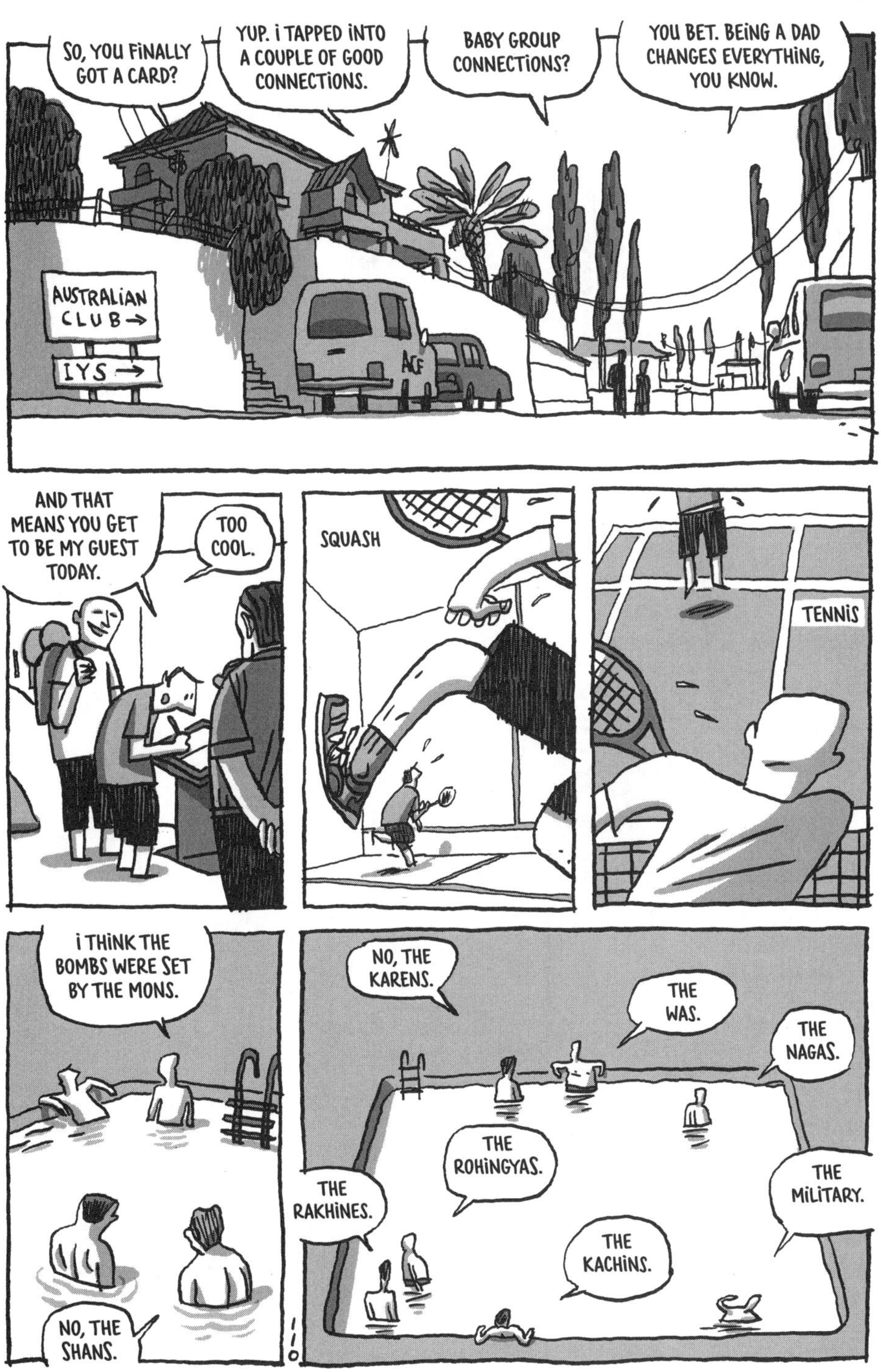
SO, YOU FINALLY GOT A CARD?
YUP. I TAPPED INTO A COUPLE OF GOOD CONNECTIONS.
BABY GROUP CONNECTIONS?
YOU BET. BEING A DAD CHANGES EVERYTHING, YOU KNOW.
AUSTRALIAN CLUB →
IYS →
AND THAT MEANS YOU GET TO BE MY GUEST TODAY.
TOO COOL.
SQUASH
TENNIS
I THINK THE BOMBS WERE SET BY THE MONS.
NO, THE SHANS.
NO, THE KARENS.
THE WAS.
THE NAGAS.
THE ROHINGYAS.
THE RAKHINES.
THE MILITARY.
THE KACHINS.

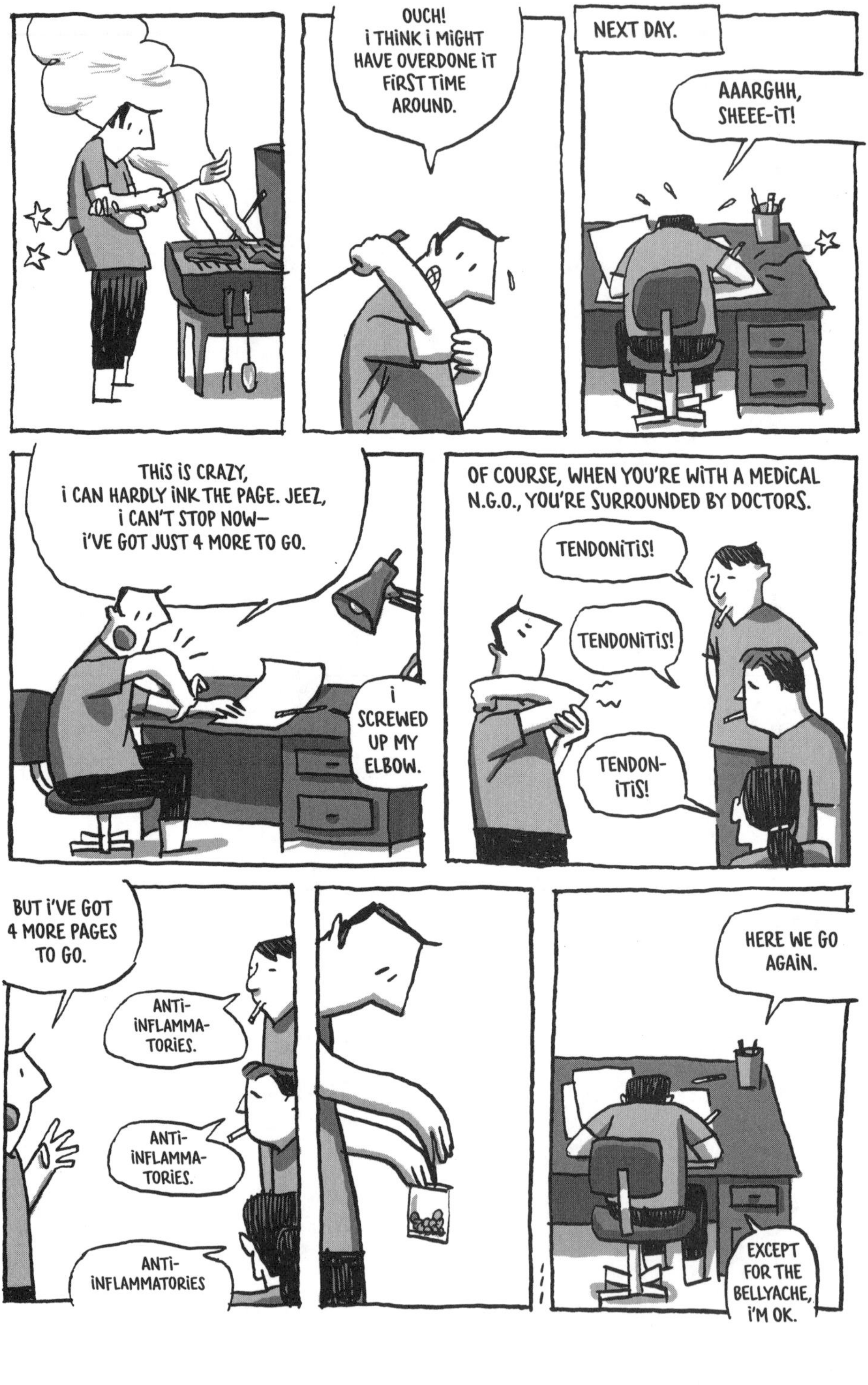

OUCH! I THINK I MIGHT HAVE OVERDONE IT FIRST TIME AROUND.
NEXT DAY.
AAARGHH, SHEEE-IT!
THIS IS CRAZY, I CAN HARDLY INK THE PAGE. JEEZ, I CAN'T STOP NOW— I'VE GOT JUST 4 MORE TO GO.
I SCREWED UP MY ELBOW.
OF COURSE, WHEN YOU'RE WITH A MEDICAL N.G.O., YOU'RE SURROUNDED BY DOCTORS.
TENDONITIS!
TENDONITIS!
TENDON-ITIS!
BUT I'VE GOT 4 MORE PAGES TO GO.
ANTI-INFLAMMA-TORIES.
ANTI-INFLAMMA-TORIES.
ANTI-INFLAMMATORIES
HERE WE GO AGAIN.
EXCEPT FOR THE BELLYACHE, I'M OK.

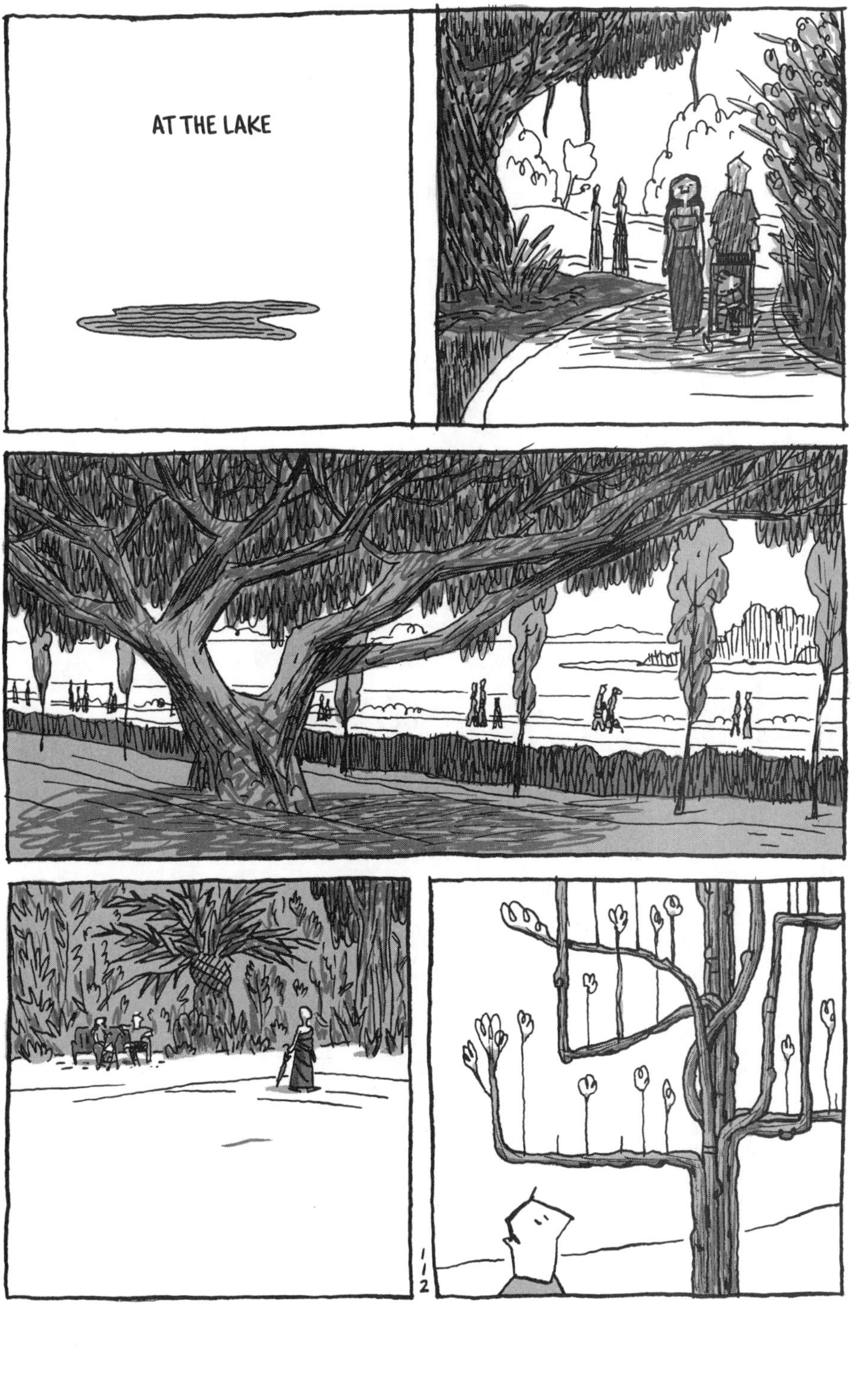
AT THE LAKE

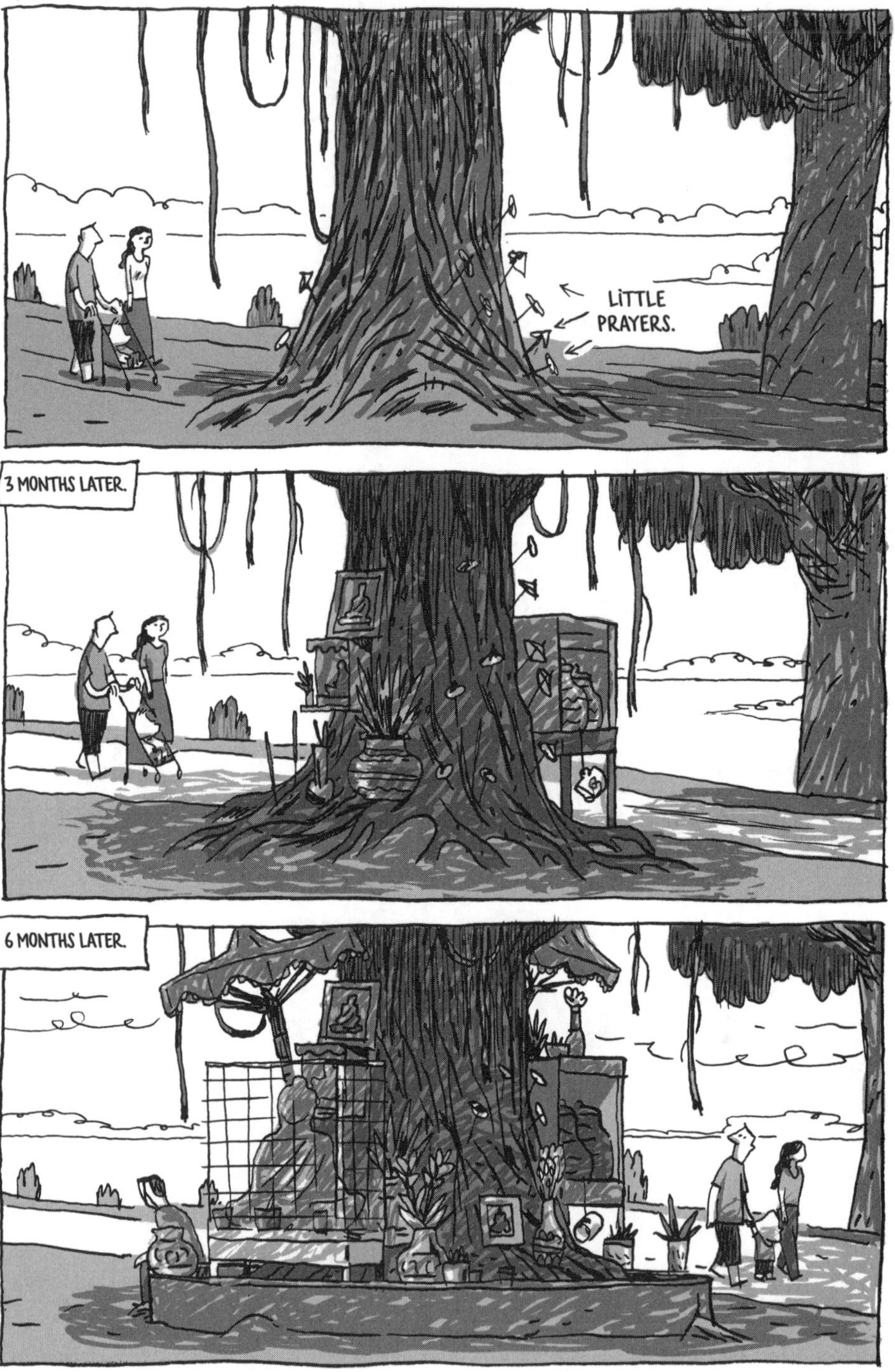
LITTLE PRAYERS.
3 MONTHS LATER.
6 MONTHS LATER.

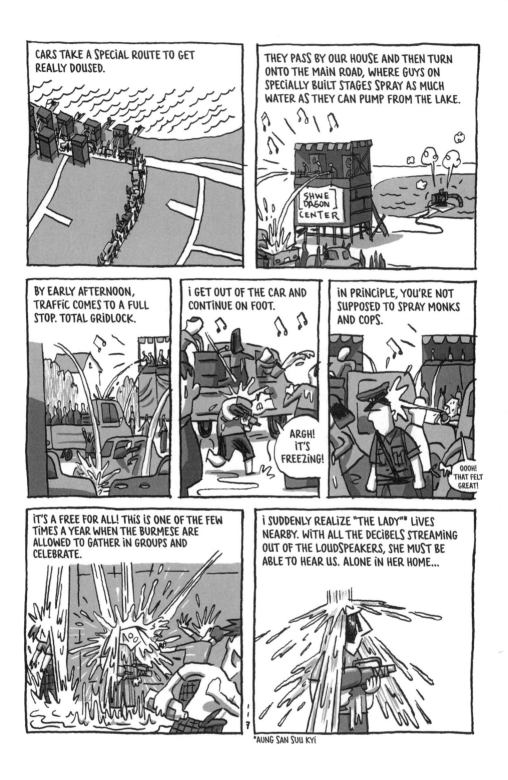

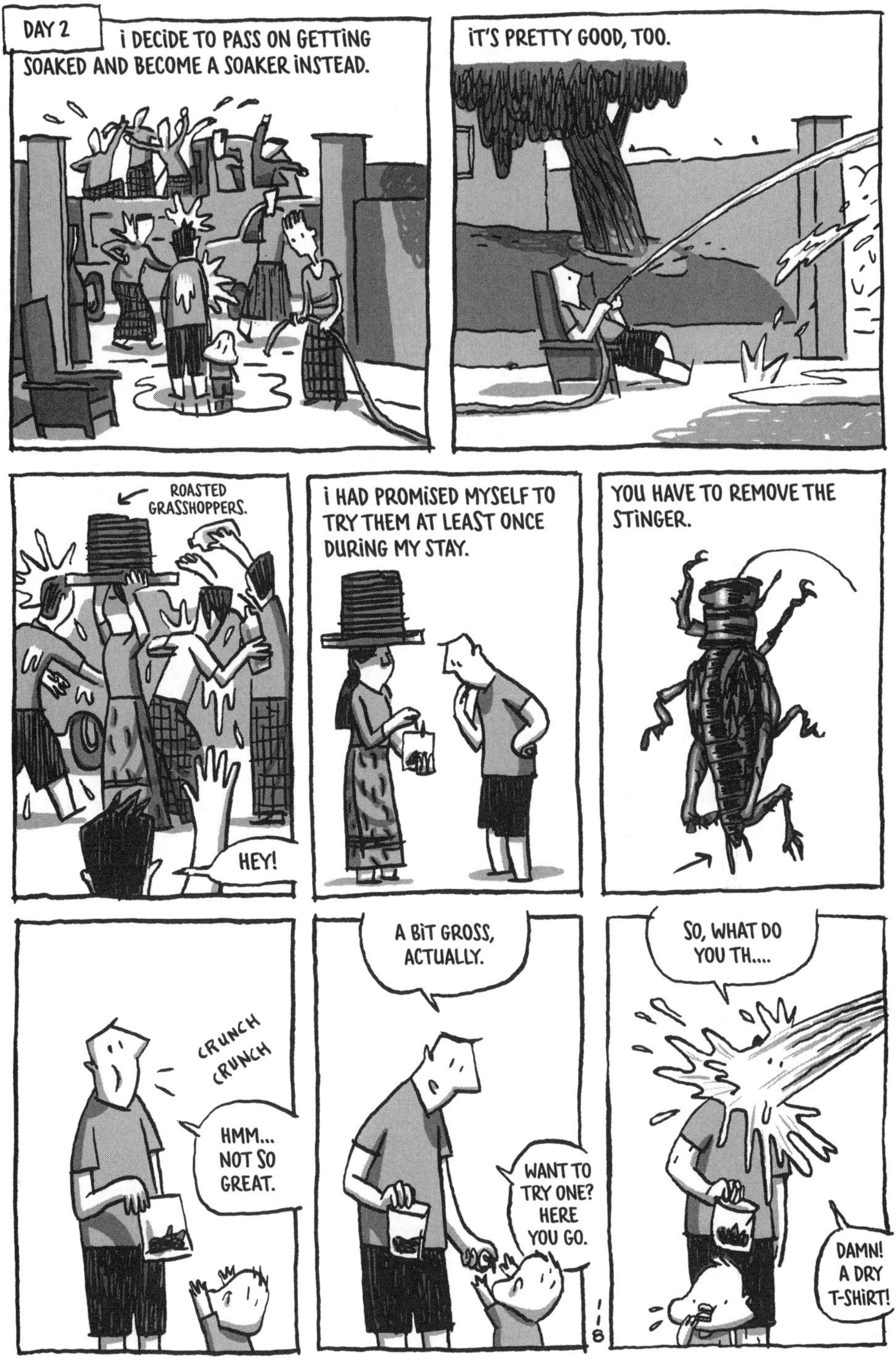
DAY 2
I DECIDE TO PASS ON GETTING SOAKED AND BECOME A SOAKER INSTEAD.
IT'S PRETTY GOOD, TOO.
ROASTED GRASSHOPPERS.
HEY!
I HAD PROMISED MYSELF TO TRY THEM AT LEAST ONCE DURING MY STAY.
YOU HAVE TO REMOVE THE STINGER.
CRUNCH CRUNCH
HMM... NOT SO GREAT.
A BIT GROSS, ACTUALLY.
WANT TO TRY ONE? HERE YOU GO.
SO, WHAT DO YOU TH....
DAMN! A DRY T-SHIRT!

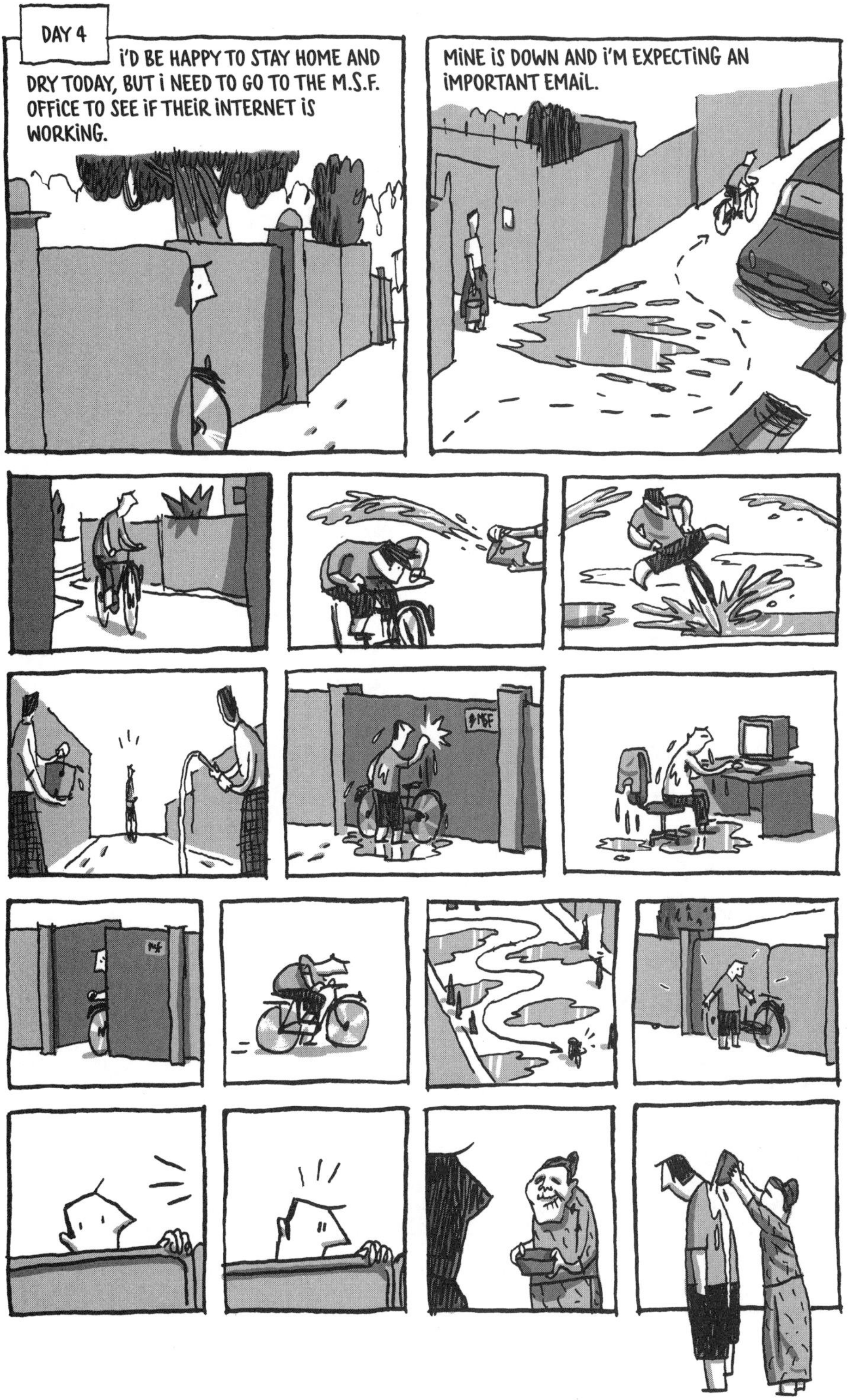
DAY 4
I'D BE HAPPY TO STAY HOME AND DRY TODAY, BUT I NEED TO GO TO THE M.S.F. OFFICE TO SEE IF THEIR INTERNET IS WORKING.
MINE IS DOWN AND I'M EXPECTING AN IMPORTANT EMAIL.
MSF

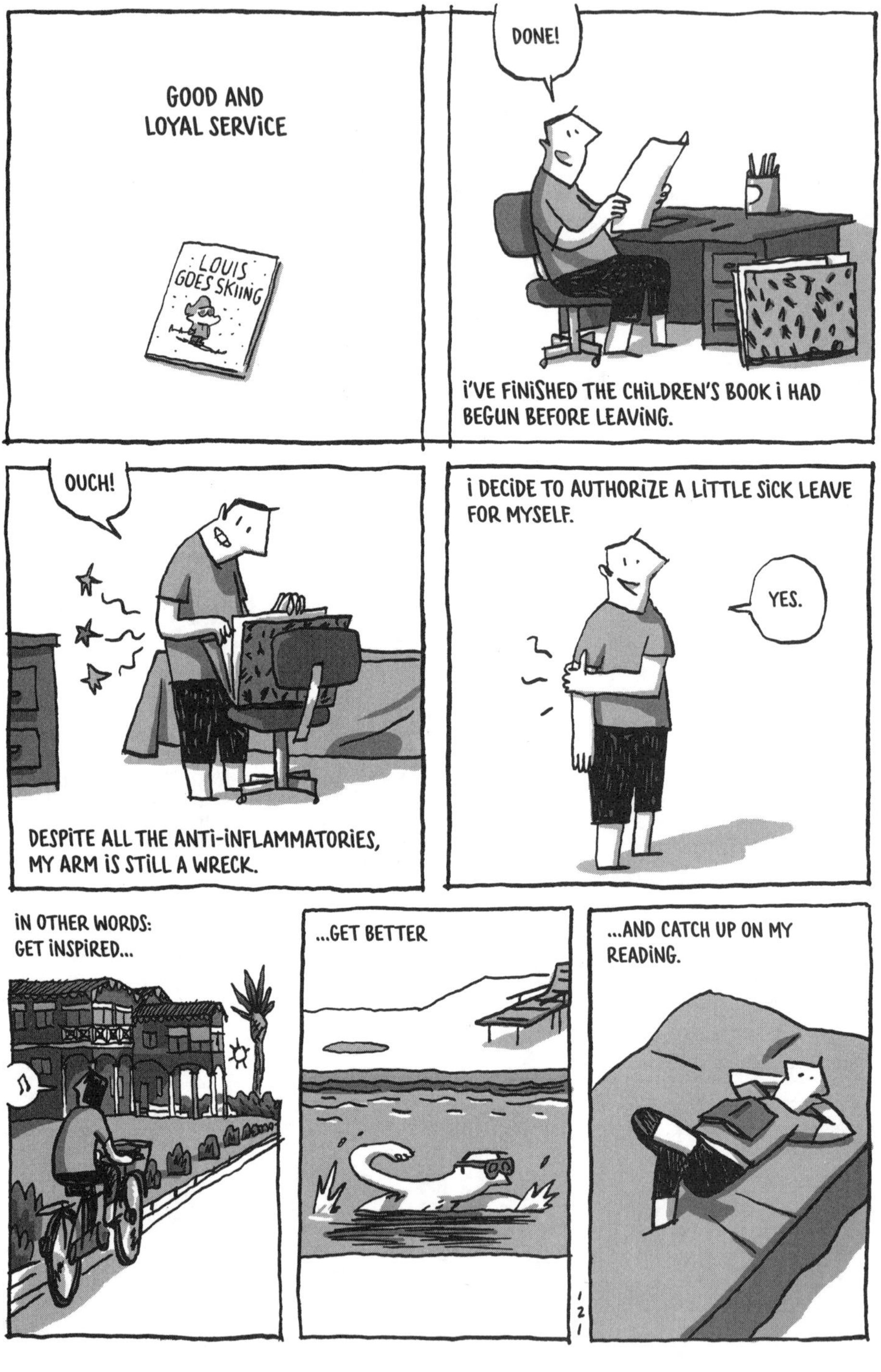
GOOD AND
LOYAL SERVICE
LOUIS
GOES SKIING
DONE!
I'VE FINISHED THE CHILDREN'S BOOK I HAD
BEGUN BEFORE LEAVING.
OUCH!
DESPITE ALL THE ANTI-INFLAMMATORIES,
MY ARM IS STILL A WRECK.
I DECIDE TO AUTHORIZE A LITTLE SICK LEAVE
FOR MYSELF.
YES.
IN OTHER WORDS:
GET INSPIRED...
...GET BETTER
...AND CATCH UP ON MY
READING.

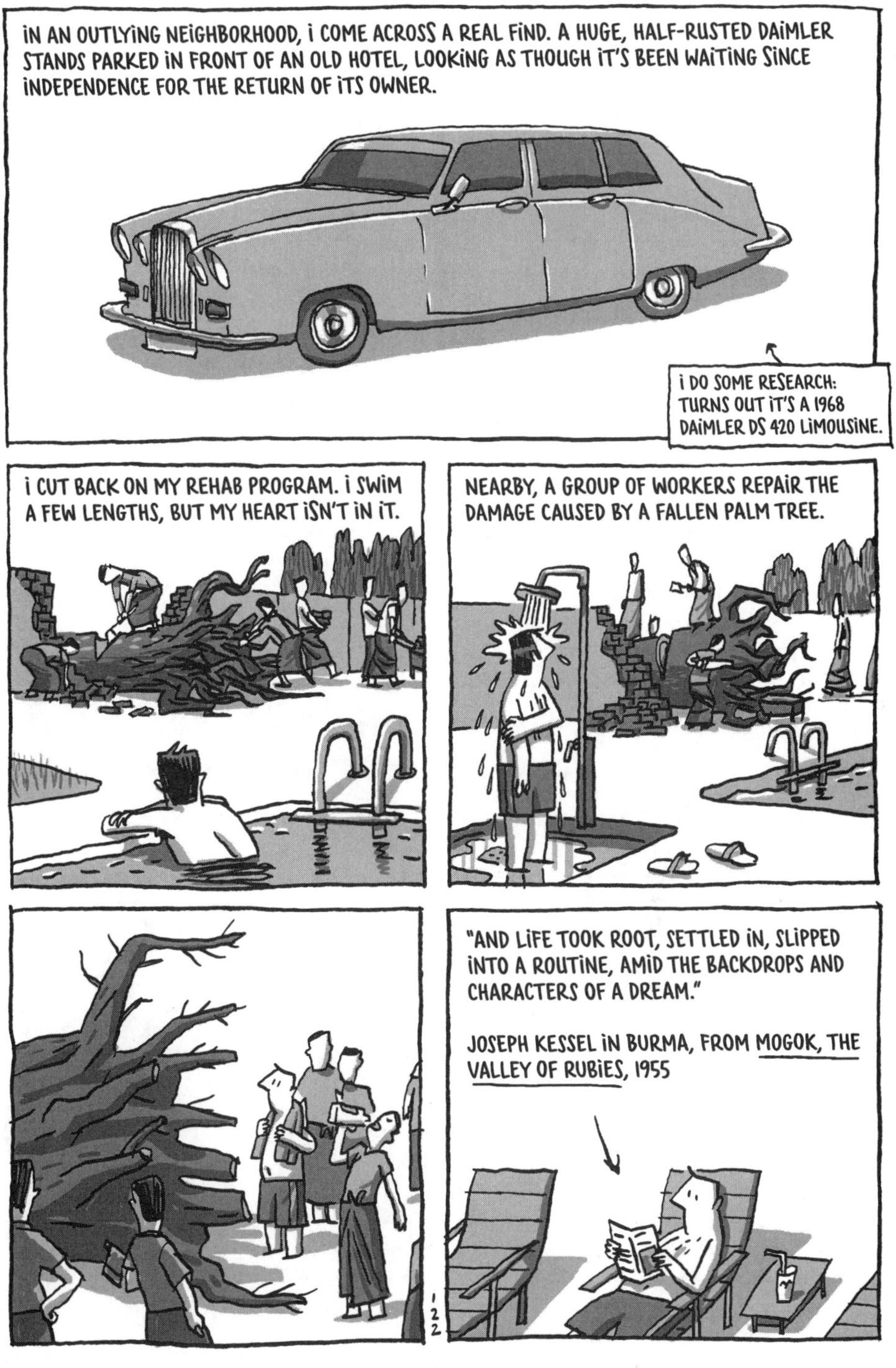
IN AN OUTLYING NEIGHBORHOOD, I COME ACROSS A REAL FIND. A HUGE, HALF-RUSTED DAIMLER STANDS PARKED IN FRONT OF AN OLD HOTEL, LOOKING AS THOUGH IT'S BEEN WAITING SINCE INDEPENDENCE FOR THE RETURN OF ITS OWNER.
I DO SOME RESEARCH: TURNS OUT IT'S A 1968 DAIMLER DS 420 LIMOUSINE.
I CUT BACK ON MY REHAB PROGRAM. I SWIM A FEW LENGTHS, BUT MY HEART ISN'T IN IT.
NEARBY, A GROUP OF WORKERS REPAIR THE DAMAGE CAUSED BY A FALLEN PALM TREE.
"AND LIFE TOOK ROOT, SETTLED IN, SLIPPED INTO A ROUTINE, AMID THE BACKDROPS AND CHARACTERS OF A DREAM."
JOSEPH KESSEL IN BURMA, FROM MOGOK, THE VALLEY OF RUBIES, 1955

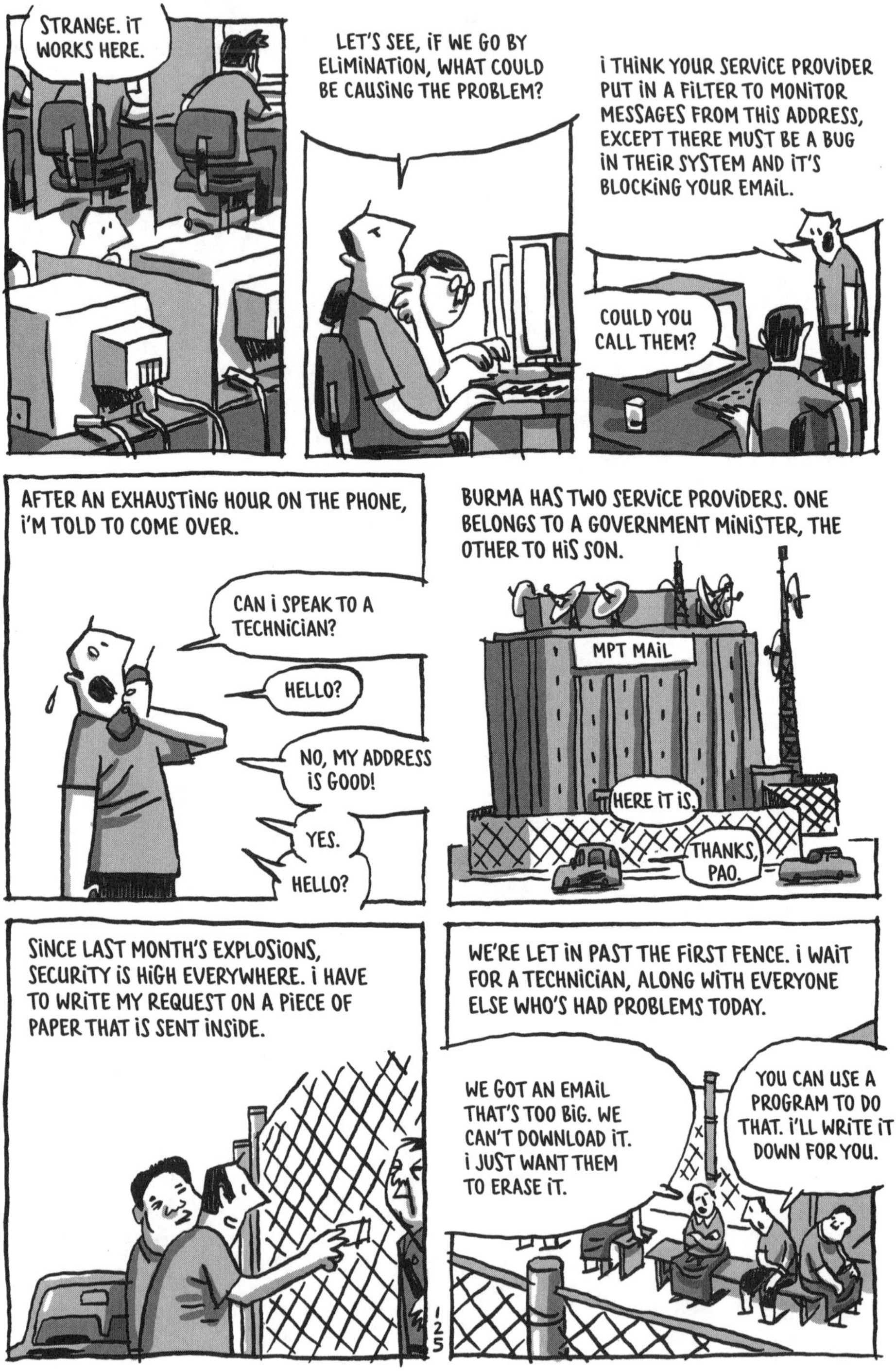
STRANGE. IT WORKS HERE.
LET'S SEE, IF WE GO BY ELIMINATION, WHAT COULD BE CAUSING THE PROBLEM?
I THINK YOUR SERVICE PROVIDER PUT IN A FILTER TO MONITOR MESSAGES FROM THIS ADDRESS, EXCEPT THERE MUST BE A BUG IN THEIR SYSTEM AND IT'S BLOCKING YOUR EMAIL.
COULD YOU CALL THEM?
AFTER AN EXHAUSTING HOUR ON THE PHONE, I'M TOLD TO COME OVER.
CAN I SPEAK TO A TECHNICIAN?
HELLO?
NO, MY ADDRESS IS GOOD!
YES.
HELLO?
BURMA HAS TWO SERVICE PROVIDERS. ONE BELONGS TO A GOVERNMENT MINISTER, THE OTHER TO HIS SON.
MPT MAIL
HERE IT IS.
THANKS, PAO.
SINCE LAST MONTH'S EXPLOSIONS, SECURITY IS HIGH EVERYWHERE. I HAVE TO WRITE MY REQUEST ON A PIECE OF PAPER THAT IS SENT INSIDE.
WE'RE LET IN PAST THE FIRST FENCE. I WAIT FOR A TECHNICIAN, ALONG WITH EVERYONE ELSE WHO'S HAD PROBLEMS TODAY.
WE GOT AN EMAIL THAT'S TOO BIG. WE CAN'T DOWNLOAD IT. I JUST WANT THEM TO ERASE IT.
YOU CAN USE A PROGRAM TO DO THAT. I'LL WRITE IT DOWN FOR YOU.

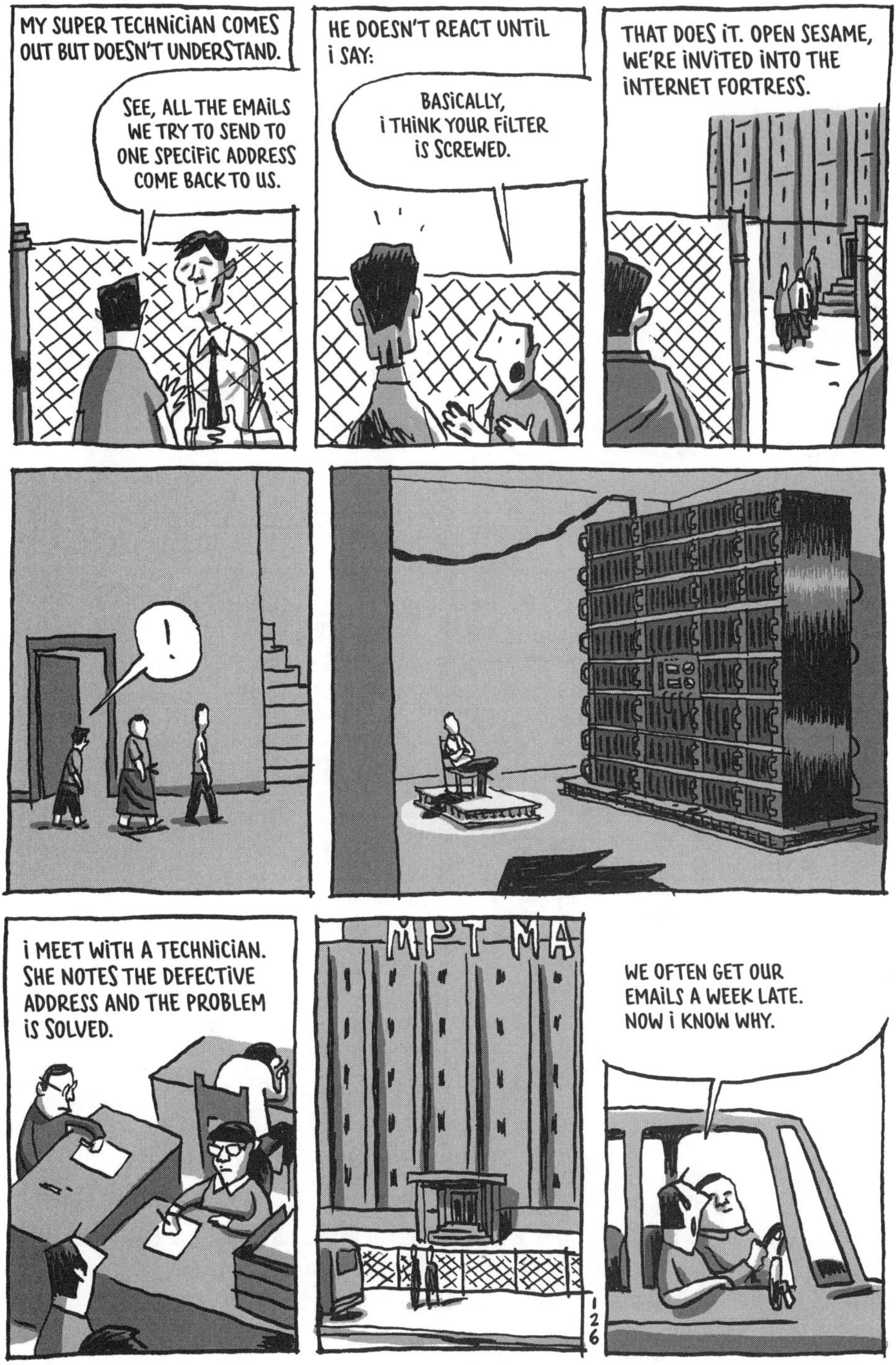
MY SUPER TECHNICIAN COMES OUT BUT DOESN'T UNDERSTAND.
SEE, ALL THE EMAILS WE TRY TO SEND TO ONE SPECIFIC ADDRESS COME BACK TO US.
HE DOESN'T REACT UNTIL I SAY:
BASICALLY, I THINK YOUR FILTER IS SCREWED.
THAT DOES IT. OPEN SESAME, WE'RE INVITED INTO THE INTERNET FORTRESS.
!
I MEET WITH A TECHNICIAN. SHE NOTES THE DEFECTIVE ADDRESS AND THE PROBLEM IS SOLVED.
MPT MA
WE OFTEN GET OUR EMAILS A WEEK LATE. NOW I KNOW WHY.

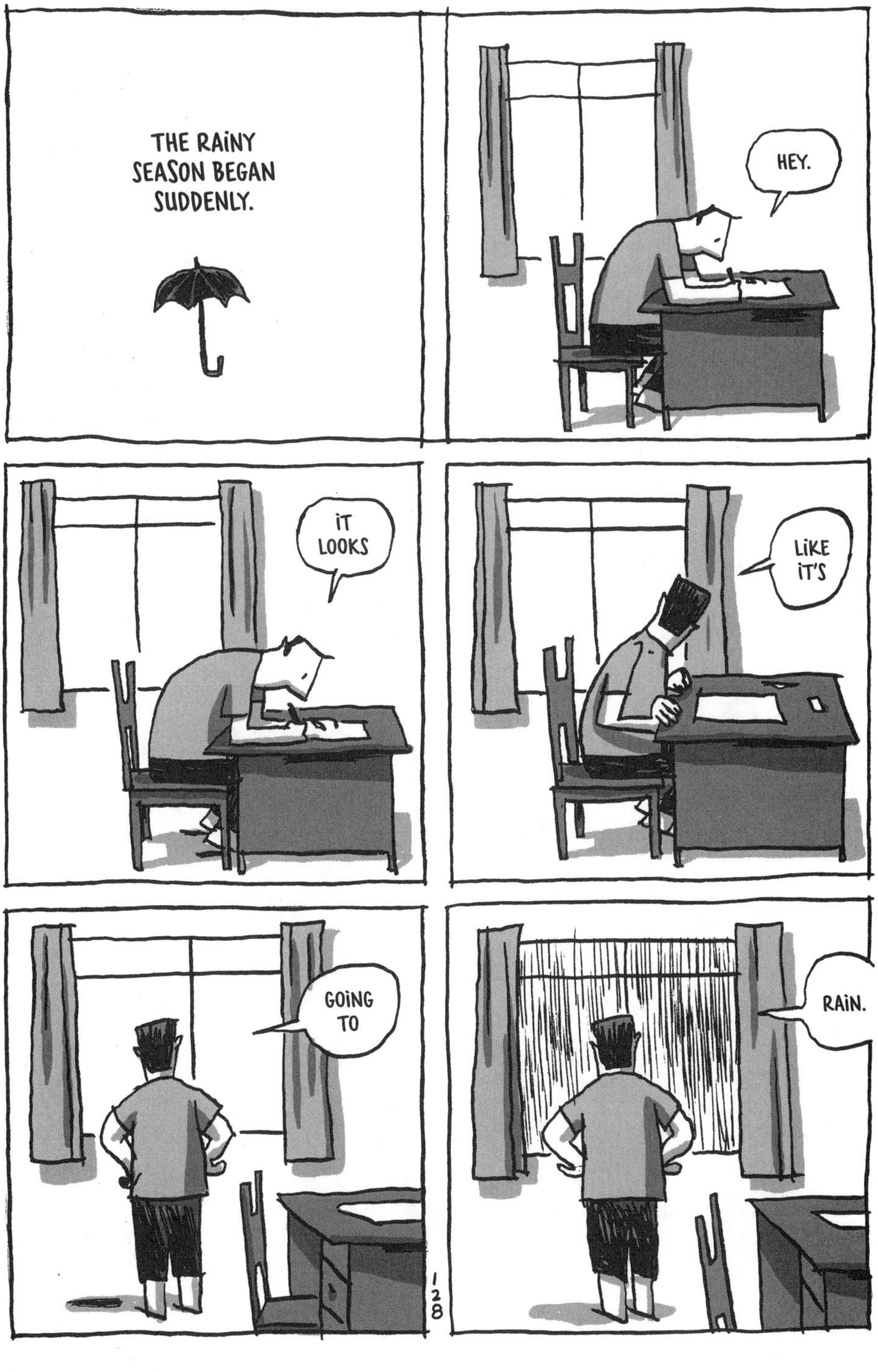
THE RAINY SEASON BEGAN SUDDENLY.
HEY.
IT LOOKS
LIKE IT'S
GOING TO
RAIN.

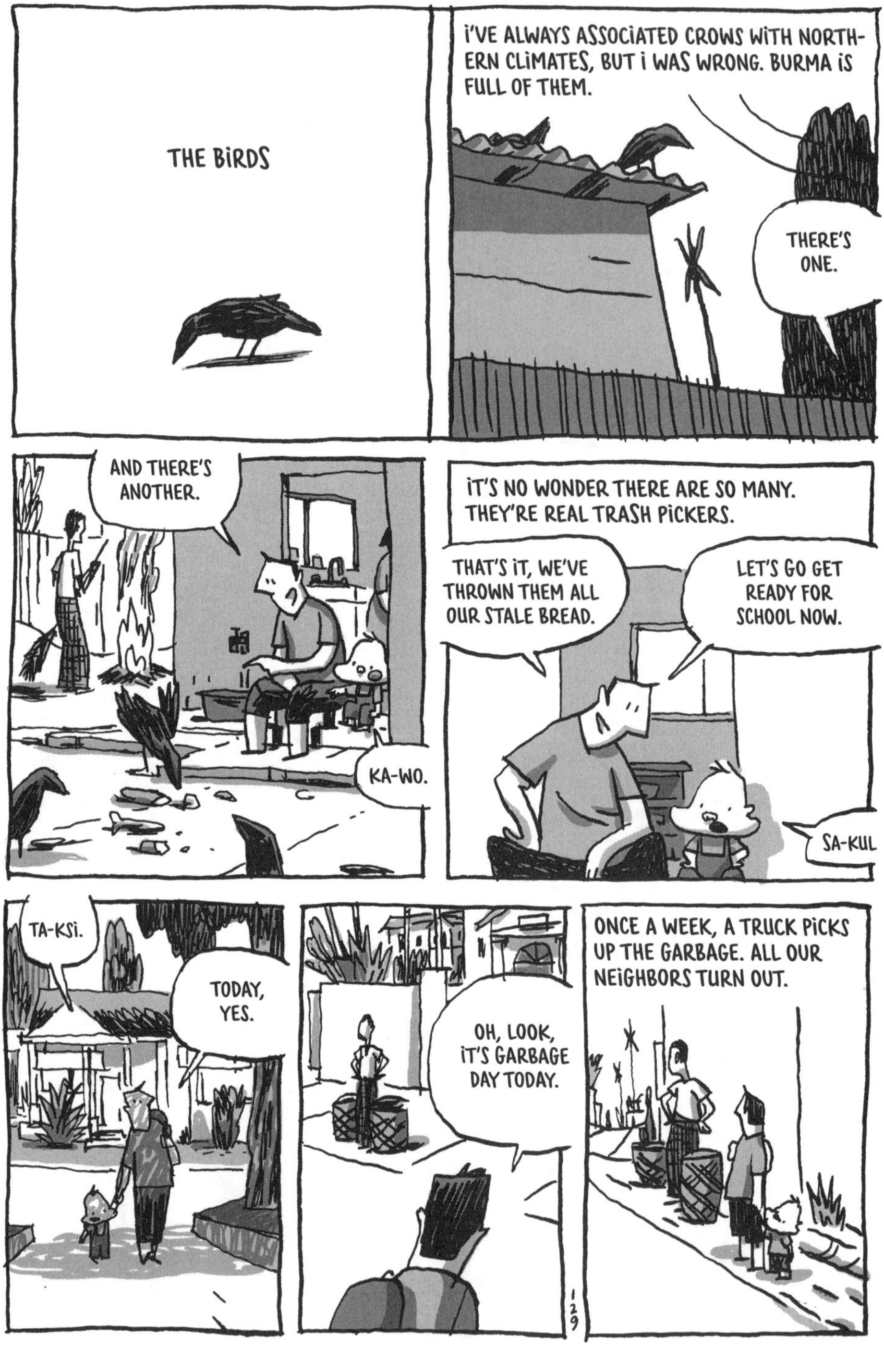
THE BIRDS
I'VE ALWAYS ASSOCIATED CROWS WITH NORTHERN CLIMATES, BUT I WAS WRONG. BURMA IS FULL OF THEM.
THERE'S ONE.
AND THERE'S ANOTHER.
KA-WO.
IT'S NO WONDER THERE ARE SO MANY. THEY'RE REAL TRASH PICKERS.
THAT'S IT, WE'VE THROWN THEM ALL OUR STALE BREAD.
LET'S GO GET READY FOR SCHOOL NOW.
SA-KUL
TA-KSI.
TODAY, YES.
OH, LOOK, IT'S GARBAGE DAY TODAY.
ONCE A WEEK, A TRUCK PICKS UP THE GARBAGE. ALL OUR NEIGHBORS TURN OUT.

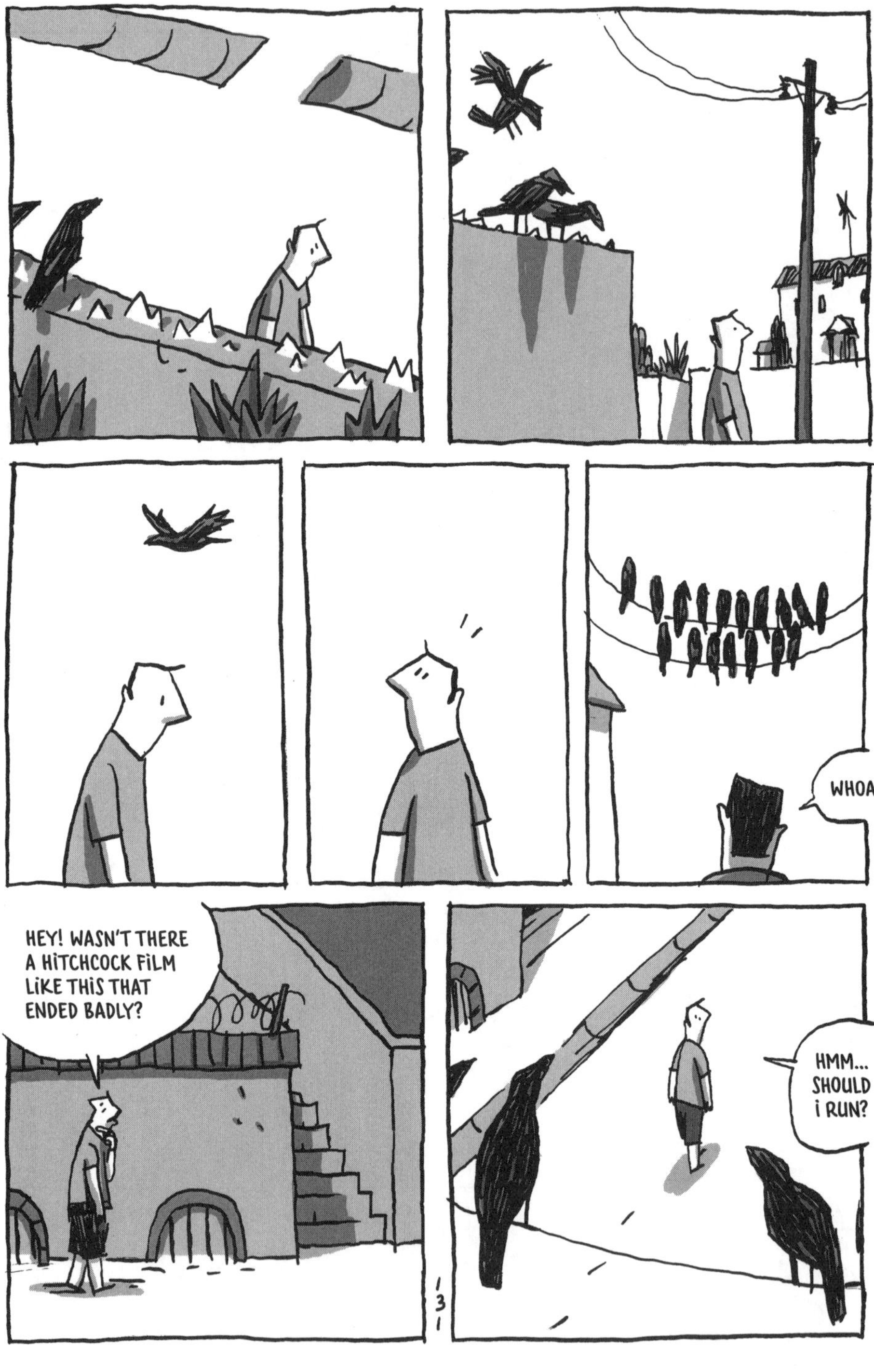
WHOA!
HEY! WASN'T THERE A HITCHCOCK FILM LIKE THIS THAT ENDED BADLY?
HMM... SHOULD I RUN?

A FEW HOURS LATER, THERE'S ANOTHER, THEN ANOTHER, AND SO ON THROUGH THE NIGHT. SOMETIMES WE HAVE TO GET OFF THE BUS.

NO WAY! I'M FED UP. LET'EM COME GET ME HERE.

AT ONE CHECKPOINT, A PASSENGER IS HELD BACK. HIS SON STAYS ON THE BUS WITH SOMEONE WHO SEEMS TO BE FAMILY. YOU CAN SEE THE WORRY ON THEIR FACES WHEN THE BUS PULLS OUT.

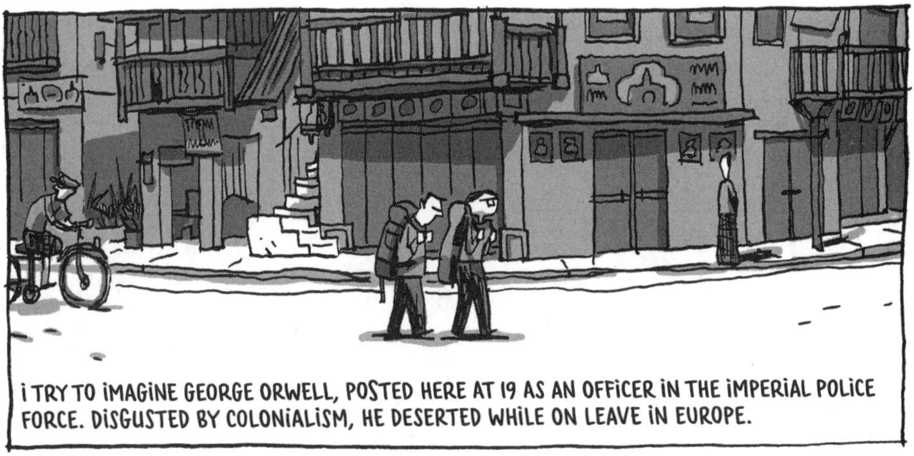
I TRY TO IMAGINE GEORGE ORWELL, POSTED HERE AT 19 AS AN OFFICER IN THE IMPERIAL POLICE FORCE. DISGUSTED BY COLONIALISM, HE DESERTED WHILE ON LEAVE IN EUROPE.

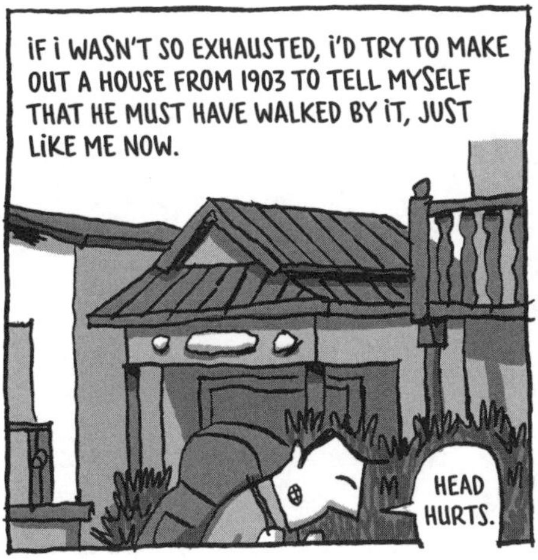
IF I WASN'T SO EXHAUSTED, I'D TRY TO MAKE OUT A HOUSE FROM 1903 TO TELL MYSELF THAT HE MUST HAVE WALKED BY IT, JUST LIKE ME NOW.
HEAD HURTS.

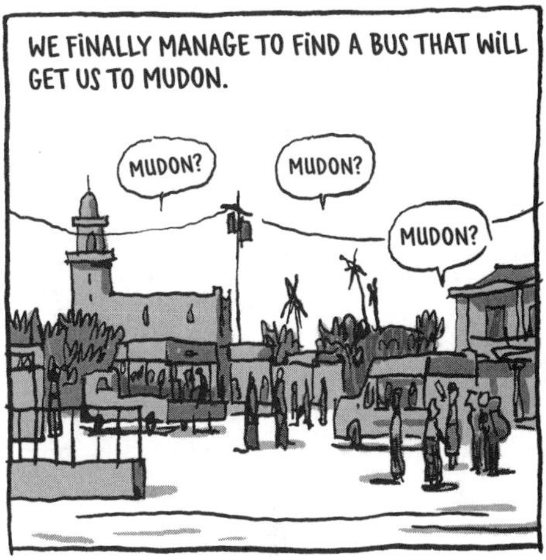
WE FINALLY MANAGE TO FIND A BUS THAT WILL GET US TO MUDON.
MUDON?
MUDON?
MUDON?

THE DRIVE IS SUPPOSED TO BE BEAUTIFUL, BUT UNFORTUNATELY I DON'T GET TO APPRECIATE IT.

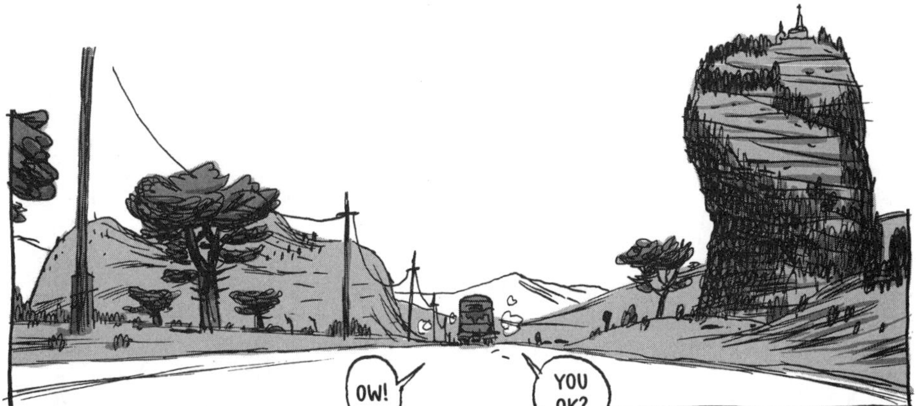
OW!
YOU OK?

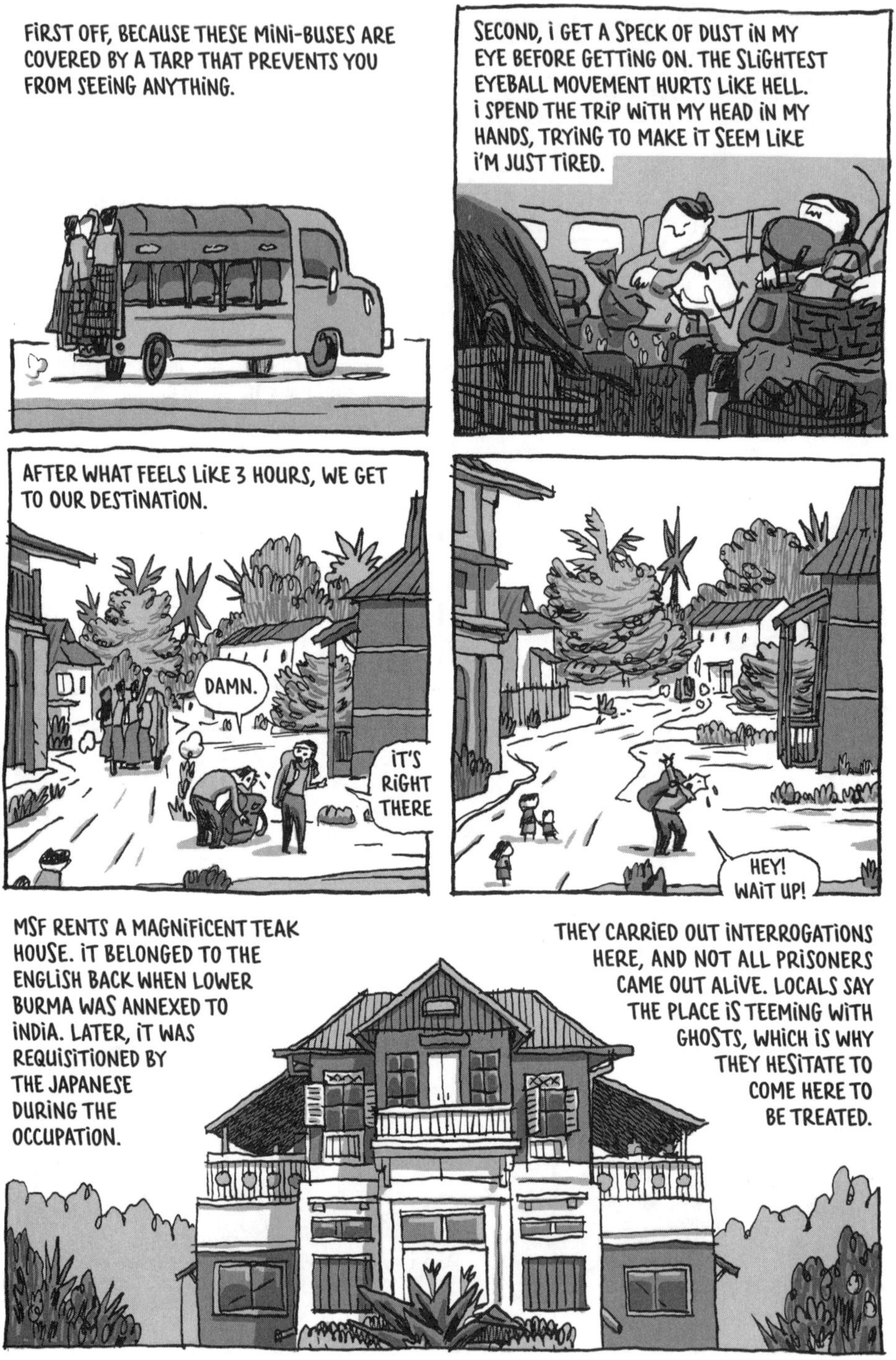
FIRST OFF, BECAUSE THESE MINI-BUSES ARE COVERED BY A TARP THAT PREVENTS YOU FROM SEEING ANYTHING.
SECOND, I GET A SPECK OF DUST IN MY EYE BEFORE GETTING ON. THE SLIGHTEST EYEBALL MOVEMENT HURTS LIKE HELL. I SPEND THE TRIP WITH MY HEAD IN MY HANDS, TRYING TO MAKE IT SEEM LIKE I'M JUST TIRED.
AFTER WHAT FEELS LIKE 3 HOURS, WE GET TO OUR DESTINATION.
DAMN.
IT'S RIGHT THERE
HEY! WAIT UP!
MSF RENTS A MAGNIFICENT TEAK HOUSE. IT BELONGED TO THE ENGLISH BACK WHEN LOWER BURMA WAS ANNEXED TO INDIA. LATER, IT WAS REQUISITIONED BY THE JAPANESE DURING THE OCCUPATION.
THEY CARRIED OUT INTERROGATIONS HERE, AND NOT ALL PRISONERS CAME OUT ALIVE. LOCALS SAY THE PLACE IS TEEMING WITH GHOSTS, WHICH IS WHY THEY HESITATE TO COME HERE TO BE TREATED.

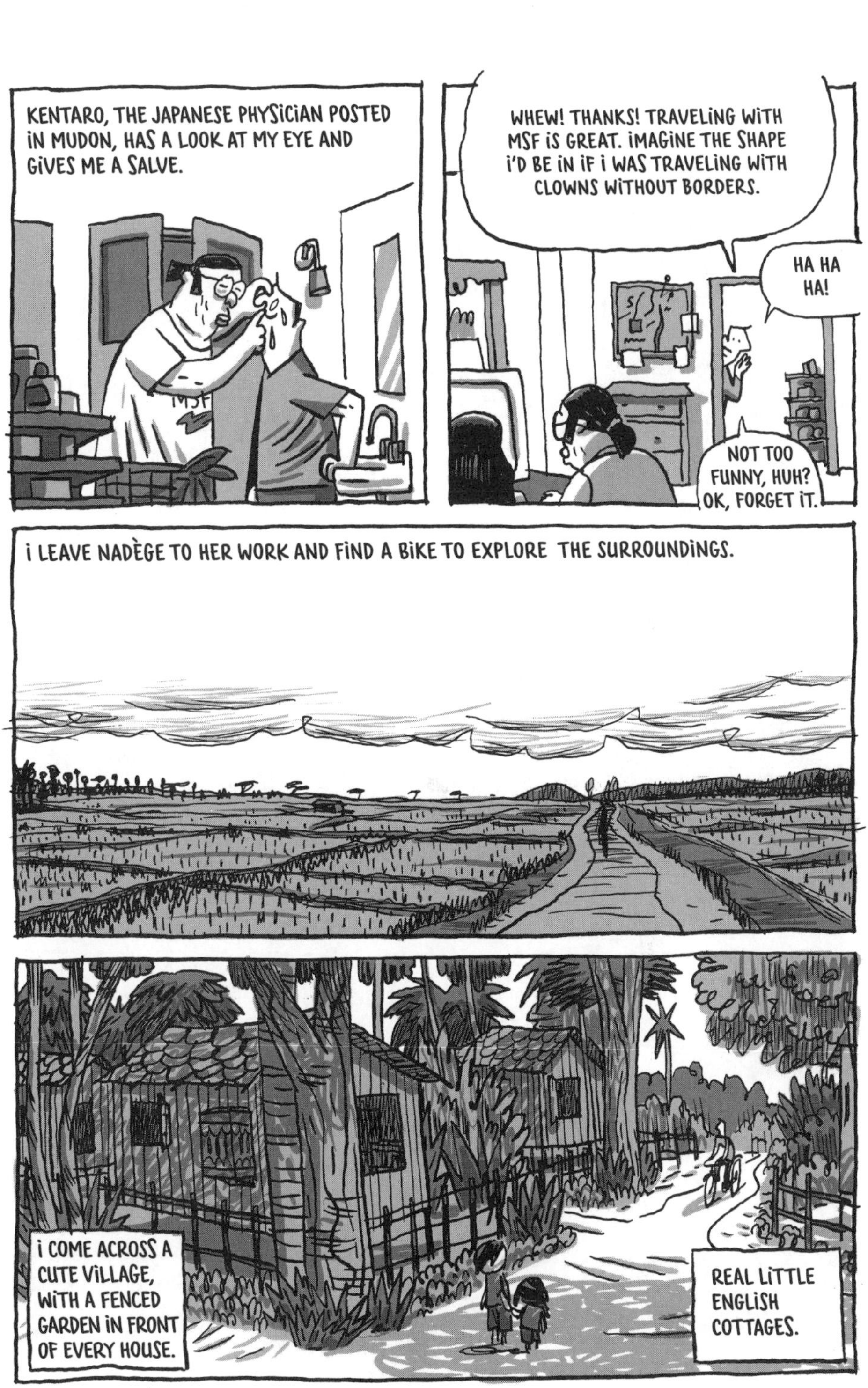
KENTARO, THE JAPANESE PHYSICIAN POSTED IN MUDON, HAS A LOOK AT MY EYE AND GIVES ME A SALVE.
MSF
WHEW! THANKS! TRAVELING WITH MSF IS GREAT. IMAGINE THE SHAPE I'D BE IN IF I WAS TRAVELING WITH CLOWNS WITHOUT BORDERS.
HA HA HA!
NOT TOO FUNNY, HUH? OK, FORGET IT.
I LEAVE NADÈGE TO HER WORK AND FIND A BIKE TO EXPLORE THE SURROUNDINGS.
I COME ACROSS A CUTE VILLAGE, WITH A FENCED GARDEN IN FRONT OF EVERY HOUSE.
REAL LITTLE ENGLISH COTTAGES.

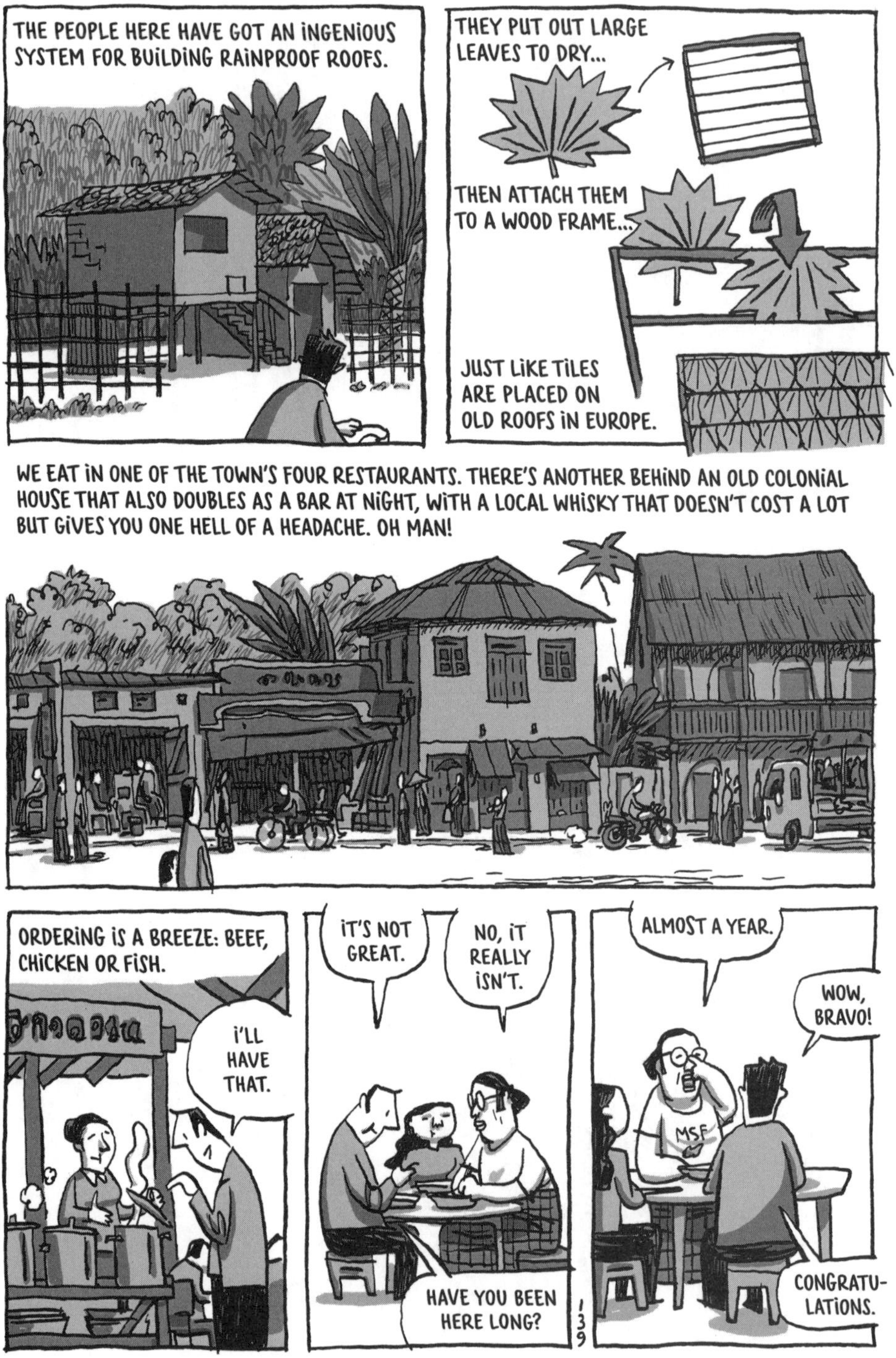
THE PEOPLE HERE HAVE GOT AN INGENIOUS SYSTEM FOR BUILDING RAINPROOF ROOFS.
THEY PUT OUT LARGE LEAVES TO DRY...
THEN ATTACH THEM TO A WOOD FRAME...
JUST LIKE TILES ARE PLACED ON OLD ROOFS IN EUROPE.
WE EAT IN ONE OF THE TOWN'S FOUR RESTAURANTS. THERE'S ANOTHER BEHIND AN OLD COLONIAL HOUSE THAT ALSO DOUBLES AS A BAR AT NIGHT, WITH A LOCAL WHISKY THAT DOESN'T COST A LOT BUT GIVES YOU ONE HELL OF A HEADACHE. OH MAN!
ORDERING IS A BREEZE: BEEF, CHICKEN OR FISH.
I'LL HAVE THAT.
IT'S NOT GREAT.
NO, IT REALLY ISN'T.
HAVE YOU BEEN HERE LONG?
ALMOST A YEAR.
WOW, BRAVO!
CONGRATULATIONS.
MSF

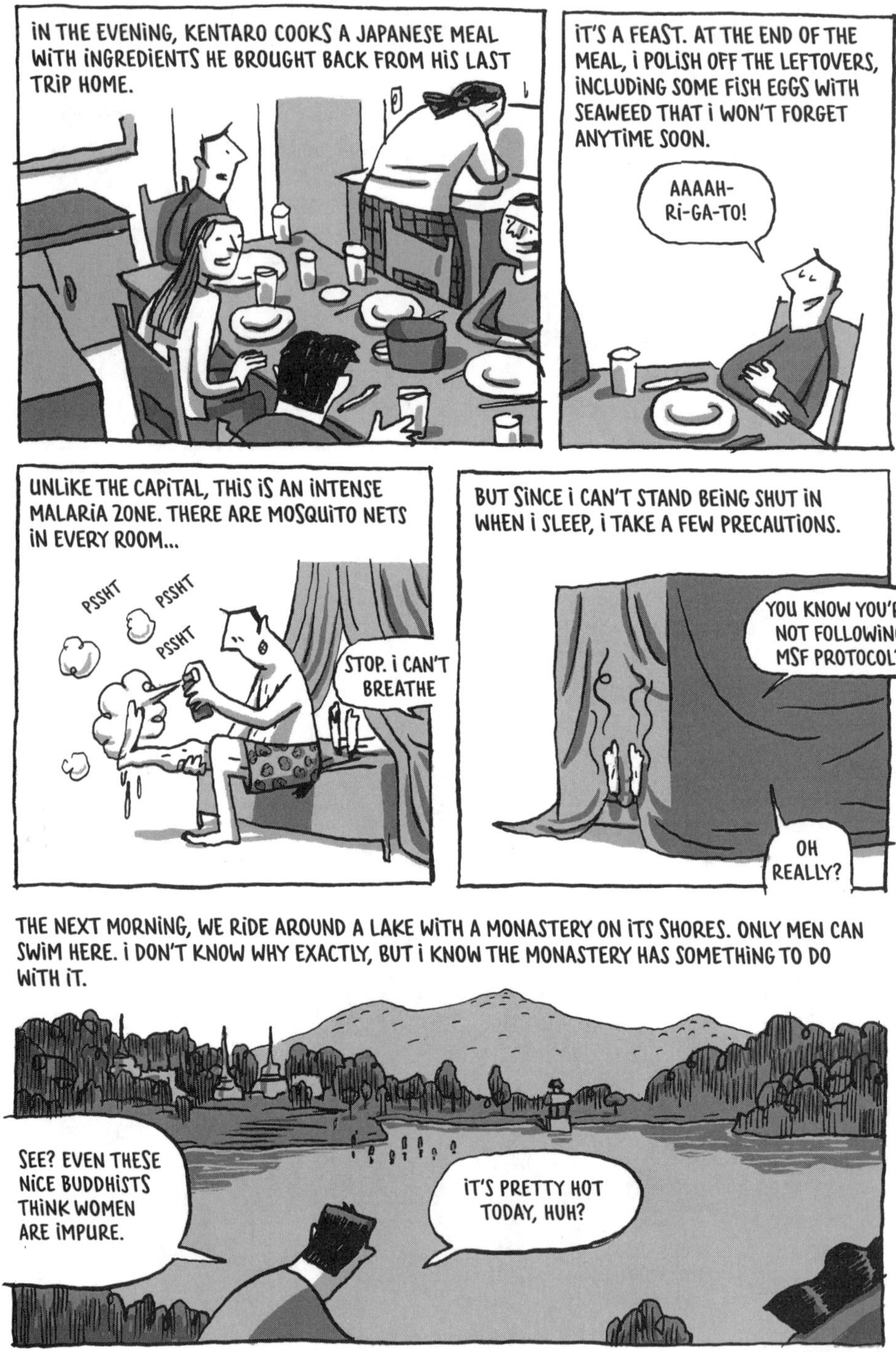
IN THE EVENING, KENTARO COOKS A JAPANESE MEAL WITH INGREDIENTS HE BROUGHT BACK FROM HIS LAST TRIP HOME.
IT'S A FEAST. AT THE END OF THE MEAL, I POLISH OFF THE LEFTOVERS, INCLUDING SOME FISH EGGS WITH SEAWEED THAT I WON'T FORGET ANYTIME SOON.
AAAAH-RI-GA-TO!
UNLIKE THE CAPITAL, THIS IS AN INTENSE MALARIA ZONE. THERE ARE MOSQUITO NETS IN EVERY ROOM...
PSSHT
PSSHT
PSSHT
STOP. I CAN'T BREATHE
BUT SINCE I CAN'T STAND BEING SHUT IN WHEN I SLEEP, I TAKE A FEW PRECAUTIONS.
YOU KNOW YOU'RE NOT FOLLOWING MSF PROTOCOL?
OH REALLY?
THE NEXT MORNING, WE RIDE AROUND A LAKE WITH A MONASTERY ON ITS SHORES. ONLY MEN CAN SWIM HERE. I DON'T KNOW WHY EXACTLY, BUT I KNOW THE MONASTERY HAS SOMETHING TO DO WITH IT.
SEE? EVEN THESE NICE BUDDHISTS THINK WOMEN ARE IMPURE.
IT'S PRETTY HOT TODAY, HUH?

IN ONE OF THE SMALL FOOD SHACKS JUTTING OVER THE LAKE, WE'RE SERVED THE BEST "MOTEE" (TRADITIONAL BREAKFAST) I'VE HAD. THE PLACE IS EMPTY, THERE'S NOT A TOURIST IN SIGHT. I FIGURE THAT MUST BE THE ONE UPSIDE OF LIVING IN A MILITARY ZONE.

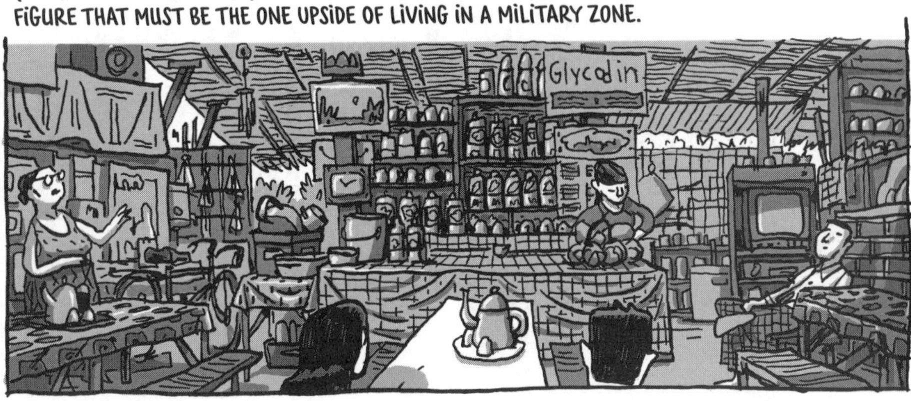
Glycodin

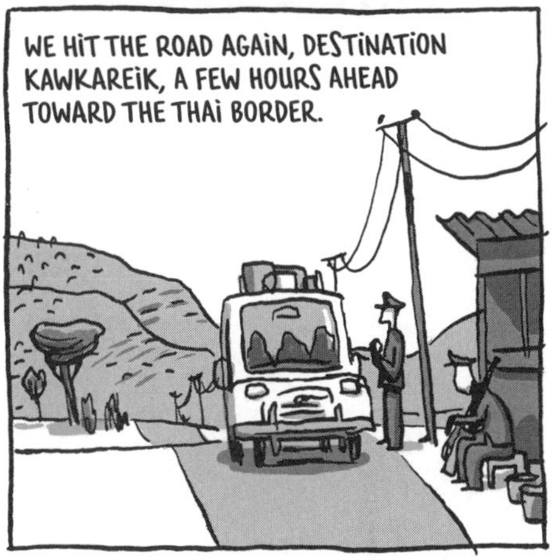
WE HIT THE ROAD AGAIN, DESTINATION KAWKAREIK, A FEW HOURS AHEAD TOWARD THE THAI BORDER.

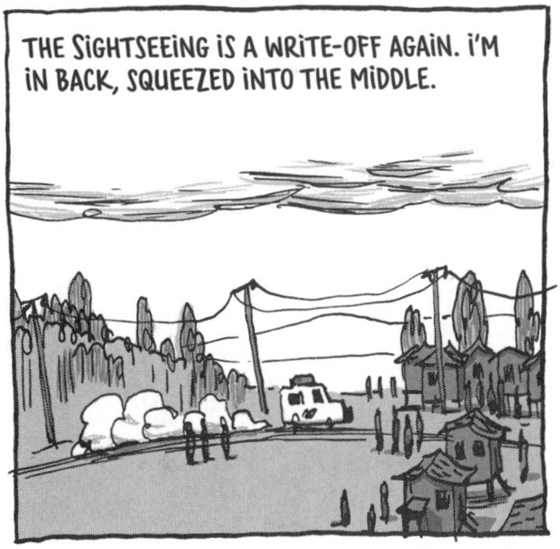
THE SIGHTSEEING IS A WRITE-OFF AGAIN. I'M IN BACK, SQUEEZED INTO THE MIDDLE.

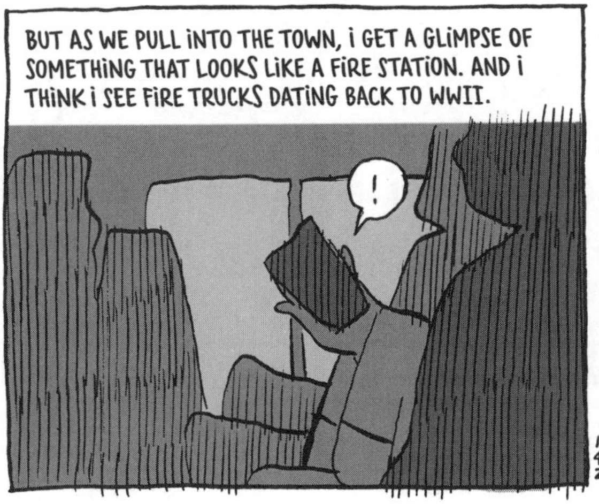
BUT AS WE PULL INTO THE TOWN, I GET A GLIMPSE OF SOMETHING THAT LOOKS LIKE A FIRE STATION. AND I THINK I SEE FIRE TRUCKS DATING BACK TO WWII.
!

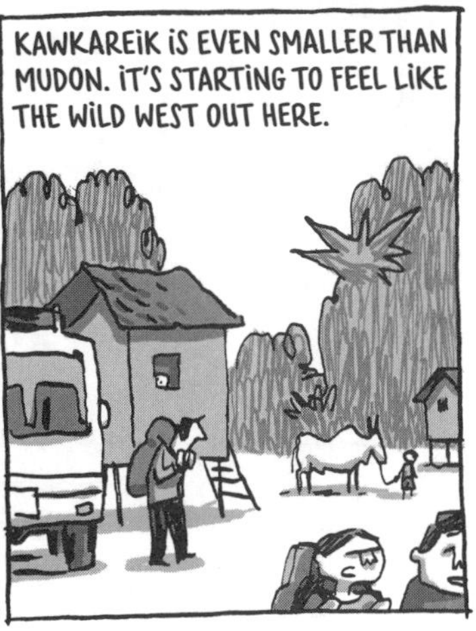
KAWKAREIK IS EVEN SMALLER THAN MUDON. IT'S STARTING TO FEEL LIKE THE WILD WEST OUT HERE.

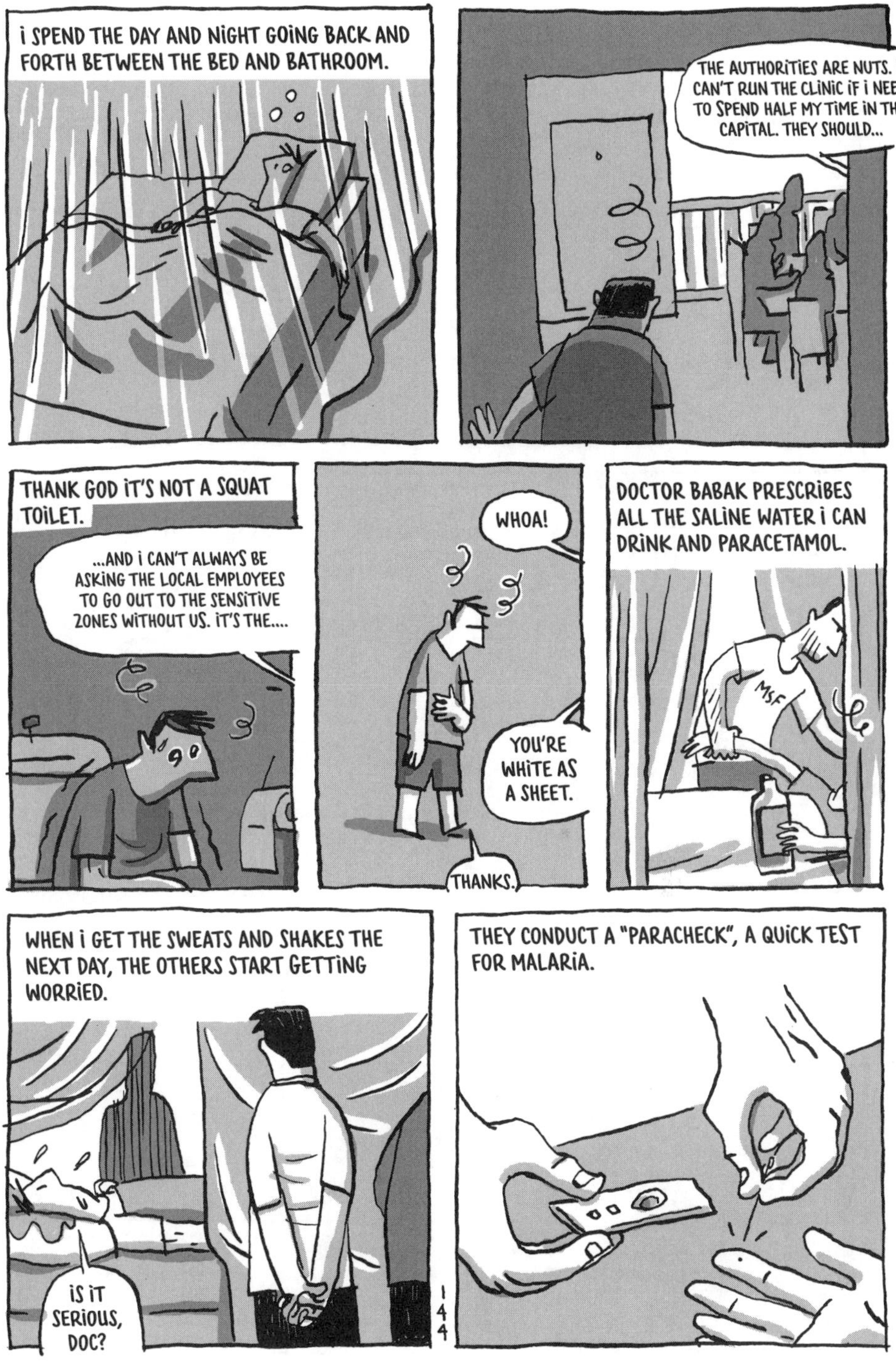

I SPEND THE DAY AND NIGHT GOING BACK AND FORTH BETWEEN THE BED AND BATHROOM.
THE AUTHORITIES ARE NUTS. I CAN'T RUN THE CLINIC IF I NEED TO SPEND HALF MY TIME IN THE CAPITAL. THEY SHOULD...
THANK GOD IT'S NOT A SQUAT TOILET.
...AND I CAN'T ALWAYS BE ASKING THE LOCAL EMPLOYEES TO GO OUT TO THE SENSITIVE ZONES WITHOUT US. IT'S THE....
WHOA!
YOU'RE WHITE AS A SHEET.
THANKS.
DOCTOR BABAK PRESCRIBES ALL THE SALINE WATER I CAN DRINK AND PARACETAMOL.
MSF
WHEN I GET THE SWEATS AND SHAKES THE NEXT DAY, THE OTHERS START GETTING WORRIED.
IS IT SERIOUS, DOC?
THEY CONDUCT A "PARACHECK", A QUICK TEST FOR MALARIA.

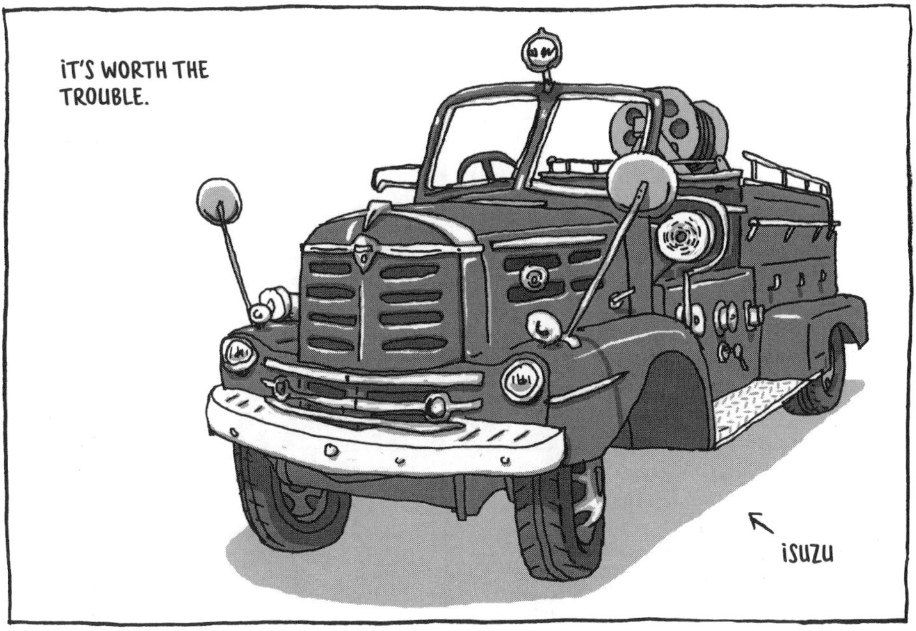
IT'S WORTH THE TROUBLE.
ISUZU

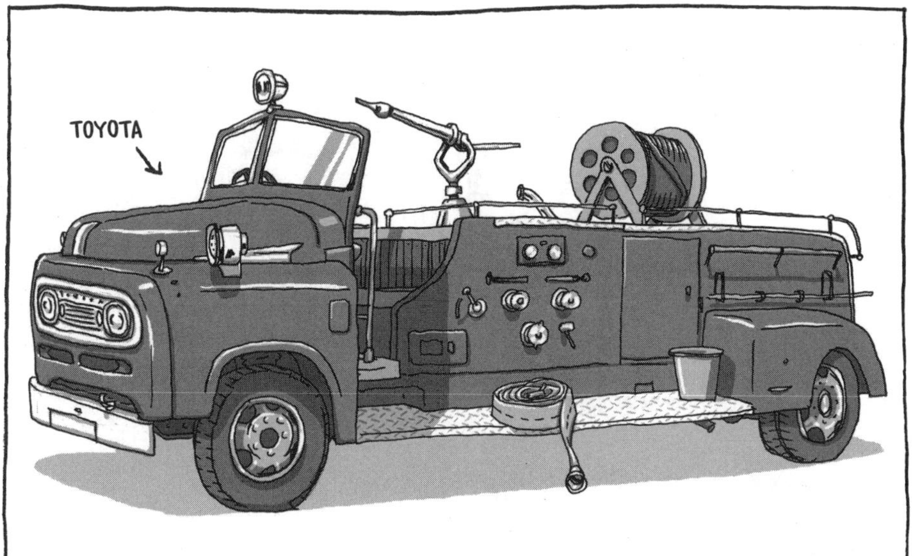
TOYOTA

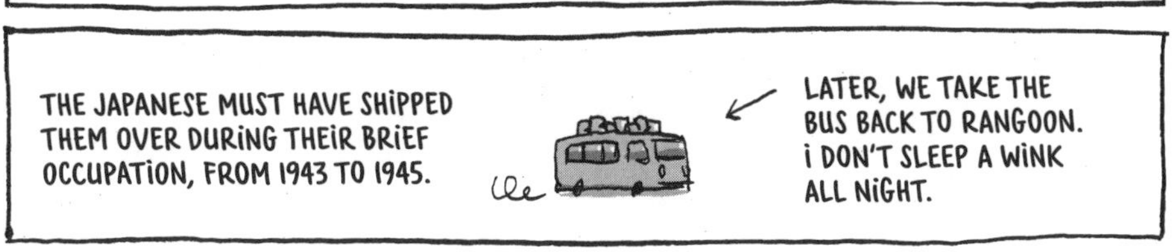
THE JAPANESE MUST HAVE SHIPPED THEM OVER DURING THEIR BRIEF OCCUPATION, FROM 1943 TO 1945.
LATER, WE TAKE THE BUS BACK TO RANGOON. I DON'T SLEEP A WINK ALL NIGHT.

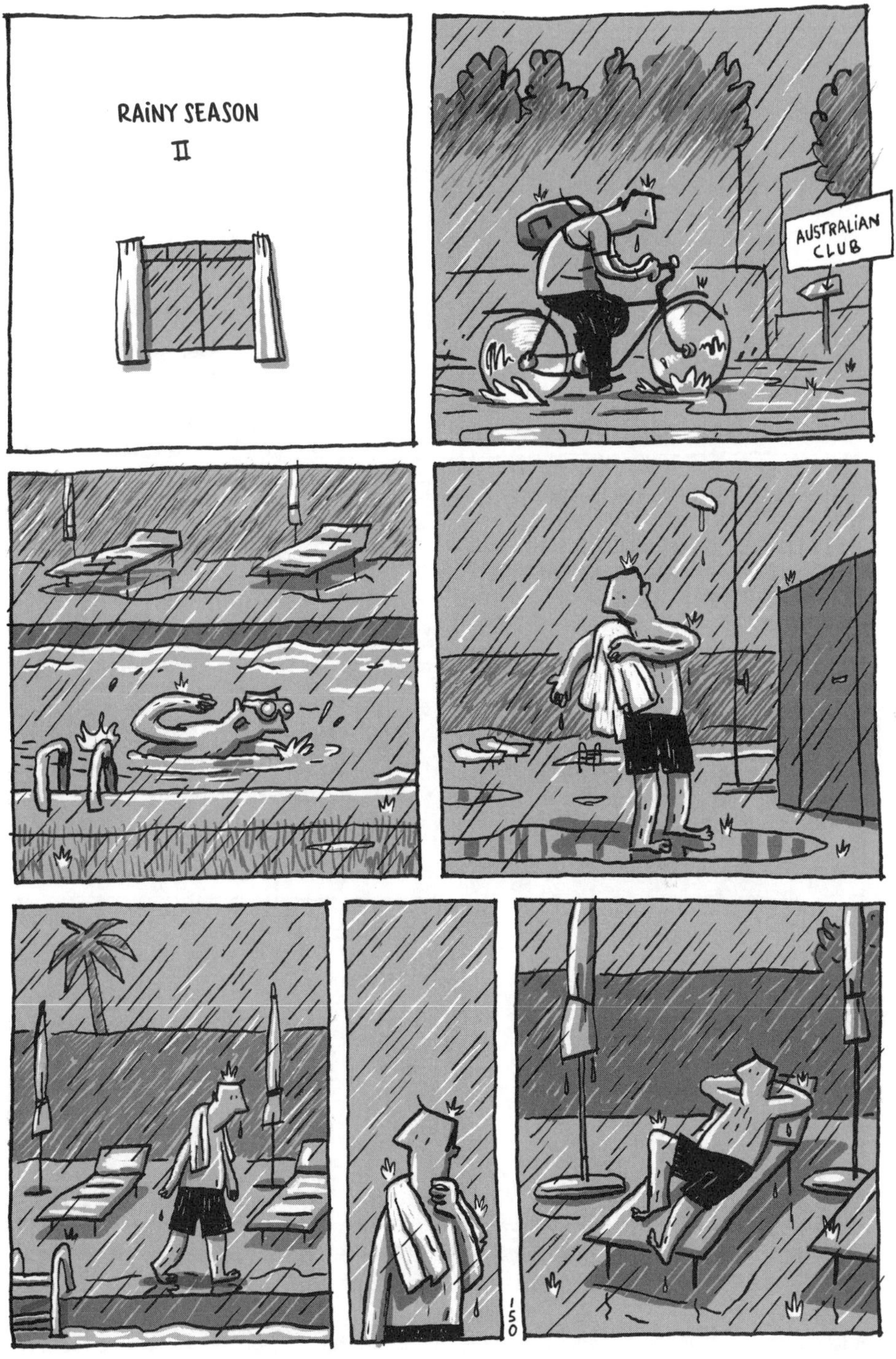
RAINY SEASON
II
AUSTRALIAN CLUB

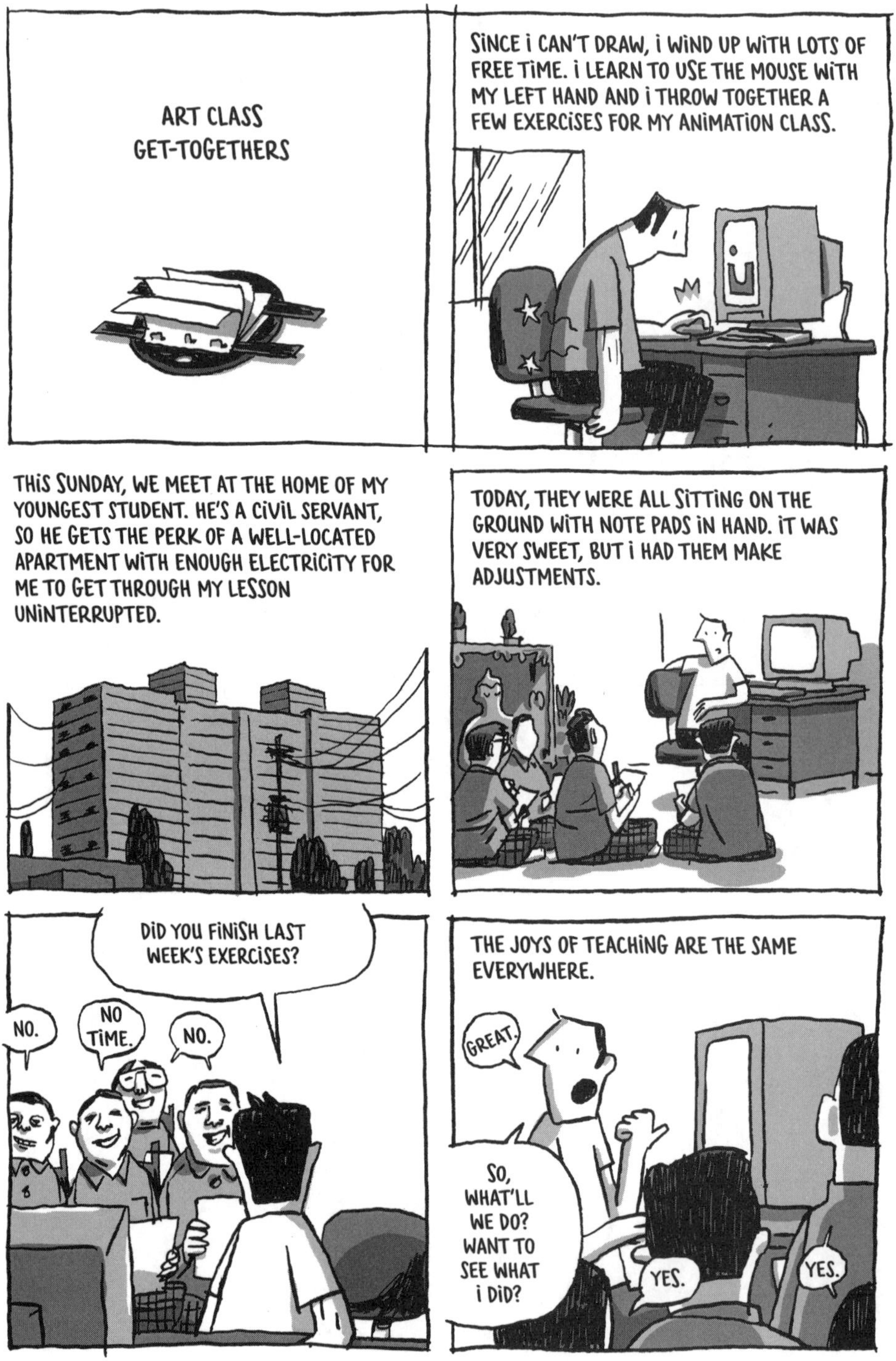
ART CLASS GET-TOGETHERS
SINCE I CAN'T DRAW, I WIND UP WITH LOTS OF FREE TIME. I LEARN TO USE THE MOUSE WITH MY LEFT HAND AND I THROW TOGETHER A FEW EXERCISES FOR MY ANIMATION CLASS.
THIS SUNDAY, WE MEET AT THE HOME OF MY YOUNGEST STUDENT. HE'S A CIVIL SERVANT, SO HE GETS THE PERK OF A WELL-LOCATED APARTMENT WITH ENOUGH ELECTRICITY FOR ME TO GET THROUGH MY LESSON UNINTERRUPTED.
TODAY, THEY WERE ALL SITTING ON THE GROUND WITH NOTE PADS IN HAND. IT WAS VERY SWEET, BUT I HAD THEM MAKE ADJUSTMENTS.
DID YOU FINISH LAST WEEK'S EXERCISES?
NO.
NO TIME.
NO.
THE JOYS OF TEACHING ARE THE SAME EVERYWHERE.
GREAT.
SO, WHAT'LL WE DO? WANT TO SEE WHAT I DID?
YES.
YES.

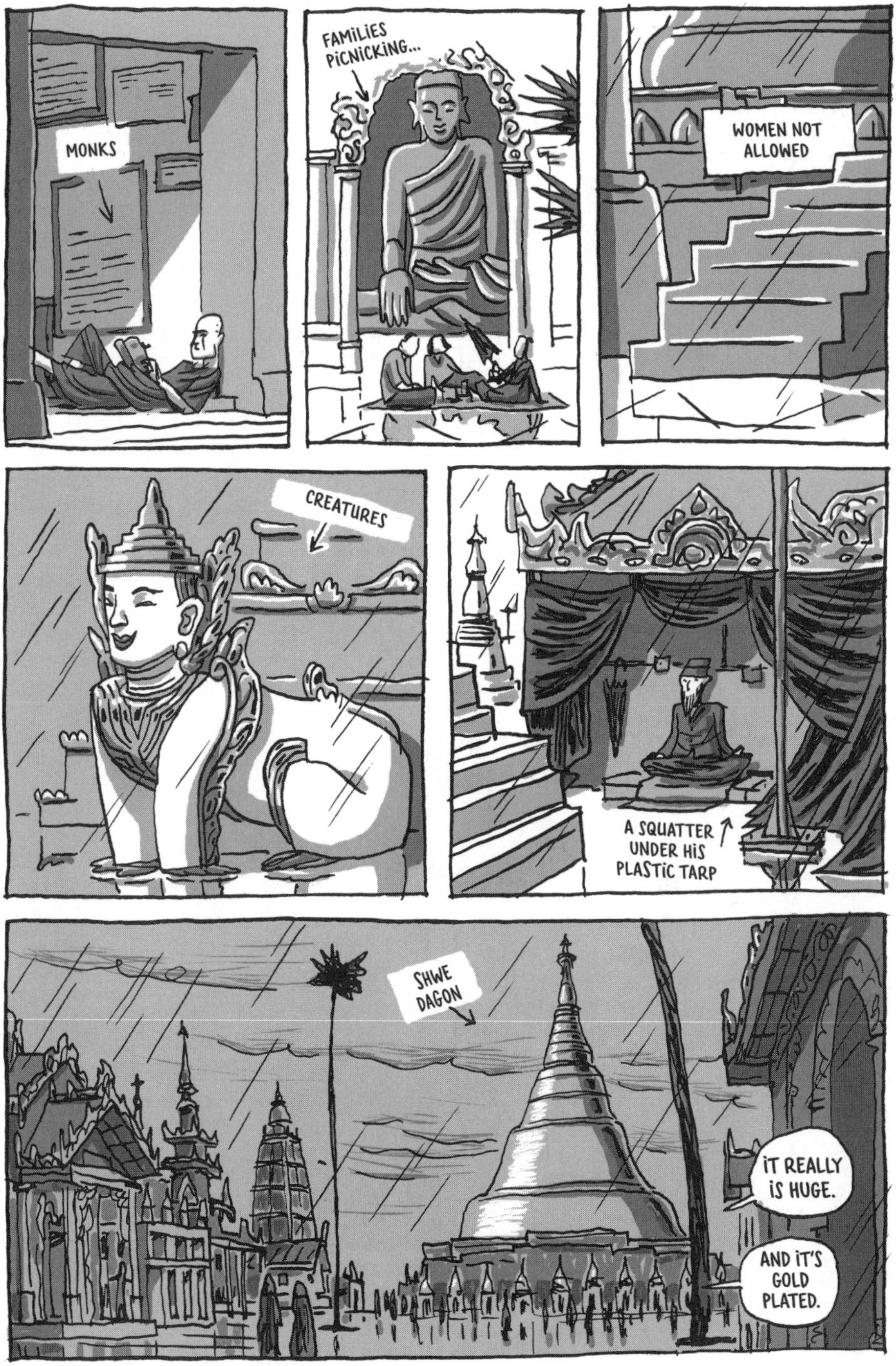
MONKS
FAMILIES PICNICKING...
WOMEN NOT ALLOWED
CREATURES
A SQUATTER UNDER HIS PLASTIC TARP
SHWE DAGON
IT REALLY IS HUGE.
AND IT'S GOLD PLATED.

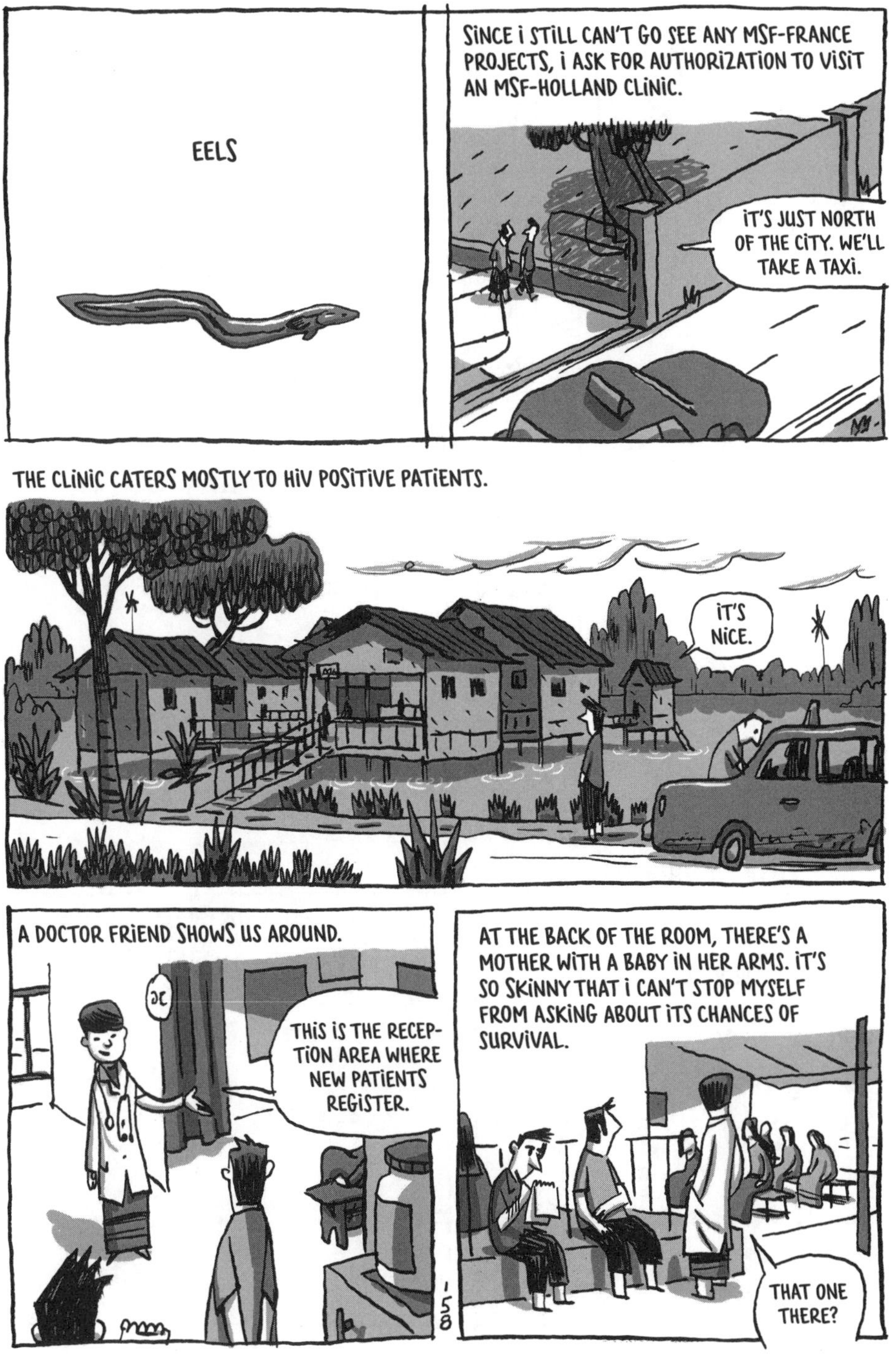
EELS
SINCE I STILL CAN'T GO SEE ANY MSF-FRANCE PROJECTS, I ASK FOR AUTHORIZATION TO VISIT AN MSF-HOLLAND CLINIC.
IT'S JUST NORTH OF THE CITY. WE'LL TAKE A TAXI.
THE CLINIC CATERS MOSTLY TO HIV POSITIVE PATIENTS.
IT'S NICE.
A DOCTOR FRIEND SHOWS US AROUND.
THIS IS THE RECEPTION AREA WHERE NEW PATIENTS REGISTER.
AT THE BACK OF THE ROOM, THERE'S A MOTHER WITH A BABY IN HER ARMS. IT'S SO SKINNY THAT I CAN'T STOP MYSELF FROM ASKING ABOUT ITS CHANCES OF SURVIVAL.
THAT ONE THERE?

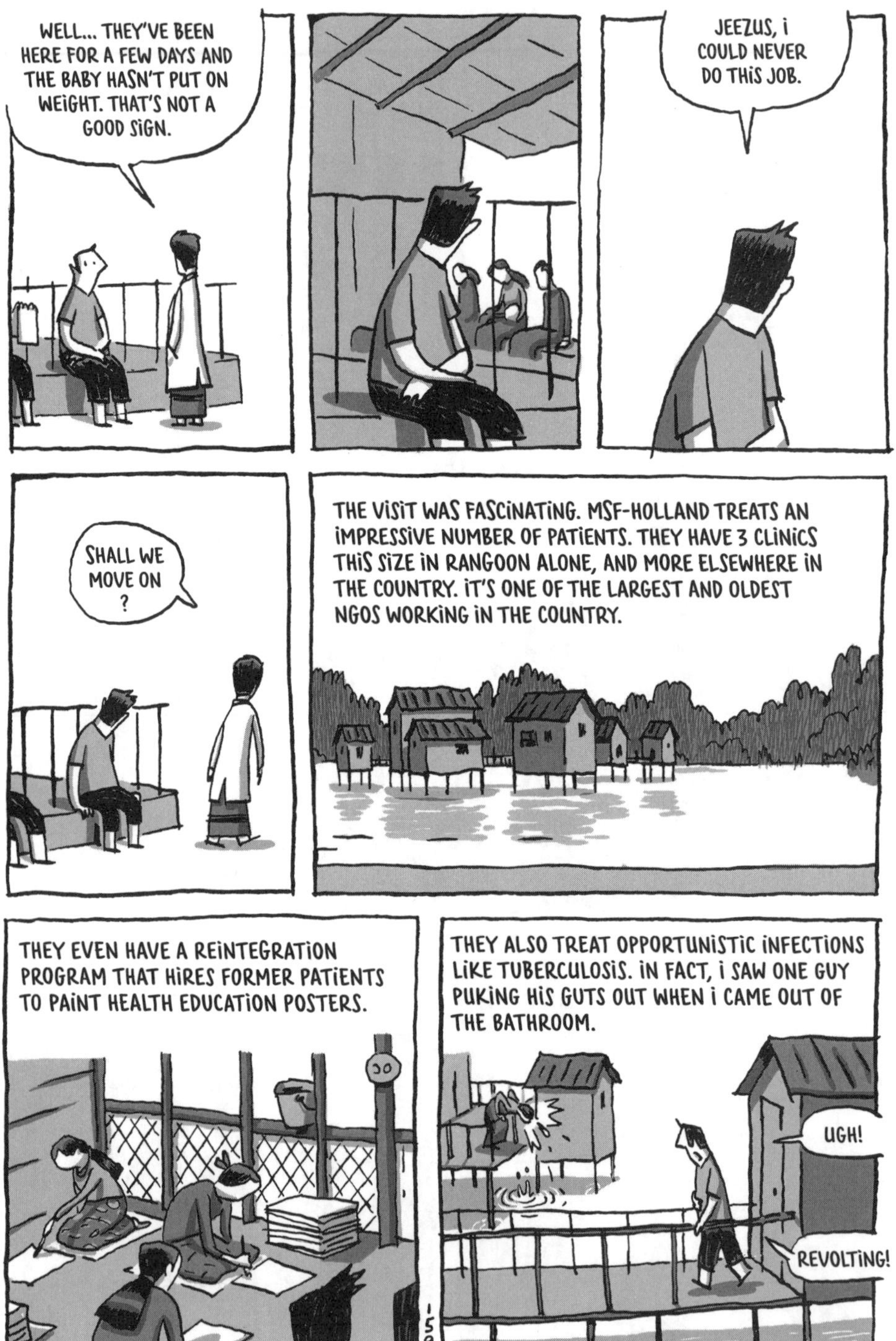
WELL... THEY'VE BEEN HERE FOR A FEW DAYS AND THE BABY HASN'T PUT ON WEIGHT. THAT'S NOT A GOOD SIGN.
JEEZUS, I COULD NEVER DO THIS JOB.
SHALL WE MOVE ON ?
THE VISIT WAS FASCINATING. MSF-HOLLAND TREATS AN IMPRESSIVE NUMBER OF PATIENTS. THEY HAVE 3 CLINICS THIS SIZE IN RANGOON ALONE, AND MORE ELSEWHERE IN THE COUNTRY. IT'S ONE OF THE LARGEST AND OLDEST NGOS WORKING IN THE COUNTRY.
THEY EVEN HAVE A REINTEGRATION PROGRAM THAT HIRES FORMER PATIENTS TO PAINT HEALTH EDUCATION POSTERS.
THEY ALSO TREAT OPPORTUNISTIC INFECTIONS LIKE TUBERCULOSIS. IN FACT, I SAW ONE GUY PUKING HIS GUTS OUT WHEN I CAME OUT OF THE BATHROOM.
UGH!
REVOLTING!

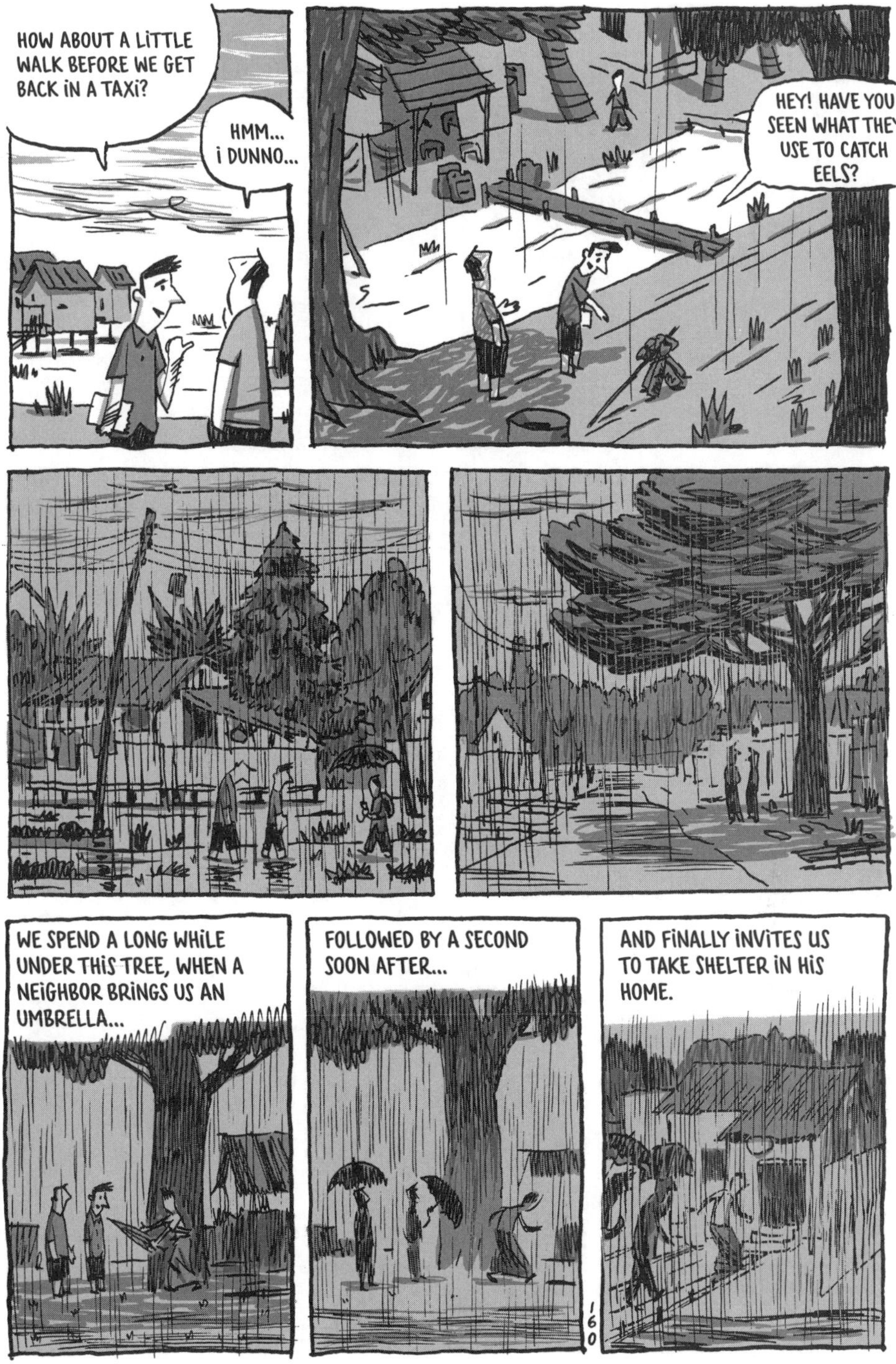
HOW ABOUT A LITTLE WALK BEFORE WE GET BACK IN A TAXI?
HMM... I DUNNO...
HEY! HAVE YOU SEEN WHAT THEY USE TO CATCH EELS?
WE SPEND A LONG WHILE UNDER THIS TREE, WHEN A NEIGHBOR BRINGS US AN UMBRELLA...
FOLLOWED BY A SECOND SOON AFTER...
AND FINALLY INVITES US TO TAKE SHELTER IN HIS HOME.

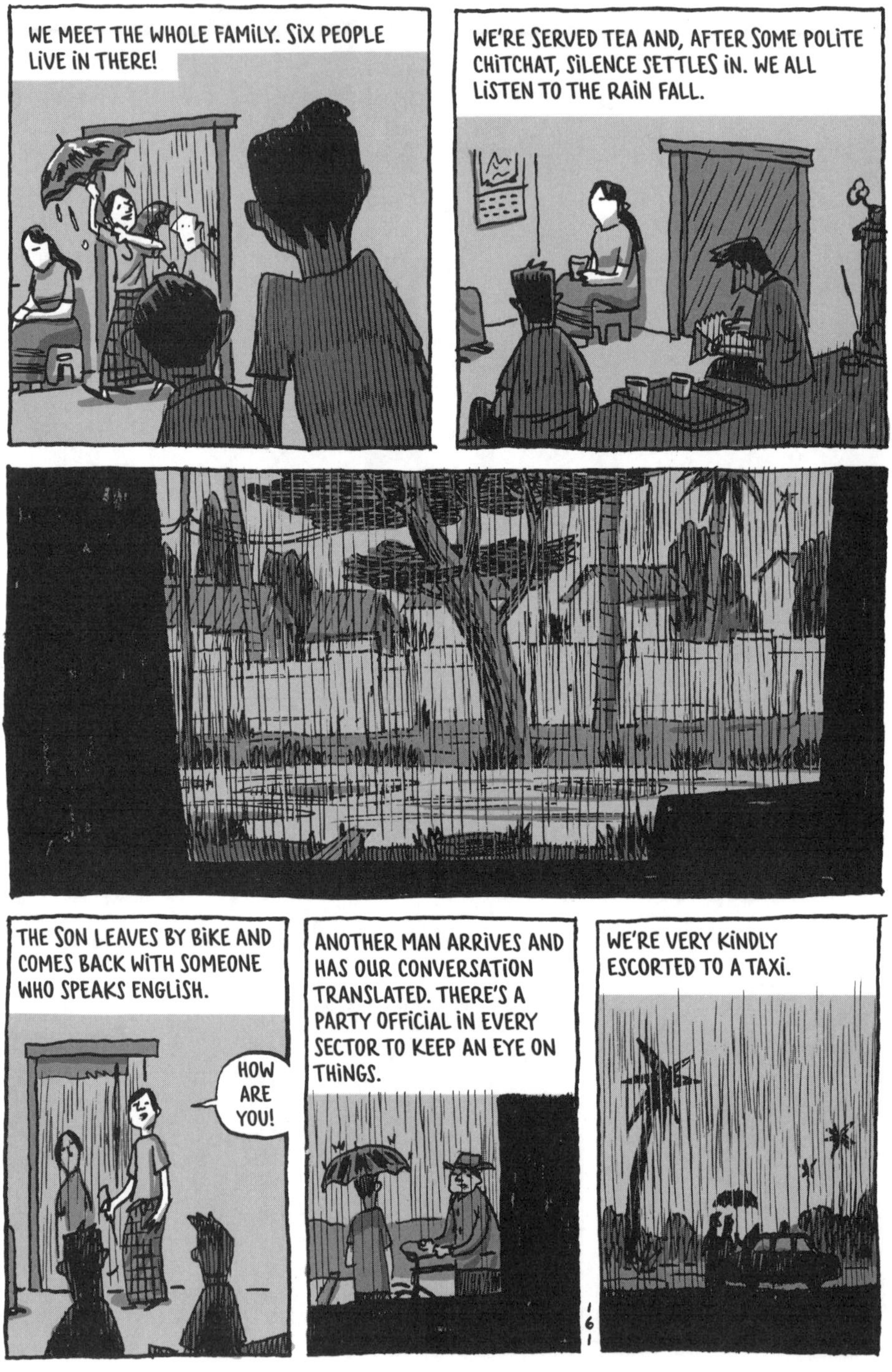
WE MEET THE WHOLE FAMILY. SIX PEOPLE LIVE IN THERE!
WE'RE SERVED TEA AND, AFTER SOME POLITE CHITCHAT, SILENCE SETTLES IN. WE ALL LISTEN TO THE RAIN FALL.
THE SON LEAVES BY BIKE AND COMES BACK WITH SOMEONE WHO SPEAKS ENGLISH.
HOW ARE YOU!
ANOTHER MAN ARRIVES AND HAS OUR CONVERSATION TRANSLATED. THERE'S A PARTY OFFICIAL IN EVERY SECTOR TO KEEP AN EYE ON THINGS.
WE'RE VERY KINDLY ESCORTED TO A TAXI.

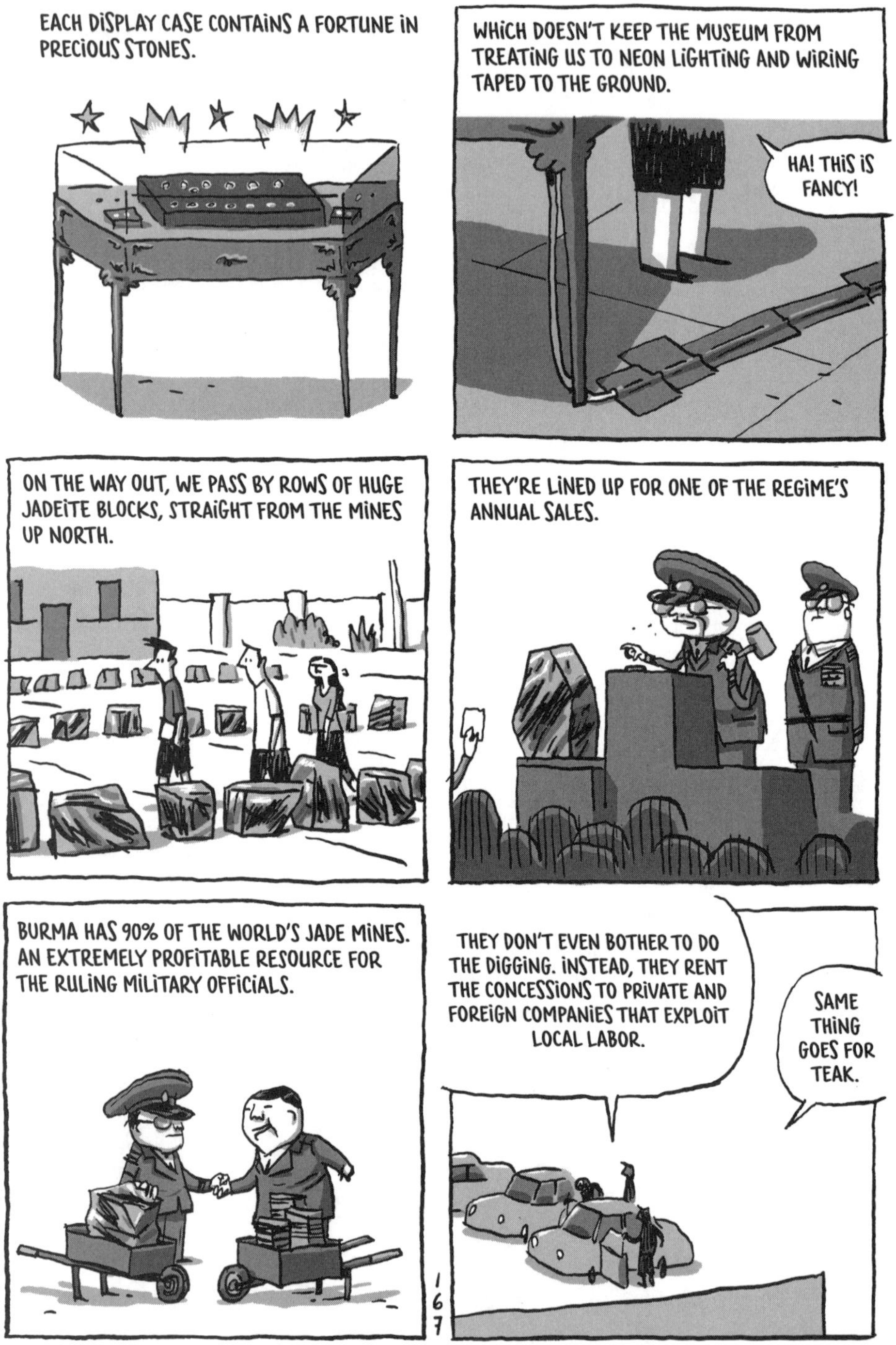
EACH DISPLAY CASE CONTAINS A FORTUNE IN PRECIOUS STONES.
WHICH DOESN'T KEEP THE MUSEUM FROM TREATING US TO NEON LIGHTING AND WIRING TAPED TO THE GROUND.
HA! THIS IS FANCY!
ON THE WAY OUT, WE PASS BY ROWS OF HUGE JADEITE BLOCKS, STRAIGHT FROM THE MINES UP NORTH.
THEY'RE LINED UP FOR ONE OF THE REGIME'S ANNUAL SALES.
BURMA HAS 90% OF THE WORLD'S JADE MINES. AN EXTREMELY PROFITABLE RESOURCE FOR THE RULING MILITARY OFFICIALS.
THEY DON'T EVEN BOTHER TO DO THE DIGGING. INSTEAD, THEY RENT THE CONCESSIONS TO PRIVATE AND FOREIGN COMPANIES THAT EXPLOIT LOCAL LABOR.
SAME THING GOES FOR TEAK.

DERAILED

THE VISIT IS OVER, JULES LEFT THIS MORNING. TIME FOR ME TO GET BACK TO MY DESK AND START DRAWING AGAIN.

OUCH, EECH.

I DON'T OVERDO IT, THOUGH, AND GO TO A BABY GROUP ORGANIZED BY ONE OF THE MOTHERS AT THE DAYCARE.

NOT BAD!

IN THE LIVING ROOM ARE TWO MAGNIFICENT WOOD BUDDHAS (REPRODUCTIONS).

JEEZ, IF WE HADN'T COME WITH BACKPACKS, I'D BRING ONE HOME AS WELL.

THE LATEST FAD FROM BANGKOK: THE KIDS PLAY WITH A ROBOT THAT DOES SOME THIRTY MOVES. IT CAN EVEN DANCE.

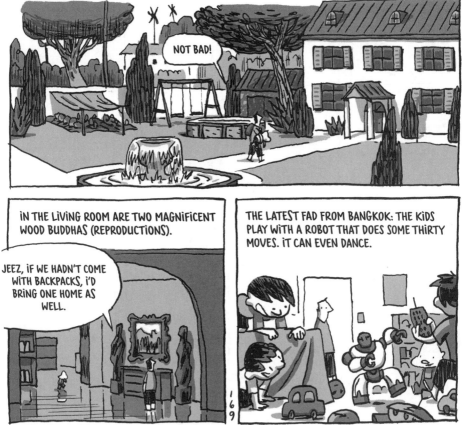

169

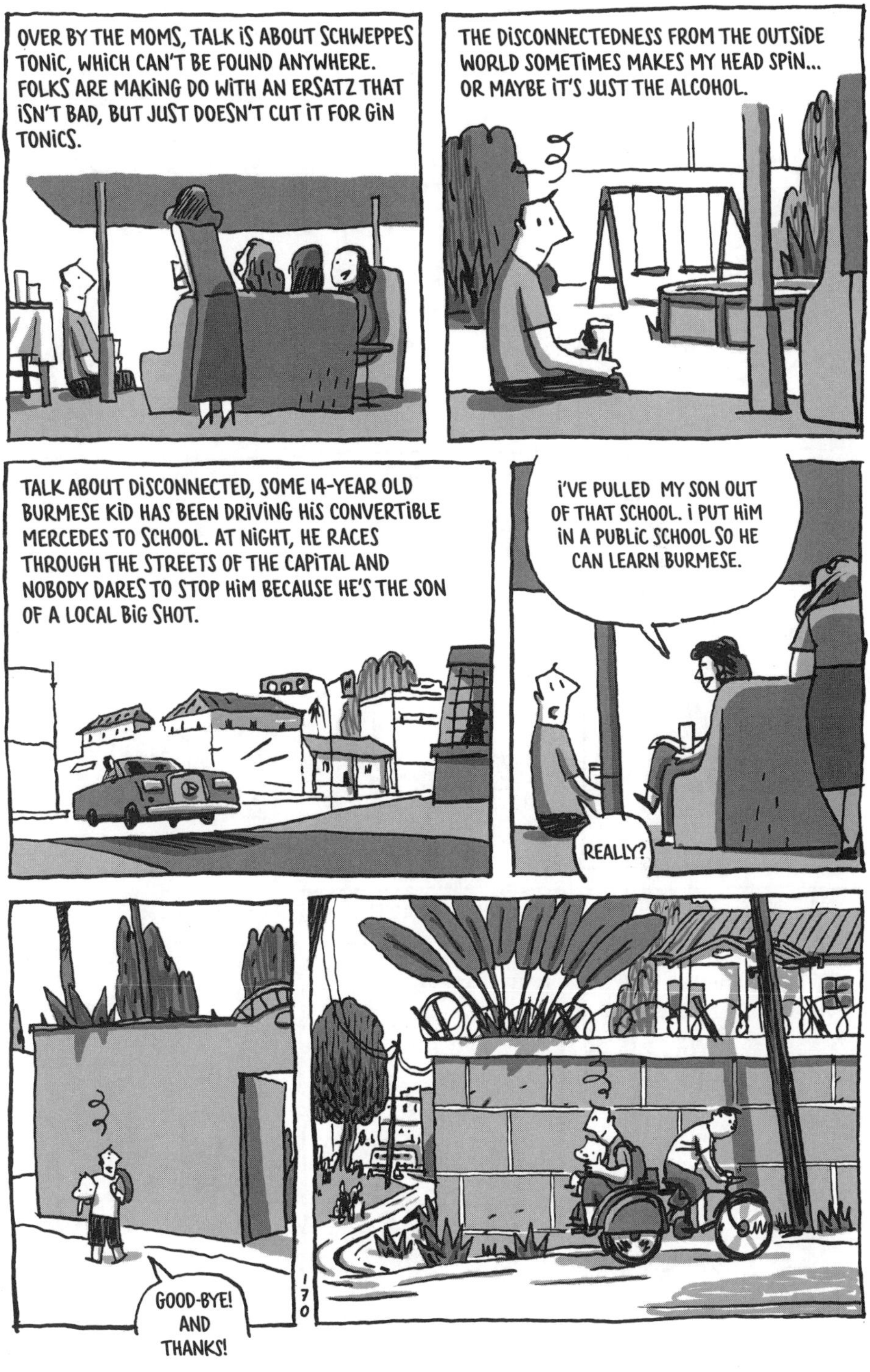
OVER BY THE MOMS, TALK IS ABOUT SCHWEPPES TONIC, WHICH CAN'T BE FOUND ANYWHERE. FOLKS ARE MAKING DO WITH AN ERSATZ THAT ISN'T BAD, BUT JUST DOESN'T CUT IT FOR GIN TONICS.
THE DISCONNECTEDNESS FROM THE OUTSIDE WORLD SOMETIMES MAKES MY HEAD SPIN... OR MAYBE IT'S JUST THE ALCOHOL.
TALK ABOUT DISCONNECTED, SOME 14-YEAR OLD BURMESE KID HAS BEEN DRIVING HIS CONVERTIBLE MERCEDES TO SCHOOL. AT NIGHT, HE RACES THROUGH THE STREETS OF THE CAPITAL AND NOBODY DARES TO STOP HIM BECAUSE HE'S THE SON OF A LOCAL BIG SHOT.
I'VE PULLED MY SON OUT OF THAT SCHOOL. I PUT HIM IN A PUBLIC SCHOOL SO HE CAN LEARN BURMESE.
REALLY?
GOOD-BYE! AND THANKS!

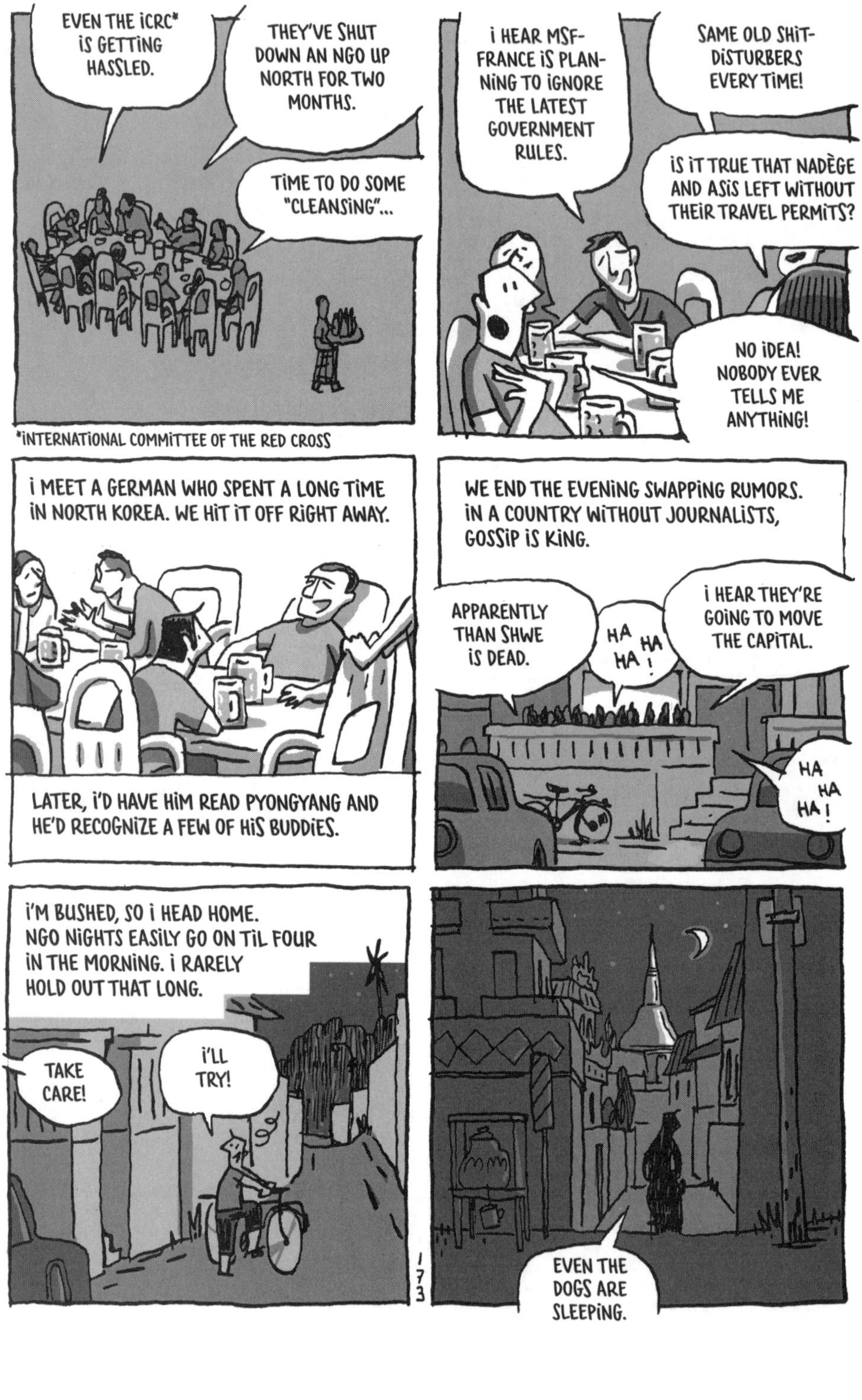
EVEN THE ICRC* IS GETTING HASSLED.
THEY'VE SHUT DOWN AN NGO UP NORTH FOR TWO MONTHS.
TIME TO DO SOME "CLEANSING"...
*INTERNATIONAL COMMITTEE OF THE RED CROSS
I HEAR MSF-FRANCE IS PLANNING TO IGNORE THE LATEST GOVERNMENT RULES.
SAME OLD SHIT-DISTURBERS EVERY TIME!
IS IT TRUE THAT NADÈGE AND ASIS LEFT WITHOUT THEIR TRAVEL PERMITS?
NO IDEA! NOBODY EVER TELLS ME ANYTHING!
I MEET A GERMAN WHO SPENT A LONG TIME IN NORTH KOREA. WE HIT IT OFF RIGHT AWAY.
LATER, I'D HAVE HIM READ PYONGYANG AND HE'D RECOGNIZE A FEW OF HIS BUDDIES.
WE END THE EVENING SWAPPING RUMORS. IN A COUNTRY WITHOUT JOURNALISTS, GOSSIP IS KING.
APPARENTLY THAN SHWE IS DEAD.
HA HA HA!
I HEAR THEY'RE GOING TO MOVE THE CAPITAL.
HA HA HA!
I'M BUSHED, SO I HEAD HOME. NGO NIGHTS EASILY GO ON TIL FOUR IN THE MORNING. I RARELY HOLD OUT THAT LONG.
TAKE CARE!
I'LL TRY!
EVEN THE DOGS ARE SLEEPING.

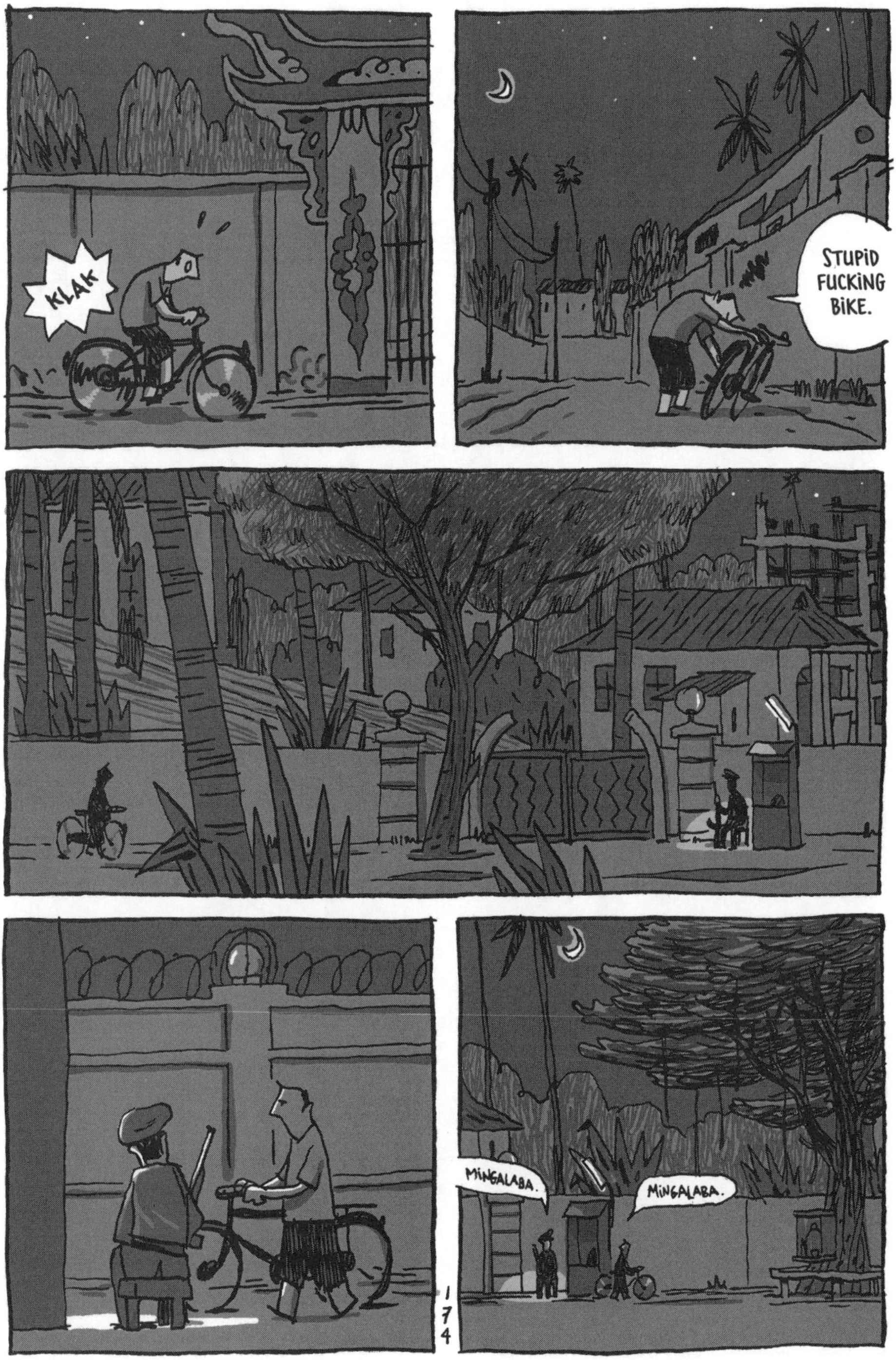
KLAK
STUPID FUCKING BIKE.
MINGALABA.
MINGALABA.

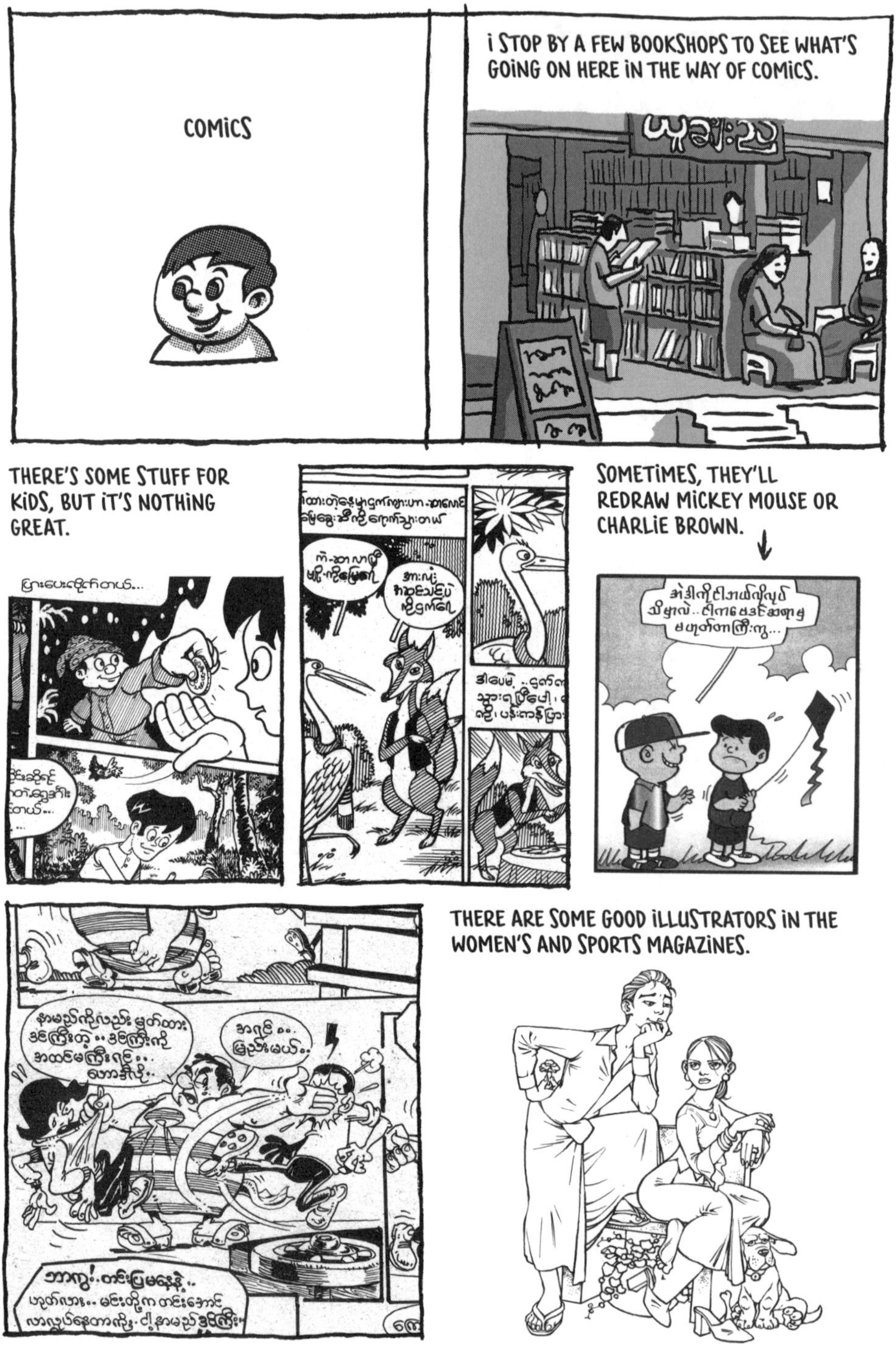
COMICS
I STOP BY A FEW BOOKSHOPS TO SEE WHAT'S GOING ON HERE IN THE WAY OF COMICS.
THERE'S SOME STUFF FOR KIDS, BUT IT'S NOTHING GREAT.
SOMETIMES, THEY'LL REDRAW MICKEY MOUSE OR CHARLIE BROWN.
THERE ARE SOME GOOD ILLUSTRATORS IN THE WOMEN'S AND SPORTS MAGAZINES.

AND EVERY NOW AND THEN, YOU COME ACROSS A REAL GEM.

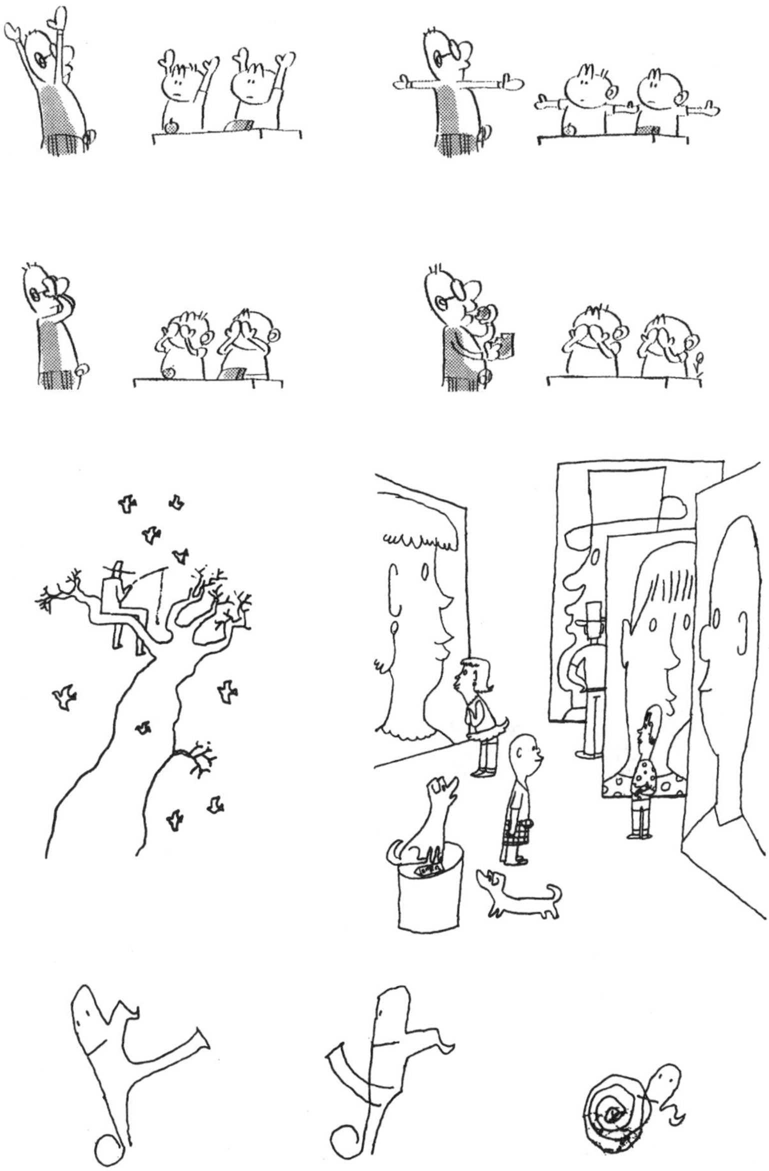

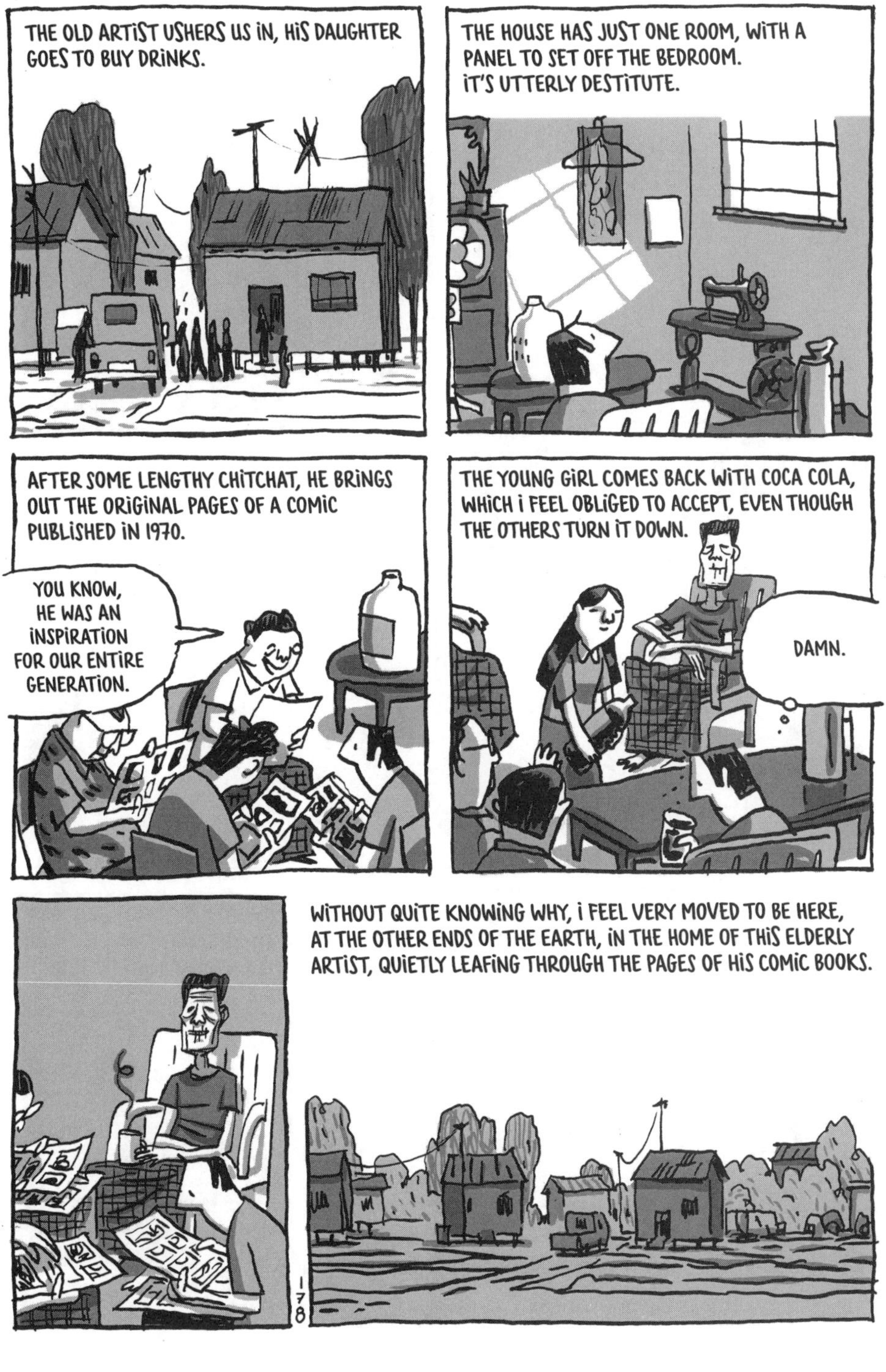
THE OLD ARTIST USHERS US IN, HIS DAUGHTER GOES TO BUY DRINKS.
THE HOUSE HAS JUST ONE ROOM, WITH A PANEL TO SET OFF THE BEDROOM. IT'S UTTERLY DESTITUTE.
AFTER SOME LENGTHY CHITCHAT, HE BRINGS OUT THE ORIGINAL PAGES OF A COMIC PUBLISHED IN 1970.
YOU KNOW, HE WAS AN INSPIRATION FOR OUR ENTIRE GENERATION.
THE YOUNG GIRL COMES BACK WITH COCA COLA, WHICH I FEEL OBLIGED TO ACCEPT, EVEN THOUGH THE OTHERS TURN IT DOWN.
DAMN.
WITHOUT QUITE KNOWING WHY, I FEEL VERY MOVED TO BE HERE, AT THE OTHER ENDS OF THE EARTH, IN THE HOME OF THIS ELDERLY ARTIST, QUIETLY LEAFING THROUGH THE PAGES OF HIS COMIC BOOKS.

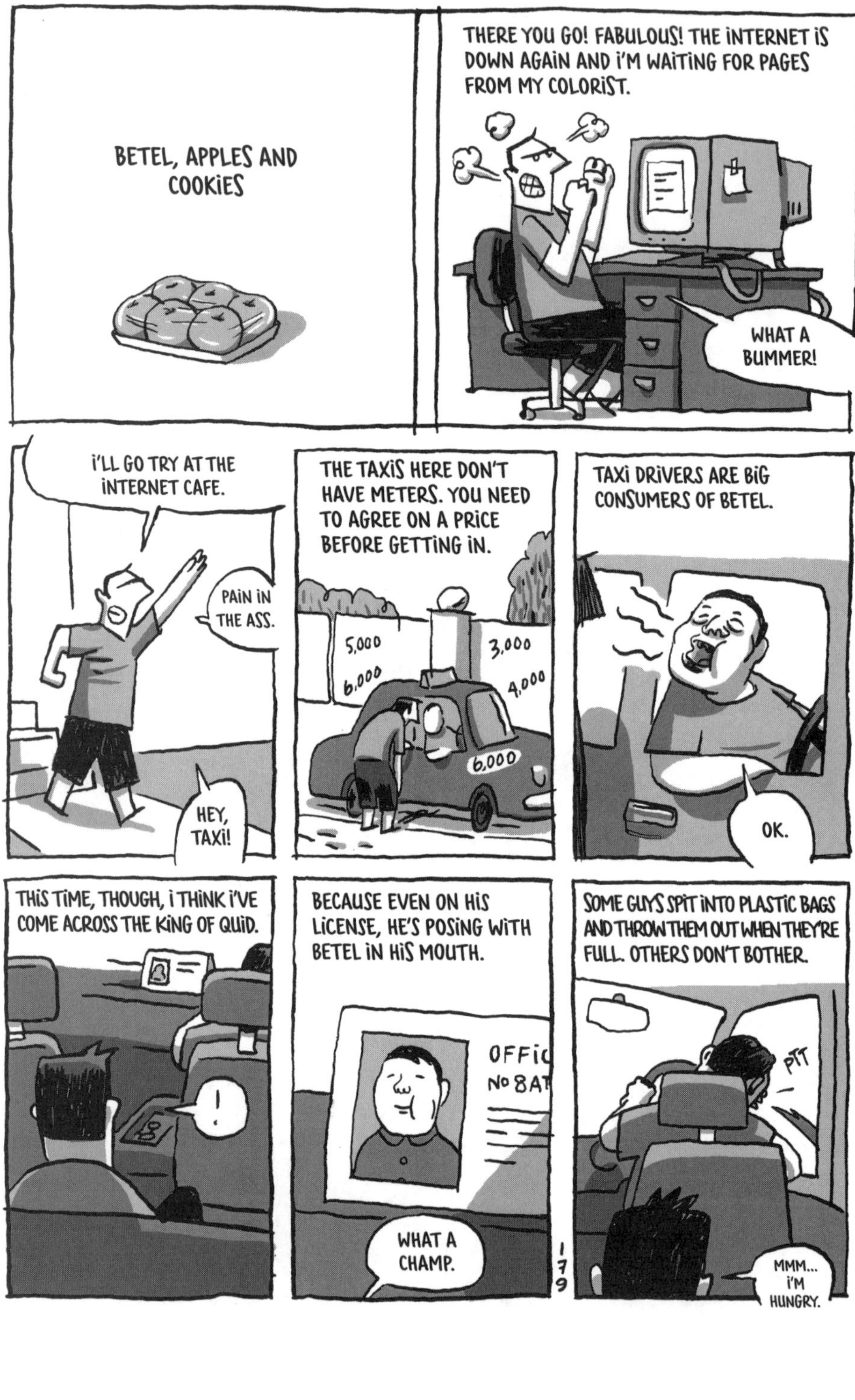
BETEL, APPLES AND COOKIES
THERE YOU GO! FABULOUS! THE INTERNET IS DOWN AGAIN AND I'M WAITING FOR PAGES FROM MY COLORIST.
WHAT A BUMMER!
I'LL GO TRY AT THE INTERNET CAFE.
PAIN IN THE ASS.
HEY, TAXI!
THE TAXIS HERE DON'T HAVE METERS. YOU NEED TO AGREE ON A PRICE BEFORE GETTING IN.
5,000
6,000
3,000
4,000
6,000
TAXI DRIVERS ARE BIG CONSUMERS OF BETEL.
OK.
THIS TIME, THOUGH, I THINK I'VE COME ACROSS THE KING OF QUID.
!
BECAUSE EVEN ON HIS LICENSE, HE'S POSING WITH BETEL IN HIS MOUTH.
OFFIC
No 8AT
WHAT A CHAMP.
SOME GUYS SPIT INTO PLASTIC BAGS AND THROW THEM OUT WHEN THEY'RE FULL. OTHERS DON'T BOTHER.
PTT
MMM... I'M HUNGRY.

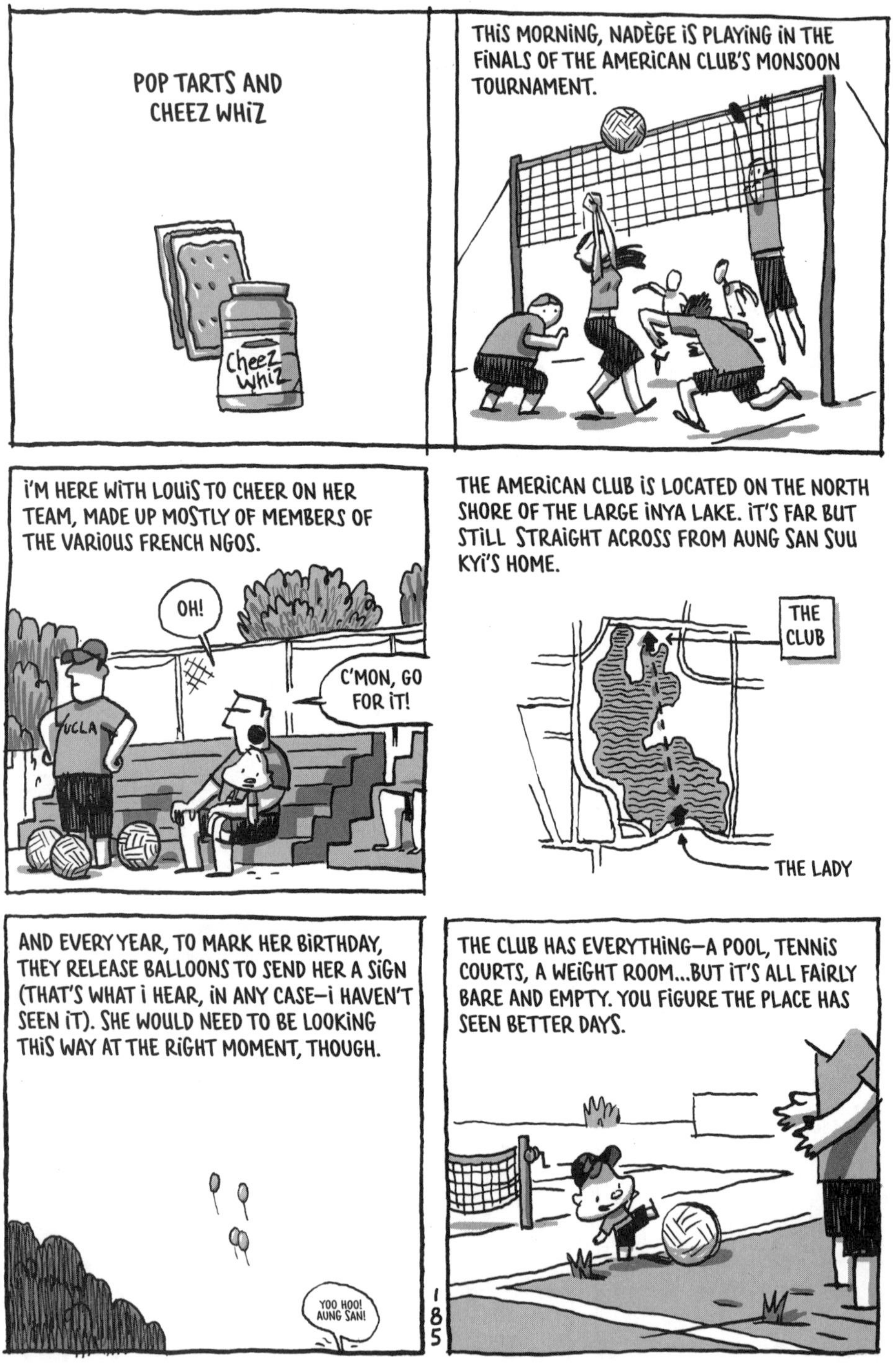
POP TARTS AND CHEEZ WHIZ
Cheez Whiz
THIS MORNING, NADÈGE IS PLAYING IN THE FINALS OF THE AMERICAN CLUB'S MONSOON TOURNAMENT.
I'M HERE WITH LOUIS TO CHEER ON HER TEAM, MADE UP MOSTLY OF MEMBERS OF THE VARIOUS FRENCH NGOS.
OH!
C'MON, GO FOR IT!
UCLA
THE AMERICAN CLUB IS LOCATED ON THE NORTH SHORE OF THE LARGE INYA LAKE. IT'S FAR BUT STILL STRAIGHT ACROSS FROM AUNG SAN SUU KYI'S HOME.
THE CLUB
THE LADY
AND EVERY YEAR, TO MARK HER BIRTHDAY, THEY RELEASE BALLOONS TO SEND HER A SIGN (THAT'S WHAT I HEAR, IN ANY CASE—I HAVEN'T SEEN IT). SHE WOULD NEED TO BE LOOKING THIS WAY AT THE RIGHT MOMENT, THOUGH.
YOO HOO! AUNG SAN!
THE CLUB HAS EVERYTHING—A POOL, TENNIS COURTS, A WEIGHT ROOM...BUT IT'S ALL FAIRLY BARE AND EMPTY. YOU FIGURE THE PLACE HAS SEEN BETTER DAYS.

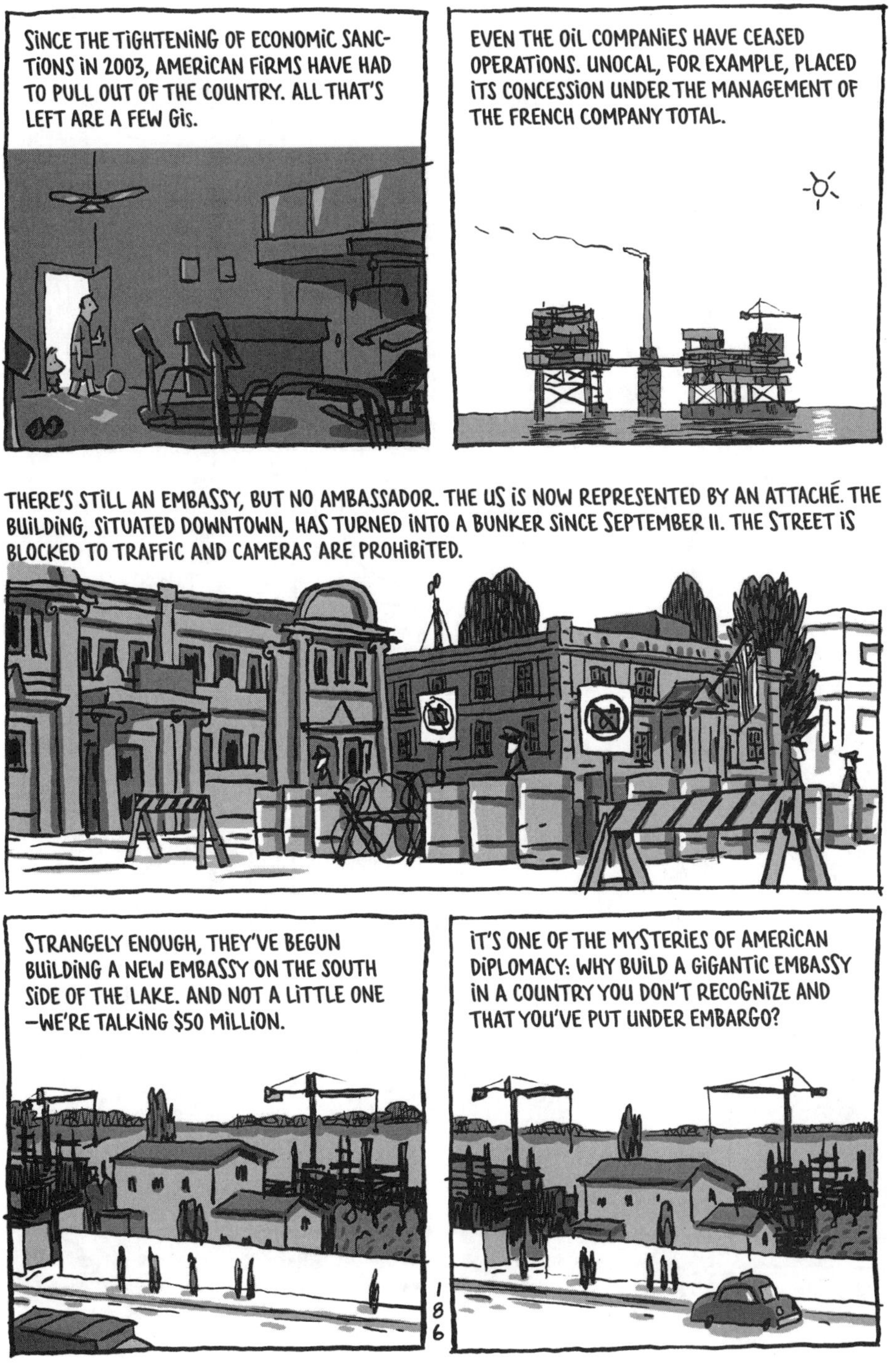
SINCE THE TIGHTENING OF ECONOMIC SANCTIONS IN 2003, AMERICAN FIRMS HAVE HAD TO PULL OUT OF THE COUNTRY. ALL THAT'S LEFT ARE A FEW GIS.
EVEN THE OIL COMPANIES HAVE CEASED OPERATIONS. UNOCAL, FOR EXAMPLE, PLACED ITS CONCESSION UNDER THE MANAGEMENT OF THE FRENCH COMPANY TOTAL.
THERE'S STILL AN EMBASSY, BUT NO AMBASSADOR. THE US IS NOW REPRESENTED BY AN ATTACHÉ. THE BUILDING, SITUATED DOWNTOWN, HAS TURNED INTO A BUNKER SINCE SEPTEMBER 11. THE STREET IS BLOCKED TO TRAFFIC AND CAMERAS ARE PROHIBITED.
STRANGELY ENOUGH, THEY'VE BEGUN BUILDING A NEW EMBASSY ON THE SOUTH SIDE OF THE LAKE. AND NOT A LITTLE ONE —WE'RE TALKING $50 MILLION.
IT'S ONE OF THE MYSTERIES OF AMERICAN DIPLOMACY: WHY BUILD A GIGANTIC EMBASSY IN A COUNTRY YOU DON'T RECOGNIZE AND THAT YOU'VE PUT UNDER EMBARGO?

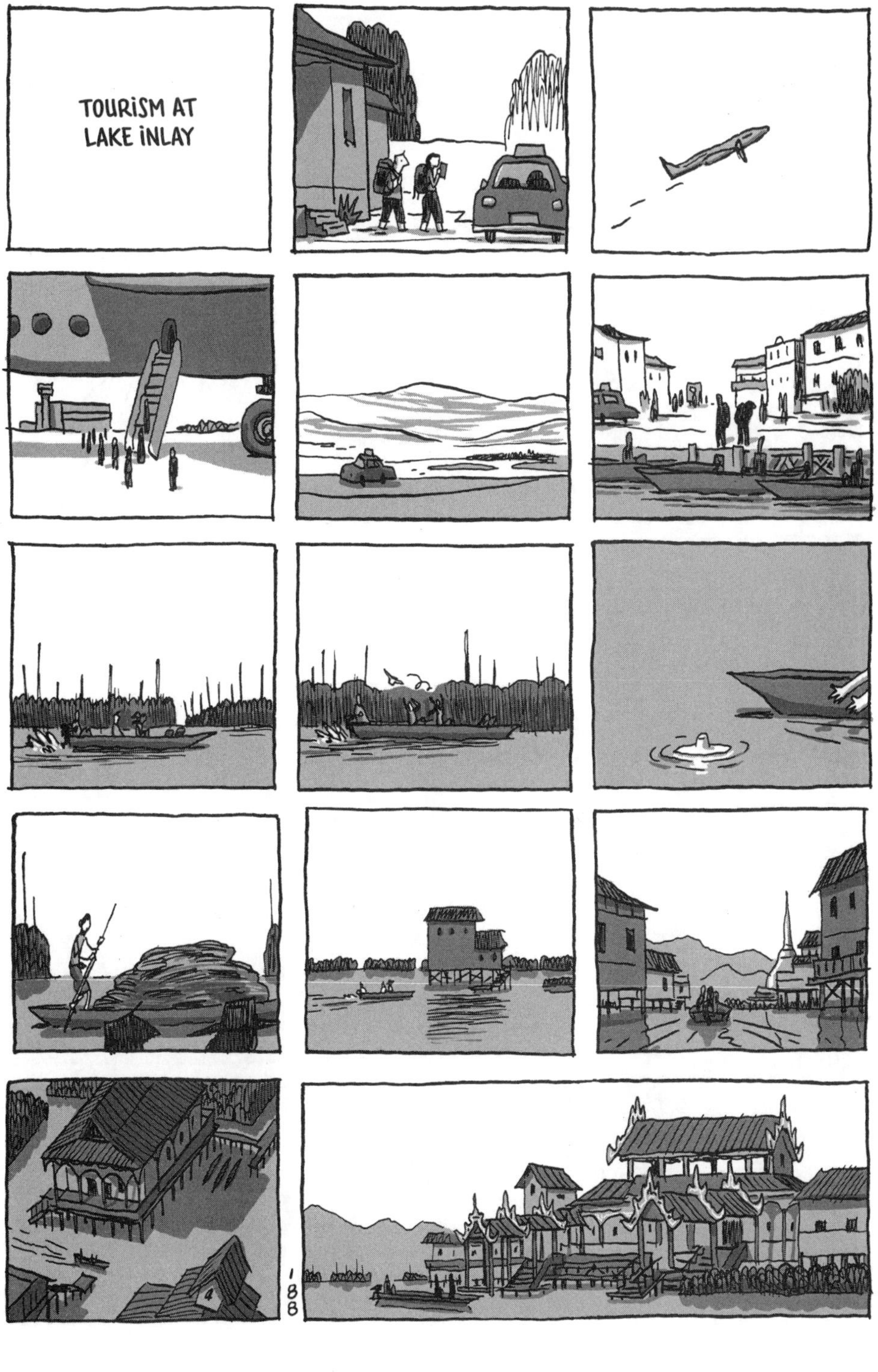
TOURISM AT
LAKE INLAY

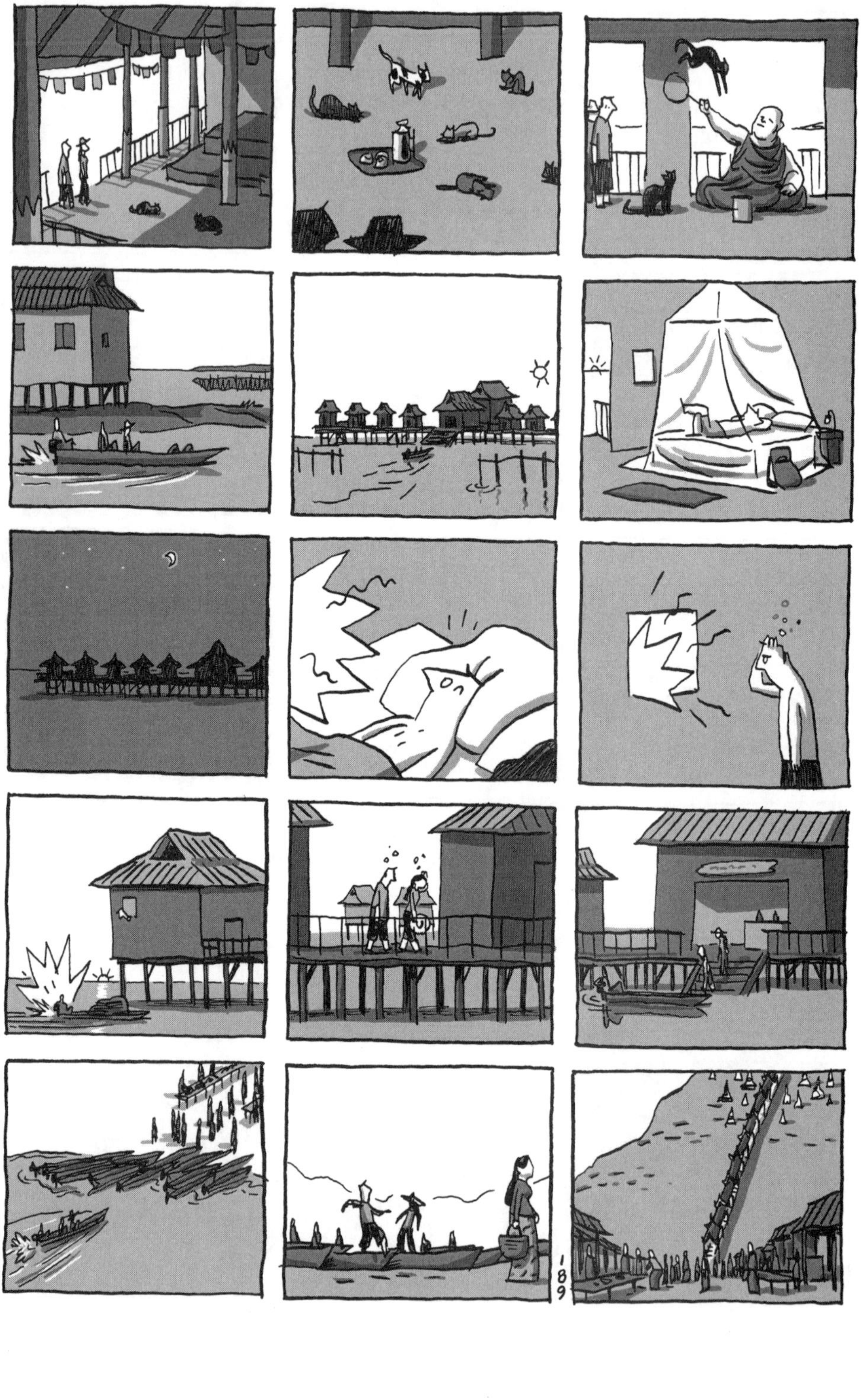

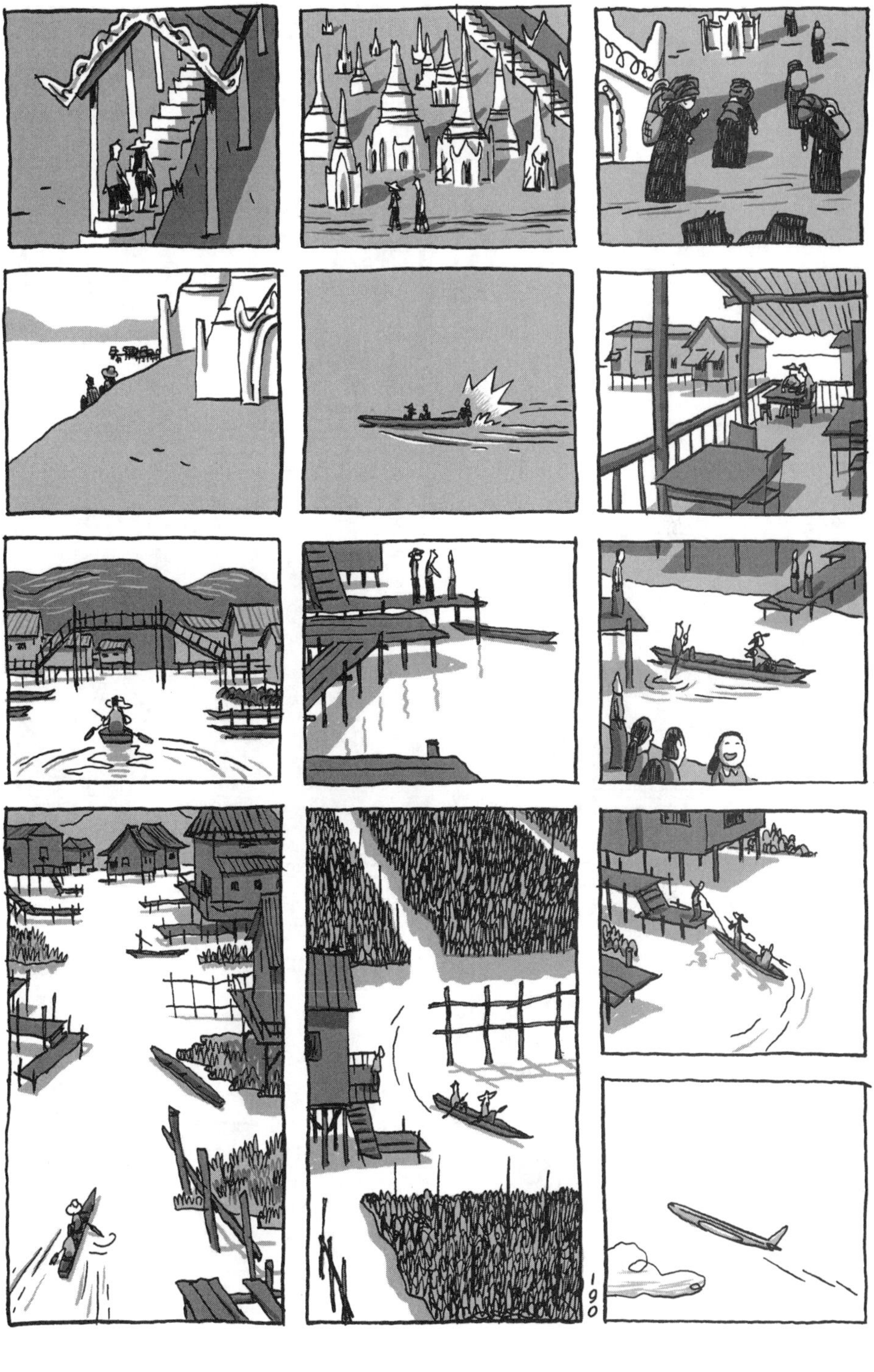

TOTAL OIL EXTRACTS NATURAL GAS FROM OFF-SHORE FIELDS IN THE YADANA REGION, SELLING IT PRIMARILY TO THAILAND VIA A PIPELINE.

CHINA
MYANMAR
LAOS
RANGOON
THAILAND
BANGKOK
CAMBODIA

YOU CAN BET THAT ITS CONSTRUCTION INVOLVED THE DISPLACEMENT OF VILLAGES AND THE USE OF FORCED LABOR. THAT'S HOW THE ARMY WORKS, WHEREVER IT GOES. EVEN TODAY.

TO BLOCK OUT THAT EPISODE, TOTAL INVESTED IN A MAJOR SOCIAL PROGRAM.

HOSPITAL
SCHOOL →
← HOSPICE
ORPHANAGE ↗

WITH THE CURRENT OIL CRISIS, MANY COUNTRIES HAVE TURNED AN EAGER EYE TO BURMA'S ENERGY RESOURCES.

INDIA
CHINA
JAPAN
SOUTH KOREA

FOR EXAMPLE, WHEN ENGLAND'S PREMIER OIL PULLED OUT OF THE COUNTRY FOLLOWING PRESSURE AND SANCTIONS, MALAYSIA'S PETRONAS TOOK ITS PLACE.

DRILLING OPERATIONS DIDN'T STOP FOR A SINGLE MOMENT.

192

JOHN, A BRIT NOW WORKING FOR PETRONAS.

THINGS ARE EASIER NOW WITH MALAYSIA. BEFORE, THERE WAS ALWAYS SOME PRESSURE GROUP STEPPING ON OUR TOES.

THEY KEPT ALL THE SAME EMPLOYEES?

PRETTY MUCH.

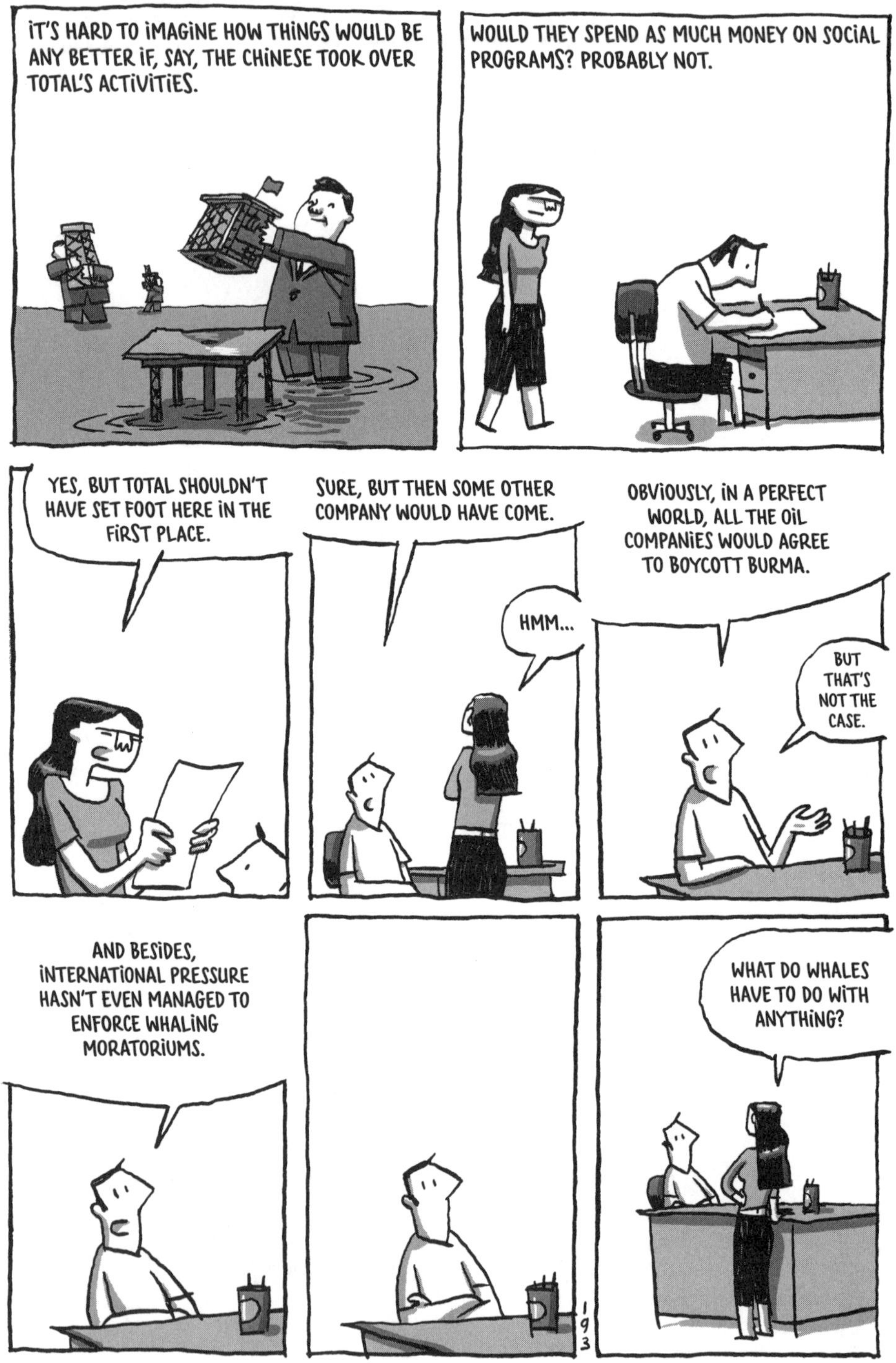
IT'S HARD TO IMAGINE HOW THINGS WOULD BE ANY BETTER IF, SAY, THE CHINESE TOOK OVER TOTAL'S ACTIVITIES.
WOULD THEY SPEND AS MUCH MONEY ON SOCIAL PROGRAMS? PROBABLY NOT.
YES, BUT TOTAL SHOULDN'T HAVE SET FOOT HERE IN THE FIRST PLACE.
SURE, BUT THEN SOME OTHER COMPANY WOULD HAVE COME.
HMM...
OBVIOUSLY, IN A PERFECT WORLD, ALL THE OIL COMPANIES WOULD AGREE TO BOYCOTT BURMA.
BUT THAT'S NOT THE CASE.
AND BESIDES, INTERNATIONAL PRESSURE HASN'T EVEN MANAGED TO ENFORCE WHALING MORATORIUMS.
WHAT DO WHALES HAVE TO DO WITH ANYTHING?

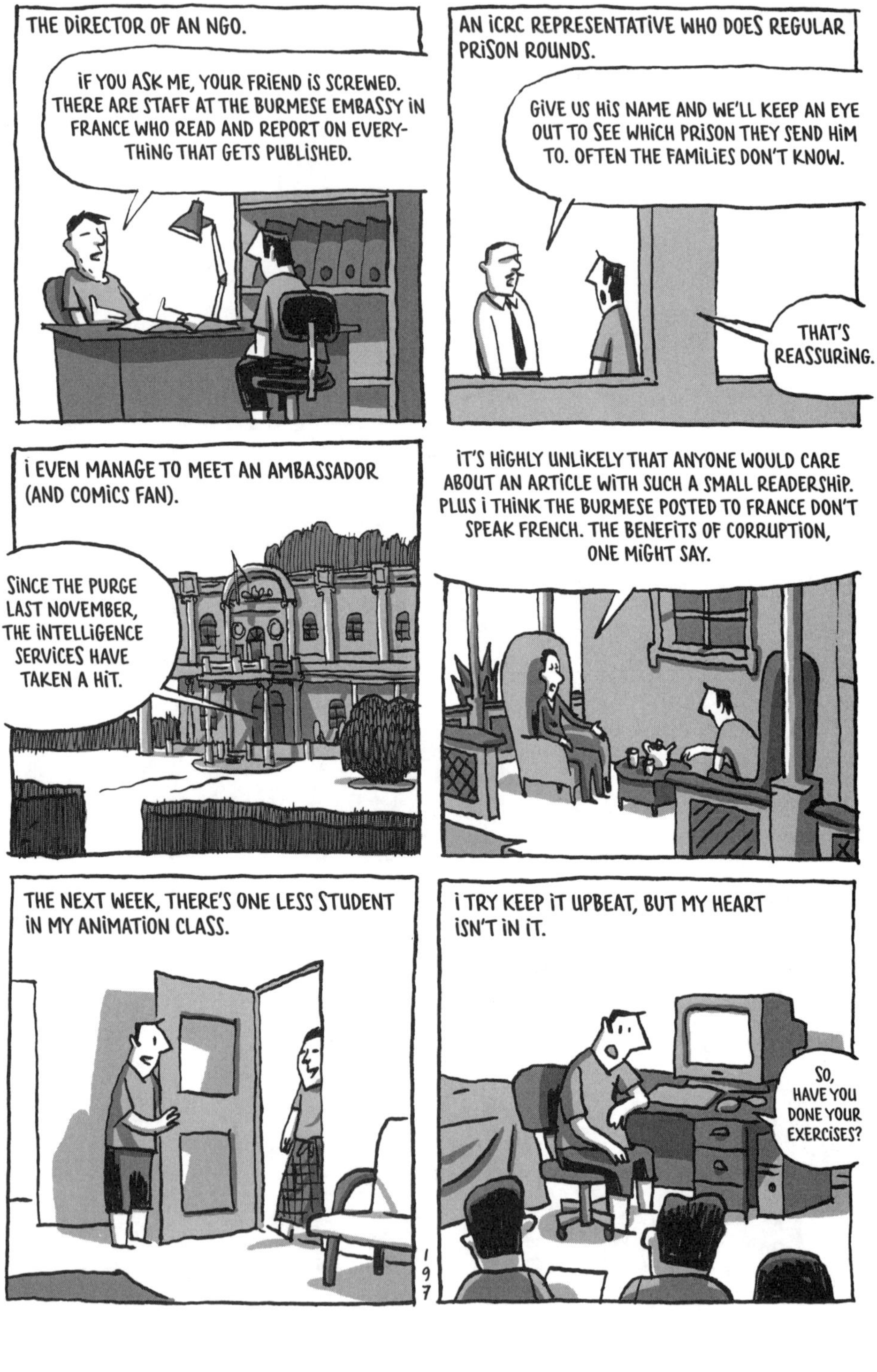
THE DIRECTOR OF AN NGO.
IF YOU ASK ME, YOUR FRIEND IS SCREWED. THERE ARE STAFF AT THE BURMESE EMBASSY IN FRANCE WHO READ AND REPORT ON EVERY-THING THAT GETS PUBLISHED.
AN ICRC REPRESENTATIVE WHO DOES REGULAR PRISON ROUNDS.
GIVE US HIS NAME AND WE'LL KEEP AN EYE OUT TO SEE WHICH PRISON THEY SEND HIM TO. OFTEN THE FAMILIES DON'T KNOW.
THAT'S REASSURING.
I EVEN MANAGE TO MEET AN AMBASSADOR (AND COMICS FAN).
SINCE THE PURGE LAST NOVEMBER, THE INTELLIGENCE SERVICES HAVE TAKEN A HIT.
IT'S HIGHLY UNLIKELY THAT ANYONE WOULD CARE ABOUT AN ARTICLE WITH SUCH A SMALL READERSHIP. PLUS I THINK THE BURMESE POSTED TO FRANCE DON'T SPEAK FRENCH. THE BENEFITS OF CORRUPTION, ONE MIGHT SAY.
THE NEXT WEEK, THERE'S ONE LESS STUDENT IN MY ANIMATION CLASS.
I TRY KEEP IT UPBEAT, BUT MY HEART ISN'T IN IT.
SO, HAVE YOU DONE YOUR EXERCISES?

I DO LEARN A FEW THINGS, THOUGH, LIKE HOW TO PRESERVE A FRESHLY AMPUTATED PART FOR REIMPLANTATION.

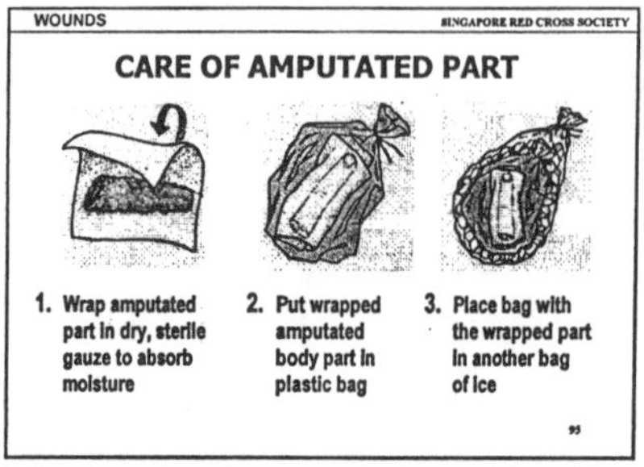
WOUNDS
SINGAPORE RED CROSS SOCIETY
CARE OF AMPUTATED PART
1. Wrap amputated part in dry, sterile gauze to absorb moisture
2. Put wrapped amputated body part in plastic bag
3. Place bag with the wrapped part in another bag of ice
95

AFTER LUNCH, I COME BACK ANYWAY FOR THE PRACTICAL EXERCISES.

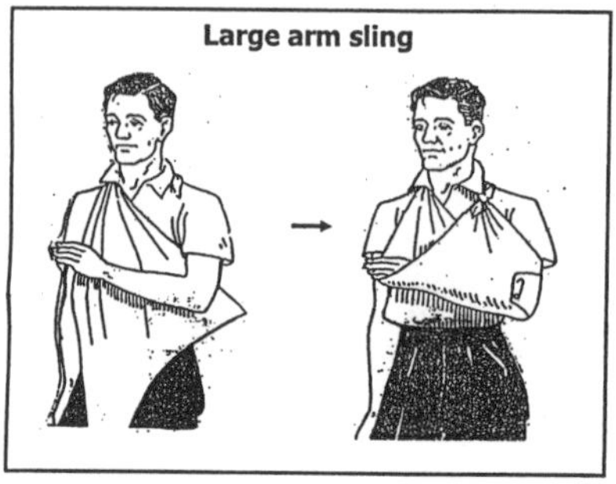
Large arm sling

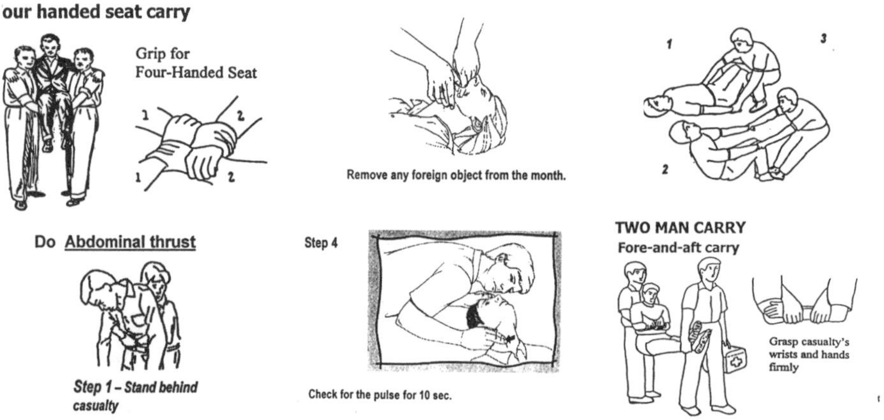
our handed seat carry
Grip for
Four-Handed Seat
1 2
1 2
Remove any foreign object from the month.
1 3
2
Do Abdominal thrust
Step 1 – Stand behind casualty
Step 4
Check for the pulse for 10 sec.
TWO MAN CARRY
Fore-and-aft carry
Grasp casualty's wrists and hands firmly

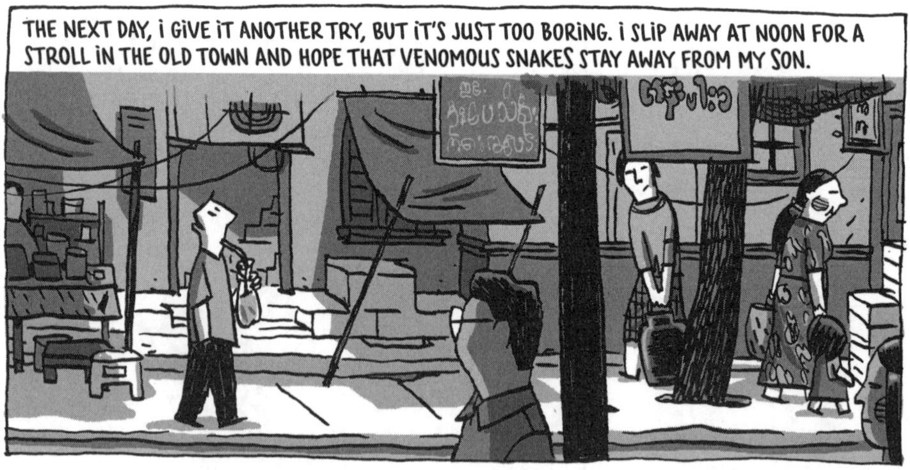
THE NEXT DAY, I GIVE IT ANOTHER TRY, BUT IT'S JUST TOO BORING. I SLIP AWAY AT NOON FOR A STROLL IN THE OLD TOWN AND HOPE THAT VENOMOUS SNAKES STAY AWAY FROM MY SON.

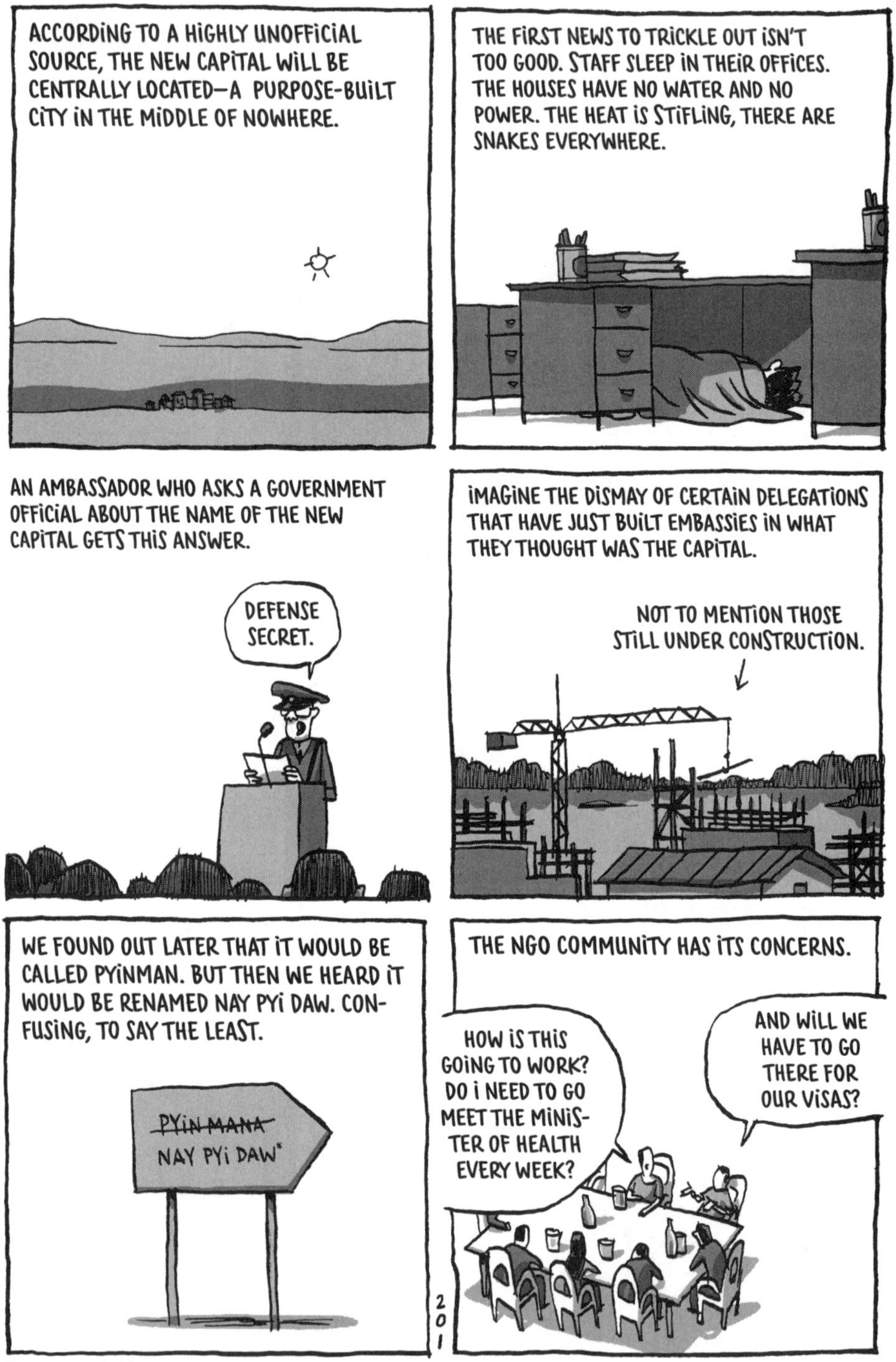
ACCORDING TO A HIGHLY UNOFFICIAL SOURCE, THE NEW CAPITAL WILL BE CENTRALLY LOCATED—A PURPOSE-BUILT CITY IN THE MIDDLE OF NOWHERE.
THE FIRST NEWS TO TRICKLE OUT ISN'T TOO GOOD. STAFF SLEEP IN THEIR OFFICES. THE HOUSES HAVE NO WATER AND NO POWER. THE HEAT IS STIFLING, THERE ARE SNAKES EVERYWHERE.
AN AMBASSADOR WHO ASKS A GOVERNMENT OFFICIAL ABOUT THE NAME OF THE NEW CAPITAL GETS THIS ANSWER.
DEFENSE SECRET.
IMAGINE THE DISMAY OF CERTAIN DELEGATIONS THAT HAVE JUST BUILT EMBASSIES IN WHAT THEY THOUGHT WAS THE CAPITAL.
NOT TO MENTION THOSE STILL UNDER CONSTRUCTION.
WE FOUND OUT LATER THAT IT WOULD BE CALLED PYINMAN. BUT THEN WE HEARD IT WOULD BE RENAMED NAY PYI DAW. CONFUSING, TO SAY THE LEAST.
~~PYIN MANA~~
NAY PYI DAW*
THE NGO COMMUNITY HAS ITS CONCERNS.
HOW IS THIS GOING TO WORK? DO I NEED TO GO MEET THE MINISTER OF HEALTH EVERY WEEK?
AND WILL WE HAVE TO GO THERE FOR OUR VISAS?

*"HOME OF KINGS"

MIND YOU, WITHOUT MAKING AN EFFORT, WE'LL HAVE LIVED IN BOTH THE CAPITAL AND THE METROPOLIS. THAT'S PRETTY COOL.

AMONG THE MANY HYPOTHESES TO EXPLAIN THE CHANGE, TWO SEEM ALMOST PLAUSIBLE.

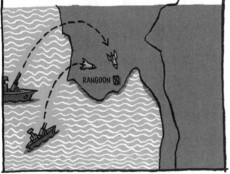

THE MILITARY THEORY: RANGOON WOULD BE TOO VULNERABLE TO THE KIND OF ATTACK EXPERIENCED BY IRAQ.

RANGOON

THE ESOTERIC THEORY: THAN SHWE'S ASTROLOGISTS APPARENTLY PREDICTED THE FALL OF RANGOON AS CAPITAL CITY. SO IT ONLY MADE SENSE TO GET AN EARLY START ON PACKING UP.

FOR THOSE WHO WANT TO BELIEVE IT, THE OFFICIAL VERSION:

THE NEW CAPITAL WILL BE BETTER SITUATED. BEING CENTRALLY LOCATED, IT WILL BE CLOSER TO ALL CITIZENS OF BURMA.

AND THAT'S THAT, IN A COUNTRY RULED BY A JUNTA, NOBODY BOTHERS WITH EXPLANATIONS. IN ANY CASE, IT'S NOT LIKE ANYONE IS GOING TO ASK TOO MANY QUESTIONS OR WRITE WHAT THEY THINK.

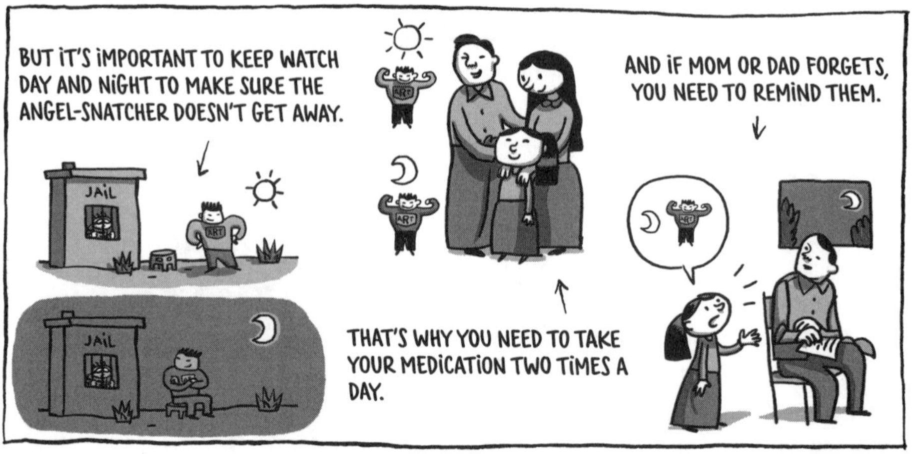
BUT IT'S IMPORTANT TO KEEP WATCH DAY AND NIGHT TO MAKE SURE THE ANGEL-SNATCHER DOESN'T GET AWAY.
JAIL
ART
JAIL
THAT'S WHY YOU NEED TO TAKE YOUR MEDICATION TWO TIMES A DAY.
AND IF MOM OR DAD FORGETS, YOU NEED TO REMIND THEM.

BURMA IS ONE OF THE WORLD'S LARGEST OPIUM PRODUCERS. IN SOME PARTS OF THE COUNTRY, HEROIN CIRCULATES MORE OR LESS FREELY. LOTS OF JUNKIES, NOT MUCH HYGIENE. THE AIDS VIRUS IS SPREADING LIKE WILDFIRE. ADD TO THAT TRANSMISSION THROUGH PROSTITUTION.

THE MANY INFECTED PEOPLE ARE CARED FOR ONLY BY FOREIGN AID GROUPS. ANTI-RETROVIRALS ARE PURCHASED IN THAILAND, WHICH MANUFACTURES GENERICS. THE CUSTOMS FORMALITIES ARE SO COMPLEX THAT IT ISN'T UNUSUAL FOR DOCTORS TO DO ONE-DAY ROUND TRIPS TO BANGKOK TO RESTOCK ON MEDICATION.

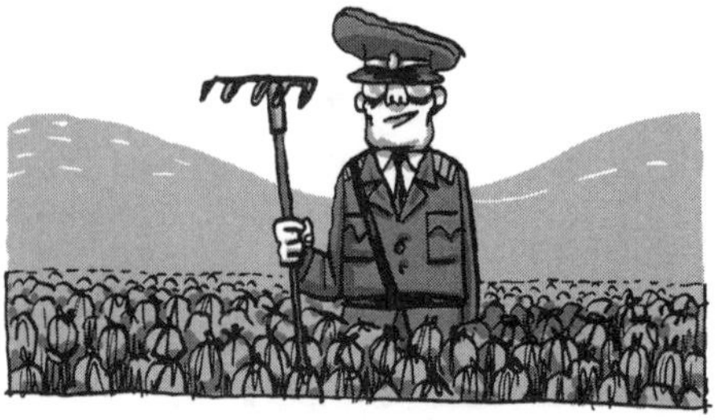

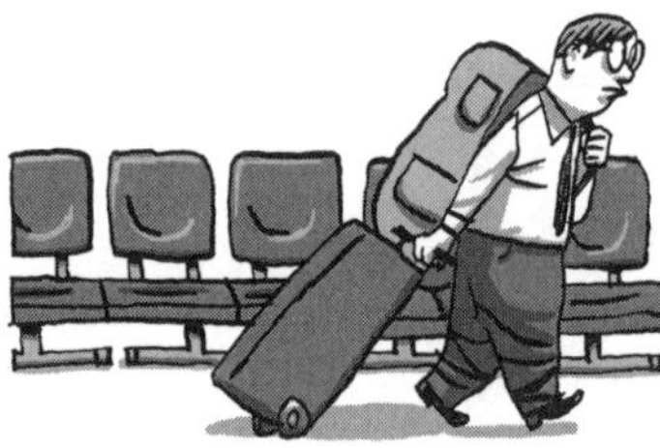

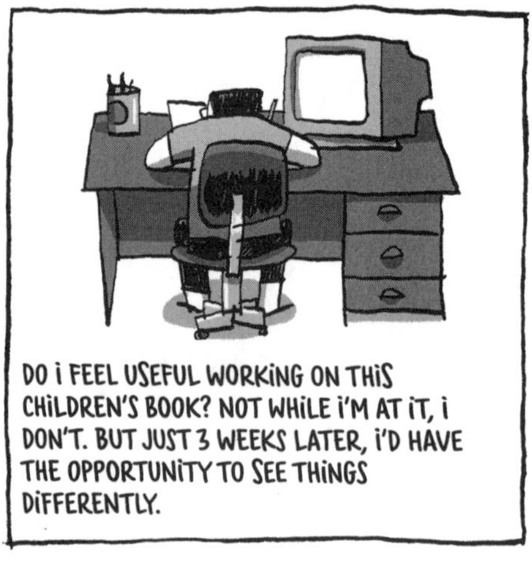
DO I FEEL USEFUL WORKING ON THIS CHILDREN'S BOOK? NOT WHILE I'M AT IT, I DON'T. BUT JUST 3 WEEKS LATER, I'D HAVE THE OPPORTUNITY TO SEE THINGS DIFFERENTLY.

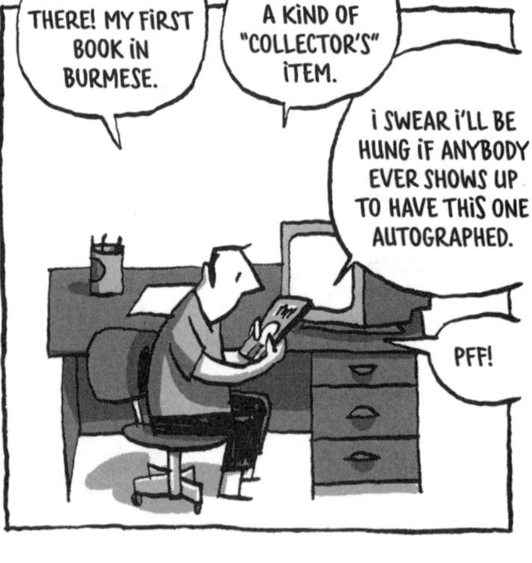
THERE! MY FIRST BOOK IN BURMESE.
A KIND OF "COLLECTOR'S" ITEM.
I SWEAR I'LL BE HUNG IF ANYBODY EVER SHOWS UP TO HAVE THIS ONE AUTOGRAPHED.
PFF!

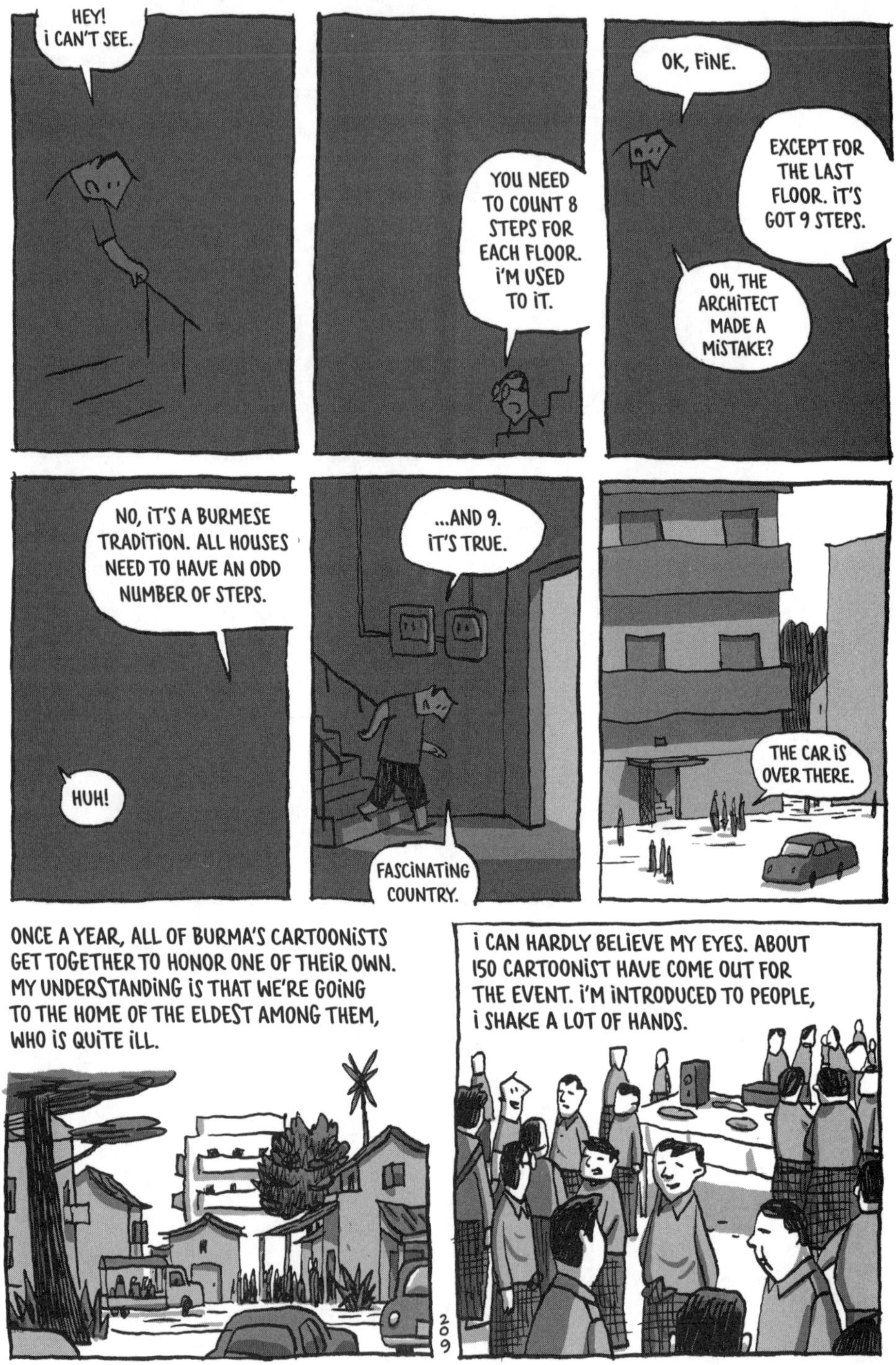
HEY!
I CAN'T SEE.
YOU NEED TO COUNT 8 STEPS FOR EACH FLOOR. I'M USED TO IT.
OK, FINE.
EXCEPT FOR THE LAST FLOOR. IT'S GOT 9 STEPS.
OH, THE ARCHITECT MADE A MISTAKE?
NO, IT'S A BURMESE TRADITION. ALL HOUSES NEED TO HAVE AN ODD NUMBER OF STEPS.
HUH!
...AND 9. IT'S TRUE.
FASCINATING COUNTRY.
THE CAR IS OVER THERE.
ONCE A YEAR, ALL OF BURMA'S CARTOONISTS GET TOGETHER TO HONOR ONE OF THEIR OWN. MY UNDERSTANDING IS THAT WE'RE GOING TO THE HOME OF THE ELDEST AMONG THEM, WHO IS QUITE ILL.
I CAN HARDLY BELIEVE MY EYES. ABOUT 150 CARTOONIST HAVE COME OUT FOR THE EVENT. I'M INTRODUCED TO PEOPLE, I SHAKE A LOT OF HANDS.

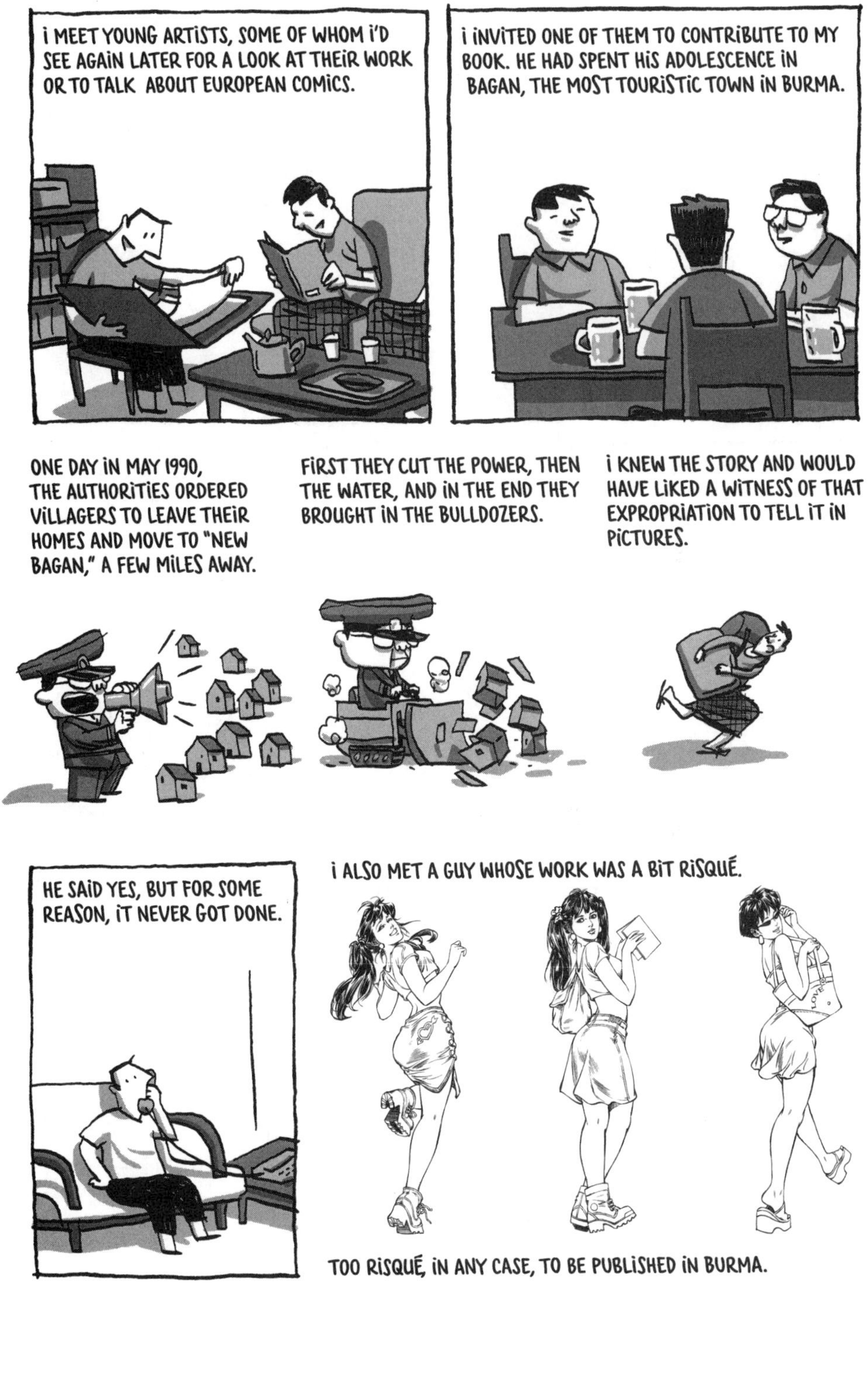
I MEET YOUNG ARTISTS, SOME OF WHOM I'D SEE AGAIN LATER FOR A LOOK AT THEIR WORK OR TO TALK ABOUT EUROPEAN COMICS.
I INVITED ONE OF THEM TO CONTRIBUTE TO MY BOOK. HE HAD SPENT HIS ADOLESCENCE IN BAGAN, THE MOST TOURISTIC TOWN IN BURMA.
ONE DAY IN MAY 1990, THE AUTHORITIES ORDERED VILLAGERS TO LEAVE THEIR HOMES AND MOVE TO "NEW BAGAN," A FEW MILES AWAY.
FIRST THEY CUT THE POWER, THEN THE WATER, AND IN THE END THEY BROUGHT IN THE BULLDOZERS.
I KNEW THE STORY AND WOULD HAVE LIKED A WITNESS OF THAT EXPROPRIATION TO TELL IT IN PICTURES.
HE SAID YES, BUT FOR SOME REASON, IT NEVER GOT DONE.
I ALSO MET A GUY WHOSE WORK WAS A BIT RISQUÉ.
LOVE
TOO RISQUÉ, IN ANY CASE, TO BE PUBLISHED IN BURMA.

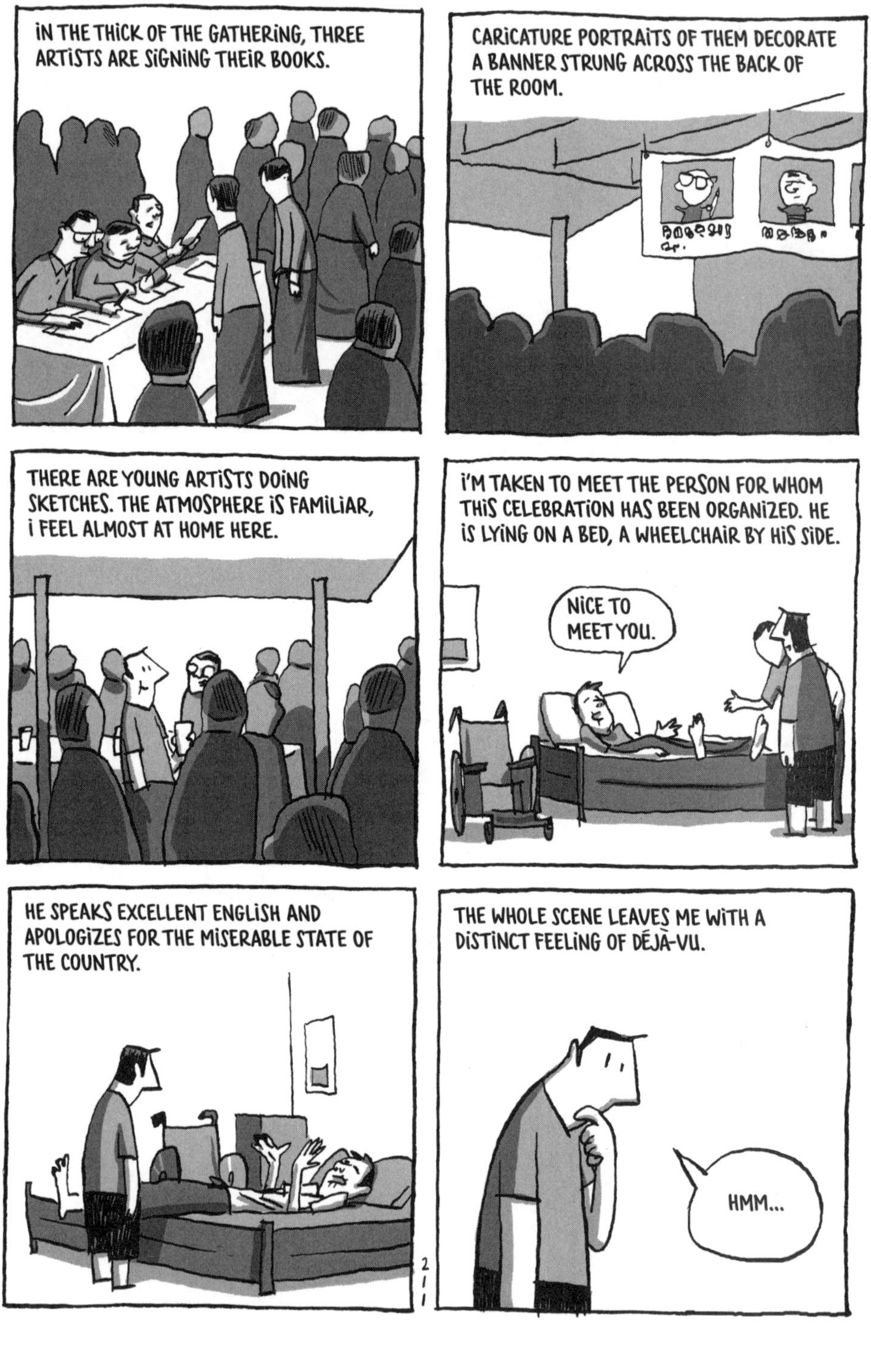
IN THE THICK OF THE GATHERING, THREE ARTISTS ARE SIGNING THEIR BOOKS.
CARICATURE PORTRAITS OF THEM DECORATE A BANNER STRUNG ACROSS THE BACK OF THE ROOM.
THERE ARE YOUNG ARTISTS DOING SKETCHES. THE ATMOSPHERE IS FAMILIAR, I FEEL ALMOST AT HOME HERE.
I'M TAKEN TO MEET THE PERSON FOR WHOM THIS CELEBRATION HAS BEEN ORGANIZED. HE IS LYING ON A BED, A WHEELCHAIR BY HIS SIDE.
NICE TO MEET YOU.
HE SPEAKS EXCELLENT ENGLISH AND APOLOGIZES FOR THE MISERABLE STATE OF THE COUNTRY.
THE WHOLE SCENE LEAVES ME WITH A DISTINCT FEELING OF DÉJÀ-VU.
HMM...

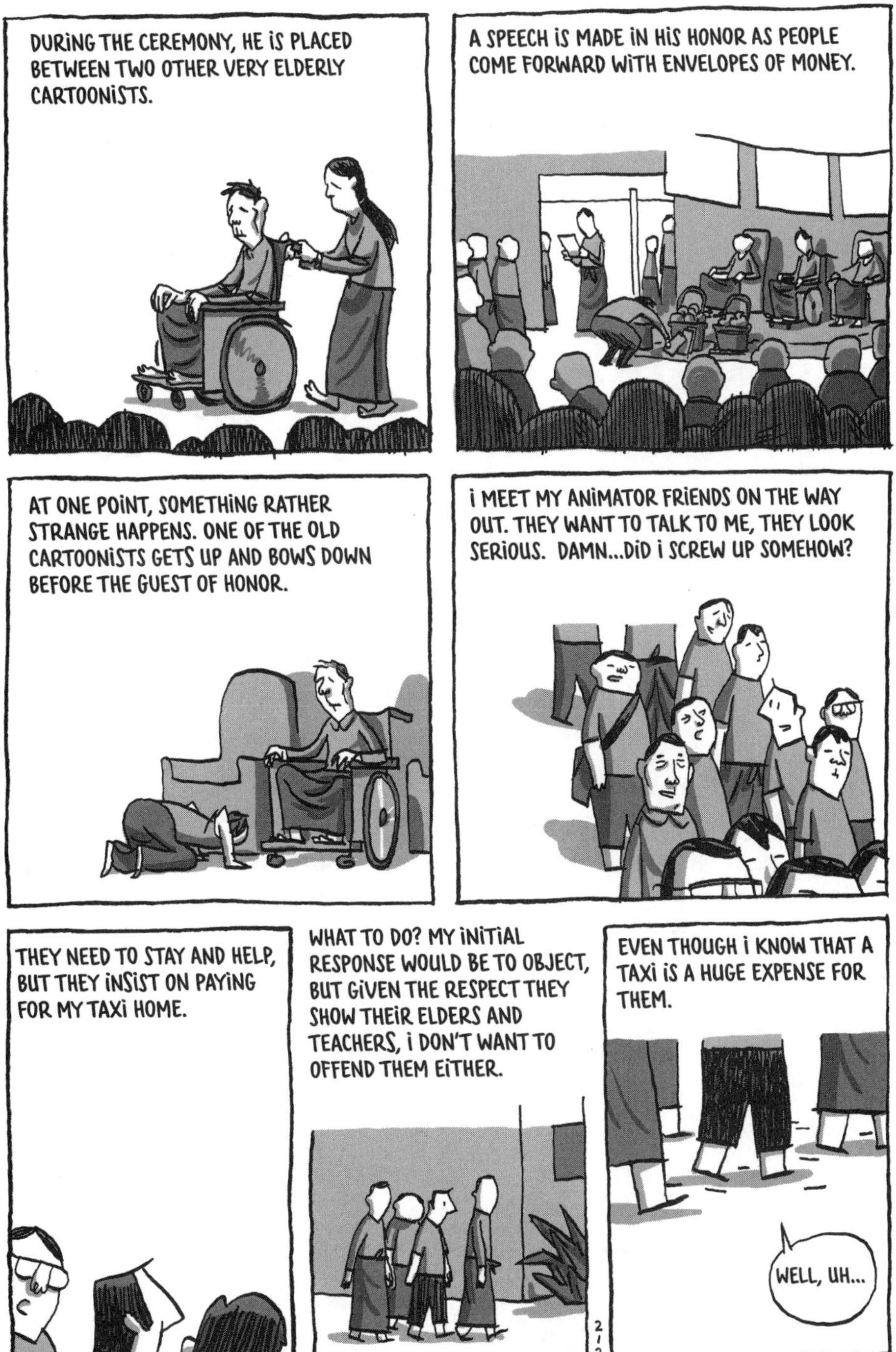
DURING THE CEREMONY, HE IS PLACED BETWEEN TWO OTHER VERY ELDERLY CARTOONISTS.
A SPEECH IS MADE IN HIS HONOR AS PEOPLE COME FORWARD WITH ENVELOPES OF MONEY.
AT ONE POINT, SOMETHING RATHER STRANGE HAPPENS. ONE OF THE OLD CARTOONISTS GETS UP AND BOWS DOWN BEFORE THE GUEST OF HONOR.
I MEET MY ANIMATOR FRIENDS ON THE WAY OUT. THEY WANT TO TALK TO ME, THEY LOOK SERIOUS. DAMN...DID I SCREW UP SOMEHOW?
THEY NEED TO STAY AND HELP, BUT THEY INSIST ON PAYING FOR MY TAXI HOME.
WHAT TO DO? MY INITIAL RESPONSE WOULD BE TO OBJECT, BUT GIVEN THE RESPECT THEY SHOW THEIR ELDERS AND TEACHERS, I DON'T WANT TO OFFEND THEM EITHER.
EVEN THOUGH I KNOW THAT A TAXI IS A HUGE EXPENSE FOR THEM.
WELL, UH...

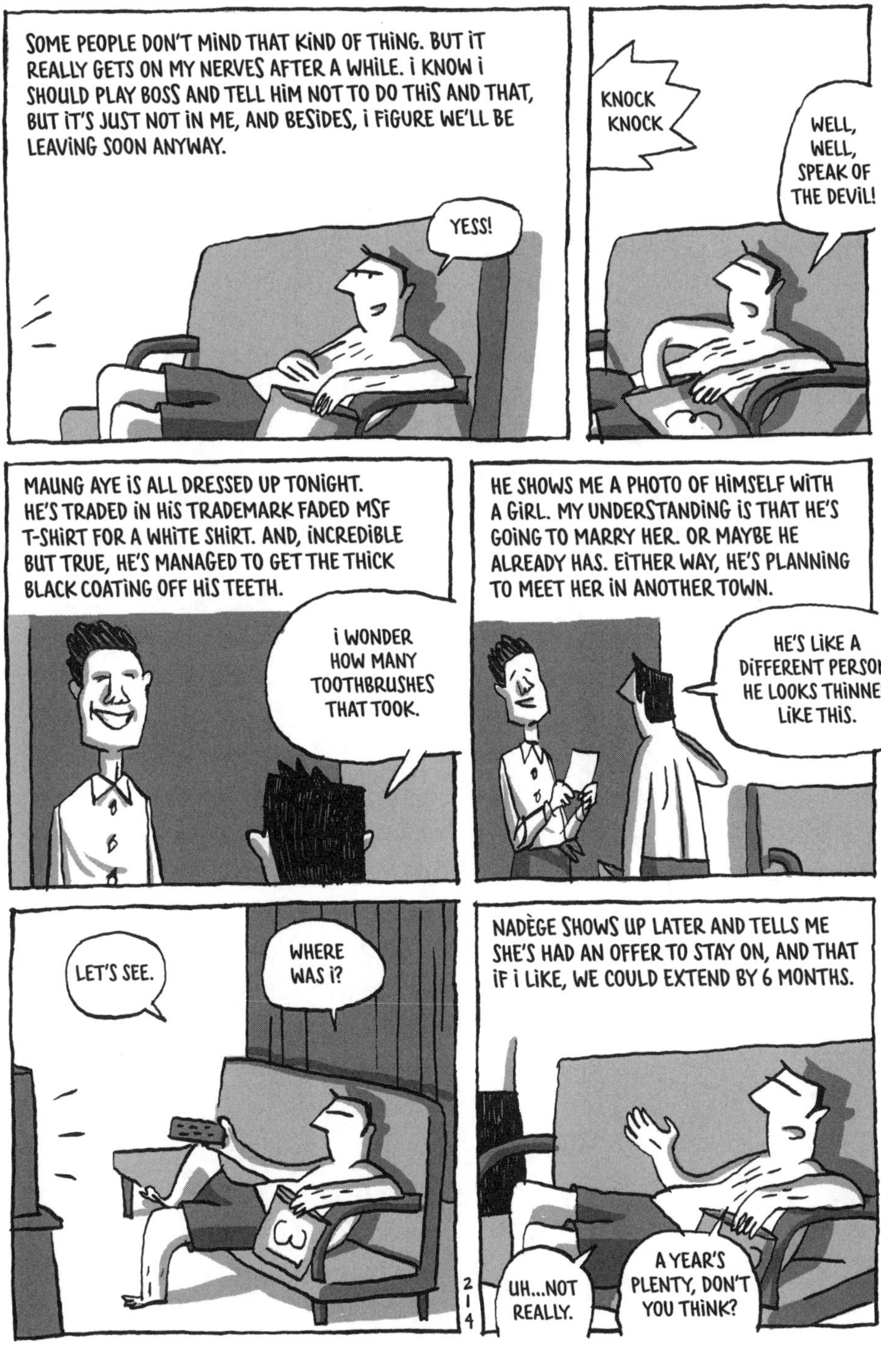
SOME PEOPLE DON'T MIND THAT KIND OF THING. BUT IT REALLY GETS ON MY NERVES AFTER A WHILE. I KNOW I SHOULD PLAY BOSS AND TELL HIM NOT TO DO THIS AND THAT, BUT IT'S JUST NOT IN ME, AND BESIDES, I FIGURE WE'LL BE LEAVING SOON ANYWAY.
YESS!
KNOCK KNOCK
WELL, WELL, SPEAK OF THE DEVIL!
MAUNG AYE IS ALL DRESSED UP TONIGHT. HE'S TRADED IN HIS TRADEMARK FADED MSF T-SHIRT FOR A WHITE SHIRT. AND, INCREDIBLE BUT TRUE, HE'S MANAGED TO GET THE THICK BLACK COATING OFF HIS TEETH.
I WONDER HOW MANY TOOTHBRUSHES THAT TOOK.
HE SHOWS ME A PHOTO OF HIMSELF WITH A GIRL. MY UNDERSTANDING IS THAT HE'S GOING TO MARRY HER. OR MAYBE HE ALREADY HAS. EITHER WAY, HE'S PLANNING TO MEET HER IN ANOTHER TOWN.
HE'S LIKE A DIFFERENT PERSON. HE LOOKS THINNER LIKE THIS.
LET'S SEE.
WHERE WAS I?
NADÈGE SHOWS UP LATER AND TELLS ME SHE'S HAD AN OFFER TO STAY ON, AND THAT IF I LIKE, WE COULD EXTEND BY 6 MONTHS.
UH...NOT REALLY.
A YEAR'S PLENTY, DON'T YOU THINK?

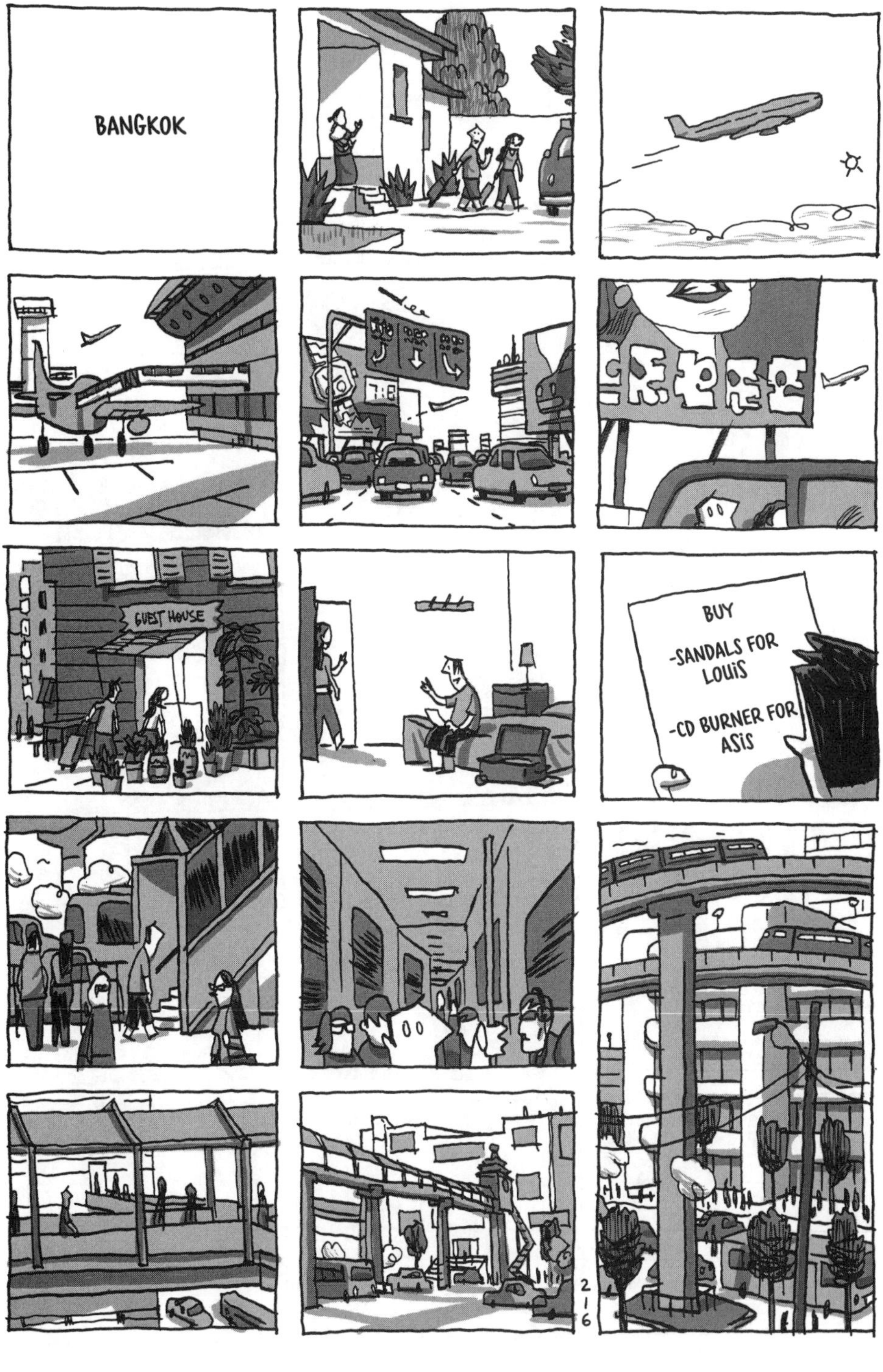
BANGKOK
GUEST HOUSE
BUY
-SANDALS FOR LOUiS
-CD BURNER FOR ASiS

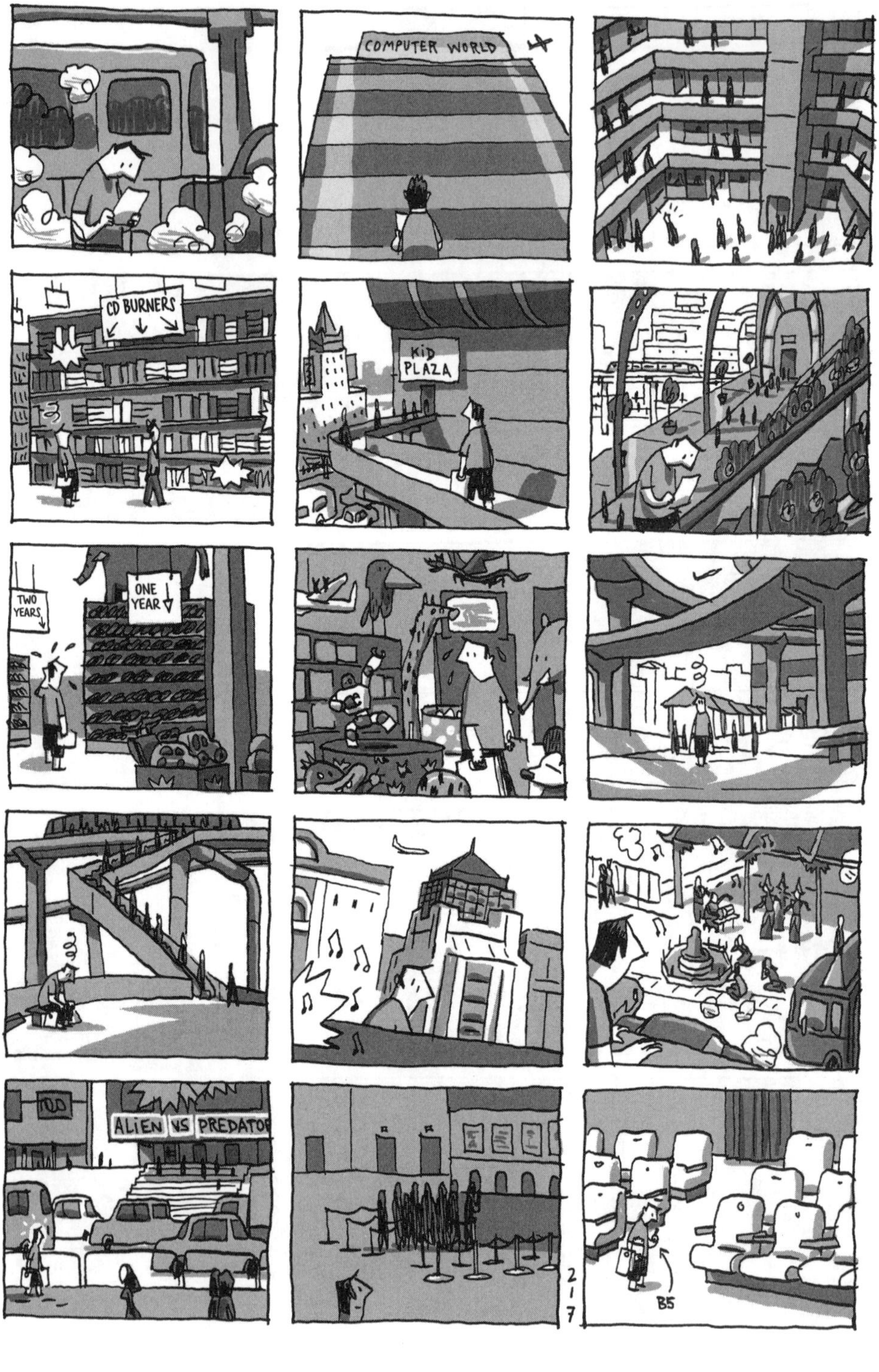
COMPUTER WORLD
CD BURNERS
KID PLAZA
TWO YEARS
ONE YEAR
ALIEN VS PREDATOR
B5

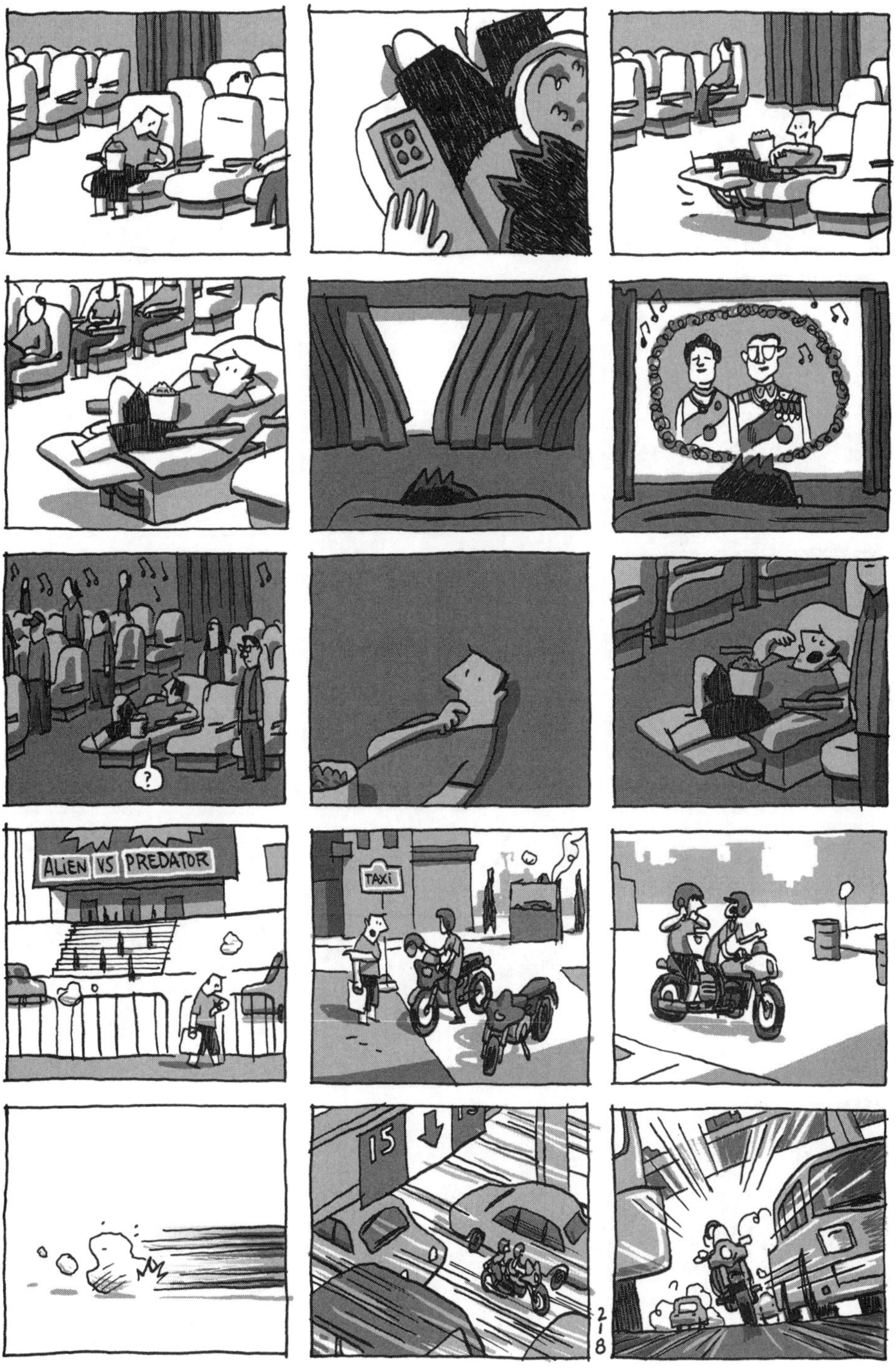

?
ALIEN VS PREDATOR
TAXI
15

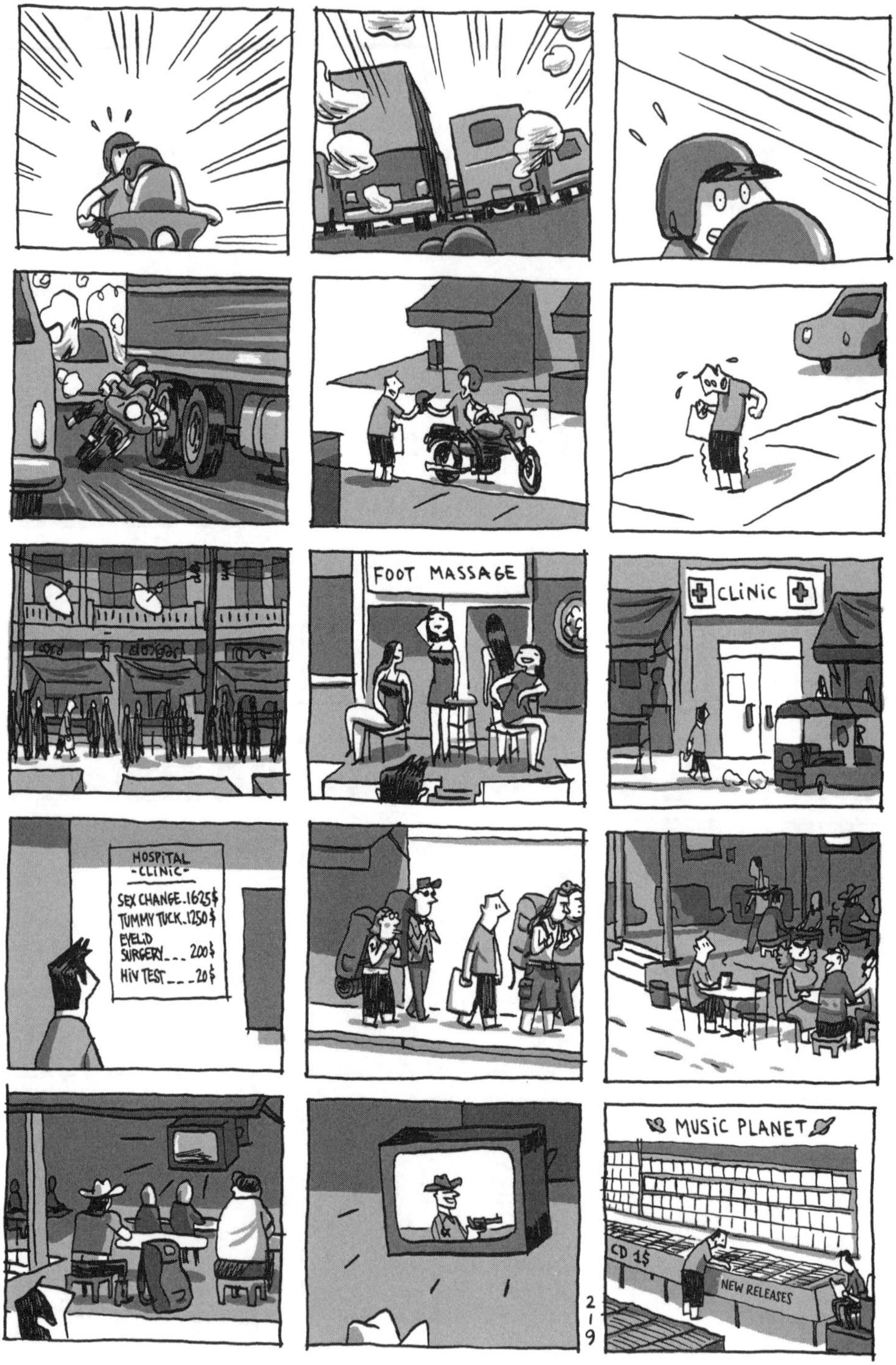
FOOT MASSAGE
CLINIC
HOSPITAL
-CLINIC-
SEX CHANGE.1625$
TUMMY TUCK.1250$
EYELID SURGERY___200$
HIV TEST___20$
MUSIC PLANET
CD 1$
NEW RELEASES

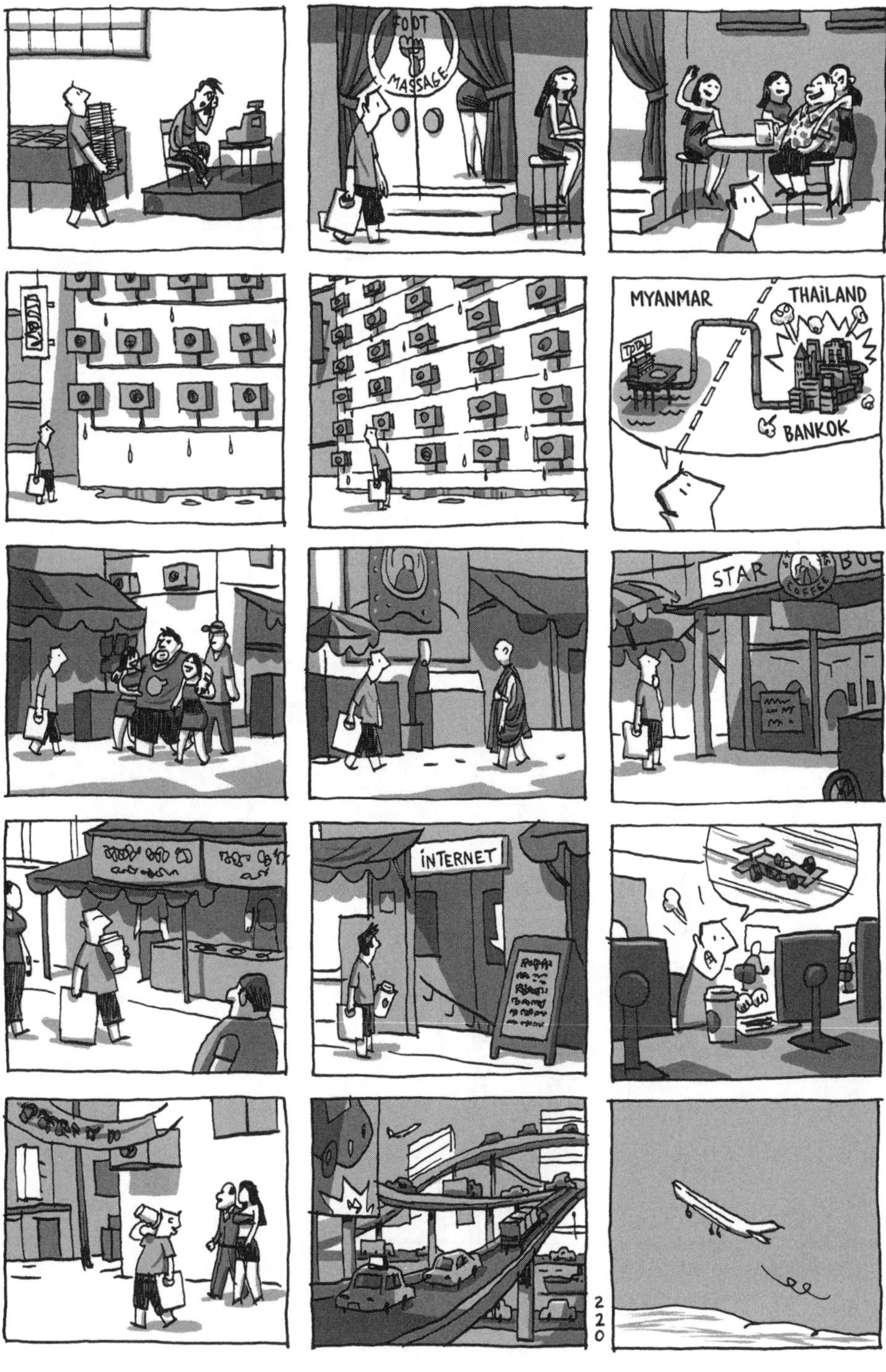
FOOT
MASSAGE
MYANMAR
THAILAND
TOTAL
BANKOK
STAR
COFFEE
INTERNET

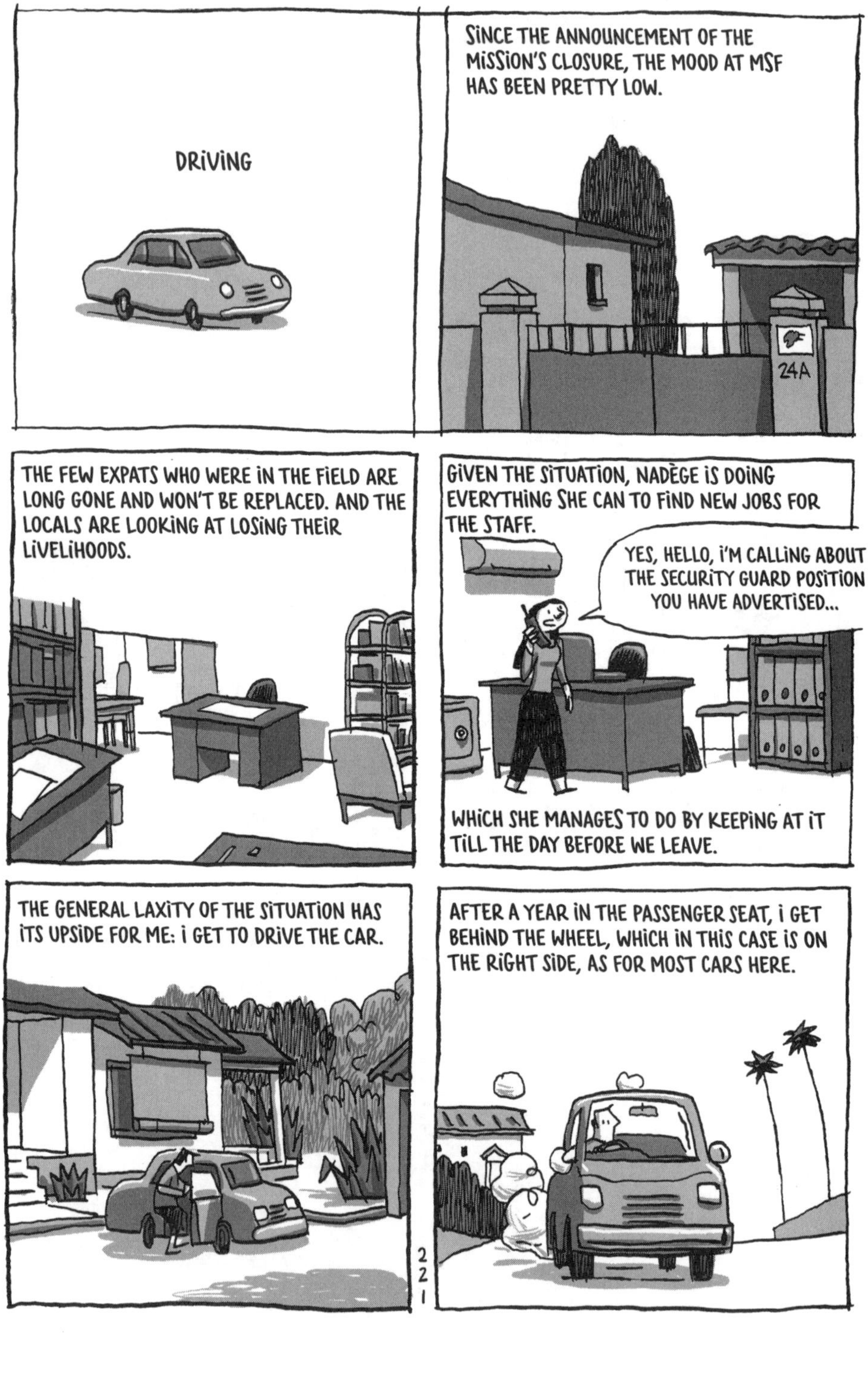
DRIVING
SINCE THE ANNOUNCEMENT OF THE MISSION'S CLOSURE, THE MOOD AT MSF HAS BEEN PRETTY LOW.
24A
THE FEW EXPATS WHO WERE IN THE FIELD ARE LONG GONE AND WON'T BE REPLACED. AND THE LOCALS ARE LOOKING AT LOSING THEIR LIVELIHOODS.
GIVEN THE SITUATION, NADÈGE IS DOING EVERYTHING SHE CAN TO FIND NEW JOBS FOR THE STAFF.
YES, HELLO, I'M CALLING ABOUT THE SECURITY GUARD POSITION YOU HAVE ADVERTISED...
WHICH SHE MANAGES TO DO BY KEEPING AT IT TILL THE DAY BEFORE WE LEAVE.
THE GENERAL LAXITY OF THE SITUATION HAS ITS UPSIDE FOR ME: I GET TO DRIVE THE CAR.
AFTER A YEAR IN THE PASSENGER SEAT, I GET BEHIND THE WHEEL, WHICH IN THIS CASE IS ON THE RIGHT SIDE, AS FOR MOST CARS HERE.

IN WHAT'S SURELY A UNIQUE SITUATION IN THE WORLD OF ROAD TRAFFIC, THE BURMESE DRIVE ON THE RIGHT, IN RIGHT-HAND DRIVE CARS—THAT'S TWICE TO THE RIGHT. FOR TWO REASONS.

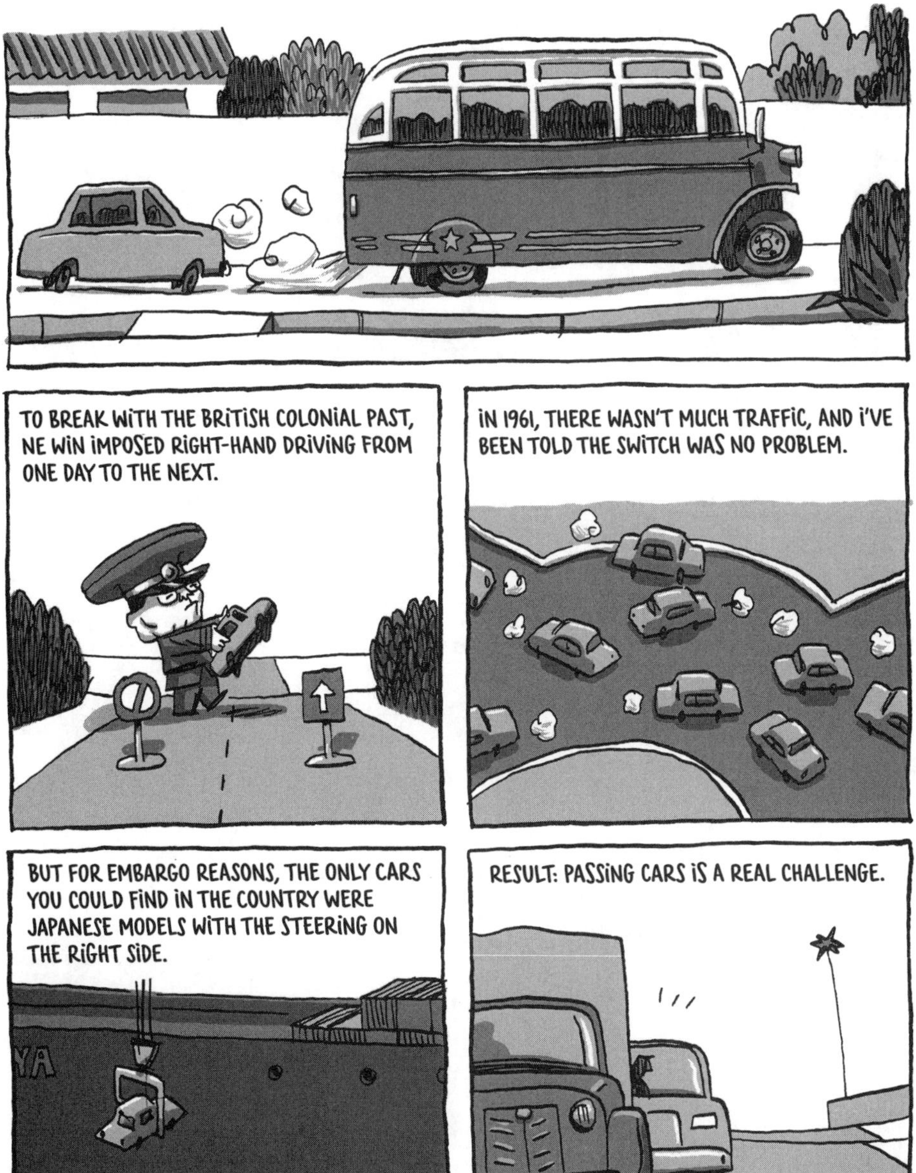

TO BREAK WITH THE BRITISH COLONIAL PAST, NE WIN IMPOSED RIGHT-HAND DRIVING FROM ONE DAY TO THE NEXT.
IN 1961, THERE WASN'T MUCH TRAFFIC, AND I'VE BEEN TOLD THE SWITCH WAS NO PROBLEM.
BUT FOR EMBARGO REASONS, THE ONLY CARS YOU COULD FIND IN THE COUNTRY WERE JAPANESE MODELS WITH THE STEERING ON THE RIGHT SIDE.
YA
RESULT: PASSING CARS IS A REAL CHALLENGE.

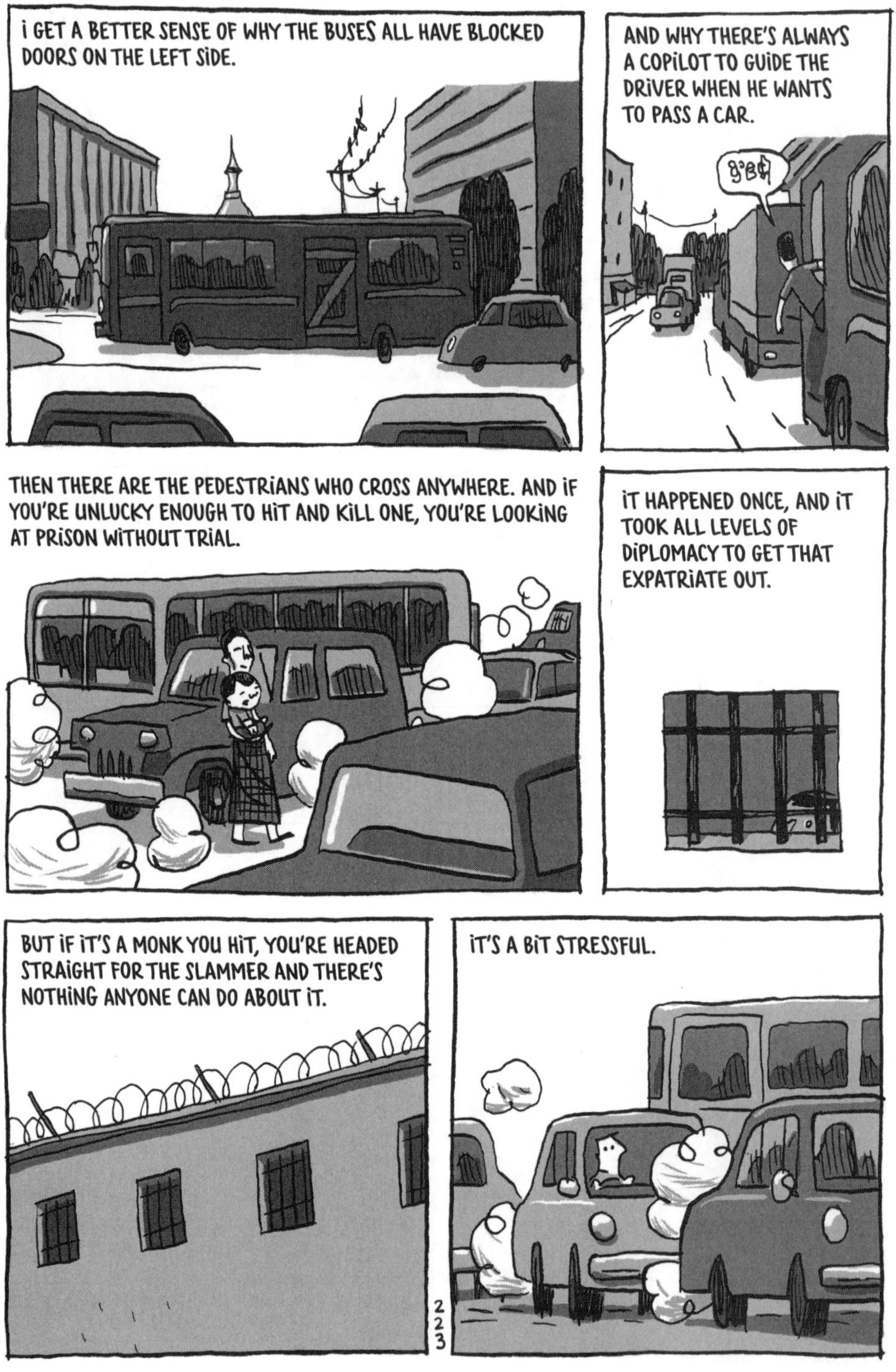
I GET A BETTER SENSE OF WHY THE BUSES ALL HAVE BLOCKED DOORS ON THE LEFT SIDE.
AND WHY THERE'S ALWAYS A COPILOT TO GUIDE THE DRIVER WHEN HE WANTS TO PASS A CAR.
THEN THERE ARE THE PEDESTRIANS WHO CROSS ANYWHERE. AND IF YOU'RE UNLUCKY ENOUGH TO HIT AND KILL ONE, YOU'RE LOOKING AT PRISON WITHOUT TRIAL.
IT HAPPENED ONCE, AND IT TOOK ALL LEVELS OF DIPLOMACY TO GET THAT EXPATRIATE OUT.
BUT IF IT'S A MONK YOU HIT, YOU'RE HEADED STRAIGHT FOR THE SLAMMER AND THERE'S NOTHING ANYONE CAN DO ABOUT IT.
IT'S A BIT STRESSFUL.

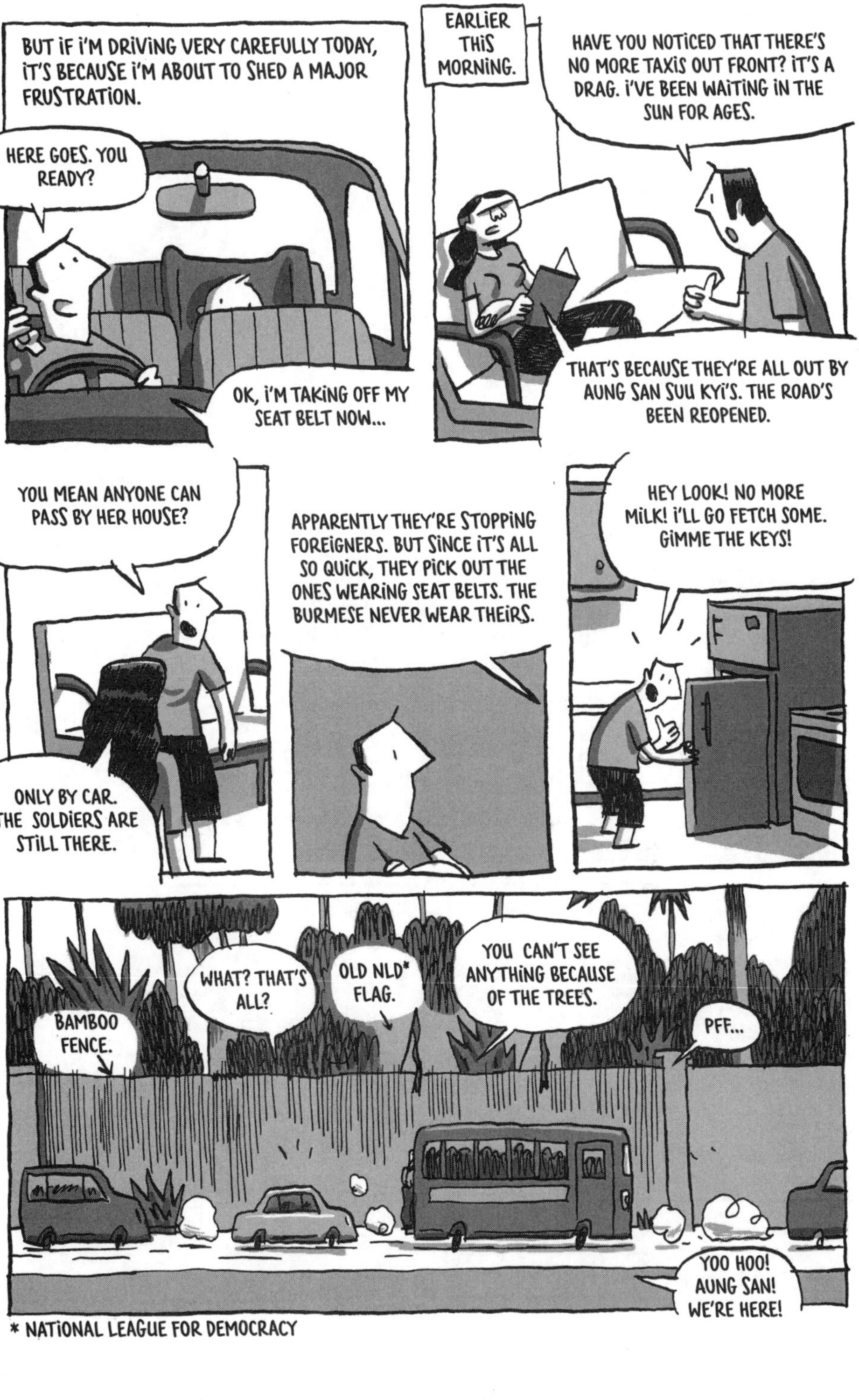
BUT IF I'M DRIVING VERY CAREFULLY TODAY, IT'S BECAUSE I'M ABOUT TO SHED A MAJOR FRUSTRATION.
HERE GOES. YOU READY?
OK, I'M TAKING OFF MY SEAT BELT NOW...
EARLIER THIS MORNING.
HAVE YOU NOTICED THAT THERE'S NO MORE TAXIS OUT FRONT? IT'S A DRAG. I'VE BEEN WAITING IN THE SUN FOR AGES.
THAT'S BECAUSE THEY'RE ALL OUT BY AUNG SAN SUU KYI'S. THE ROAD'S BEEN REOPENED.
YOU MEAN ANYONE CAN PASS BY HER HOUSE?
ONLY BY CAR. THE SOLDIERS ARE STILL THERE.
APPARENTLY THEY'RE STOPPING FOREIGNERS. BUT SINCE IT'S ALL SO QUICK, THEY PICK OUT THE ONES WEARING SEAT BELTS. THE BURMESE NEVER WEAR THEIRS.
HEY LOOK! NO MORE MILK! I'LL GO FETCH SOME. GIMME THE KEYS!
BAMBOO FENCE.
WHAT? THAT'S ALL?
OLD NLD* FLAG.
YOU CAN'T SEE ANYTHING BECAUSE OF THE TREES.
PFF...
YOO HOO! AUNG SAN! WE'RE HERE!

* NATIONAL LEAGUE FOR DEMOCRACY

BACK IN THE FIELD

I'M GOING OUT INTO THE FIELD FOR A SECOND AND LAST TIME BEFORE THE MISSION SHUTS DOWN.

THIS TIME, I'VE BROUGHT A HAT.

ASIS

BUT I STILL DON'T HAVE A PERMIT TO TRAVEL IN THE ZONES WHERE THE MSF CLINICS ARE LOCATED, SO WE ARRANGE WITH ASIS THAT I'LL SLEEP IN MOULMEIN, THE TOURIST TOWN, AND THEN JOIN THEM ON THEIR VISITS DURING THE DAY.

THE NIGHT IS PRETTY GOOD, I'M LESS COLD THAN LAST TIME.

KUNG FU FILM →

TOWEL

BUT EARLY THE NEXT DAY...

225

OUR BUS STALLS A FEW MILES FROM OUR DESTINATION. WE START BY WAITING FOR REPAIRS, BUT END UP, LIKE ALL THE OTHER PASSENGERS, STOPPING LOCAL BUSES TO FINISH OUR JOURNEY.

ASIS AND NADÉGE, WITH THEIR DARKER COMPLEXIONS, BLEND INTO THE CROWD. PEOPLE TALK TO THEM IN BURMESE. THEY PRETEND TO UNDERSTAND AND COLLECT THEIR CHANGE.

OF COURSE, I LOOK LIKE A STRANDED TOURIST AND A KIND TRANSLATOR OFFERS HIS HELP.

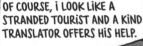

HE EXPLAINS...
YOU WANT TAKE WITH VILLAGE?

UH... YES, OKAY. THANKS.

OH!

LET'S SEE: NO...OPIUM, SHOOTING UP OR SMOKING ...IS THAT A CIGARETTE?

WE GET TO OUR DESTINATION A FEW HOURS LATE. AN MSF CAR COMES TO TAKE US TO MUDON. I'LL NEED TO MAKE THE TRIP BACK TONIGHT TO SLEEP AT THE HOTEL.

THINGS ARE MUCH QUIETER NOW IN THE BIG HOUSE IN MUDON. THE EXPATS HAVE LEFT AND ACTIVITIES HAVE WOUND DOWN. FOR ALL THE STAFF HERE, IT'S THE END OF AN ERA.

ASIS STAYS TO DO INVENTORY WHILE I LEAVE WITH NADÈGE TO VISIT THE FAMOUS CLINICS.

WE DRIVE PAST MILES OF RICE PADDIES.

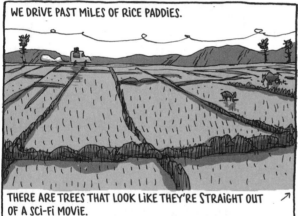

THERE ARE TREES THAT LOOK LIKE THEY'RE STRAIGHT OUT OF A SCI-FI MOVIE. ↗

NEXT, WE PASS BY A SERIES OF RUBBER PLANTATIONS.

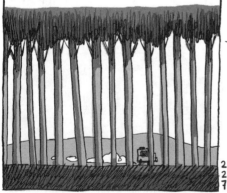

SEE, THE PLANTATION WORKERS OFTEN GET SICK BECAUSE THEY HARVEST THE SAP AT NIGHTFALL, AND THAT'S WHEN MALARIA-CARRYING MOSQUITOES ARE ACTIVE.

IS THIS IT?

227

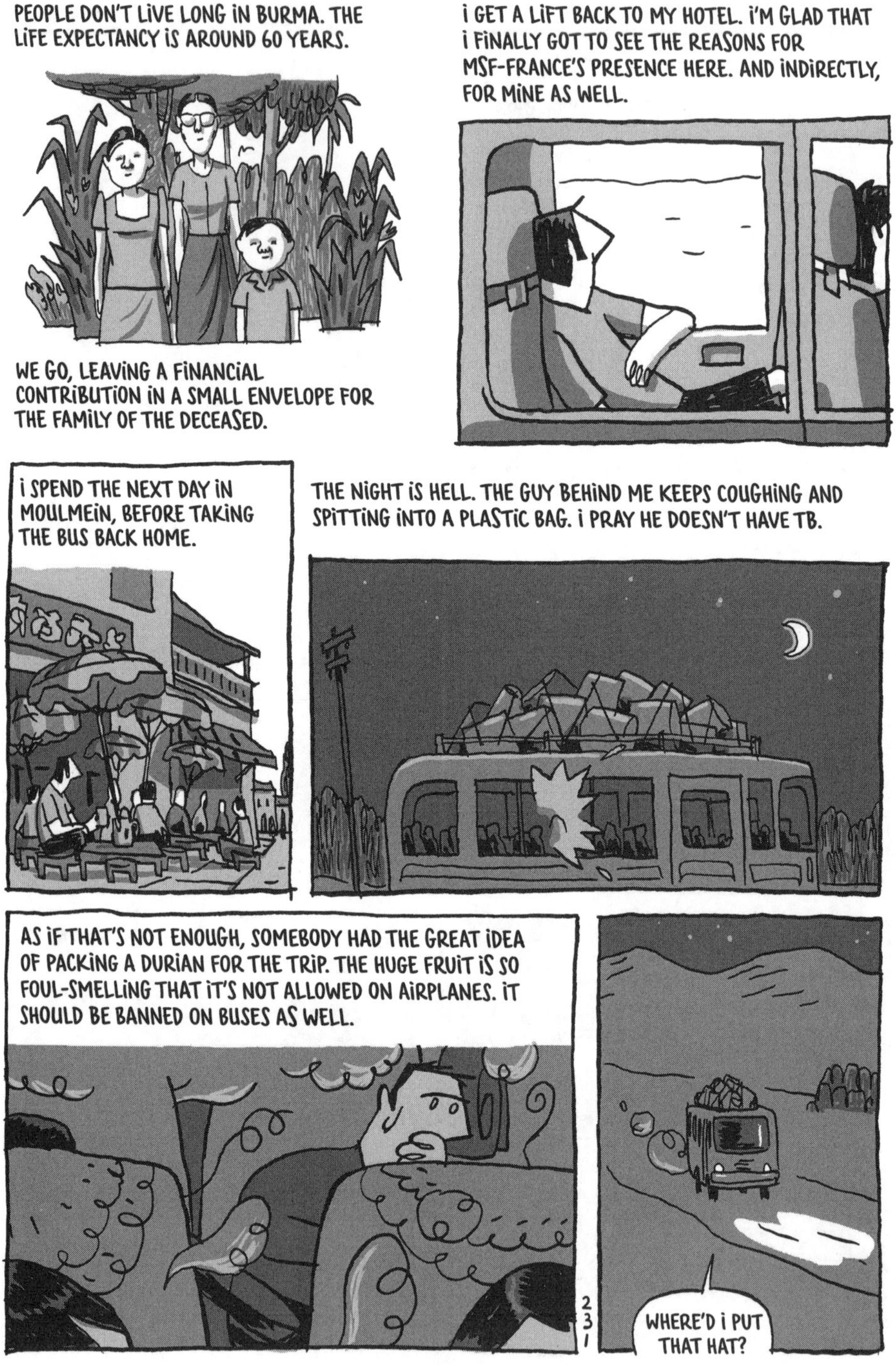
PEOPLE DON'T LIVE LONG IN BURMA. THE LIFE EXPECTANCY IS AROUND 60 YEARS.
WE GO, LEAVING A FINANCIAL CONTRIBUTION IN A SMALL ENVELOPE FOR THE FAMILY OF THE DECEASED.
I GET A LIFT BACK TO MY HOTEL. I'M GLAD THAT I FINALLY GOT TO SEE THE REASONS FOR MSF-FRANCE'S PRESENCE HERE. AND INDIRECTLY, FOR MINE AS WELL.
I SPEND THE NEXT DAY IN MOULMEIN, BEFORE TAKING THE BUS BACK HOME.
THE NIGHT IS HELL. THE GUY BEHIND ME KEEPS COUGHING AND SPITTING INTO A PLASTIC BAG. I PRAY HE DOESN'T HAVE TB.
AS IF THAT'S NOT ENOUGH, SOMEBODY HAD THE GREAT IDEA OF PACKING A DURIAN FOR THE TRIP. THE HUGE FRUIT IS SO FOUL-SMELLING THAT IT'S NOT ALLOWED ON AIRPLANES. IT SHOULD BE BANNED ON BUSES AS WELL.
WHERE'D I PUT THAT HAT?

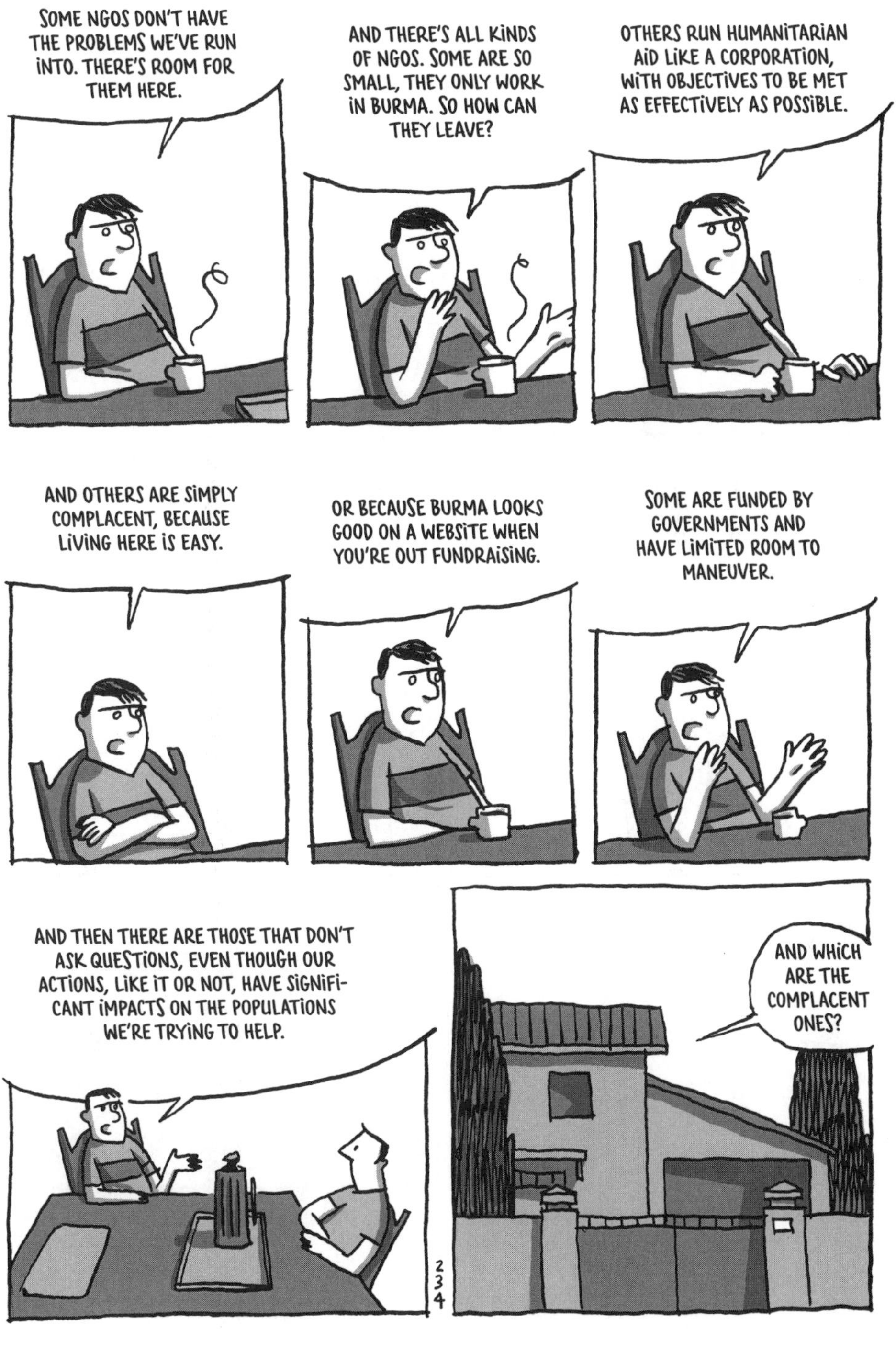
SOME NGOS DON'T HAVE THE PROBLEMS WE'VE RUN INTO. THERE'S ROOM FOR THEM HERE.
AND THERE'S ALL KINDS OF NGOS. SOME ARE SO SMALL, THEY ONLY WORK IN BURMA. SO HOW CAN THEY LEAVE?
OTHERS RUN HUMANITARIAN AID LIKE A CORPORATION, WITH OBJECTIVES TO BE MET AS EFFECTIVELY AS POSSIBLE.
AND OTHERS ARE SIMPLY COMPLACENT, BECAUSE LIVING HERE IS EASY.
OR BECAUSE BURMA LOOKS GOOD ON A WEBSITE WHEN YOU'RE OUT FUNDRAISING.
SOME ARE FUNDED BY GOVERNMENTS AND HAVE LIMITED ROOM TO MANEUVER.
AND THEN THERE ARE THOSE THAT DON'T ASK QUESTIONS, EVEN THOUGH OUR ACTIONS, LIKE IT OR NOT, HAVE SIGNIFI-CANT IMPACTS ON THE POPULATIONS WE'RE TRYING TO HELP.
AND WHICH ARE THE COMPLACENT ONES?

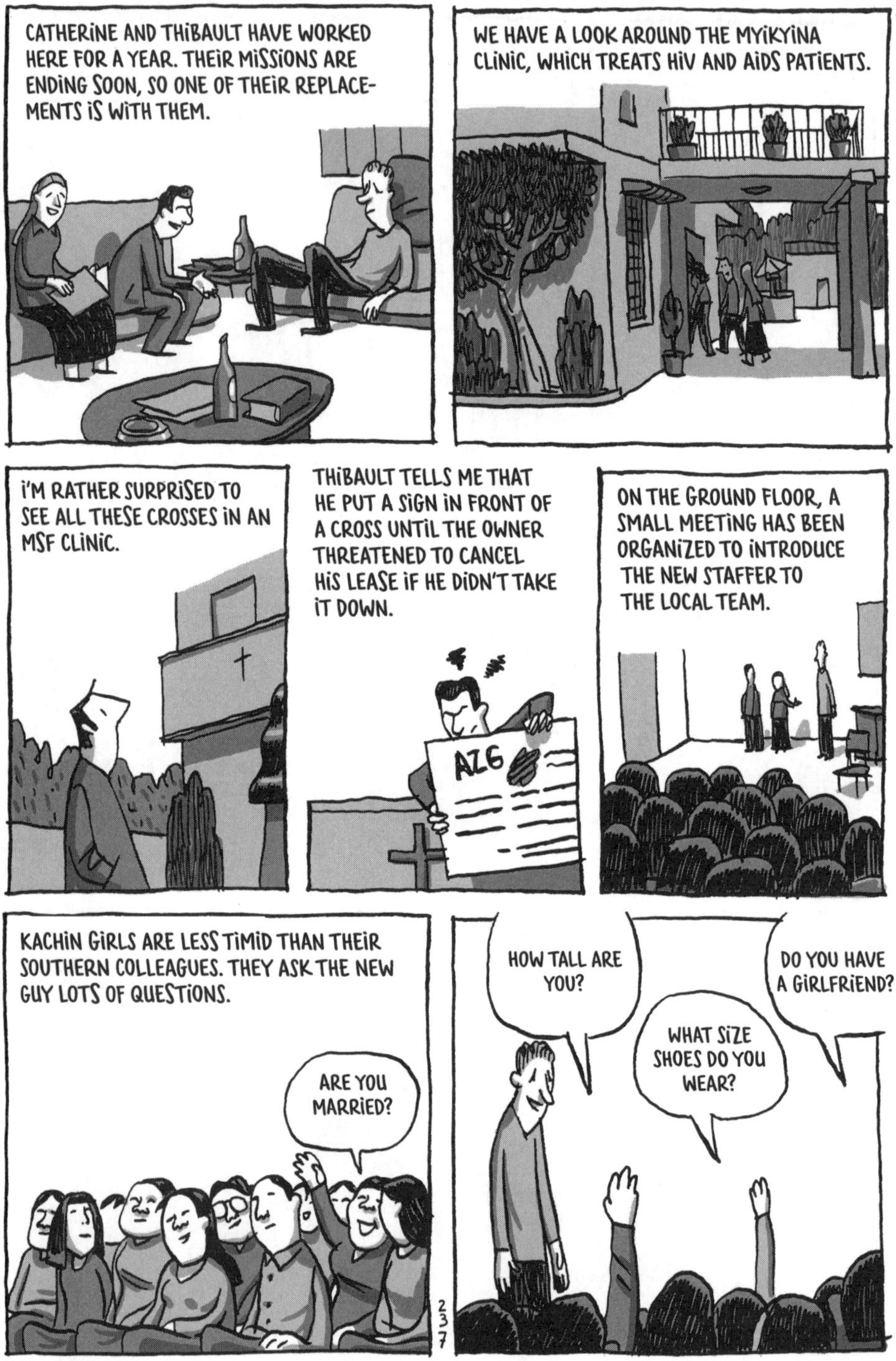
CATHERINE AND THIBAULT HAVE WORKED HERE FOR A YEAR. THEIR MISSIONS ARE ENDING SOON, SO ONE OF THEIR REPLACEMENTS IS WITH THEM.
WE HAVE A LOOK AROUND THE MYIKYINA CLINIC, WHICH TREATS HIV AND AIDS PATIENTS.
I'M RATHER SURPRISED TO SEE ALL THESE CROSSES IN AN MSF CLINIC.
THIBAULT TELLS ME THAT HE PUT A SIGN IN FRONT OF A CROSS UNTIL THE OWNER THREATENED TO CANCEL HIS LEASE IF HE DIDN'T TAKE IT DOWN.
AZG
ON THE GROUND FLOOR, A SMALL MEETING HAS BEEN ORGANIZED TO INTRODUCE THE NEW STAFFER TO THE LOCAL TEAM.
KACHIN GIRLS ARE LESS TIMID THAN THEIR SOUTHERN COLLEAGUES. THEY ASK THE NEW GUY LOTS OF QUESTIONS.
ARE YOU MARRIED?
HOW TALL ARE YOU?
WHAT SIZE SHOES DO YOU WEAR?
DO YOU HAVE A GIRLFRIEND?

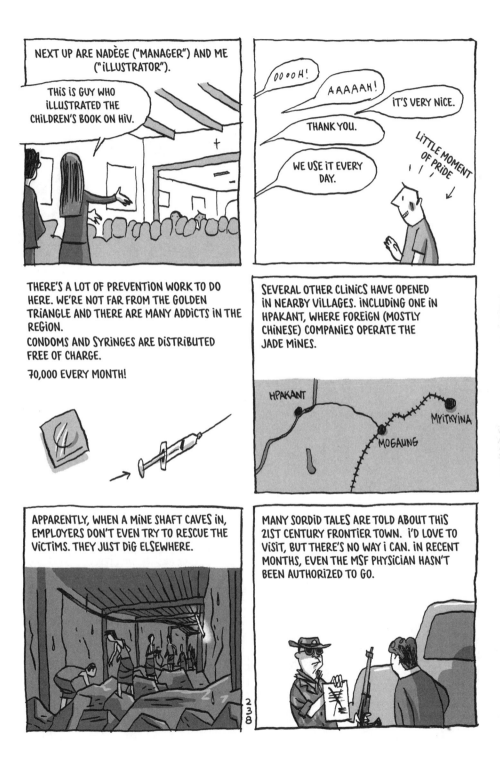

NEXT UP ARE NADÈGE ("MANAGER") AND ME ("ILLUSTRATOR").

THIS IS GUY WHO ILLUSTRATED THE CHILDREN'S BOOK ON HIV.

OOOOH!

AAAAAH!

IT'S VERY NICE.

THANK YOU.

WE USE IT EVERY DAY.

LITTLE MOMENT OF PRIDE

THERE'S A LOT OF PREVENTION WORK TO DO HERE. WE'RE NOT FAR FROM THE GOLDEN TRIANGLE AND THERE ARE MANY ADDICTS IN THE REGION.
CONDOMS AND SYRINGES ARE DISTRIBUTED FREE OF CHARGE.

70,000 EVERY MONTH!

SEVERAL OTHER CLINICS HAVE OPENED IN NEARBY VILLAGES. INCLUDING ONE IN HPAKANT, WHERE FOREIGN (MOSTLY CHINESE) COMPANIES OPERATE THE JADE MINES.

HPAKANT

MYITKYINA

MOGAUNG

APPARENTLY, WHEN A MINE SHAFT CAVES IN, EMPLOYERS DON'T EVEN TRY TO RESCUE THE VICTIMS. THEY JUST DIG ELSEWHERE.

MANY SORDID TALES ARE TOLD ABOUT THIS 21ST CENTURY FRONTIER TOWN. I'D LOVE TO VISIT, BUT THERE'S NO WAY I CAN. IN RECENT MONTHS, EVEN THE MSF PHYSICIAN HASN'T BEEN AUTHORIZED TO GO.

238

THAT'S CHINA OVER THERE.

OH, HEY, WE REALLY ARE NEXT DOOR.

SINCE WE CAN'T VISIT HPAKANT, WE GO FOR A RIDE IN THE COUNTRYSIDE.

I THINK THIS IS A CEMETERY FOR THE VICTIMS OF BURMA'S STRUGGLE FOR INDEPENDENCE.

AND WHAT'S THIS?

I DON'T KNOW.

WE COME ACROSS A MYSTERIOUS STRUCTURE.

IT'S A LITTLE ROOM, WITH A CHAIR IN THE MIDDLE.

THERE'S OTHERS.

LET'S SEE.

IT'S GOT TWO FLOORS.

WITH AN INNER COURTYARD.

WITH SMALL ROOMS EVERYWHERE.

AND A CHAIR IN EACH ROOM.

THERE'S A CROSS HERE!

HEY, I'VE GOT IT! IT'S A PLACE OF PRAYER.

ASTONISHING LAYOUT, HUH?

IT'S LIKE YOU'RE IN A JODOROWSKY* COMIC.

...AND WITH FERVENT WORSHIPPERS IN EVERY ROOM, A MYSTICAL ENERGY TAKES HOLD OF THE BUILDING, WHICH STARTS TO SPIN AND LIFTS OFF LIKE A UFO.

DON'T YOU THINK?

240

*FAMOUS SCIENCE FICTION COMICS WRITER

WE GO BACK TO THE GROUND FLOOR, WHERE THE REGULARS HAVE ARRIVED. THERE ARE 3 SPRAWLED OUT ON MATS, 2 PLAYING PING PONG IN THE COURTYARD AND ONE LEANING AGAINST A COLUMN, TRYING TO TAKE AN OLD GUITAR DOWN FROM ITS HOOK.

THE VILLAGE IS DEAD SILENT, NOT A SOUL IN SIGHT.

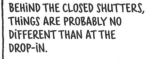

BEHIND THE CLOSED SHUTTERS, THINGS ARE PROBABLY NO DIFFERENT THAN AT THE DROP-IN.

IT MAKES YOU WONDER HOW THE GOVERNMENT CAN PUT UP WITH SUCH A SITUATION.

IN MY HUMBLE OPINION, IT SUITS THE GOVERNMENT FINE. THEY'D PROBABLY PREFER TO SEE YOUNG KACHINS STONED TO THE GILLS THAN TAKING UP ARMS AND JOINING THE RANKS OF THE RESISTANCE.

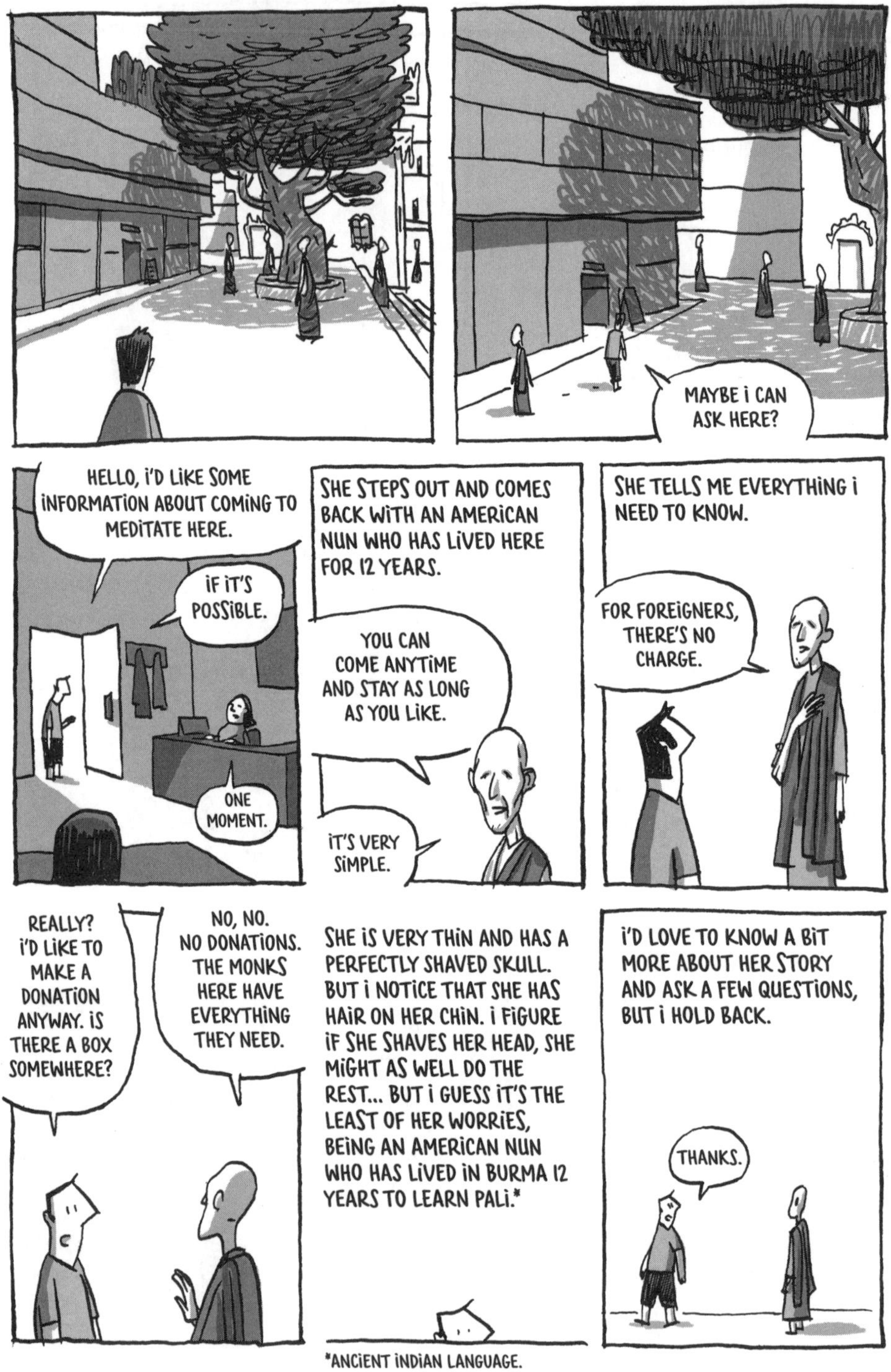
MAYBE I CAN ASK HERE?
HELLO, I'D LIKE SOME INFORMATION ABOUT COMING TO MEDITATE HERE.
IF IT'S POSSIBLE.
ONE MOMENT.
SHE STEPS OUT AND COMES BACK WITH AN AMERICAN NUN WHO HAS LIVED HERE FOR 12 YEARS.
YOU CAN COME ANYTIME AND STAY AS LONG AS YOU LIKE.
IT'S VERY SIMPLE.
SHE TELLS ME EVERYTHING I NEED TO KNOW.
FOR FOREIGNERS, THERE'S NO CHARGE.
REALLY? I'D LIKE TO MAKE A DONATION ANYWAY. IS THERE A BOX SOMEWHERE?
NO, NO. NO DONATIONS. THE MONKS HERE HAVE EVERYTHING THEY NEED.
SHE IS VERY THIN AND HAS A PERFECTLY SHAVED SKULL. BUT I NOTICE THAT SHE HAS HAIR ON HER CHIN. I FIGURE IF SHE SHAVES HER HEAD, SHE MIGHT AS WELL DO THE REST... BUT I GUESS IT'S THE LEAST OF HER WORRIES, BEING AN AMERICAN NUN WHO HAS LIVED IN BURMA 12 YEARS TO LEARN PALI.*
I'D LOVE TO KNOW A BIT MORE ABOUT HER STORY AND ASK A FEW QUESTIONS, BUT I HOLD BACK.
THANKS.

*ANCIENT INDIAN LANGUAGE.

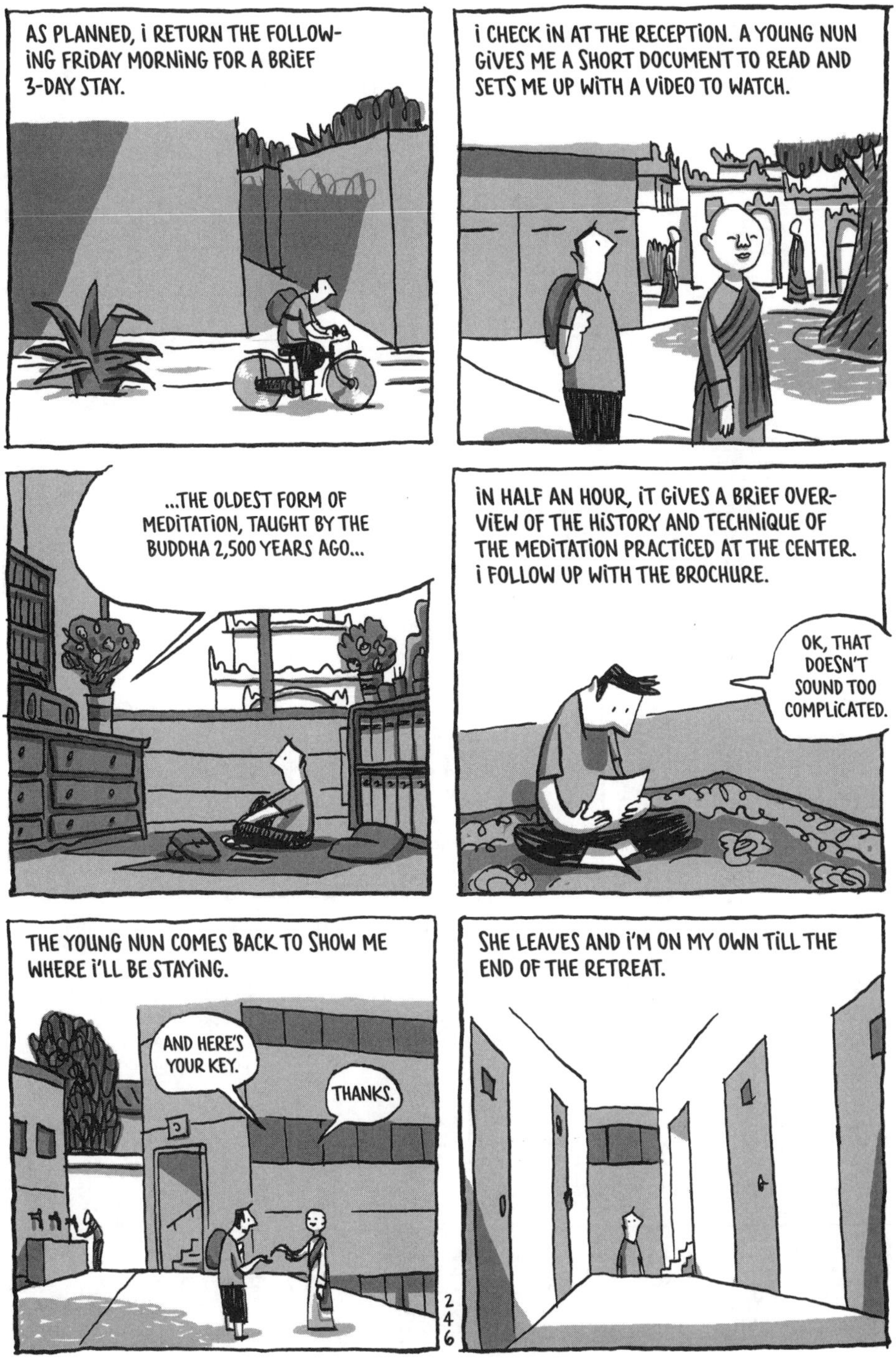
AS PLANNED, I RETURN THE FOLLOWING FRIDAY MORNING FOR A BRIEF 3-DAY STAY.
I CHECK IN AT THE RECEPTION. A YOUNG NUN GIVES ME A SHORT DOCUMENT TO READ AND SETS ME UP WITH A VIDEO TO WATCH.
...THE OLDEST FORM OF MEDITATION, TAUGHT BY THE BUDDHA 2,500 YEARS AGO...
IN HALF AN HOUR, IT GIVES A BRIEF OVERVIEW OF THE HISTORY AND TECHNIQUE OF THE MEDITATION PRACTICED AT THE CENTER. I FOLLOW UP WITH THE BROCHURE.
OK, THAT DOESN'T SOUND TOO COMPLICATED.
THE YOUNG NUN COMES BACK TO SHOW ME WHERE I'LL BE STAYING.
AND HERE'S YOUR KEY.
THANKS.
SHE LEAVES AND I'M ON MY OWN TILL THE END OF THE RETREAT.

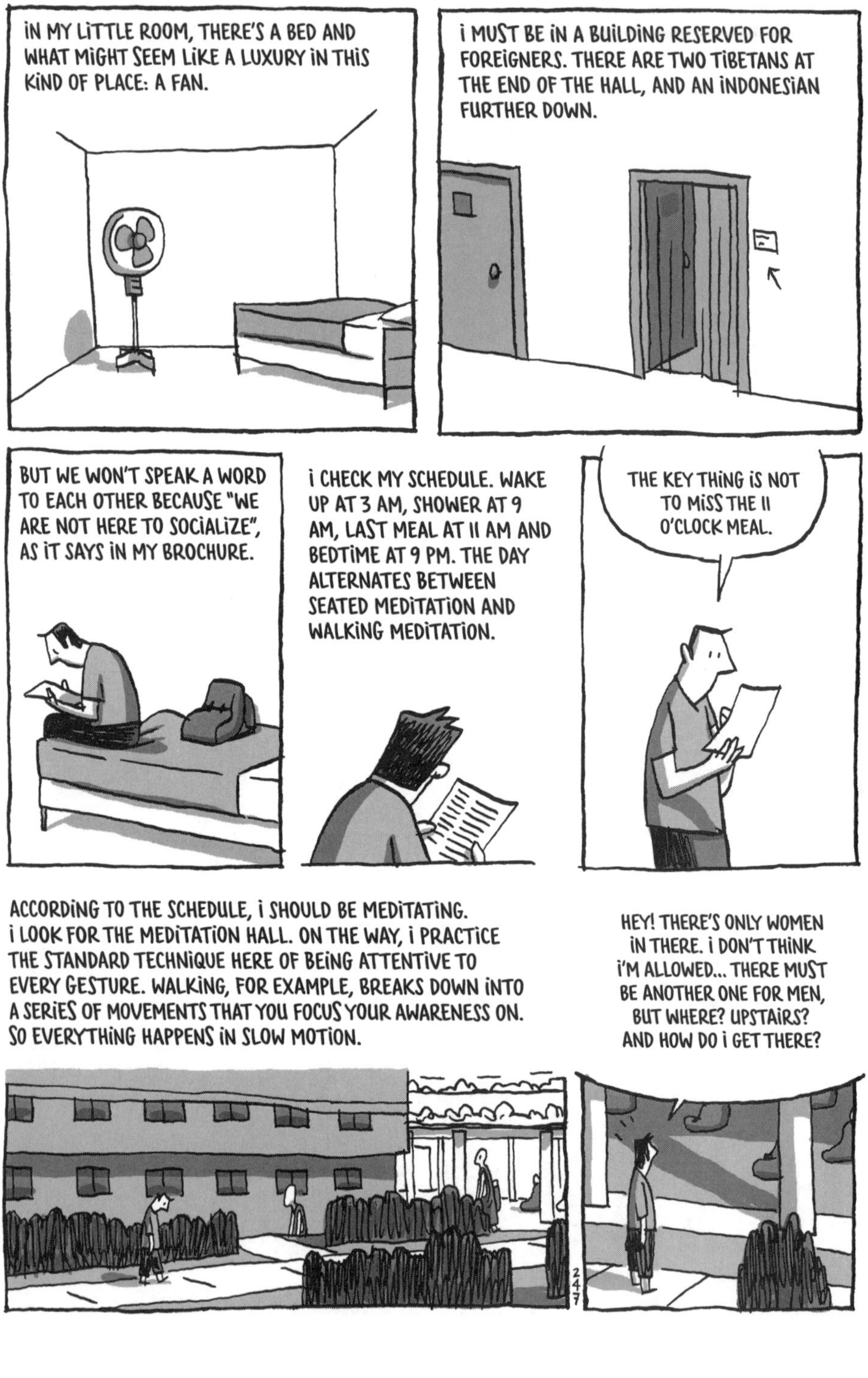
IN MY LITTLE ROOM, THERE'S A BED AND WHAT MIGHT SEEM LIKE A LUXURY IN THIS KIND OF PLACE: A FAN.
I MUST BE IN A BUILDING RESERVED FOR FOREIGNERS. THERE ARE TWO TIBETANS AT THE END OF THE HALL, AND AN INDONESIAN FURTHER DOWN.
BUT WE WON'T SPEAK A WORD TO EACH OTHER BECAUSE "WE ARE NOT HERE TO SOCIALIZE", AS IT SAYS IN MY BROCHURE.
I CHECK MY SCHEDULE. WAKE UP AT 3 AM, SHOWER AT 9 AM, LAST MEAL AT 11 AM AND BEDTIME AT 9 PM. THE DAY ALTERNATES BETWEEN SEATED MEDITATION AND WALKING MEDITATION.
THE KEY THING IS NOT TO MISS THE 11 O'CLOCK MEAL.
ACCORDING TO THE SCHEDULE, I SHOULD BE MEDITATING. I LOOK FOR THE MEDITATION HALL. ON THE WAY, I PRACTICE THE STANDARD TECHNIQUE HERE OF BEING ATTENTIVE TO EVERY GESTURE. WALKING, FOR EXAMPLE, BREAKS DOWN INTO A SERIES OF MOVEMENTS THAT YOU FOCUS YOUR AWARENESS ON. SO EVERYTHING HAPPENS IN SLOW MOTION.
HEY! THERE'S ONLY WOMEN IN THERE. I DON'T THINK I'M ALLOWED... THERE MUST BE ANOTHER ONE FOR MEN, BUT WHERE? UPSTAIRS? AND HOW DO I GET THERE?

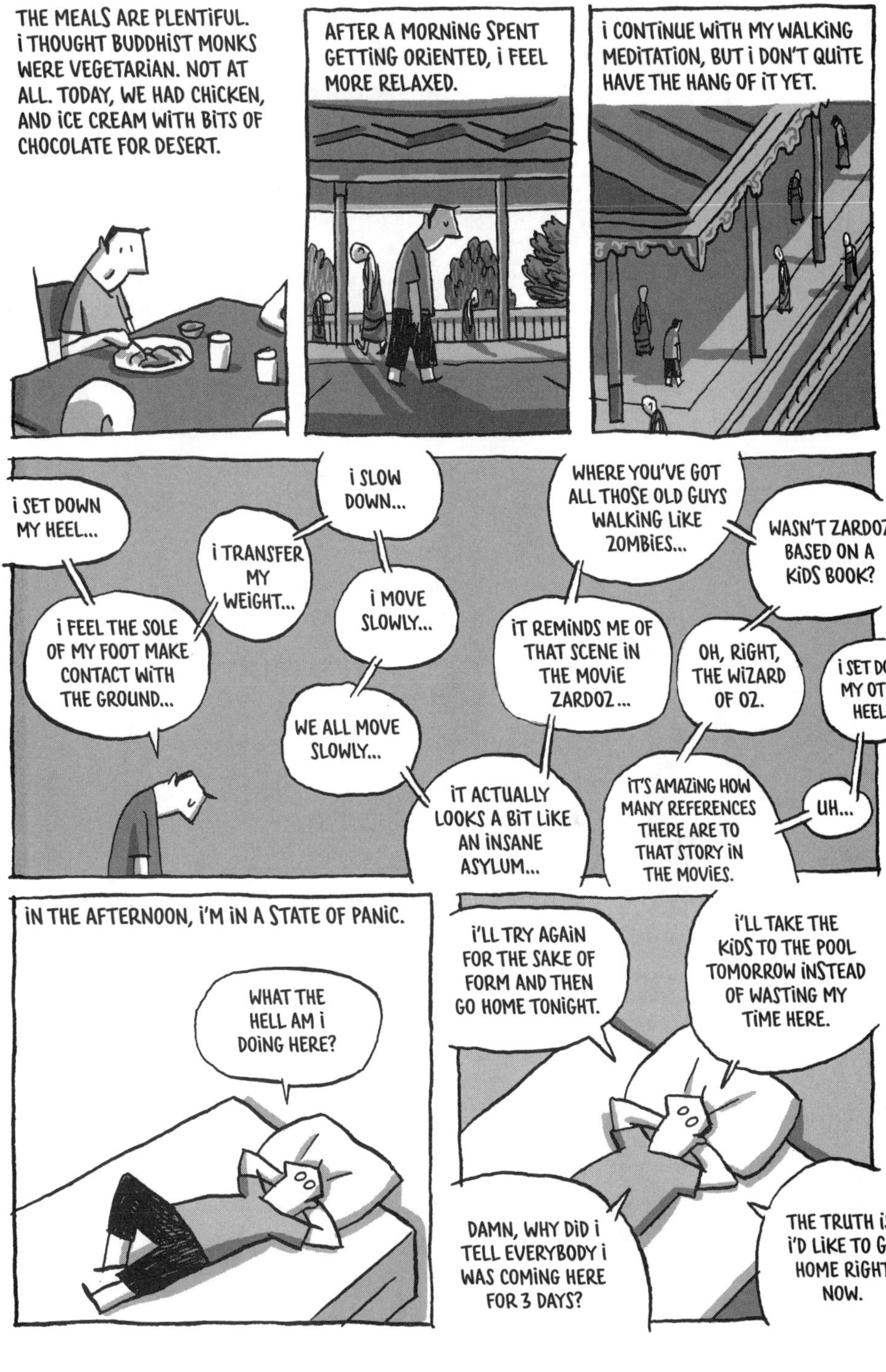
THE MEALS ARE PLENTIFUL. I THOUGHT BUDDHIST MONKS WERE VEGETARIAN. NOT AT ALL. TODAY, WE HAD CHICKEN, AND ICE CREAM WITH BITS OF CHOCOLATE FOR DESERT.
AFTER A MORNING SPENT GETTING ORIENTED, I FEEL MORE RELAXED.
I CONTINUE WITH MY WALKING MEDITATION, BUT I DON'T QUITE HAVE THE HANG OF IT YET.
I SET DOWN MY HEEL...
I FEEL THE SOLE OF MY FOOT MAKE CONTACT WITH THE GROUND...
I TRANSFER MY WEIGHT...
I SLOW DOWN...
I MOVE SLOWLY...
WE ALL MOVE SLOWLY...
IT ACTUALLY LOOKS A BIT LIKE AN INSANE ASYLUM...
IT REMINDS ME OF THAT SCENE IN THE MOVIE ZARDOZ...
WHERE YOU'VE GOT ALL THOSE OLD GUYS WALKING LIKE ZOMBIES...
WASN'T ZARDOZ BASED ON A KIDS BOOK?
OH, RIGHT, THE WIZARD OF OZ.
IT'S AMAZING HOW MANY REFERENCES THERE ARE TO THAT STORY IN THE MOVIES.
UH...
I SET DOWN MY OTHER HEEL...
IN THE AFTERNOON, I'M IN A STATE OF PANIC.
WHAT THE HELL AM I DOING HERE?
I'LL TRY AGAIN FOR THE SAKE OF FORM AND THEN GO HOME TONIGHT.
I'LL TAKE THE KIDS TO THE POOL TOMORROW INSTEAD OF WASTING MY TIME HERE.
DAMN, WHY DID I TELL EVERYBODY I WAS COMING HERE FOR 3 DAYS?
THE TRUTH IS, I'D LIKE TO GO HOME RIGHT NOW.

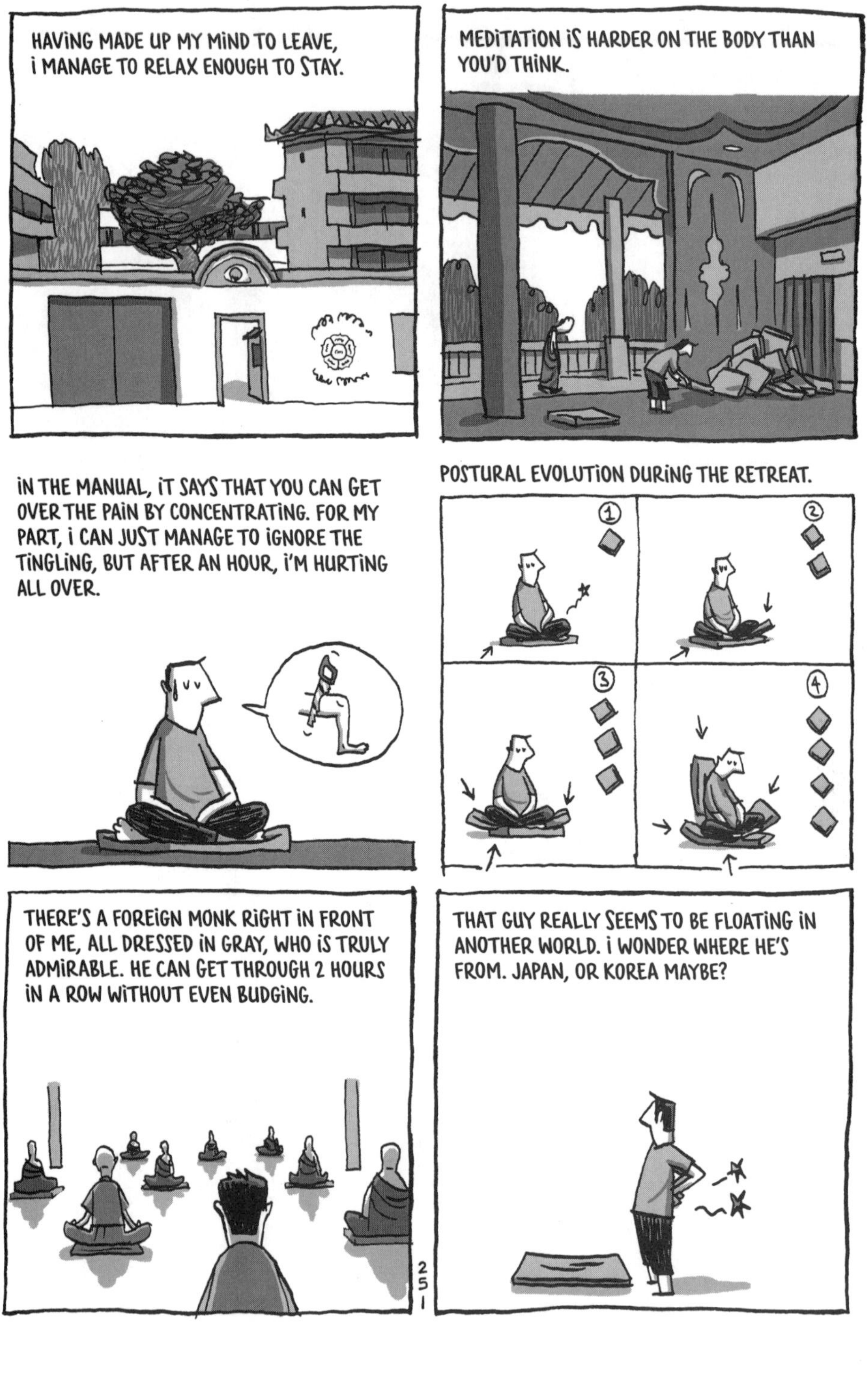
HAVING MADE UP MY MIND TO LEAVE, I MANAGE TO RELAX ENOUGH TO STAY.
MEDITATION IS HARDER ON THE BODY THAN YOU'D THINK.
IN THE MANUAL, IT SAYS THAT YOU CAN GET OVER THE PAIN BY CONCENTRATING. FOR MY PART, I CAN JUST MANAGE TO IGNORE THE TINGLING, BUT AFTER AN HOUR, I'M HURTING ALL OVER.
POSTURAL EVOLUTION DURING THE RETREAT.
1
2
3
4
THERE'S A FOREIGN MONK RIGHT IN FRONT OF ME, ALL DRESSED IN GRAY, WHO IS TRULY ADMIRABLE. HE CAN GET THROUGH 2 HOURS IN A ROW WITHOUT EVEN BUDGING.
THAT GUY REALLY SEEMS TO BE FLOATING IN ANOTHER WORLD. I WONDER WHERE HE'S FROM. JAPAN, OR KOREA MAYBE?

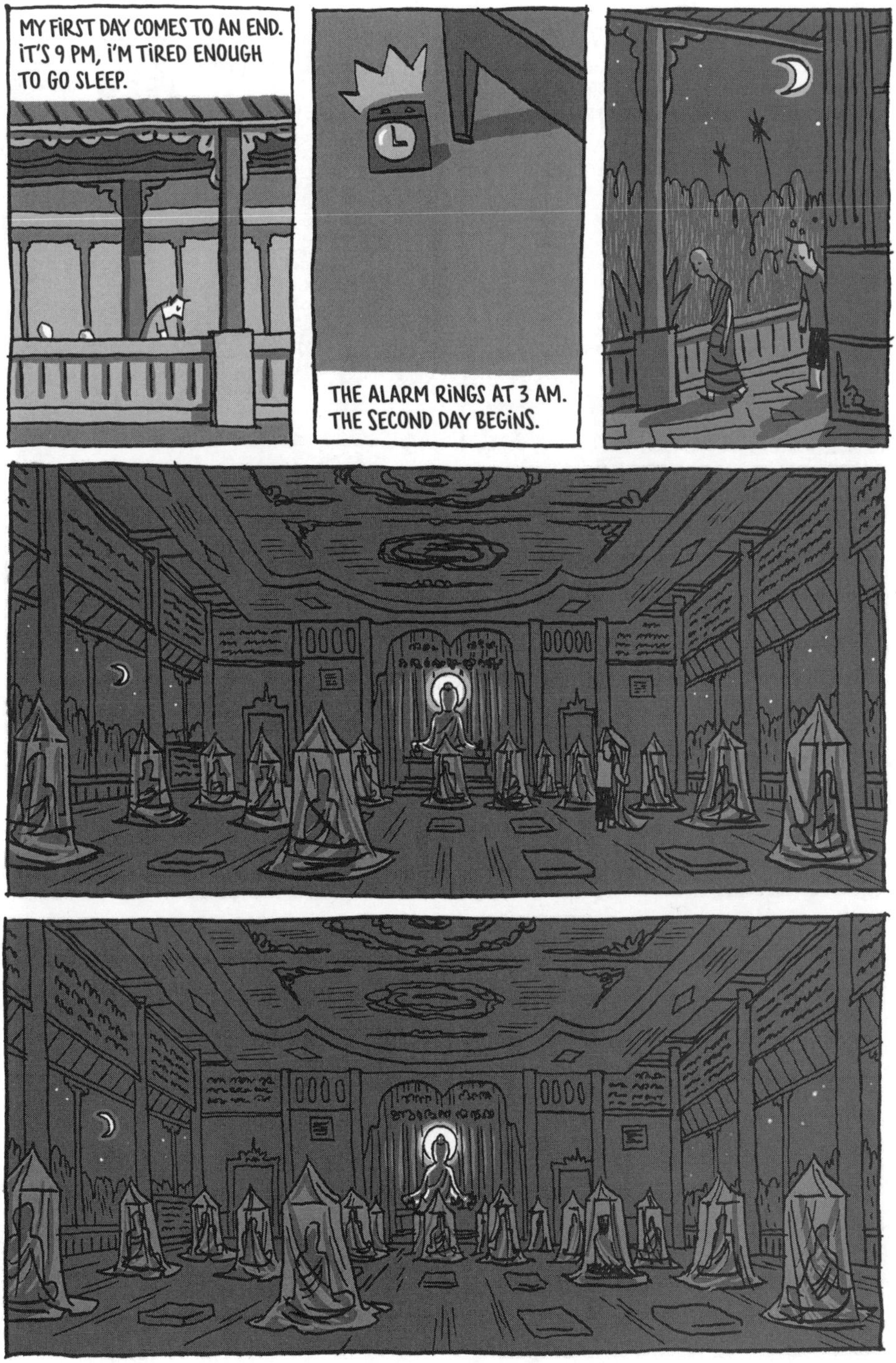
MY FIRST DAY COMES TO AN END. IT'S 9 PM, I'M TIRED ENOUGH TO GO SLEEP.
THE ALARM RINGS AT 3 AM. THE SECOND DAY BEGINS.

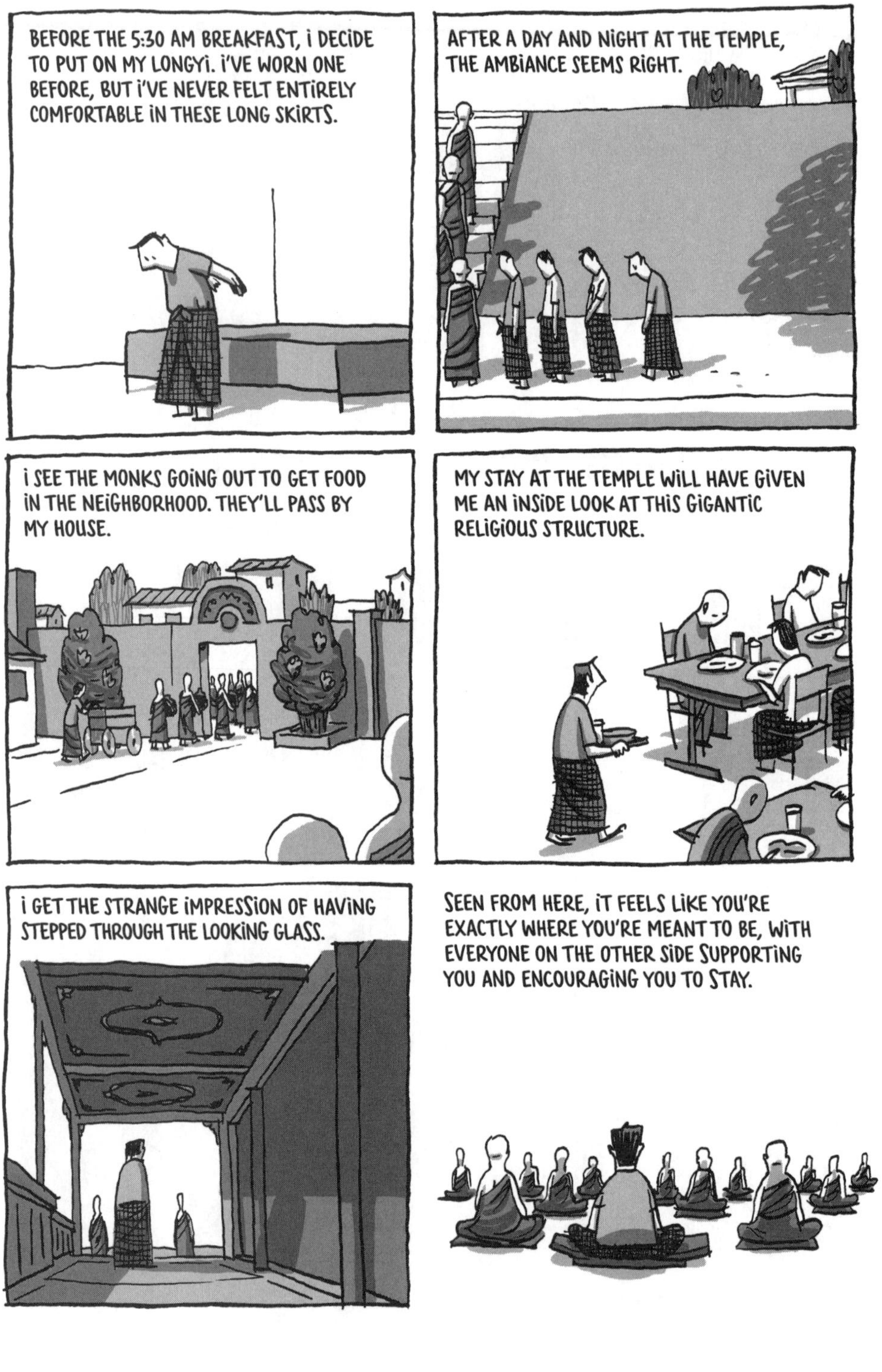
BEFORE THE 5:30 AM BREAKFAST, I DECIDE TO PUT ON MY LONGYI. I'VE WORN ONE BEFORE, BUT I'VE NEVER FELT ENTIRELY COMFORTABLE IN THESE LONG SKIRTS.
AFTER A DAY AND NIGHT AT THE TEMPLE, THE AMBIANCE SEEMS RIGHT.
I SEE THE MONKS GOING OUT TO GET FOOD IN THE NEIGHBORHOOD. THEY'LL PASS BY MY HOUSE.
MY STAY AT THE TEMPLE WILL HAVE GIVEN ME AN INSIDE LOOK AT THIS GIGANTIC RELIGIOUS STRUCTURE.
I GET THE STRANGE IMPRESSION OF HAVING STEPPED THROUGH THE LOOKING GLASS.
SEEN FROM HERE, IT FEELS LIKE YOU'RE EXACTLY WHERE YOU'RE MEANT TO BE, WITH EVERYONE ON THE OTHER SIDE SUPPORTING YOU AND ENCOURAGING YOU TO STAY.

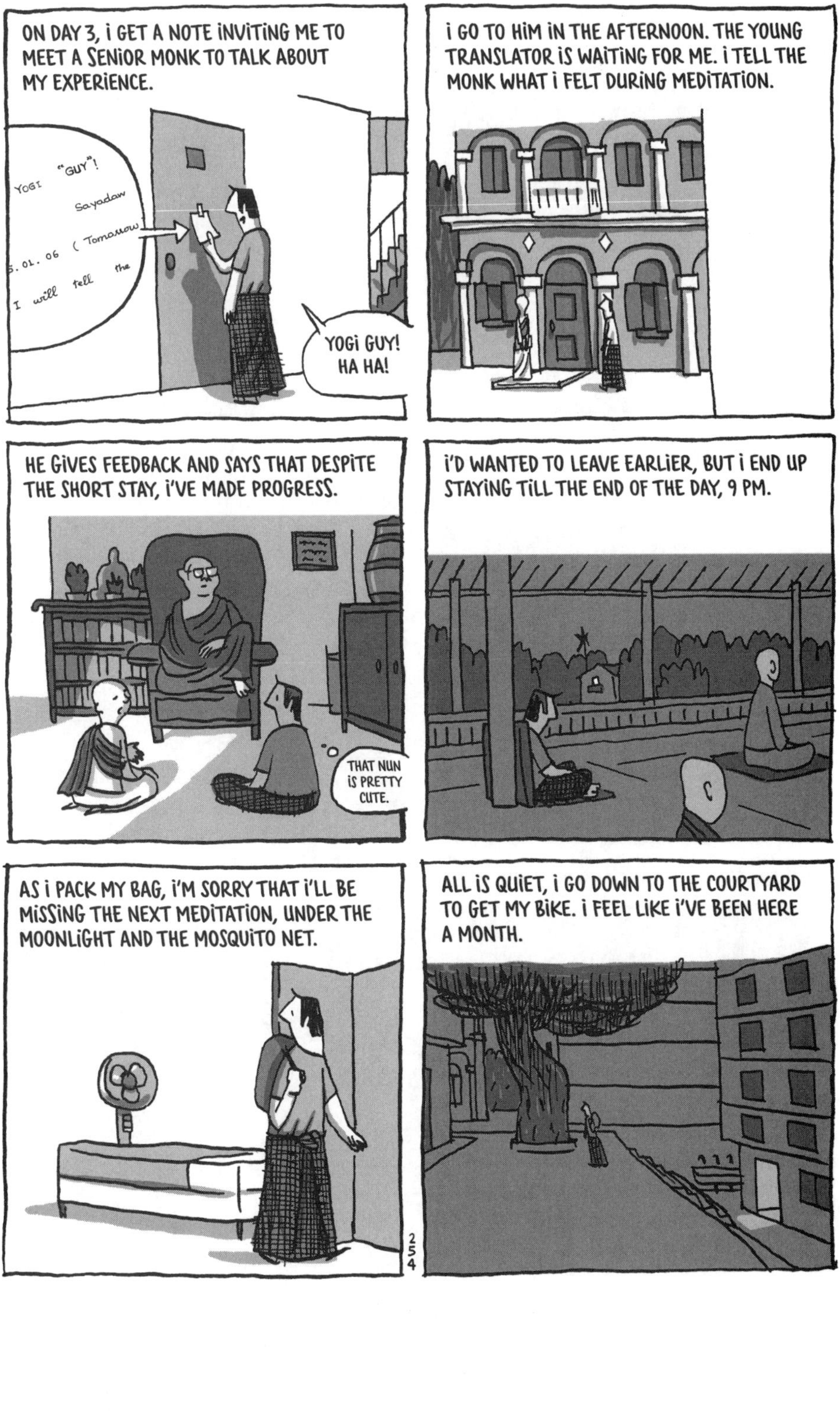
ON DAY 3, i GET A NOTE iNViTiNG ME TO MEET A SENiOR MONK TO TALK ABOUT MY EXPERiENCE.
YOGI "GUY"!
Sayadaw
5.01.06 (Tomorrow
I will tell the
YOGi GUY! HA HA!
i GO TO HiM iN THE AFTERNOON. THE YOUNG TRANSLATOR iS WAiTiNG FOR ME. i TELL THE MONK WHAT i FELT DURiNG MEDiTATiON.
HE GiVES FEEDBACK AND SAYS THAT DESPiTE THE SHORT STAY, i'VE MADE PROGRESS.
THAT NUN iS PRETTY CUTE.
i'D WANTED TO LEAVE EARLiER, BUT i END UP STAYiNG TiLL THE END OF THE DAY, 9 PM.
AS i PACK MY BAG, i'M SORRY THAT i'LL BE MiSSiNG THE NEXT MEDiTATiON, UNDER THE MOONLiGHT AND THE MOSQUiTO NET.
ALL iS QUiET, i GO DOWN TO THE COURTYARD TO GET MY BiKE. i FEEL LiKE i'VE BEEN HERE A MONTH.

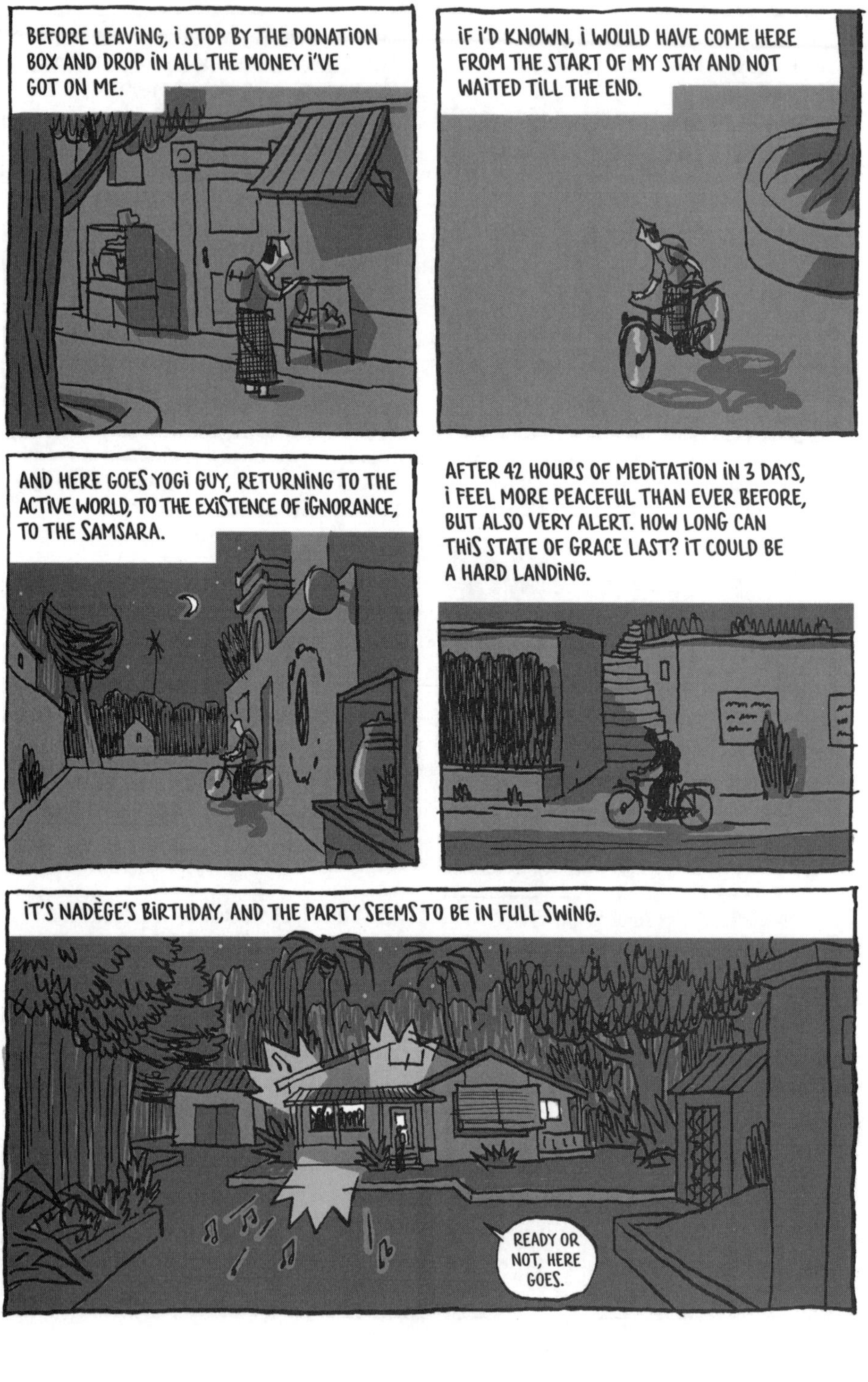
BEFORE LEAVING, I STOP BY THE DONATION BOX AND DROP IN ALL THE MONEY I'VE GOT ON ME.
IF I'D KNOWN, I WOULD HAVE COME HERE FROM THE START OF MY STAY AND NOT WAITED TILL THE END.
AND HERE GOES YOGI GUY, RETURNING TO THE ACTIVE WORLD, TO THE EXISTENCE OF IGNORANCE, TO THE SAMSARA.
AFTER 42 HOURS OF MEDITATION IN 3 DAYS, I FEEL MORE PEACEFUL THAN EVER BEFORE, BUT ALSO VERY ALERT. HOW LONG CAN THIS STATE OF GRACE LAST? IT COULD BE A HARD LANDING.
IT'S NADÈGE'S BIRTHDAY, AND THE PARTY SEEMS TO BE IN FULL SWING.
READY OR NOT, HERE GOES.

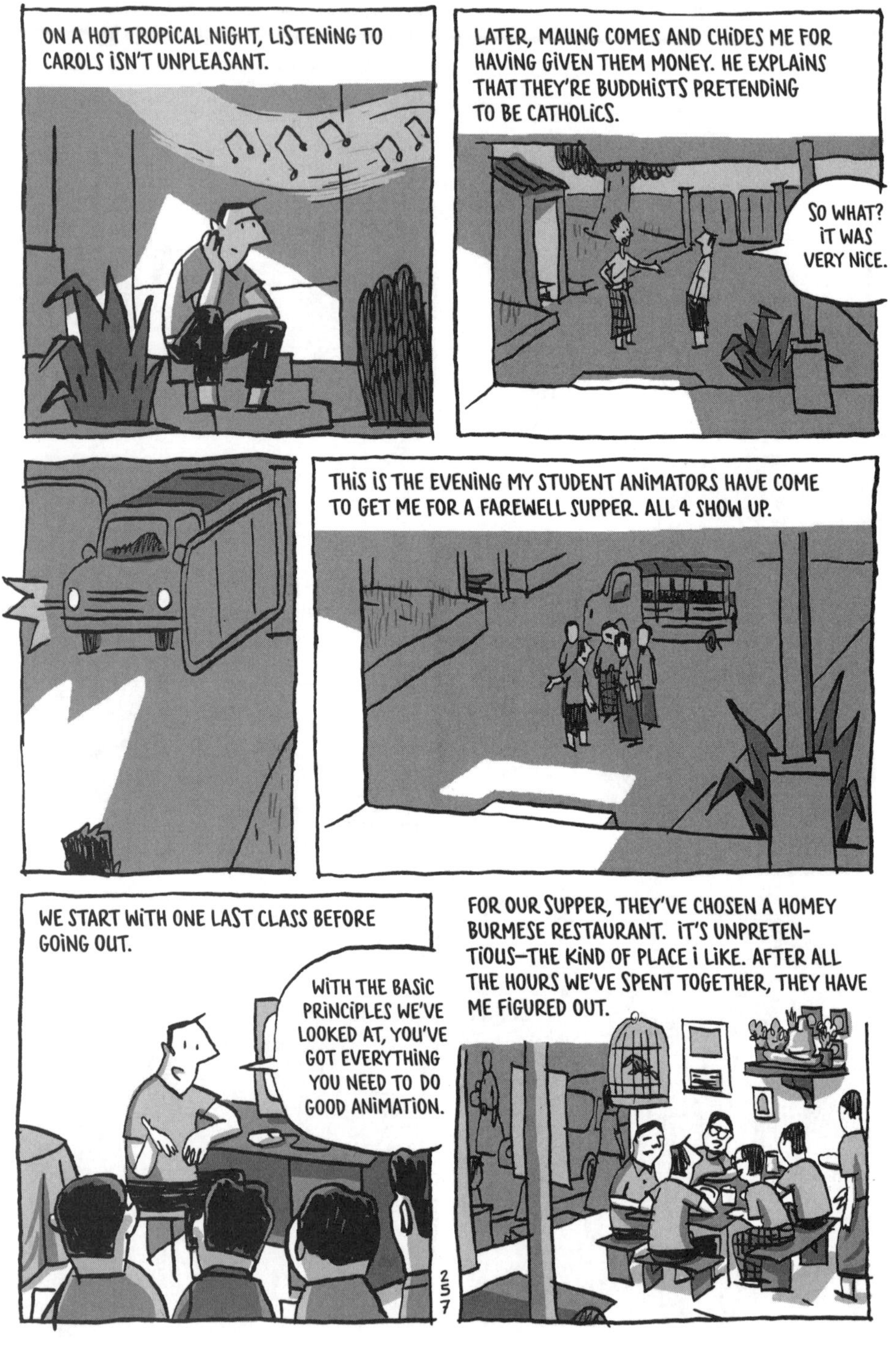
ON A HOT TROPICAL NIGHT, LISTENING TO CAROLS ISN'T UNPLEASANT.
LATER, MAUNG COMES AND CHIDES ME FOR HAVING GIVEN THEM MONEY. HE EXPLAINS THAT THEY'RE BUDDHISTS PRETENDING TO BE CATHOLICS.
SO WHAT? IT WAS VERY NICE.
THIS IS THE EVENING MY STUDENT ANIMATORS HAVE COME TO GET ME FOR A FAREWELL SUPPER. ALL 4 SHOW UP.
WE START WITH ONE LAST CLASS BEFORE GOING OUT.
WITH THE BASIC PRINCIPLES WE'VE LOOKED AT, YOU'VE GOT EVERYTHING YOU NEED TO DO GOOD ANIMATION.
FOR OUR SUPPER, THEY'VE CHOSEN A HOMEY BURMESE RESTAURANT. IT'S UNPRETENTIOUS—THE KIND OF PLACE I LIKE. AFTER ALL THE HOURS WE'VE SPENT TOGETHER, THEY HAVE ME FIGURED OUT.

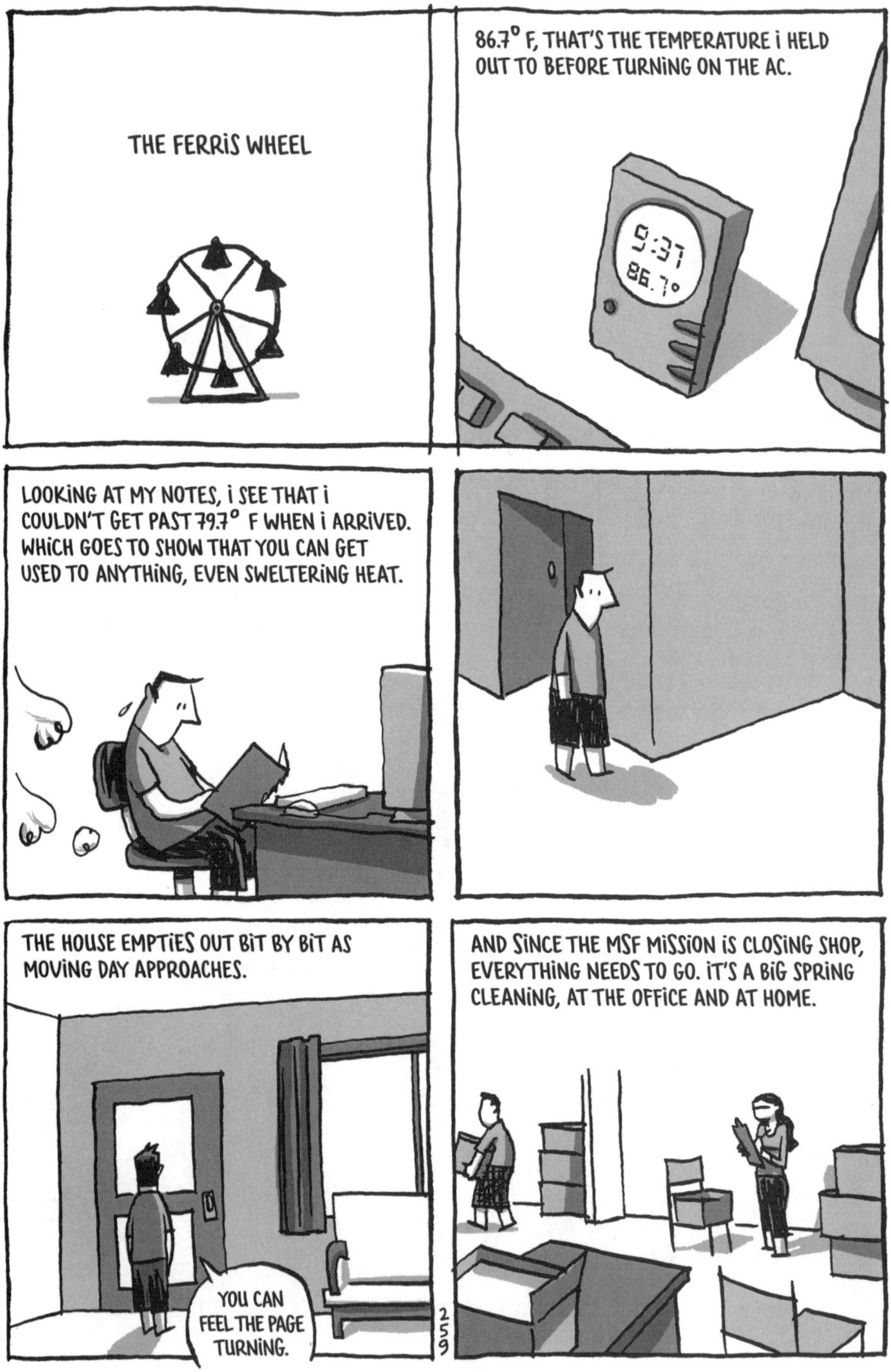
THE FERRIS WHEEL
86.7° F, THAT'S THE TEMPERATURE I HELD OUT TO BEFORE TURNING ON THE AC.
9:37
86.7°
LOOKING AT MY NOTES, I SEE THAT I COULDN'T GET PAST 79.7° F WHEN I ARRIVED. WHICH GOES TO SHOW THAT YOU CAN GET USED TO ANYTHING, EVEN SWELTERING HEAT.
THE HOUSE EMPTIES OUT BIT BY BIT AS MOVING DAY APPROACHES.
YOU CAN FEEL THE PAGE TURNING.
AND SINCE THE MSF MISSION IS CLOSING SHOP, EVERYTHING NEEDS TO GO. IT'S A BIG SPRING CLEANING, AT THE OFFICE AND AT HOME.

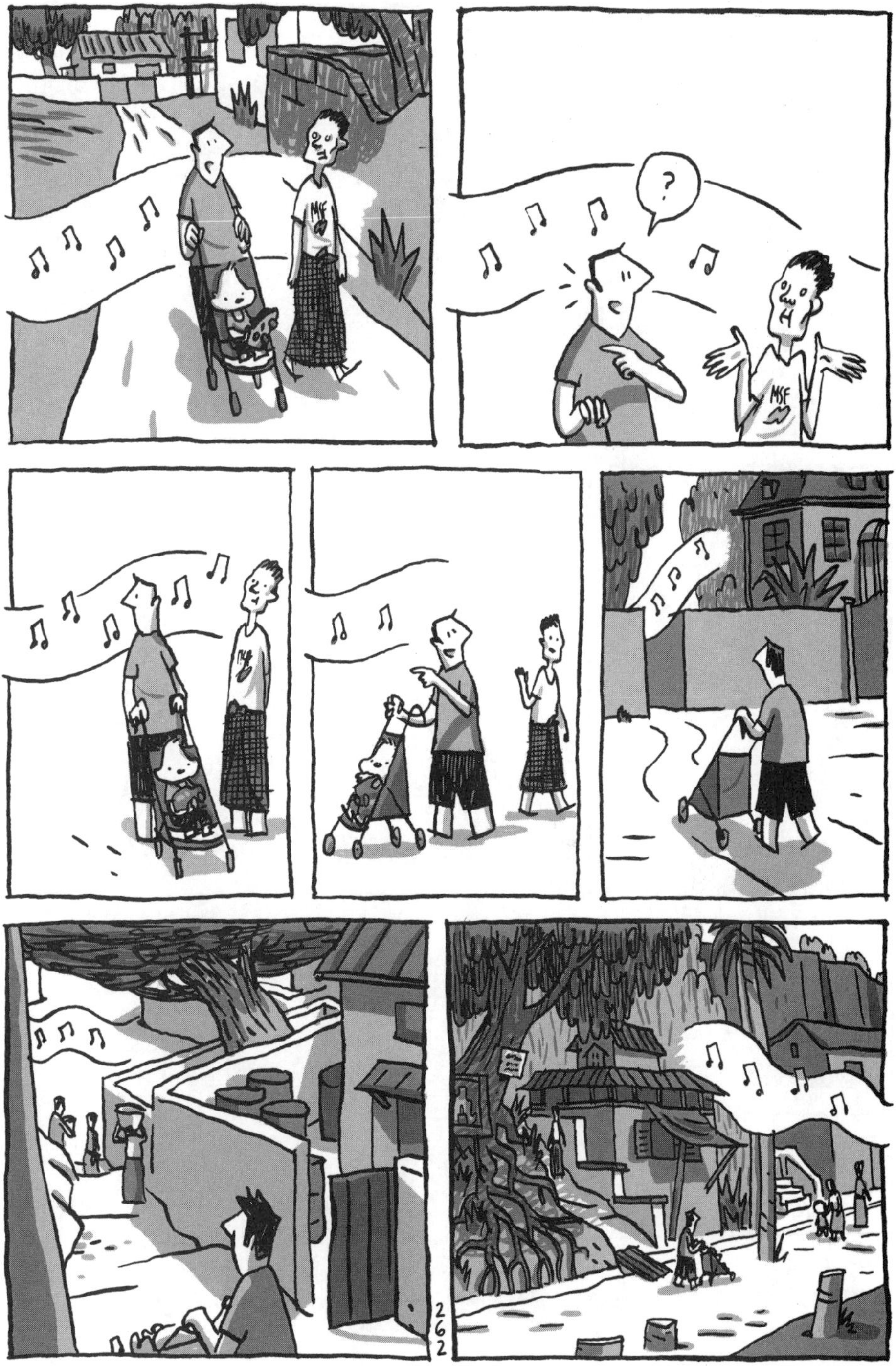
?
MSF

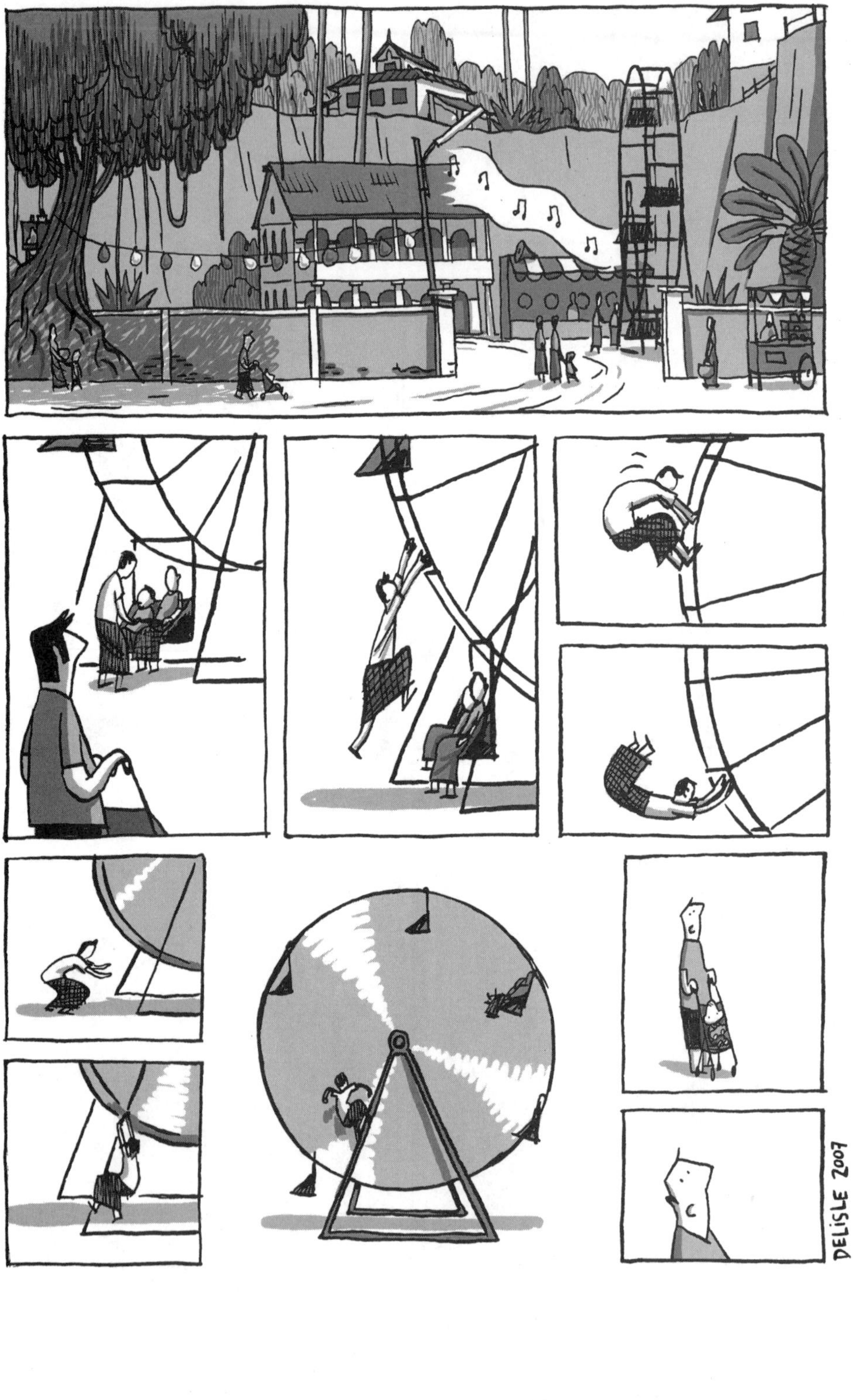
DELISLE 2007